A DANCE BETWEEN FLAMES

OTHER BOOKS BY THE AUTHOR

NON-FICTION

Martin Allen is Missing
The Journey Back from Hell
Berlin to Bucharest
in preparation: *An Honourable Defeat*

FICTION

City of the Horizon
City of Dreams
City of the Dead

A DANCE
BETWEEN FLAMES

Berlin Between the Wars

Anton Gill

Carroll & Graf Publishers, Inc.
New York

FOR RICHARD
'God preserve friendship! You could almost think you were not alone.'

Kurt Tucholsky

Copyright © 1993 by Anton Gill

Published by arrangement with John Murray (Publishers) Ltd.

First Carroll & Graf edition April 1994

Carroll & Graf Publishers, Inc.
260 Fifth Avenue
New York, NY 10001

Library of Congress Cataloging-in-Publication Data

Gill, Anton.
    A dance between flames : Berlin between the wars / Anton Gill.
        p.   cm.
    ISBN 0-7867-0063-7 : $23.00
    1. Berlin (Germany)—History—1918–1945.   2. Berlin (Germany)—
Intellectual life.   3. Berlin (Germany)—Social life and customs.
I. Title
DD880.G48   1994
943.1'55085—dc20   94-1265
                                                                    CIP

Manufactured in the United States of America

Contents

Illustrations

MAPS *page*

CREDITS

The author and publishers wish to thank the following for permission to reproduce photographs:

Iron Hindenburg: Ullstein Bilderdienst, Berlin (UB). Kaiser Wilhelm: Archiv fur Kunst und Geschichte, Berlin (AKG). Liebknecht: Märkische Museum, Berlin (MM). Luxemburg: AKG. Armoured train: AKG. Soldiers on Brandenburg Gate: MM. Kapp in aeroplane: MM. Kessler: Bildarchiv Preussische Kulturbesitz, Berlin (BPK). Stinnes: UB. Einstein: UB. Slum room: AKG. Street acrobat: AKG. *Paar am Tisch* by Richard Ziegler, from the Marvin and Janet Fishman Collection: AKG. *Das Letzte Glas* by Lutz Ehrenberger: AKG. Walldorf by Gunter Böhmer: Berlinische Galerie (BG). Lion: UB. Gert by Jeanne Mammen: BG. Berber by Otto Dix: Galerie der Stadt Stuttgart, © Otto Dix-Stiftung, Vaduz. Baker: UB. Muguette: UB. Tiller girls: UB. Haller Review: BPK. Haller poster by Ludwig Kainer: AKG. Stresemann: UB. Rathenau by Emil Orlik: Berlin Museum (BM). Dada exhibition: BPK. *A German Mother* by Käthe Kollwitz: BPK. *Match-seller* by Otto Dix: BPK. *Woman Carrying a Bucket* by Heinrich Zille: BM. *National Socialist Statue* by Josef Thorak: BPK. Kollwitz by Hänse Herrmann: AKG.

Liebermann by Conrad Felixmuller: BG. Grosz self-portrait: BM. Einstein Tower: BPK. Columbushaus: Landesbildstelle, Berlin (L). Mercedes by Erdmann & Rossi: L. Streamlined car by Aerodynamischen Versuchsantalt Göttingen: L. 'Zeppelin of the tracks' by Franz Kruckenberg: L. Teapot by Marianne Brandt: Bauhaus Archiv (BA). Kiosk by Herbert Bayer: BA. 'Abstract figure' by Oskar Schlemmer: Staatsgalerie Stuttgart © Raman C. Schlemmer.

Brecht: UB. Kästner: UB. Tucholsky: UB. Zuckmayer: UB. Massary: AKG. Durieux: BM. Bergner: BM. Garbo: UB. Reinhardt: UB. Interior of Grosses Schauspielhaus by Hans Poelzig: BPK. Jessner by Rudolf Grossmann: BM. Kerr: UB. Still from *The Cabinet of Dr Caligari*: UB. Still from *Nosferatu*: UB. Still from *Metropolis*: BPK. Lang and Helm: UB. Albers, Valetti and Dietrich: AKG. Dietrich poster: AKG. Furtwängler: UB. Klemperer and Hindemith: UB. Lenya and Weill: UB. Hirschfeld: AKG. Gennat: UB. *Ringverein*: BPK. Scheller: UB. Haarmann: AKG. Klante: UB. Cycle race: L. Schmeling: BPK. Campbell: L. Olympic women: UB. Riefenstahl: UB. Javelin thrower from *Olympiade*: BPK. 'Seven-month children': AKG. Women's wrestling club: L. Cycling club: L. Fitness club: L. Unity Mitford: BPK. National Boycott Day: L. Torchlit SA procession: MM. Bookburning: L. Hitler's salute from *The Triumph of the Will*: UB.

Acknowledgements

MANY PEOPLE HAVE helped me with this book. Between them they represent as many facets of life as Berlin itself. I should like to thank: M. Abraham, Gisela Armstrong, Andreas Austilat, Jonathan Barker, Prof. Boleslaw Barlog, Gerda Bassenge, Arnold Bauer, Lutz Becker, Birgit Brandau, Bern Brent, Gunn Brinson, Prof. Theodor Eschenburg, Peter Ewence, Joachim C. Fest, Alfred Joachim Fischer, Prof. Dr Dr Ossip K. Flechtheim; my father, George Gill and my wife, Nicola Gill; Berthold Goldschmidt, Alan Gunn, Ludwig, Freiherr von Hammerstein, Henni Handler, Liz Heasman, Mrs Bernhard Heiliger, Prof. Dr Walter Huder, Fr. Prof. Huder, Mr and Mrs Hans Jackson, Richard Johnson, Dominique Jubien, Erich Kaufman, Dr Lothar Kettenacker, Wolfgang Koch, the late Hans Lietzau, Prof. Ernst G. Lowenthal, Dr Cecile Lowenthal-Hensel, Mark Lucas, Grant McIntyre, Kunigunda Messerschmitt, Werner Messerschmitt, Juliet Milne, Bernhard Minetti, the late Christopher Moller, Jo Morley, Erna Nelki, the late Wolfgang Nelki, Prof. Julius Posener, Dr Gerd Radde, Sybil Rares-Schüster, Curt Riess, Connie Rosenstiel, Edwin Rosenstiel, Günther Ruschin, Dr Helga Russow, Inge Fehr Samson, Dr Waldemar Schröder, Steffie Spira, Elizabeth Cross Stanton, the late John Stanton, Joe Steeples, Klaus Täubert, Anthony Vivis, Illa Walter, Heddy Wassermann, Stephen White, Christa Wichmann, Peter Wickham, Ilse Wolff and Prof. Grete von Zieritz.

I also acknowledge the help given me by many institutions and organizations, and thank the Akademie der Künste, Berlin; the Amerika-Gedenk-Bibliothek; the Archiv für Kunst und Geschichte, Berlin (Justus Göpel and Jürgen Raible); ARD; the Association of Jewish Refugees; *Aufbau*; the Austrian Institute, London; the Bauhaus Museum, Berlin;

the Berlin Museum (Dr Dominic Bartmann); the Berliner Geschichts-
werkschaft e.V.; the *Berliner Zeitung*; the Berlinische Galerie e.V.; the
Bildarchiv Preussischer Kulturbesitz (Fr. Klein); the British Library,
London; Deutsche Künstlerhilfe; Deutsche Kinemathek Berlin (Herr
Theis); the *Frankfurter Allgemeine Zeitung*; the German Embassy, Lon-
don; the Goethe-Institut London, and especially Regine Friederici and
its library staff; the Historische Kommission zu Berlin e.V.; the
Jüdisches Museum zu Berlin; the Landesarchiv Berlin (Dr Dettmer,
Dr Christiane Schuchard and Dr Wetzel); Landesbildstelle Berlin
(Fr. Kusserow); the Märkisches Museum (Herr Hansen, Fr. Reiszmann
and Fr. Zettler); the Musicians' Benevolent Fund, London (Martin
Williams); Norddeutscher Rundfunk; PEN Zentrum Deutschland;
Presse und Informationsamt des Landes Berlin; the Preussischer
Staatsbibliothek (Dr Kobi); the Preussisches Geheimes Staatsarchiv
(Dr Iselin Gundermann); the Stadtarchiv Berlin (Eveline Schmidt); the
Stiftung Preussischer Kulturbesitz; *Der Tagesspiegel*; Ullstein Bilder-
dienst (Herr Frentz); Westdeutscher Rundfunk; the Wiener Library,
London; and ZDF.

The twenty-one years covered in this book span a period of great
activity and complexity. Berlin came into its own and enjoyed a short,
hectic summer before the clouds closed in again. The anecdotes,
Dokumentation, and history books which cover the period are legion. I
hope I have identified the most interesting aspects, and that I have ironed
out as many as possible of the inconsistencies that inevitably crop up in
such a vast quantity of information. The contents of this book represent
the tip of a very large iceberg. Errors that remain must be laid at my
door, and I apologize for them.

Author's Note

████████ IN GERMANY, THE surname of a person plus his title (the designation of his profession) is frequently used, and the Christian name is not. Thus it has sometimes been difficult to discover a person's full name, but examples of this in the text are few. In the course of my research I have found different spellings of the same person's name (or of newspapers, or other proper names) occurring in different books. Where possible I have resolved discrepancies by going back to original documents (e.g., the *Berliner Illustrirte* – which by tradition spelt *illustrierte* without its middle 'e'); otherwise I have simply adopted the form which I have found to be most frequently used. The same goes for disagreement on dates, though it has been relatively easy to confirm correct ones in most cases. Less easy has been the rationalization of Berlin street-names, some of which changed four times between 1918 and 1945. Many of the Weimar names were restored after the collapse of the Third Reich, but Berlin was so thoroughly bombed and destroyed that in the centre of town little of the original street pattern remains. Three decades of division by the Berlin Wall did not help an already complicated situation, and in former East Berlin many streets were named after Communist heroes; some of those streets are now once again renamed.

German officialdom is very fond of acronyms. Where these occur I have given, wherever possible, the full German name and an English translation, either in the text or in a note. The same goes for abbreviations of titles; for example, GESTAPO is a contraction of GEheime STAatsPOlizei (Secret State Police). A feature of German life is the admonitory couplet, still to be seen on tube train notices, for example. Where these occur I have usually given them in German, with a translation either in the text or in a note.

Germans still use titles with more formality than we do. If someone is a professor and also a Ph.D., he will be called 'Professor Doktor'. If he has two or three doctorates, they will all be set down, at least on paper: Prof. Dr Dr Dr was what Max Reinhardt was entitled to put in front of his name.

When writing of the large sums of money – in numerical terms at least – in circulation during the period of inflation, when I mention a billion I mean one thousand million. That is the sense of the German *Milliarde*.

Some of the people in this book are far more familiar to Germans than to the English-speaking world. Most of them deserve books to themselves. Many of them *have* books to themselves. Where I have felt that they need more of an introduction than the narrative allows, I have taken refuge in discreet explanations in the notes, and have sometimes suggested an autobiography or a biography.

To deal with Berlin's history between 1918 and 1939 properly, one would need ten years' research and one would produce ten volumes. But while what is exhaustive is academically best, it isn't necessarily what everyone wants. In this single volume it has not been possible to cover every aspect of the city's life, or indeed to give everything that is covered the same emphasis. Wherever I can, I have referred the reader to specialized books dealing with all areas, both in the Bibliography and in the Notes. As you read this work, my personal interests and predilections will inevitably become clear, though I have tried to rein them in, in the interests of balance. The Bibliography is based on personal choice, but I have indicated to readers who really want to dig deeply into this period where more extensive bibliographies can be found. To take the most advantage of the space available to me, I have on the whole avoided listing unpublished or archive file sources – interested readers should consult either the institutions noted in the Acknowledgements, or more specialized works than this.

I have followed events in roughly chronological order; but sometimes I have preferred to deal with a subject in its entirety rather than break it up across a number of chapters. The main example of this is the chapter which is almost entirely devoted to theatre during the Weimar period. It is hard to overestimate the importance theatre played in the lives of Berliners. People of all classes and all backgrounds were enthusiastic and inveterate theatregoers. That there could be actors' and even critics' strikes is proof of this.

Most of my sources were written in German. Where I am aware of English translations, I have noted them. All otherwise unacknowledged translations from German are my own.

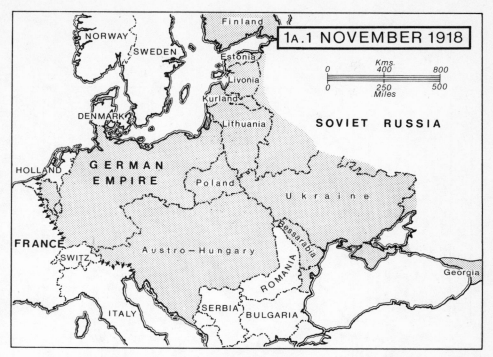

1A.1 NOVEMBER 1918

NORWAY

SWEDEN

Finland

Estonia

Livonia

Kurland

Lithuania

DENMARK

SOVIET RUSSIA

HOLLAND

GERMAN EMPIRE

Poland

U k r a i n e

FRANCE

SWITZ

Austro—Hungary

Bessarabia

ROMANIA

Georgia

ITALY

SERBIA

BULGARIA

Kms.
0   400   800
0   250   500
Miles

1B. DECEMBER 1921

NORWAY

SWEDEN

FINLAND

ESTONIA

LATVIA

LITHUANIA

DENMARK

GERMANY

SOVIET RUSSIA

HOLLAND

BELGIUM

GERMANY

P O L A N D

FRANCE

CZECHOSLOVAKIA

SWITZ

AUSTRIA

HUNGARY

ROMANIA

ITALY

YUGOSLAVIA

BULGARIA

GREECE

Kms.
0   400   800
0   250   500
Miles

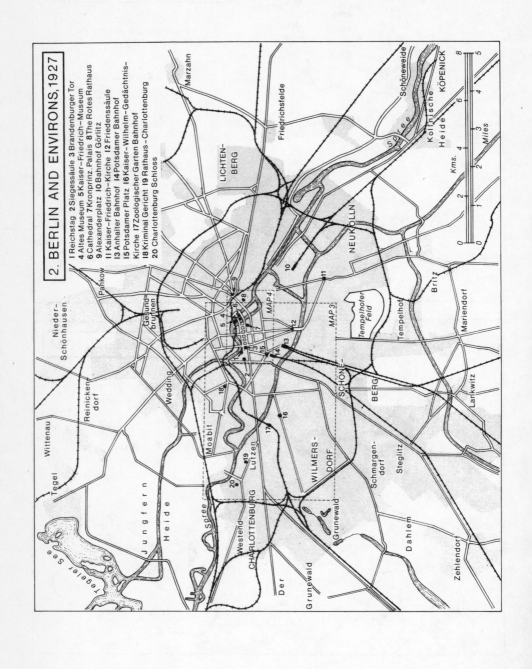

2. BERLIN AND ENVIRONS, 1927

1 Reichstag 2 Siegessäule 3 Brandenburger Tor
4 Altes Museum 5 Kaiser–Friedrich–Museum
6 Cathedral 7 Kronprinz. Palais 8 The Rotes Rathaus
9 Alexanderplatz 10 Bahnhof Görlitz
11 Kaiser–Friedrich–Kirche 12 Friedenssäule
13 Anhalter Bahnhof 14 Potsdamer Bahnhof
15 Potsdamer Platz 16 Kaiser–Wilhelm–Gedächtnis–
Kirche 17 Zoologischer Garten Bahnhof
18 Kriminal Gericht 19 Rathaus–Charlottenburg
20 Charlottenburg Schloss

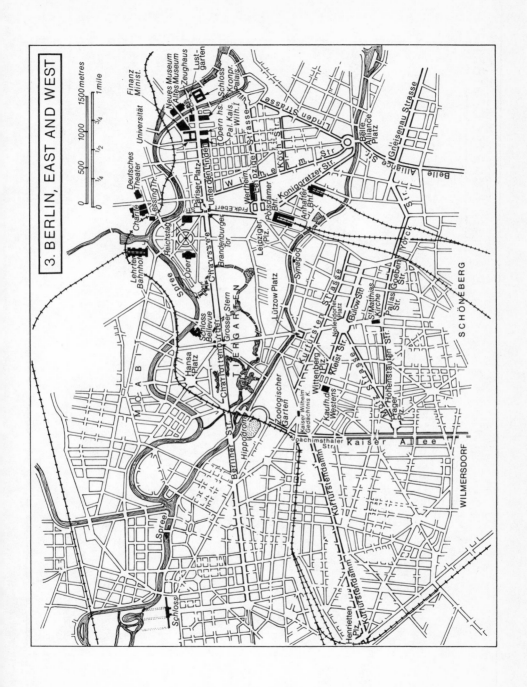

3. BERLIN, EAST AND WEST

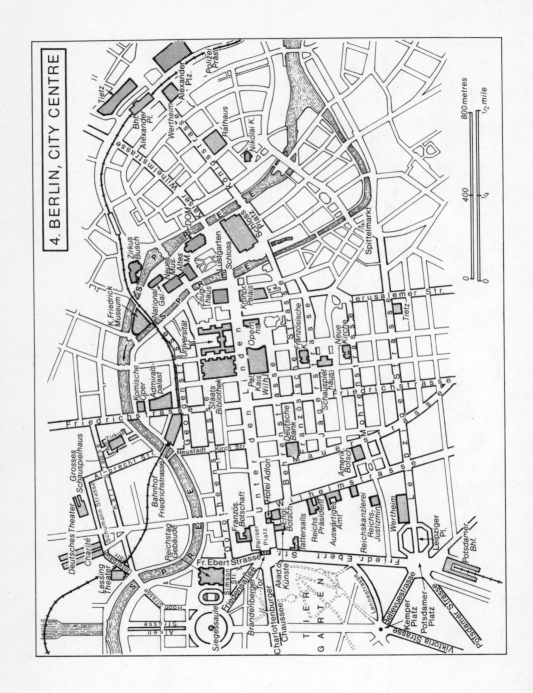

4. BERLIN, CITY CENTRE

800 metres
400
0
½ mile
¼

Tietz
Bhf.
Alexander Pl.
Polizei Präsi.
Wertheim
Wilhelmstrasse
Rathaus
Nikolai K.
Königstrasse
Zirkus Busch
Neues Mus.
Altes M.
N.M.
DOM
Schloss
Lustgarten
Schloss
Spittelmarkt
K. Friedrich Museum
National Gal.
P
Zeughaus
Kronpr. Palais
Jerusalemer Str.
Tietz
Universität
Linden
Opern hst.
Französische
Neue Kirche
Komische Oper
Admirals palast
Staats Bibliothek
Pal. Kais. Wilh.
Schauspiel haus
Deutsche Bank
Friedrichstrasse
Georgenstr.
Kirch Str.
Franzö s.
Mauerstr.
Mohrenstr.
Jäger str.
Friedrichstrasse
Grosses Schauspielhaus
Zirkus
Neustadt
Amerik. Botsch.
Wertheim
Deutsches Theater
Charité
Albrecht Str.
Bahnhof Friedrichstrasse
Schumann Strasse
Hotel Adlon
Engl. Botsch.
Reichs Präsident
Auswärtiges Amt
Reichskanzlerei
Reichs-Justizmin.
Leipziger Pl.
Potsdamer Bhf.
Reichstag Gebäude
Lessing Theater
Dorotheenstr.
Französ. Botschaft
Parisel Platz
Tattersalls
Unter den
S P R E E
Simson Str.
Fr. Ebert Strasse
Brandenberger Tor
Akad. d. Künste
Friedensallee
Siegessäule
Charlottenburger Chaussee
Friedr. Ebert
T I E R G A R T E N
Lennéstrasse
Bellevuestrasse
Kemper Platz
Potsdamer Platz
Viktoria Strasse
Potsdamer Strasse
Alsen Strasse
Roon Strasse

TWILIGHT

Glow-worm, glow-worm, glimmer, glimmer,
Glow-worm, glow-worm, shimmer, shimmer;
Lead us all along the road
That leads to happiness' abode.

Paul Lincke, music-hall song, *c.* 1890.

The oath sworn on the Colours has become a fiction.

First Quartermaster-General Wilhelm Gröner,
November, 1918

1 Götterdämmerung

A WAR ENDS in rags and dust.

On 9 November 1918 crowds of workers who had started a revolution outside Berlin were descending on the city. Within hours, Germany had been declared a republic from a window of the Reichstag building; and the Kaiser, under pressure from his high command, had abdicated. Few ordinary Berliners knew exactly what was going on, or what would happen next.

Lorenz Adlon, Berlin's top restaurateur and founder of the hotel which bore his name at Number 1, Unter den Linden, overlooking the Brandenburg Gate, put on his morning coat and called for his top hat. Then he left the hotel and walked to Rothe's, the florists. At that time of maximum deprivation the shop could only offer him wild flowers, but he bought them all and had them made into a formal bouquet, as carefully as if they had been 'Maréchal Niel' roses. Carrying them he made for the Brandenburg Gate, an incongruously elegant figure among the tattered Berliners and the mutilated soldiers openly selling their guns next to peasant women offering turnips and firewood.

The old man stood to attention in front of the Gate, looking towards the central pillars. He drew a few glances, but nobody interfered with him until a policeman who recognized him asked what he was doing.

'I am waiting for His Imperial and Royal Highness to return to his capital, following his great victory. I want to be the first to congratulate him when he rides through the Brandenburg Gate.'

By this time Louis Adlon, Lorenz's son, had appeared; he led his father gently back to the hotel. It was hard to break the truth to him, that the old gods had died.[1]

The soldiers returning to Berlin were tired and broken. The actress

Steffie Spira, who was ten years old then, remembers: 'My sister and I went with bouquets to the Brandenburg Gate, very much against my mother's will, to see the returning soldiers march home. But it was a sad occasion – people cried, and even the children sensed the unhappiness. I gave a soldier my little bouquet and he looked at me and just said, "Good luck to you, little miss." I will never forget the grief in his eyes. The men looked so battered; their uniforms were worn out, and ragged, and filthy.'[2] Grete von Zieritz, who arrived in the city from Graz as an eighteen-year-old music student in 1917, remembers too: 'I went out of curiosity to the Royal Schloss and saw how the sailors tried to break down the iron doors. And the troops returning from the war – they were broken men. We watched them march with Hindenburg under the Brandenburg Gate and down Unter den Linden with tears in our eyes. There was a sense of doom in the air.'[3]

Until 1918, Germany had not suffered a military defeat for a century. In that time, the collection of states which made up the German nation had been fused by Bismarck into the Second Reich, and Berlin, capital of Prussia since the eighteenth century, had become its capital in 1871. It was a young city and, until well into the nineteenth century, a small one. It had none of the developed society of London or Paris; the court in nearby Potsdam was the centre of social life, and Wilhelm II, like Hitler after him, disliked Berlin and its free-thinking, insubordinate inhabitants.

In one sense, Berlin has always been a divided city. The Westend is smart. Away to the south-west are the equally smart, leafy suburbs of Dahlem, Lichterfelde, Steglitz and Zehlendorf. Immediately to the west of the city centre are Tiergarten, Charlottenburg and Wilmersdorf, comfortable middle-class districts. The workers lived in the districts to the north and east where the fingers of hunger and cold reached first. The artist Käthe Kollwitz lived far from the glitter of the centre, in Berlin North, where her doctor husband had his practice, and where she worked on drawings of the poor for her series *The War*. By contrast, Grete von Zieritz lived in the Westend. She spent the last two years of the war going to concerts in Berlin: 'I went to ninety-three, and I never returned to Graz, as had been my original intention.' She adds: 'You cannot imagine the richness of cultural life in Berlin during the last few months of the war.' When she arrived at Anhalter Station in 1917, the first thing to confront her was 'an enormous poster advertising a *Liederabend* (an evening of songs) with Hugo Wolff. I had always admired him and it was very moving, like a welcome.'[4]

Bloody as it had been, the First World War was not the 'total war' visited on the world after 1942: technology had not yet made such a thing possible. It was the wish of the German administration during the war that cultural ambassadors of the Reich should take German art to coun-tries not in conflict with the Fatherland. So German orchestras and theatre companies toured abroad, and in Berlin, far from the trenches and the mustard gas, the barbed wire and the whiz-bangs, the concert halls were open. In this city of painful contrasts, the rich ate and played as if nothing had happened.

Scientists were able to keep up professional relations across enemy lines. In 1914 Albert Einstein, then 35, moved to Berlin from Switzerland at the invitation of Max Planck, to become director of the Astrophysical Department of the Kaiser-Wilhelm-Institut in Dahlem. From there he published his General Theory of Relativity in 1915, which naturally received international attention. The theory was recognized as brilliant by those who could understand it, but a cardinal problem was how to prove it. In March 1917 the British Astronomer Royal, Sir Frank Dyson, with a splendid disregard for the war that hap-pened to stand between them, suggested to his German colleague that an eclipse of the sun on 29 March 1919 'would provide an excellent chance for such proof, since the darkened sun would pass through an excep-tionally bright group of stars, the Hyades'.[5] The light rays from the stars could be measured as they moved close to the sun at the moment of eclipse.

But it was not given to everyone to remain aloof from the conflict. A short war – of six weeks – had been planned for, and so supremely confi-dent was the high command that no contingency measures were taken. Rationing was not introduced until 1915, by which time supplies, hindered by the British naval blockade, were already short. Rations grew smaller as the war progressed, and as early as the beginning of 1916 there was trouble on the streets of the capital. Demonstrations became regular occurrences.

Most revolutions are based on bread. The longer the war lasted, and the less food there was, the deeper the gulf between the two halves of the city became. Notionally, everyone got the same. Daily rations per adult at the end of 1916 were 270 grams of bread, 35 grams of meat, 25 grams of sugar and 11 grams of dripping. Every fortnight each person was sup-posed to get one egg and, whenever possible, 10 pounds of potatoes. In practice the bread was made of turnips and the meat was half bone, half gristle. The dripping was thin and the sugar was usually saccharine. By as early as August 1916 no more milk or cheese was to be had on the open market, and potatoes were largely replaced by swedes. Most things there were to eat were ersatz, and in May 1916 the *Berliner Tageblatt*, sailing very close to the censorship laws forbidding adverse comments on the lack of food, observed that there was no rubbish that couldn't be turned into food, even if it were only ersatz pepper.[6]

Black marketeers throve like maggots on an apple. On the open market, rations of butter were available at 2.50 marks a pound. Under the counter you could get as much as you liked for ten times that price – but most people went without, starved, froze, and cursed the war. Health suffered, especially among the very young and the very old. The city council set up soup kitchens, but they couldn't cope with the demand. In the shops, new produce appeared for sale: crows, squirrels, even woodpeckers. 'But if you had the money you could go into the back room of almost any restaurant and get roast goose and strawberries and cream, and wash it all down with as much beer and champagne as you could hold,' says a Berliner who remembers that time. 'Meanwhile, ordinary people were making do on sparrow stew.'

The people who had to live on such food – getting a thousand calories or less a day – also had to work in the arms factories, for which there was no more heating coal. The nadir was reached in the 'turnip winter' of 1916/17, when the temperature in central Berlin fell to −22°C. The wooden scaffolding which surrounded the 'Iron Hindenburg' statue at the foot of the Victory Column disappeared bit by bit as people made off with the planks for fuel. Both column and statue were viewed by Berliners with their customary cynicism. The column had been erected to mark the successful campaigns of 1864, 1866 and 1870, but the golden-winged Goddess of Victory above the heads of the starving, freezing citizens now seemed as remote as those glorious days. The statue of Hindenburg, carved in Russian alder, was more recent. Erected in 1914, it was a gimmick to collect money for the war effort: people would pay for a nail to hammer into the statue – a golden nail cost a hundred marks, a silver, five, and an iron, one. The figure was never fully 'nailed', and as the war progressed fewer and fewer people visited it. Once the scaffolding and even the wooden steps within it had been stolen for firewood, the Tiergarten authorities wanted the huge twelve-metre-high statue removed. However, nobody would take responsibility for it. Later it was dismantled into the twenty-one blocks which made it up, carted to a warehouse in the north of the city, and used for fuel. The head was discovered on a dump in 1938.

Women ran Berlin. They drove the buses, the trams and the delivery vans; they laid railway-lines and built roads; they worked in the docks and in the slaughterhouses. As always, it was the women who took responsibility for feeding their families. People said wryly, 'When old Bill's [the Kaiser's] lady wife queues for spuds, then the war'll be over.'

In Berlin, a new recipe appeared for stew made of tree bark. Meanwhile, on 16 April 1917 Wilhelm II sat down to dinner in Bad Kreuznach with officers of his High Command; their menu was:

Garnished consommé
Weinheimer Riesling 1911
Haut Brion 1907
Ragout of eggs and wild mushrooms
Niersteiner Auslese 1904
Saddle of venison with fresh young vegetables
Cream sauce
Muller Extra
Pears Regency
Burgundy 1881
Sliced toasted cheese
Tokaji essencia
Coffee

But the Kaiser was not in a good mood. The United States had entered the war against him as a result of his decision to make U-boat attacks even on neutral merchant shipping, and now there was more bad news: 200,000 munitions workers had gone on strike in Berlin. His Majesty was appalled. 'Gentlemen,' he said, 'I require you to take the most drastic measures necessary against these impossible Berliners.' In the event the strike, sparked by a reduction of 25 per cent (not the first) in the bread ration, collapsed quickly in the face of military intervention. But it was the first mass strike, and the workers took heart from it. Ironically, four days earlier and under conditions of high security, Lenin had set off for Russia from Berlin's Stettiner Station, with the blessing and under the protection of the Imperial German Army. The plan was simple: Lenin was to start a revolution in Russia; the Tsar would be brought down; and Russia would then sign a peace treaty with Germany which would be advantageous to the Reich. The officer in charge of Lenin's safe-conduct was Quartermaster-General Erich von Ludendorff, blinkered in his loyalty, a military genius, and a champion of the Right. Within five years Adolf Hitler was to be his closest political associate.

Germany before the First World War was a relatively enlightened state, but it was not a democracy. After the war, one of the hardest tasks facing the leaders of what is now known as the Weimar Republic was to introduce democratic ideas to a wrecked, disillusioned people whose instinct was to cling to the values they knew: order, military authority, and government by a 'father figure' – an instinct which was to have appalling consequences when Hitler presented himself as the successor of Bismarck and Hindenburg. But even before its low cost of living and its easy morals (born of desperation and cynicism) made it a Mecca for the world in all its aspects, Berlin was a centre of left-wing liberalism.[7] The emergent progressive parties could always count on electoral victory here. Before the First World War, Bismarck spoke angrily and contemptuously of the 'circle of progressives' in power in Berlin. As an industrial centre, it naturally had a strong workers' movement; in 1875, the socialists unified themselves in the Socialist Workers' Party, renamed the SPD (Sozialdemokratische Partei Deutschlands) in 1890. Though not initially powerful, it was regarded by the Establishment as so dangerously revolutionary that when the half-mad Karl Nobiling made his pointless and obviously independent assassination attempt on Wilhelm I in the summer of 1878, Bismarck was swift to lay the blame at its door. He pushed through a law banning socialist organizations of any kind, even socialist gatherings and publications. This law remained in force until 1890, but its effect was small. Support for the Left grew steadily in the capital during the last decade of the nineteenth century, and 'Red' Berlin's reputation was born.

By Monday 28 January 1918, the workers of Berlin had had enough; they began a new strike, one such as the city had never seen before. Four hundred and fourteen strikers' representatives were elected, and these in turn nominated an eleven-strong action committee. Their demands included an immediate peace negotiation on all fronts, the release of all political prisoners, improved provision of foodstuffs, and immediate democratization of the political system. Five hundred thousand workers took part, and they enjoyed the support of both the SPD and the far-left USPD – the Independent SPD – of Karl Liebknecht, who had been joined by the Polish Communist Rosa Luxemburg. Late in 1916, these two had founded the Spartakusbund (Spartacists) – effectively, the activist branch of the USPD – which on 1 January 1919 became the German Communist Party (KPD). Strike-breaking drivers were chased from their trams, which were overturned. The police could not contain the demonstrations, and civil unrest reached the brink of civil war. But the time was still not ripe. Once again, the army managed to crush the strike, and within a week factories were functioning normally. People would have recalled the cabaret song *The Revolutionary*, written by Erich Mühsam as early as 1907:

> He cleaned the gas lamps on the street,
> That's what he did to make ends meet.
> The rest of the time it was a different story,
> This lad, you see, was a Revolutionary.
>
> He talked revolution day and night,
> Shouted 'Power to the people!' with all his might.
> He pushed his beret over one ear
> And swore he'd sell his life so dear.
>
> The revolutionaries marched down the middle of the street.
> The houses shook to their marching feet,

While all along the pavements gleamed
The brave gas lamps our hero cleaned.

But the marchers had designs
On those polished lamps so fine.
'Quick, pull them down,' the leader said,
'We'll use them for a barricade.'

'Oh please don't touch, oh can't you see,
Those lamp-posts mean so much to me.'
He begged, he pleaded, he cajoled,
When all else failed, he then grew bold . . .

'Leave them alone. If they don't work
You'll leave the bourgeois in the dark!
If you behave in this reckless way,
Them I'm no longer going to play.'

The others simply roared with laughter,
And took the lamp-posts they were after,
While our hero slunk away,
Sat in a corner and began to cry.

After this he stayed at home,
Working on a learned tome
On HOW TO OVERTHROW SOCIETY
WHILE TREATING LAMP-POSTS WITH DUE PROPRIETY.[8]

Meanwhile, though the days of Wilhelmine Germany were numbered, the ruling class fantasized about an empire that would extend to the oilfields of Baku, the Balkans, the Near East, Africa, Belgium, Northern France, Holland and Scandinavia. No sooner had the ploy of supporting Lenin paid off, than the bickering began over who would get what of the considerable land gains Germany made from Russia under the ensuing treaty of Brest–Litovsk. Poland, Lithuania, half of Estonia, the Ukraine, Livonia, Kurland . . . the list went on, as Lenin was for the present in no position to bargain. With a supreme disregard for the historical realities surrounding them in their own country and on the Western Front, the Duke of Urach plotted with Matthias Erzberger – who within months was to lead the German delegation to Compiègne to sign the Armistice – to become King of Lithuania; Prince Friedrich Karl von Hessen, a brother-in-law of the Kaiser, had it in mind to be King of Finland; and the Kaiser himself, who had heard that there were great herds of aurochs in Kurland,[9] decided to turn that country into his own personal game preserve (the Kaiser was a good draughtsman, and had already designed the coat of arms he would use as its Duke).[10]

It was thirty years earlier, on 15 June 1888, that Friedrich III, second emperor of the Second Reich, died of cancer after a reign of ninety-five days. Although it had long been clear that he would ascend the throne only as a dying man, the liberal faction hoped that at least he would be able to set in motion an irrevocable process towards constitutionalism. During the long period he spent as Crown Prince, he had awoken great hopes. As early as his twenty-second year, he had protested at Bismarck's reactionary measures against the press, and at his policies *vis-à-vis* constitutional reform. He had a horror of war which was not mollified by Germany's successes in the 1860s. And he bade fair to become the country's first constitutional monarch, and to change the whole face of Germany's political system by curbing the absolute rights of the aristocracy, abolishing the three-tier voting system related to class, and opening appointments within the civil service to all. Friedrich understood that industrialization, a rising middle class, greater educational opportunities, and the legacy of the revolutions of 1848, had undermined the old order forever, but unfortunately his son did not inherit his liberal instincts. The Crown Prince, soon to become Wilhelm II, viewed the future with dismay. Even his moustache was modelled on that of an ancestor who had made his country an absolute monarchy. He saw the *status quo* in Germany threatened by his father and by what he regarded as the free-thinking of his English mother Victoria, Princess Royal of England, who shared her husband's principles.

As Friedrich lay dying in the New Palace in the park of Sanssouci in Potsdam, his son called out the Guard-Hussars from their barracks to surround the palace. Henceforward, no one was to take messages or documents in or out.[11] The moment he received news of his father's death, Wilhelm sent trusted army officers and secret policemen into the palace. Every desk, every drawer, every corner was searched for documents which might be construed as harmful to the old *status quo*. They looked behind paintings and under rugs. Nothing – apparently – was found.

Wilhelm now reigned with false triumph in what became increasingly a fool's paradise. He harked back to the old, 'great' days of German history, even going so far as to hold costume balls at the castle of Malbork, the mighty fourteenth-century seat of the Teutonic Knights, with himself naturally in the role of the Grand Master.[12] His crowning folly was to force, by reason of his policies, the resignation of Bismarck, thereby throwing away the services of the one man whose sense of the realities of contemporary society might have saved Germany from the chaos awaiting it. Bismarck was never too grand to learn; Wilhelm always was.

The First World War, which Germans had been led to believe was a war of defence, dragged on not for a matter of weeks, but for four years. Even as early as March 1915 it was going so badly that Grand-Admiral von Tirpitz[13] suggested that the Kaiser should dismiss his Chancellor and Chief of the Great General Staff and himself go into temporary retirement, after appointing Field Marshal Paul von Hindenburg[14] Dictator of the Reich. The army had always been regarded as Germany's backbone; even Bismarck had had trouble asserting his authority over it. However, he had gone some way to establishing a balance of power between the politicians and the military; the First World War gave the generals the advantage.

Helmuth von Moltke, Chief of the General Staff at the outbreak of war, achieved no outstanding military successes and was unable to overcome the civilian authority. His successor, General von Falkenhayn, respected Parliament but was replaced after the débâcle of Verdun, on the advice of the Chancellor, Bethmann Hollweg, by the two commanders who were the real heroes of the war. Paul von Hindenburg and his Quartermaster-General, Erich von Ludendorff, had gained the confidence of the people by their early victories on the Russian front at Tannenberg and the Masurian Lakes.[15] Hindenburg, who had come out of retirement to command the Eighth Army, was a father figure of the kind so beloved by the Germans, and so fatal to them. He had the charisma and *gravitas* that the Kaiser so evidently lacked. According to the playwright Carl Zuckmayer, there was an 'Iron Hindenburg' statue in every market town in Germany. From August 1916 until the end of the war, Hindenburg and Ludendorff effectively ruled Germany, demonstrating how politically incompetent good soldiers can be.[16] Their vainglorious decisions, not least to introduce, against strenuous diplomatic and political advice, all-out U-boat aggression, sealed the fate of Germany. Perhaps Germany had to experience the depths of disaster before something better could emerge. While tracing the last crazy months of 1918, which culminated in revolution in Berlin and in the country very nearly becoming a Soviet state, one has to remember that no effective tradition of democracy existed, however much it might have been desired by progressive thinkers; and that any attempt to introduce its principles was met with horror by the Establishment. 'Germany's very future requires political rights for the general population, in order that the just and joyous political collaboration of the masses may be obtained,' said Bethmann Hollweg to the Lower House of the Prussian Legislature on 14 March 1917. He was met by icy silence on the Right.[17]

Even when news started to come in of the Russian revolution the Kaiser, well under the thumb of his two generals, was still reluctant to implement reforms; only a few sops to democracy were contained in his Easter Message of 2 April. Ludendorff, never a man to mince words, called this 'kowtowing to the Russian revolutionaries'; as late as December he was writing, 'In my opinion the war has given us no grounds for democratization or republicanization . . . On the contrary, I consider such a policy of yielding to the spirit of the age extraordinarily dangerous. Its consequences will inevitably lead us to disaster.'[18] In the meantime, the devious but respected Centrist leader, Matthias Erzberger, had made a speech to the Reichstag advocating a negotiated peace. Based on military and diplomatic advice, it polarized opinion. Hindenburg started intriguing to get Bethmann Hollweg ousted. The peace lobby also wished to see the unfortunate Chancellor go. They believed him too weak to push a peace settlement through. Bethmann Hollweg was replaced. But the war continued.

Spurred on by this success, and dismissive of the mood of the working classes in Berlin and of the increasing pessimism of their soldiers in the field, Hindenburg and Ludendorff, secure from Russian attack, now planned a major offensive on the Western Front. They hoped to crush the Allies – and possibly negotiate a favourable peace – before American forces could properly establish themselves. It didn't work. Three offensives by Ludendorff brought the German army to the Marne, but the men were exhausted, disillusioned and hungry. Meanwhile, fresh, well-fed Americans poured in, armed with the most modern equipment. From July 1918 it was downhill all the way for Germany, although the generals continued to believe that maintaining a defensive war would force the enemy to terms of peace.[19] By September even the Kaiser was convinced that the war should end, but the generals insisted that both the monarchy and the pre-war frontiers must be preserved. They spoke of a revolution from above and, ironically, the panic reforms they now introduced went further than any previously suggested: parliamentary government and universal suffrage were introduced in October 1918. But it was all too late.

The chancellorship had passed to a reluctant Prince Max von Baden – reluctant, because he realized that his main task would be to sue for peace. Von Baden, a cousin of the Kaiser, was a liberal, better known as the patron of education who made it possible for Kurt Hahn to establish a school at Salem, one of his castles. (Hahn later came to Britain as a fugitive from the Nazis; among the schools he established, Gordonstoun is the most famous by virtue of its association with the British Royal family.) Von Baden knew that to achieve the most merciful terms he had to go to the Allies with a cabinet which demonstrated the new democracy Germany had, to save her skin, ushered in. He expected no clemency from the French, but had hopes of the Americans and the British. Ironically, Ludendorff and Hindenburg were able to hide behind the skirts of the parliamentary democracy they had created, and avoid taking the blame for the downfall of their country. They emerged smelling, if not of roses, at least not of sulphur. But the Allies insisted on terms that would preclude any possible resumption of hostilities by Germany. This was a hope to which Hindenburg and Ludendorff had clung, and they now made a last-ditch attempt to seize the initiative for themselves and renew the war. As a result, von Baden was able to obtain Ludendorff's dismissal; Hindenburg had managed to distance himself from his more outspoken colleague in time. (Ludendorff, in fear of attack from the revolutionary forces in his disintegrating country, or even of being handed over to the Allies as a war criminal, subsequently fled in great haste, disguised in false beard and dark blue sun-glasses, to neutral Sweden.) Meanwhile the US President, Woodrow Wilson, refused to deal with either military or monarchy. If the Germans refused these terms, an unconditional surrender would be demanded forthwith: this requirement effectively scotched any possibility of retaining the Kaiser on his throne.

The armed forces were now breaking up. The ordinary conscripted soldiers were demoralized, cynical and disillusioned after four years of dirty war coupled with the rigid discipline and social injustice of the German army. Inevitably, there was a popular swing to the Left. These men were no longer *kaisertreu*: in fact, they wanted to boot the Kaiser out as fast as possible. The situation worsened when Wilhelm II set off for the battle front HQ at Spa in Belgium on 29 October 1918. His naval commanders, frustrated by lack of action since the battle of the Skagerrak left them blockaded by the British, now decided to break out. The U-boat war over, they sought a final battle with the enemy. But on the same day that the Kaiser left for the Front, the naval stokers went on strike with such unanimity that their commanders' orders had to be rescinded. By 4 November the red flag flew from every warship at Kiel, and groups of revolutionary sailors started to wander south, east and west into Germany, kindling revolt in Bremen, Lübeck, Hamburg, and eventually Berlin. On 6 November, von Baden decided that further delay would be dangerous. Better to lose something than to lose everything. He determined to set off for Spa immediately to ask the Kaiser for his abdication. Before leaving Berlin, and in order to protect himself against a revolution in the city while he was away, he confided his intention to Friedrich Ebert, the SPD representative in the Reichstag, and Philipp Scheidemann, another leading Social Democrat. Both men were ready to support von Baden, but were given an ultimatum by their own party, new to real power and obstreperous in it, that the SPD would withdraw from the newly-formed coalition government if the Emperor and the Crown Prince had not abdicated by noon on 8 November. This was the following day, and revolution was spreading like a conflagration from one town to another throughout the country. On 8 November a republic was declared in Munich, deposing the Bavarian Wittelsbach dynasty. Shortly afterwards, the Berlin working-class district of Neukölln also declared itself an independent republic. Brunswick's liberal Duke, husband of the Kaiser's only daughter, renounced his title.

And still Wilhelm II resisted abdication. He resisted it vigorously: 'My abdication is out of the question! The army and the people are firmly behind me! It's just that damned Berlin that's against me!'[20] Von Baden came back to Berlin empty-handed. It may be that Wilhelm thought he could return from Spa at the head of the armies and restore order by force; but even he must have seen that those armies were collapsing around him.[21] The generals, though well aware of the situation in Berlin, waited until the morning of 9 November before they too asked the Kaiser to relinquish the throne. On the night of 8 November the government telegraphed to Spa that the rebellion could not be checked if the abdication were not announced in the morning papers: in a futile play for time, Hindenburg replied that the All-Highest had retired to bed, and could not be disturbed.

Unwilling to do so himself, Hindenburg persuaded Ludendorff's successor, General Gröner, to put the ultimatum to the Kaiser. This Gröner did, in the full knowledge that he was possibly saving Hindenburg's reputation with the army at the expense of his own; he was motivated by a modest patriotism, and by a conviction that Hindenburg's image must remain unsullied for the good of the military. Gröner was the son of an NCO in the Württemberg army; a career soldier and a brilliant staff officer, he was a greater realist than any of his noble Prussian colleagues, and a good deal more honourable than many of them.

Finally, too late to prevent the SPD from leaving the government, the Kaiser bowed to the inevitable; by now crowds of workers were marching towards Berlin. Many soldiers in the city were still loyal to the government, but no one wanted to lead them against the rebels. No one knew who was in charge. Von Baden learned of the abdication by telephone at 11 a.m. on 9 November. Determined to save the institution of monarchy at least, he announced at noon that the Emperor had relinquished the throne, and that the Crown Prince had declined to succeed him. In the event, this proved an academic exercise. As soon as the news broke the SPD, as the strongest party, announced to him they were taking over the government. Von Baden was obliged, not unwillingly, to give up the chancellorship. To his successor Ebert, a former saddler, he said, 'Herr Ebert, I commit the German nation to the care of your heart.' Ebert replied, 'I have lost two sons in the defence of this nation.'

As a footnote to these momentous events, the text of Wilhelm's abdication now came through: he abdicated as Emperor, but not as King of Prussia. This was a pathetic clutching at straws, since the latter was subsumed within the former. While lunching at Spa he learned, between the fish and the meat courses, that his abdication had been accepted. 'Treachery! Damned, shameless treachery!' he yelled. But the following day he was on a little train heading for a long and not uncomfortable exile at Doorn, in neutral Holland. There is no serious evidence of penitence for the destruction and mass slaughter he had brought about. But is such a thing ever to be expected in such men? If the words of the old German army song lamenting the fallen, *I Had a Comrade*, ever passed through his mind, they would not have reproached him. In any event, the Republic was now a reality.

A cultural revolution had preceded the political one which ended the Second Reich and Wilhelm, for all his fulminations against the New Art, and despite the wide censorship facilities at the disposal of his police, had failed to suppress it. The Kaiser's taste in artistic matters was conventional, stuffy and reactionary, as was his wife's. Although the Hohenzollerns were music-lovers, Empress Auguste Viktoria attempted to prevent the production of Richard Strauss's *Salome* in 1905 (she actually succeeded in keeping *Der Rosenkavalier* off the stage in Germany). Berlin had a strong musical and operatic tradition, but modern trends were not encouraged.

In 1882 the Berliner Philharmonic Orchestra was founded, and attracted among its guest conductors Brahms, Grieg, Mahler, Richard Strauss and Tchaikovsky. The Royal Opera was one of the best in Europe in the 1890s, and Leoncavallo was a personal friend of Wilhelm II. In 1896 the Theater des Westens opened in Charlottenburg as a home for light opera, and the Komische Oper on Weidendammer Brücke opened in 1905 with Offenbach's *Tales of Hoffmann*.

One of the great centres of the artistic renaissance-cum-revolution was at Friedrichshagen, to the immediate south-east of Berlin. There, from the 1880s on, a poets' colony was founded by the brothers Heinrich and Julius Hart, men of letters and critics who tried to encourage young talent. Gerhart Hauptmann was one writer to profit from their nurturing. Wilhelm II disliked this movement – naturalism was unpopular at court – and went so far as to describe Hauptmann's *The Weavers* as 'the literature of the gutter'; but the new artistic movement throve on adversity. Hauptmann had made his name as Germany's leading playwright at the age of 27 with his first play, *Before Sunrise*, and he retained his pre-eminence, receiving the Nobel Prize twenty-three years later, in 1912. As early as 1893 Prince Chlodwig zu Hohenlohe-Schillingsfürst (who became Chancellor in the following year) was inveighing against Hauptmann's *Hannele's Road to Heaven*, a symbolic tragedy of the lower depths of working-class life. He wrote in his diary: 'A monstrous . . . piece of work, social-democratic-realistic . . . fully of sickly, sentimental mysticism . . . Afterwards we went to Borchardt's, to get ourselves back into a human frame of mind with champagne and caviare.'[22]

Thomas Mann had made his name with *Buddenbrooks* in 1901 (when he was 26); he went on to win the Nobel Prize in 1929. His elder brother Heinrich published *Professor Unrat* in 1905; twenty-four years later the film of the novel, *The Blue Angel,* simultaneously launched and immortalized Marlene Dietrich. The new publishing houses of Ernst Rowohlt and Kurt Wolff were on the *qui vive* for original, non-establishment talent. Two new magazines, Franz Pfemfert's *Aktion* (1911–1932), and Herwarth Walden's *Sturm* (1910–1932), encouraged new Expressionist writing and, in the latter case, art as well. Walter Hasenclever's play *The Son* was written in 1914, and performed first in Prague and then in Dresden in 1916 – privately in Dresden, as the piece had promptly been banned in Germany. The writer was 26, and his work was the first of many after the war which dealt with a son's rebellion against an authoritarian father. It was 'as prophetic of the Weimar style as Marc's *Blue Horses*'.[23]

Max Reinhardt, who in 1905, at the age of 32, took over the direction of the Deutsches Theater, had fully developed his style by 1914, and his position as king of German theatre was being challenged before the Weimar Republic was more than a few years old. Later the Nazis drove him from the city which he had helped make the theatre centre of the world. The Free Theatre was founded in 1889 to give club performances of plays which had attracted the attention of the censor, and a year later the People's Theatre appeared. This great theatre was the brain-child of a group led by the Social Democrat writer Bruno Wille, born of discussions in the debating-club Alte Tante (Old Auntie – a stock character in German folklore; the name served as camouflage against Bismarck's anti-socialist law). The idea was to bring plays to the working classes and the poor, who would become members of the People's Theatre on payment of a small subscription; theatres were rented for one Sunday in the month to put on productions.[24] Membership quickly grew to 70,000, and the People's Theatre decided to acquire its own house. The New People's Theatre opened on 30 August 1910 with Ibsen's *Pillars of the Community,* and the theatre was later associated with the greatest luminaries of left-wing drama in Germany.

Established art was less happy. The dominant painter of the court was the President of the Prussian Academy of Art, Anton von Werner, who went in for large historical canvases and such subjects as the *Opening of Parliament by Wilhelm II* (1889), whose title says it all. The official sculptor, Reinhold Bergas, must at least have had a sense of humour. He was commissioned to provide a series of statues of German heroes for the Siegesallee in Berlin (Berliners at once nicknamed it 'Puppet Alley');

there was much amusement over the Court's indignation when it was revealed that the model for one statue had been the social critic, artist and cartoonist of Berlin's low-life, Heinrich Zille. At any rate, he had a noble beard.

The artistic flagship of the Weimar Republic, the Bauhaus, was foreshadowed in some of its ideas by Jugendstil – the German art nouveau. Jugendstil took its name from the Munich magazine *Jugend* (Youth) and advocated the joining of forces and blending of disciplines of architects, artists, artisans and technicians. In May 1898 a loose association of some sixty-five artists broke away from the Academy and formed the Berlin Secession, partly in protest against Wilhelm II's dictatorial desire to lock art within conservative and formal bounds. Among them was Max Liebermann, Berlin born and bred. The most important new ideas ushered in by this forerunner of Expressionism – Liebermann himself was an Impressionist – were to do with the abandonment of the stiff and photographic realism preferred by the Kaiser (and later by Hitler), and the introduction of themes related to real life and its problems. Modern art and modern thinking also attracted to the capital great innovative painters of a slightly older generation, like Lovis Corinth and Max Slevogt, as well as the much older artist, the diminutive Adolf von Menzel; these bridged the gap between the old guard and the new.

Elsewhere in Germany, new life was about to burst through. Vassily Kandinsky's revolutionary manifesto, *Concerning the Spiritual in Art*, appeared in 1912, and the Expressionist Movement was fully fledged before the First World War. One of its greatest exponents, Franz Marc (whose *Blue Horses* vies with Van Gogh's *Sunflowers* as the most reproduced painting ever), died in the conflict in 1916, aged 36. In Munich Der Blaue Reiter (The Blue Rider) was founded by Kandinsky and Marc in 1911, to be disbanded during the First World War. This breakaway group attracted, among others, August Macke and Paul Klee; Klee later joined the Bauhaus group. (Blue was a favourite colour of many German Romantic poets, especially Novalis, and of the mystical Expressionists; and one of Kandinsky's early pictures – of 1903, and now in the Bührle Collection – was entitled *Der Blaue Reiter*.) The principal inspirations of Die Brücke (The Bridge) group which flourished in Dresden between 1905 and 1913 were the Fauves, Gauguin, Van Gogh, Munch, and primitive tribal art. Despite its short life it cast a long shadow, influencing the graphic arts, and the woodcut in particular. (The origin of the name is obscure – though the fact that Nietzsche's work was a central inspiration to the group, and the bridge is a major symbol in his *Thus Spake Zarathustra*, is one possible explanation.)

The clean lines and spare, uncluttered functionalism of the Bauhaus could not be in sharper contrast to the red brick or sandstone Gothic

Baroque of the Wilhelmine Establishment, a most striking example of which is the Kaiser-Wilhelm-Gedächtniskirche, whose ruined spire stands as a memorial of the Second World War.

One building which unified the Kaiser and his unruly Berliners in dislike was the Reichstag, built in 1894. This top-heavy and over-ornate grey pile was immediately dubbed 'the first-class hearse'. In a letter to a friend Wilhelm II called it the *Reichsaffenhaus* (the Reich Monkey House); he was, however, probably referring to its contents rather than its looks.[25] In the midst of such wedding-cakery, it is refreshing to discover the architect Peter Behrens and his pupils, who included Walter Gropius, Mies van der Rohe and Le Corbusier, creating buildings whose looks will always be associated with the new century.

The progressive movement in Berlin encouraged the early development of artists who were to influence and spill over into the Weimar Republic. The last decade of the nineteenth century and the first decade of the twentieth were the ones in which the breakthroughs were made. The First World War was an interruption of an unstoppable process.

MORNING

A large number of people came towards me along Leipziger
Strasse. They were running away. I asked them what they
were fleeing from. One or two of them shouted that
counter-revolutionary troops had been sent up from Potsdam,
and there was shooting. I turned into Wilhelmstrasse, but
heard nothing, though by all accounts there should have been
shooting in Potsdamer Platz at about that time. I got home
about 1 a.m. That was the end of the first day of the
revolution, which in the course of a few hours had seen the
fall of the house of Hohenzollern, the collapse of the Imperial
Army, and the end of the society we had known up until
then. One of the most memorable and terrible days in
German history.

– Harry, Graf Kessler, diary entry,
Saturday 9 November 1918.

No pig could find its way around this sty.
What's true is false, what's fake is not,
And everything is stewing in the pot,
And pain's a laugh, and pleasure makes them cry,
And up is down, and front's behind.
Just shake your head – or lose your mind.

– Erich Kästner, *Ragoût fin de siècle*
(translated by Koka Koala)

2 Death and Resurrection

■■■■■■■ WHEN BERLIN BECAME the centre and focus of the revolution, people took bolts of red cloth from the department stores around Alexanderplatz and soon red flags were draped from public buildings, including the Town Hall. Power took to the streets, and did not leave them for fifteen months, although the revolution of the far left foundered sooner. On 9 November, a Communist takeover of Germany was a real threat. Friedrich Ebert, now Chancellor, and Philipp Scheidemann sat uneasily in the Reichstag restaurant – at separate tables, for they had no strong feelings of amity for each other – and ate potato soup. Neither knew how to respond to the demands being made of them, with ever greater urgency, to say something – something encouraging, reassuring – to the seething mob outside the windows. The most worrying news was that Karl Liebknecht was preparing to proclaim a Soviet state. The 1 p.m. edition of the *Berliner Zeitung am Mittag* was on the streets, and its headline announced the abdication. Something had to be done. But what? Both men knew that someone had to take control. Finally Philipp Scheidemann, who with his white imperial beard and strong features looked more like a poet or an actor than a politician, walked across to the windows and opened one wide. Noticing him, the crowd quietened. Scheidemann pronounced in a clear voice: 'The people have won all along the line! Long live the German Republic!'[1]

This declaration saved the situation, at least for the moment. But it smacked of what Berliners called *een falscha Irrtum* – a cock-up. Ebert and the right wing of the SPD hadn't wanted a revolution. They hadn't even wanted a republic. But they certainly didn't want Liebknecht's Socialist Republic – which nonetheless was proclaimed a few hours later from the very balcony of the Schloss from which the Kaiser had proclaimed mobilization in 1914. Among those who reported it was the 24-year-old Ben Hecht of the Chicago *Daily News*. Liebknecht subsequently moved to the offices of the conservative newspaper, the *Lokal Anzeiger*, and took them over as the base of his new revolutionary publication, *Die Rote Fahne* (The Red Flag).

Ebert was furious with Scheidemann for being importunate, but there is no knowing what greater confusion might have reigned if he had not spoken at all. In any case, there was a terrible mess to be sorted out. People were buying guns from conscripts eager for cash to buy food. Former Imperial officers caught in the streets had their decorations and epaulettes torn off. The SPD viewed all this with dismay. They had wanted bourgeois democracy and social reform and now had to set about achieving them, not in an orderly way, but out of chaos. To complicate matters further the regular army, garrisoned dangerously close, in Potsdam, largely retained its right-wing elements. Many of the conscripts, the soldiers and sailors who now roved the streets in semi-disciplined and resentful bands, were fanatically attached to Communist ideals. Others simply had no homes to go to; those who had, returned to their wives, families, jobs, or smallholdings with all possible speed.

Now the revolution paused for breath. On 10 November Theodor Wolff, Berlin's most eminent editor, wrote in one of his famous Sunday leaders in the *Berliner Tageblatt*: 'The greatest of all revolutions has, like a sudden tempest, swept away the Imperial regime and all that it stood for. One can call this the greatest of all revolutions because never before has so strongly-built and solidly-walled a Bastille been taken at a stroke.' And indeed, so far, for all the menace and confusion, it had not been what one might call a bloody affair. Wolff also wrote: 'A week ago, there existed a military and civil administrative apparatus so four-square, so tightly-knit, and so deep-rooted that it looked as if it could withstand the changing times ... In the offices and the ministries an apparently unassailable bureaucracy seemed to reign. Early in the morning in Berlin everything was still in place. Later the same day nothing was left of it at all.'2 As it transpired, the old apparatus was all too unshaken – though this proved to be to the benefit as much as to the disadvantage of the fledgling regime.

The SPD had its headquarters in the building belonging to its paper, *Vorwärts* (Forwards), in Lindenstrasse. Party organization was excellent, and the SPD held another strong card in that they enjoyed the support of the majority of the German army, right-wing elements notwithstanding. Even so, a large number of far-left workers' and soldiers' councils sprang up in Berlin, independently, and not always in agreement. Even the barracks were in the hands of revolutionary soldiers, and the police had sensibly vanished from the scene. Without executive power or direction, however, many of these councils disbanded in the course of a few days, and the city authorities were able to make their first moves against the anarchy on the streets as early as the evening of 9 November. It was vital to re-establish order, suppress looting, and protect the food-distribution system. In the midst of the infighting, a people's committee representing the SPD, Liebknecht's Independents and the trades unions was set up to implement an exhortation by SPD city councillor Johannes Sassenbach, that 'Order and calm are necessary concomitants to the successful conclusion of the revolution. Citizens are requested to keep off the streets wherever possible and certainly after dark.' The city councillors were liberal progressives but were careful not to call themselves revolutionaries, preferring instead 'people's representatives'; they struggled to maintain the ordinary infrastructure of the city through thick and thin. Vigilante groups appeared to make up for the lack of police.

The Police Praesidium was taken over by the Sparticist Emil Eichhorn, who now declared himself Chief of the Berlin police. The Spartacists themselves were based at the former Prussian Chamber of Deputies, but the most important left-wing revolutionary centre was the Zirkus Busch, on the banks of the Spree near the Stock Exchange. Not a circus in the usual sense, this was a theatre-in-the-round and so made a useful debating chamber. (After the Reichstag fire, the Nazis used the Kroll Opera in the same way.)

Ebert's first attempts to make himself master of the situation by invoking the army's aid failed miserably. The conscripted divisions returning to Berlin melted away as soon as they reached the city, and a projected attack on revolutionary sailors from Kiel who had installed themselves in the Marstall – the former Imperial stables behind the Schloss – came to nothing when the women, the elderly and the children of the city took the sailors' part and alerted workers' groups, who sent armed reinforcements from the factories. A demonstration by left-wing veterans interrupted a procession of returning regular troops. In the meantime General Gröner, at Spa, had been in touch with Ebert via the secret telephone link Max von Baden had used in his frantic attempts to persuade the Kaiser to abdicate. In return for the new government's promise to back the officer corps, a ratification of Hindenburg's position as commander-in-chief and a commitment to suppress Bolshevism, Gröner offered the army's help in restoring discipline in Berlin (and, by extension, the country) as well as its support for the government. Ebert was too desperate and too grateful to do anything but agree unconditionally, and Gröner at a stroke thus ensured the survival and the integrity of the regular Imperial armed forces. The deal lamed the revolution at birth.

The army remained the backbone of the country, and subsequent events merely strengthened its position.

Within a month of the Armistice on 11 November, General Gröner had brought two million troops home to Germany. By late December there was some hope of using what remained of the army to restore order in Berlin. Ebert welcomed them at the Brandenburg Gate with a high-sounding speech describing them as 'undefeated on the field of battle', thereby tightening the bonds which bound his government to them.[3] Hindenburg, by dissociating himself from the signing of the Armistice, had managed to keep his reputation, but the problem of maintaining the solidarity of the old officer corps was not so easily solved. Within days of the army's return a National Congress of Workers' and Soldiers' Councils had convened in Berlin, claiming to represent the full interests of the German people. Although dominated by the SPD, it none the less passed a resolution demanding that officers be elected by the soldiery, that all marks of rank and other insignia be abandoned, and that the old Imperial Army be phased out in favour of a new People's Army. Gröner put immediate pressure on Ebert. With his chief aide, Kurt von Schleicher (whose role as the most powerful *éminence grise* of the Weimar Republic was about to begin), he rode to Berlin in full dress uniform and told the provisional Chancellor precisely what the military's attitude to such a proposal was. Ebert knew he had to go along with the army, and fortunately was able to defuse the situation by simply ignoring the Congress's demands. Equally fortunately, the Congress itself was more immediately interested in confirming Ebert's position and working towards full elections for a new National Assembly.

But the Weimar Republic was doomed from birth. Even as the plans for the new democracy were being drawn up, the forces of reaction were crystallizing. Hermann Göring, then a Luftwaffe captain with the highest German decoration for bravery, the *Pour le Mérite*, publicly voiced his grievances against what he saw as a pusillanimous new regime, and later, in *Mein Kampf*, Adolf Hitler recalled with characteristic rodomontade his own bitterness at this period – bitterness which impelled him to enter politics.[4]

The Schloss and the Marstall were still occupied by revolutionary sailors. Ebert had as yet no means of ejecting them by force so, shortly before Christmas, playing for time, he offered them 125,000 marks as 'payment for guarding the Schloss'; the sailors were to reduce their force to 600, all of them to move into the Marstall. They demanded a further 80,000 marks as a 'Christmas bonus'; Ebert gave way to this, repeating his condition that the Schloss be vacated. The sailors, with the backing of the people, thereupon occupied the Chancellery building itself. They kidnapped the military governor of Berlin, the civilian SPD delegate

Otto Wels, and two associates, took them back to the Schloss and beat them up.

The sailors had gained control of the Chancellery's telephone switchboard, but did not know of the secret line to army headquarters (by now relocated at Kassel). Ebert telephoned Gröner for help and reached Schleicher, who arranged for a detachment of General von Lequis' Horse Guards to ride from Potsdam to the government's aid. Meanwhile, Ebert continued to negotiate. The sailors were persuaded to agree to leave the Chancellery in return for their Christmas bonus; but they then got wind of the army's intended intervention. To allay their anger Ebert now desperately tried to get Gröner to call von Lequis' men off; but Gröner would not agree. Eight hundred cavalry, reinforced by 1,000 infantry who had been encamped in the large Tiergarten park, now prepared to lay siege. The sailors released Wels and his companions but, emboldened by the promise of reinforcements, refused to surrender. As the troops occupied the Schloss, after giving it an artillery battering such as it had not experienced during the whole of the war, the sailors retreated to the Marstall. To the government's fury the police, under the command of Emil Eichhorn, remained neutral.

By the morning of Christmas Eve the sailors were on the point of surrender and begged a short truce. Now occurred a bizarre *volte-face*. During the battle Spartacists, alarmed at this show of force by the army and anxious to undermine it if possible, had stirred people up, spreading fears of a counter-revolution from the Right. As soon as the troops stopped firing, thousands swept into the square surrounding the beleaguered buildings and began to talk to the soldiers. There was little the officers could do to maintain discipline; swayed by popular argument, large numbers of troops began to waver. Some even abandoned their weapons. To preserve what they could under the circumstances, the officers formed up their men and marched them away. It was a disastrous blow for the army, and for the government which had sided with it. Ebert felt the initiative slide away from him. There was a Dada-esque element in the fact that all this was happening on 24 December – in Germany the most important day of Christmas. Only tens of metres away crowds were unconcernedly doing their last-minute shopping, cabarets and theatres were open, and those with money were spending it freely. This was the first peace-time Christmas for five years, and for most people no revolution was going to stop them enjoying it.

Watching it all was Harry, Graf Kessler. He was born in Paris on 23 May 1868 and died, almost forgotten, in exile in provincial France in December 1937.[5] He was the son of the German director of the Paris branch of a German bank, ennobled in 1879, and of an Irish mother, Alice Harriet Blosse-Lynch, a notable beauty who had enjoyed a long (and platonic) friendship with Wilhelm I. Harry Kessler was educated in Paris, Ascot and Hamburg and grew up a true cosmopolitan. Enormously wealthy in his own right, he became a patron of the arts, ran a high-quality printing and publishing company, the Cranach Press, from his country home at Weimar, championed modern art and design, wrote well and widely, was involved in politics on the Left (he was nicknamed 'the Red Count' and hated by the Right), and by Christmas 1918 had just returned from a short spell as German Ambassador to Poland. Elegant, handsome and urbane, never marrying, Kessler knew everyone from Virginia Woolf to Richard Strauss, from Max Reinhardt to Albert Einstein. In his autobiography the Communist artist George Grosz, whose life Kessler had saved at the end of the war, writes of him warmly as 'perhaps the last real gentleman to cross my path'.

Kessler's diary entry for 24 December notes the destruction of the Schloss, and the Christmas crowd's lack of concern:

In the Lustgarten[6] an enormous crowd wandered undisturbed. The great entrance [of the Schloss] facing the Lustgarten is quite shot up; one of its columns lies shattered on the ground; the iron doors hang askew, bent and shot through. The balcony over them, from which the Kaiser made his speech on 4 August 1914, hangs down, smashed up. The windows in the façade are empty and dark, all broken . . . Saddest of all are the beautiful Baroque caryatids which support the balcony: one Michelangelo-esque arm lies shot away, and the expressive heads look more pathetically bowed down than ever . . . During the playing-out of these bloody events Christmas trading carries on undisturbed. Barrel-organs play in the Friedrichstrasse, street-peddlers offer indoor fireworks, cinnamon-cakes and tinsel. The jewellers on Unter den Linden are all open, without a care in the world, their windows brightly lit. In Leipziger Strasse the usual Christmas crowds flock to Wertheim's, Kayser's,[7] and so on. Quite certainly in thousands of homes the Christmas trees will be lit, and the children will be playing under them with the presents they've had from Daddy, Mummy, and their dear Aunt. And at the same time corpses lie in the Marstall, and the new wounds of the Schloss and the German State gape in the Christmas night.

The Spartacists pressed home their success. On Christmas Day a mass rally was called. Kessler wrote:

In the afternoon there was a massive . . . demonstration which took place between Siegesallee and the Schloss, where the people fraternized with the victorious sailors. Then the crowd moved on to the offices of *Vorwärts*. They occupied the building and printed flyers with the title *The Red Vorwärts*. The flyer announced: 'Today, 25 December 1918, *Vorwärts* was occupied by us, the revolutionary workers, on behalf of the new power born with the revolution of 9 November. Long live the revolutionary naval division, the revolutionary proletariat, the socialist international world revolution. Down with the Ebert–Scheidemann government! All power to the Workers' and Soldiers' Soviets! Arm the workers! Disarm the bourgeoisie and their minions! Signed: the Revolutionary Representatives and Administration of Great Berlin.' The whole thing was done on red paper.

Following the Schloss débâcle, Ebert's government seemed doomed. Liebknecht was riding high, and even the more intellectual and cautious Rosa Luxemburg was swept along. The three weeks following Christmas were weeks of civil war in Berlin as forces – both civilian and military – loyal to the government struggled desperately for power with the Spartacists. At the same time shops, theatres, and cabarets were open. The rich turned their backs on the chaos in the streets, losing themselves in an orgy of tinselly pleasure.

Grosz describes his impressions as a homecoming soldier thus:

> In that year, 1919, as we walked through the dark streets of Berlin, we ducked in and out of the tall doorways keeping close to the small porters' lodges – many people, unable to bear their frightened and cooped-up existence, had made for the roof-tops and would take pot-shots at anything they saw, whether birds or people. They had obviously lost all sense of proportion, for one day, when one of these snipers was caught and confronted with a man he had shot in the arm, he said only: 'But sergeant, I was sure that one was a big pigeon.'[8]

On 1 January 1919, as Harry Kessler sat down in a restaurant to dine, it was invaded by a deputation of striking waiters, demanding their colleagues join them in an ultimatum to the restaurant manager: concede to their demands, or face closure. 'The strikers wore red cards tucked into their hatbands.' Within five minutes the manager had done a deal, and service could continue. On 8 January Spartacists occupied houses in Mohrenstrasse, while government troops lay in wait in the darkened Kaiserhof Hotel. But just down the road, in Potsdamer Platz, everything was open as usual: the great café-restaurants were all brilliantly lit and packed. On 17 January Kessler went to a cabaret; during one number, a shot rang out. No one paid the least attention.

> And that's how big city society responds to the revolution. The life Berlin society leads is so elementary that even a revolution of world significance like the present one barely makes an impression on it. The Babylonian, immeasurable depth of chaos and violence in Berlin has only now become clear to me, through the revolution. I see that this monstrous movement, within the even more monstrous to-ing and fro-ing of the whole seething city, just makes little local impressions. It's as if Berlin were an elephant, and the revolution were a penknife. It sticks into the elephant, which shakes itself, but then strides on, as if nothing in the world had happened.

Returning soldiers were still pouring into the city and setting up their gun-stalls. Grosz's cousin bought six Mauser .98s, and Grosz himself was able to pick up a brand-new Lüger. 'The times were certainly out of joint. All moral restraints seemed to have melted away. A flood of vice, pornography and prostitution swept the entire country. "Je m'en fous" was what everyone thought – "It's time we had a bit of fun." '9 Six weeks into 1919, Kessler noted: 'I was hauled off by acquaintances to a place where you can dance until dawn. There are hundreds like it in Berlin now. The best description of this second phase of the revolution . . . is "dancing on a volcano" .'10

But there was no question of fun for a government fighting for its life. Early in January Ebert called in his colleague Gustav Noske from Kiel, where Noske, an expert in military affairs and acting Minister of Defence, had been engaged in the efficient putting-down of the naval mutiny. Noske, like Ebert, had been a craftsman (a basket-weaver and a master butcher), and shared the same moderate socialist outlook. A brilliant organizer, he was prepared to co-operate with the army and the officer corps to relieve the country of the 'Communist menace'. Although his arrival signalled the beginning of the end for that menace, the struggle continued vigorously for several months, and flickered on throughout the Weimar Republic.

The great weakness of the Spartacus movement was that its dominant figure was not the intelligent and realistic Rosa Luxemburg, but Karl Liebknecht. He was ambitious, he had very little charisma, he was too optimistic of success too soon, and he was not well-enough informed of what was happening away from Berlin among his enemies. He thought he could seize power by sheer force of revolution, in emulation of his Russian counterparts. He was wrong.

In the army town of Zossen, about fifty kilometres south-west of Berlin, General Ludwig von Maercker had been working for the past month on a secret plan of Schleicher's to salvage the remains of the Imperial regiments and form them into a coherent new army. The idea was to form mobile 'storm units'. Maercker had taken four thousand men and created a so-called Volunteer Rifle Corps. This was just one of a number of units of *Freikorps* – right-wing divisions of veteran soldiers under wartime commanders, bent on supporting the interests of the army and the old *status quo*. They were employed on the basis of a monthly renewable contract, and had the right to elect representatives as spokesmen on matters of pay, leave, and other conditions of service.

Noske was appointed Army Minister – 'someone's got to be the bloodhound', was his not unenthusiastic comment. On Saturday 4 January he and Ebert were invited by General Walther von Lüttwitz, responsible for the military in Berlin, to review Maercker's troops. The deal, as before,

was that the Republic should be defended at the expense of the Revolution – any revolution; from now on the Weimar Republic, for all the
good it in fact achieved, was compromised. Ebert and Noske were
jubilant as they drove back to Berlin. They seemed finally to have the
weapon they needed: reliable troops. 'Everything's going to be all right
now,' Noske told Ebert. They did not waste time. That same day the
government attempted to oust the self-appointed police chief, Emil
Eichhorn, from the Police Praesidium. For most Berliners he represented the very opposite of a force for public order. Kessler described
him as 'a figure out of operetta, whose answer to riots in the streets was
to arm the rioters, and who served the government without denying
himself his salary from Russia'.[11] Eichhorn refused to be dislodged, and
a week of violent revolutionary activity began – Spartacus Week.

On Sunday night a revolutionary committee was formed, within the
Police Praesidium, of fifty-three left-wing leaders. They worked as fast
as the government had and by Monday morning had organized a general
strike which closed down the majority of Berlin's factories, public
transport, and electricity stations. A quarter of a million demonstrators
took to the streets, occupying the railway stations and several newspaper
offices; there were armed men on top of the Brandenburg Gate. This
time the rest of the city couldn't quite as easily behave as if nothing were
happening. Liebknecht was sure he would be able to push his opportunity home; Rosa Luxemburg was appalled by his rashness, but could
do nothing; the die was cast. Noske withdrew to the safety of Dahlem,
and began to organize the counter-attack. He was ready a week later. On
11 January he marched back to the city centre at the head of 3,000
Freikorps troops. This time there was no repetition of the siege of the
Schloss. The Freikorps established a base at the old Moabit barracks
north of Tiergarten, and a force was dispatched to take the Police
Praesidium. Smashing down the doors, they burst into the building and
shot anyone they encountered. On the following day systematic
mopping-up operations eliminated every pocket of Communist resistance, and Liebknecht's rag-bag army was shattered. By 14 January,
Liebknecht and Rosa Luxemburg had retreated to a flat in Wilmersdorf
from where they attempted to rally their all but spent forces. It didn't last
long. They were betrayed, and within twenty-four hours a detachment
of Horse Guards had arrested them both and taken them to Army Headquarters at the Eden Hotel.

Their interrogation was conducted by Captain Waldemar Pabst. No
one will ever know the exact truth of what happened, but it is beyond
doubt that both Liebknecht and the lame Rosa Luxemburg were brutally
beaten. Several hours later they were driven off, ostensibly to be taken
into custody at Moabit Prison pending trial. But the army had already

decided that they were too dangerous to be allowed to live. The car carrying Liebknecht pulled up in a dark side road off the Tiergarten, and he
was shot dead. The body was delivered to a nearby hospital as an anonymous victim of the violence of the last few days. Pabst was officially
informed that Liebknecht had been shot 'while trying to escape'. Rosa
Luxemburg was so badly beaten up that her body had to be more
thoroughly disposed of. Her brains were blown out, and her body thrown
into the Landwehrkanal some way from the centre of town. The story
was that the car had been stopped by an angry crowd demanding
vengeance on the Communist leader: the army detail had been obliged
to surrender their prisoner. Rumours went around that she was still alive,
until her bloated and barely recognizable body was discovered in the
canal on 31 May.

A Berliner born in 1913, who now lives in London, remembers that
time. Both his parents were leading figures in the Spartacist movement.

> My parents died when I was five-and-a-half, and I spent my time roaming
> the streets. I lived in the streets; there was nobody to look after me. My
> parents were ardent Spartacists – my mother's nickname was the Red Queen
> of Neukölln, and they're described as a 'Spartacist-Couple' in the death
> notices . . . On the day of their death, [they] told me that they had to go to
> a meeting, and packed me off to a neighbour. This was nothing new. I
> remember it was 11 January 1919. At about eight o'clock at night the
> neighbour took me back to the flat and unlocked the door. I remember that
> she was startled to see that the gas light had been left on. I pushed past her
> and came upon the scene which is forever etched upon my memory. I saw
> my mother in her bed by the window. Her head appeared enlarged to me,
> and there was blood. I ran out of the room crying.

Unable to face the future, his parents had killed themselves. His father
had shot his mother, and then himself. But his mother was only
wounded. 'She had been able to get up and tidy her husband's corpse
before lying down on the bed to die. But she did not die for two months,
though she never spoke again, as the bullet had shattered her vocal cords.
In hospital she tried to slash her wrists. She wanted to see me. I didn't
want to see her.' The suicide note still exists. It is written by his father
in pencil on the back of an old form, neatly torn up into squares to use
as rough paper: 'Dear son, do not curse us . . .' This man has had a very
successful career in England, but has been undergoing therapy for most
of his life – one tragedy among the many of those days.

On 19 January national elections took place, from which the Communists held aloof; the SPD were elected with a big enough majority for
Ebert to set about creating a legitimate parliamentary government, and
with it a new Constitution. He was aware that the people had voted not
so much for him as for what the republican revolution had so far

achieved: truly democratic voting rights which included women and young people, an eight-hour working day, unemployment benefit, freedom of speech plus an end to censorship, and the cessation of aristocratic privileges. Berlin remained in such a state of tension that as part of the security measures even dancing had been forbidden. A National Assembly was convened in Weimar, 200-odd kilometres to the south-west, on 6 February.

February also saw the return of Ludendorff to Germany. He wrote to his wife with characteristic bluntness: 'It would be the greatest stupidity if the revolutionaries [the provisional government] were to allow us all to remain alive. Why, if ever I come to power again, there will be no pardon. Then, with an easy conscience, I would have Ebert, Scheidemann and co. hanged, and watch them dangle.'[12]

Weimar was safe and provincial, and it was also symbolic: the cradle of pan-German culture and humanism. Goethe had lived there for most of his life, and the city had also been home to Cranach, Schiller and Liszt. Once installed there, the National Assembly knew that speed was essential to stabilize both its own position, and national security. No formal peace had yet been signed with the Allies, but the question of reparations would soon be on the horizon. At the same time, Berlin continued insecure. Russian influence was feared, and while the extreme Left was largely crushed, strikes and fighting continued.

On 11 February Friedrich Ebert won the election for provisional President, a result which reflected party political balance, and also Ebert's standing in the eyes of his peers. Even the conservative *Kölnische Zeitung* recognized his decency and honour.[13] Snobs may have been distressed to see a saddler as Head of State, but realists were pleased to see a path opened up at last for talent, regardless of background. Plump, unassuming, but doggedly conscientious, Ebert personified a new German ideal. A coalition cabinet was created from the parties which had won the most seats: the SPD (together with the Independents) had 185, the Centre Party 88, and the Democrats 75. Any inclusion of the Right or pro-monarchist parties would have alarmed the Allies, who naturally were watching closely, and Ebert had a delicate path to tread. Scheidemann became Chancellor, Noske took over the new army, or Reichswehr, and the Minister of the Interior was a lawyer, Hugo Preuss.

Preuss had been an eminent teacher at Friedrich-Wilhelm University in Berlin, but as a Jew had never been granted a Chair there. Perhaps his typically *Berlinerisch* biting wit and sarcasm had also had something to do with it; he later gained a professorship at the more tolerant and liberal Commercial University, just before the outbreak of the First World War. An ardent advocate of German unity, he also understood how important it was for Germany to emerge from the shadow of authoritarianism and develop its own genuine democracy, if it were ever to play a real part in world affairs. After a three-day debate, Preuss began drafting a new Constitution. Its 177 Articles set out to resolve, as far as possible, differences of opinion between the Right and the Left, while maintaining a certain integrity. One bone of contention was universal suffrage; even a liberal like Karl Severing later observed: 'The extension of franchise to younger people [the previous age limit was 25] and to women would, in a well-established democracy, mean the further enrichment of the democratic concept of the state. But in 1919 these changes wrought confusion rather than education.'[14] German women later voted in their millions for Hitler, who proposed to strip them of all their rights and made no secret of his idea of their role in society.

Another difficulty was the choice of a new flag. A proposal that the Imperial black, white and red be replaced by the revolutionary black, red and gold of 1848 promptly caused a split between the Right and the Left. The new colours were adopted by a vote of 190 to 110; the old flag was retained for the Merchant Navy – a measure which mollified neither the far right nor the Nationalists. The Imperial colours reappeared in 1933 as the background to Hitler's swastika.

Harry Kessler, in Weimar for the Assembly (by now transformed into a Reichstag proper), gives a thumbnail sketch of the new leaders gathered in the theatre co-opted for their use:

> The 'Gothic Room', which serves as a conference room for the members of the government, and is supposed to recall the Houses of Parliament at Westminster, has been knocked together on the stage behind the Presidential Chair out of stage flats from *Lohengrin* and club armchairs. Here the regal proletarian Scheidemann, puffed up like a peacock in his tuppeny-ha'penny pomp, strolls up and down, arm-in-arm with Preuss and Erzberger, advising and consulting on State business. In the lightest draught the painted Gothic pews around them wobble. I joined them today. Erzberger, with his loose cheeks and cunning, lecherous mouth, welcomed me roguishly. He always looks like someone who's just eaten well and is doling out the tips to the waiters. Scheidemann is vainglorious in his concertina'd trousers. Preuss is quite simply a monster. The three of them together are Extract of German Philistinism.[15]

Returning to Berlin a few days later, Kessler found little to encourage hope for the future. Trams were running, but because of strikes there were few newspapers. There was still fighting around the Police Praesidium, now occupied by a Freikorps unit under Walter von Reinhardt. Officers of the Freikorps were to be seen in the streets, epaulettes on: gone were the days of soldiers stripping officers of their insignia. On 6 March Kessler wrote: 'Just today they've been bill-posting the walls: "Who has the prettiest legs in Berlin? Little Darlings' Caviare

Ball." As I write, the electricity goes off. The strike has reached the electricity works.' By 8 March the newspapers were back on the streets, but in the following days Kessler describes a soldier brutally whipping one of a group of prisoners being loaded into a lorry outside the Chancellery – the prisoner had been found in possession of papers belonging to three vanished officers; elsewhere, a sergeant of the Reinhardt Regiment is shot by Spartacists on the street; Spartacists ambush two soldiers and throw them into the canal; other soldiers have their throats cut. Kessler concludes, 'Every horror of the most pitiless civil war is perpetrated by each side. The hatred and bitterness which are being sown now will bear fruit. The innocent will pay for the cruelty. It is the beginnings of Bolshevism!' But in the very next sentence, 'The electricity is on again. All the cabarets, bars, theatres and dance-halls are open.'

By 10 March Noske had declared martial law and decreed that any unauthorized person bearing arms would be shot out of hand. Professor Julius Posener remembers that his own artist father joined the Bürgerwehr (militia) and, at 56, learned to shoot. On sentry duty on a railway embankment he fired the first shot in anger of his life – and the last. Thinking he saw a hand reach over the edge of the embankment as if someone were climbing up onto it from below, he shouted 'Halt! Who goes there?' Getting no reply, he fired. 'He got a bull's-eye,' recalls Posener. 'There wasn't much left of the hedgehog . . .'

In the rich west of the city, people were saying that all Spartacists should be lined up and shot; in east Berlin, they were saying the same thing of government troops. At one point the Imperial standard was raised on the Schloss and one Freikorps group demanded that the Kaiser's son August-Wilhelm be declared Emperor.[16] George Grosz, threatened with arrest, fled from his studio and for a few days lived the life of a fugitive. Kessler was especially appalled by the out-of-hand slaughter of 24 young revolutionary sailors.

By mid-spring Noske had won, but it was a bitter victory. Thousands of people had been killed, and Berlin was demoralized as never during the war. Among those executed was Leo Jogiches, Rosa Luxemburg's former lover, who, ironically, had advocated a peaceful resistance. Perhaps worst of all, a profound ideological disaffection with the government now grew up. In his urgent desire to establish order, Ebert used means too harsh and did not, in the end, achieve more than a shaky and transient 'stability'.

Berlin was not only Germany's capital; it quickly grew to be the principal industrial centre too. But in the winter of 1918/19 unemployment in the city stood at around 250,000 and this figure, huge by pre-war standards,

was to rise dramatically in the troubled times ahead. At the beginning of
the Second Reich, in 1871, Berlin had not yet spread to encompass its
neighbouring towns.[17] Its population stood at 800,000, and the area it
covered was 60 square kilometres. There was little sprawl outside the city
limits (Arnold Bauer, who has lived in the same house in Charlottenburg
since 1920, points out that even today the countryside begins immediately Berlin stops).[18] By 1918 the city had a population of around two
million – which fell gradually but steadily to 1,779,000 in 1939 – and it
covered 90 square kilometres. When its adjoining towns and villages
were incorporated in 1920 Greater Berlin (as it then became) was the biggest city in Europe after London. The towns added to Berlin had themselves seen spectacular population increases: Charlottenburg had 20,000
inhabitants in 1871, and 325,000 in 1919; Grunewald was a tiny community of 32 souls in 1871; by 1919, 6,448 people were living there.[19]
The turn of the century saw the fastest growth, despite the decrease in
Old Berlin's population. Suburbs like Pankow and Reinickendorf sprang
up in the 1920s, and by 1939 only Weissensee and Zehlendorf of the
twenty administrative districts of Greater Berlin had fewer than 100,000
inhabitants. The rises in population were due less to births than to migra-
tion, as people came to the industrial centre from the land to seek better
work. There is an old saying that most true Berliners actually come from
Silesia, but city records show that the majority then came from the province of Brandenburg. By 1925, the total population of Greater Berlin had
reached four million.

Expansion led to vigorous building programmes, not all of them good.
Flats for the poor were erected more or less hastily in blocks surrounding
narrow courtyards – some are still to be seen in working-class districts
like Neukölln. They offered the lowest possible quality of life, and a
short life-expectancy. Particularly grim were the so-called cellar-flats.
There were about 20,000 of these in 1910, occupied by 60,000 people.
Most workers' flats comprised two small rooms: a kitchen and a bed-
sitting room. There was rarely a private lavatory, to say nothing of a
bathroom. In 1910 many households numbered five people, so that conditions everywhere were hopelessly overcrowded. It was a different story
for the rich. Vast fortunes were made by local farmers and landowners
who could sell their land for building, and the idea of the garden city was
imported from England for middle-class developments. Villa colonies
had been started as early as the 1860s in Nikolaussee, Schlachtensee,
Wannsee and Zehlendorf, made possible by the development of a suburban railway network second to none. An exceptional garden city
development was built at Staaken for workers at the Spandau armaments
works, and can be taken as the model for later, similar attempts by the
Weimar Republic to improve living conditions for the working class.

Martin Wagner championed the creation and preservation of parkland, for which Berlin is still known.

Berlin was a city of modern technology. Industries were attracted by its pioneering water, gas and electrical systems. As early as 1856 the English firm of Fox and Crampton was running Berlin's waterworks. Electricity was first installed in the city in 1884, and the first power station proper opened in 1885. The heavy engineering firm of Borsig opened works near the Tegeler See, and the electrical company founded by Werner Siemens was established at Nonnenwiesen. By 1873 the Aktiengesellschaft für Anilinfabrikation, better known today simply as AGFA, had been set up. Emil Rathenau, who had bought from Edison the right to exploit its electrical patents in Europe, set up his giant AEG company as a rival to Siemens. Rathenau's son Walther became one of the greatest, and most tragic, political figures of the Weimar Republic.

The first electric trams were running by 1881 (Wilhelm II never allowed them on Unter den Linden), and the first underground trains appeared in October 1908, though initially the high fares restricted them exclusively to middle and upper class passengers. Development of elegant new districts began in the 1890s in the west of the city: Charlottenburg, Friedenau, Schöneberg, Steglitz and Wilmersdorf. Further out were Dahlem, Grunewald and Lichterfelde. In these districts, later, members of the Bauhaus had opportunities to build according to their new ideas of domestic architecture.

It was Berlin's industrial expansion as much as its proximity to the German 'Versailles' of Potsdam that in 1871 persuaded Bismarck to select it over Kassel (the stronghold of the military) as the Reich capital. His choice did not please the aristocracy, who correctly saw in the town a growing power-base for the middle and working classes and their free-thinking ideas. During the troubles that succeeded the end of the First World War, unemployment leapt from 20,000 to 300,000 in the area covered by Greater Berlin. This was 25 per cent of the total unemployment for the country, although Berlin's inhabitants only represented about 6.25 per cent of its population. The startling increase was caused by the great influx of war refugees and returning soldiers. Somehow or other, despite the disruption and throughout even the darkest days, post was still delivered, telephone lines (usually) stayed open, and food, drink and fuel were regularly distributed. By the end of 1919 the city authorities had reduced unemployment by 20 per cent. Universal suffrage, brought in in 1919, gave the SPD and the Independents together a clear two-thirds majority in local government, though the electoral turn-out was a cynical 57.46 per cent. The results confirmed aristocratic suspicions of the capital. The 'Red' Town Hall in Königsstrasse, with its

74-metre-high tower, was so-called for its politics, now, as well as for its brickwork.

The fighting in the city during the months following November 1918 brought great suffering to the population. There is an abiding image in the report of an observer who came with Herbert Hoover's mission to help the Berlin poor. Visiting a hospital for children suffering from hunger oedema and starvation, he saw 'tiny faces, with large dull eyes, overshadowed by huge puffed, rickety foreheads, their small arms just skin and bones, and above the crooked legs with their dislocated joints the swollen, pointed stomachs . . . "You see this child here," the physician in charge explained; "it consumed an incredible amount of bread, and yet it did not get any stronger. I found out that it hid all the bread it received underneath its straw mattress. The fear of hunger was so deeply rooted in the child that it collected the stores instead of eating the food: a misguided animal instinct made the dread of hunger worse than the actual pangs." '[20] Images of starving children are everywhere to be found in Käthe Kollwitz's drawings of man's inhumanity to man. She herself lost one of her two sons, Peter, in 1914, when he was 18 years old. She had always been attracted to depicting the poor and the working classes and then, unlike her close contemporary Heinrich Zille, only the dark side of their lives. 'The joyous side simply did not appeal to me,' she states.[21] She was the daughter of a lay preacher; perhaps it is worth noting the inscription on her grandfather's grave: 'Man is not here to be happy, but to do his duty.' She moved to Berlin on her marriage in 1891, and occupied the same house until 1943. It was not a close marriage, but it was a companionable one. Käthe took on much of the suffering of the poor, and indeed her own life was full of grief. Her doctor husband sacrificed his entire life to the care of his working-class patients and died, exhausted, in 1940.

The war and the death of her son politicized Käthe's originally aesthetic attraction to working-class subjects. In 1918 she wrote: 'That these young men whose lives were just beginning should be thrown into the war to die by legions – can this be justified? There has been enough dying! Let not another man fall! . . . *Seed for the planting must not be ground.*' Six weeks later she heard Richard Strauss conduct Beethoven's Ninth Symphony: '. . . I was carried away, swept up out of the partisan dust to heights of purest joy. Yes, in the Ninth there is socialism in its purest form. That is humanity, glowing darkly like a rose, its deepest chalice drenched with sunlight.'[22]

The effect of the upheavals of 1918 and 1919 on artists and intellectuals, to both the Left and the Right, was enormously stimulating, and the cultural innovation which had begun before the war now surged forward. That the forces of the Right would ultimately gain the upper hand, leading in 1933 to a massive exodus of talent, would be Germany's loss, and the rest of the world's (predominantly America's) gain. In November 1918 a group of artists in Berlin formed themselves into the November-gruppe, in support of the new republic. The German-American painter Lyonel Feininger was among those who signed the Novembergruppe manifesto, underwriting innovation and reconstruction; but Ebert's alliance with the army, and Noske's brutal suppression of the Spartacists, very quickly left them disaffected. As early as December the poet Rainer Maria Rilke wrote: 'Under the pretence of a great upheaval, the old want of character persists.'[23] Käthe Kollwitz and George Grosz were pursued by the authorities for their unadorned, highly critical presentation of continuing social injustice. On 16 March Kessler confided to his diary:

> This morning I visited Grosz in his studio to give him the money for the painting I have bought from him. After letting me into the hallway, he asked me to wait there for a moment, as a friend who had spent the night in the studio had to make his getaway; probably a Communist on the run.
>
> Grosz told me that many artists and intellectuals (Einstein for example) were fleeing from house to house. The government had determined ruthlessly to rob the Communists of their spiritual leaders . . . then he related one or two of his own experiences during the last few days [when he himself had been on the run] which he had obviously found deeply shattering: battling Spartacists, even convicts, whose enthusiasm and courage-unto-death were unbelievable. Fanaticism for an idea. Through this he had come to a quite new understanding of the proletariat. The artist, the intellectual, should modestly put himself in his proper place. Even more appalling: he had seen a lieutenant shoot a soldier dead, merely because the man had no papers and answered back insolently. The man's comrades had wept – either from rage or grief. [Grosz] declares himself to be a Spartacist now. Force is necessary to push ideas through; otherwise there will be no overcoming the inertia of the bourgeoisie.

Later the same day, talking with Georg Bernhard of the liberal paper *Vossische Zeitung*, Kessler noted: 'That this discredited, blood-spattered government can hold out much longer seems to Bernhard to be out of the question. The only thing is that there is no one among the Communists who comes close to being a statesman. Rosa Luxemburg would have been the only person in the Party who might have been able to rule Germany.'[24]

If liberals like Kessler were outraged, the middle class in the main was grateful to have the ship of state back on an even keel. It preferred order to freedom, and within a very short time a nostalgia for the old days was being widely expressed. The new Republic did not seem to have the authority of the old Reich, and Ebert and Noske sacrificed a good deal of dignity when in the course of the grim year of 1919 a photograph of them bathing at Warnemünde appeared on the front cover of the *Berliner Illustrirte Zeitung*. 'One serves the Republic, but one does not love it,' muttered the historian Hans Dehlbrück. More serious was the developing myth of the 'stab in the back': the army had been betrayed by the republican politicians. This seriously undermined their credibility, particularly after the signing of the Treaty of Versailles – a necessary evil which brought the government almost universal opprobrium at home. In the end, Hitler would call them the 'November criminals'.

Another problem for the SPD was lack of experience. None of the party's members had ever run a country before, and this was a country brought to its knees by a disastrous war which had earned it the mistrust and in some cases the hatred of its neighbours. The SPD found it difficult to assert government authority after the panicky abuse of power which had characterized the crushing of the far left, and it was equally difficult for anyone to admire the SPD, beyond those few far-sighted intellectuals who saw what the party represented and could become (rather than what it was), and who understood how much better that would be than what had gone before. Alas, the majority (even in 'Red' Berlin), disappointed after the first euphoria, began to look almost immediately for a strong leader – a father figure. That search, coupled with a parliamentary system which ensured such a proliferation of political parties that no single one could wield enough power to rule adequately, left the Weimar leaders at a disadvantage.

The intellectuals of the Right included Oswald Spengler and Moeller van den Bruck.[25] Van den Bruck was one of the leading lights of the June Club, an exclusive Berlin debating society leaning to the centre Right and affiliated with the Herrenklub – which later attracted much ill-fame by its association with Franz von Papen, in the final days of the Weimar Republic; he was a theorist fascinated by foreign policy and bored by the prospect of putting the German house in order. In 1923 – two years before his suicide – he published *The Third Reich*: it was in no way a model for government, rather a disquisition on van den Bruck's interest in the mystical nature of the number 3. Such dabbling with mysticism was not new, and remained a feature of the thinking of the German Right, in particular. That the Nazis called their regime after it was probably a coincidence; but it could also be a grim example of Anatole France's dictum that the popular success of a book almost always rests upon a misunderstanding between author and reader.

Spengler's two-volume *Decline of the West* (1918, 1922) is a flawed book which prophesied the decline of the western world and the rise of African and Asian powers, maintaining that growth and decline in the course of history was characteristic not only of nations and empires but of whole continents. He also wrote *Preussentum und Sozialismus* (Prussian-ness and Socialism), an immediate best-seller on its publication in 1920, in which he argued that the Prussia of Frederick the Great was in fact a socialist state. Spengler's strength lay in his ability to expound socialism agreeably. In his hands it became, not a Marxist bogey but instead a bourgeois phenomenon. No matter that socialists themselves objected to the comparison with classical Prussia: the book reminded everyone about the most glorious period in Prussia's – and, by extension, Germany's – history. Spengler was a nationalist without being a National Socialist, and a believer in the German race without being an anti-Semite; but that was not necessarily how he was read. The Nazis also invoked the spirit of Frederick the Great, in a kind of warped justification of their claim to be restoring its former greatness to Germany.

These books were harbingers of a renewed hankering for greatness. Meanwhile, after the débâcle of the war and the horrors of the following winter, most people just wanted to enjoy themselves.

3 A Phoenix Arisen

THE FIRST MEETING of the National Assembly con-
vened at Weimar had barely been called to order before a large, bearded
man rose. His speech was a mixture of nonsense and obscenity. Oblivious
to commands to shut up and sit down, he insisted the Weimar Republic
was a Dadaist demonstration and, before being noisily ejected, he
nominated himself its President. People knew him. The police already
had him registered as insane. He was Johannes Baader, an architect, and
Chief Dada of Berlin. To understand what he was up to, it is necessary
to go back a little, and speak of other men.[1]

Hugo Ball was 29 years old when he arrived in Zurich in 1915, a
fugitive from Munich. He had volunteered a year earlier, but quickly
became disillusioned with the war. With his mistress (later his wife), the
diseuse Emmy Hennings, he started a cabaret in a seedy Zurich bar – by
coincidence, opposite the *pension* where Lenin was then lodging. They
called it the Cabaret Voltaire, as an ironic reflection on the fate of reason
in the face of war. The club once established, Ball cast about for fellow-
thinkers – not difficult to find, as Zurich had become a magnet for many
fleeing the fighting. Centred on the Voltaire, and led by Ball, with the
Strasburg poet and painter Hans Arp and the Romanian poet Tristan
Tzara, a movement was born which came to be called Dada. No one
knows where the name comes from. The Slavonic 'yes', repeated for
emphasis? The French nursery word for a horse (gee-gee, horsy)? An
expression of the unorganized chaos of creation? Or nothing at all? Dada
precisely reflected the need some artists felt to cure the madness of the
warring world by turning it on its head. It found its forms in sculpture,
painting and poetry, and went hand in hand with early cabaret. Its
manifesto was simple: *Kunst ist Scheisse* (Art is Shit). Its aim was to pull
no punches.

One of the principal players was Richard Hülsenbeck, a medical student who had previously met Ball in Berlin, where he claims the seeds of Dada were sown. Hülsenbeck managed to avoid military service by persuading a friendly doctor to declare him insane, then made his way to Zurich and wound up at the Voltaire as a kind of master-of-ceremonies, or *conférencier*. His act involved beating a drum and reciting vaguely threatening nonsense poems. (In the fullness of time, Hülsenbeck ended his life as a psychotherapist in New York.) At first, recited poetry was the main medium for Dadaism; it peaked early, in a performance by Hugo Ball which marked the pinnacle of his career. '[I was] dressed in a tight-fitting cylindrical pillar of shiny blue cardboard which reached to my hips so that I looked like an obelisk. Above this, I wore a huge cardboard coat collar, scarlet inside and gold outside, which was fastened at my neck in such a way that I could flap it like a pair of wings by moving my elbows. I also wore a high, cylindrical, blue-and-white striped witch-doctor's hat.'[2] Thus dressed, he went on stage and recited the following poem:

> Gadji beri bimba
> glandridi lauli lonni cadori
> gadjama bim beri glassala
> gladrid glassala tuffim

Ball wasn't being especially original; the great German nonsense poet Christian Morgenstern had already written *Das grosse Lalula*:

> Kroklokwafzi? Sememem
> Seiokronto-prafriplo:
> Bifzi, bafzi; hulalemi:
> Quasti basti bo . . .
> Lalu, lalu lalu lalu la!

and Edward Lear had had a go in *Mr and Mrs Spikky Sparrow*. But Ball caused a storm, and had to be carried off stage, immobilized inside his costume, at the end of his act.

By the time of that performance, the Cabaret Voltaire had already been closed down by the police – following one complaint too many from the good Swiss burghers who lived in its vicinity. At the end of the war, the artists who had for a time stood stolid Zurich on its nose returned to places with broader horizons. Some went to Paris, where Dada pursued an apolitical course. Hugo Ball gave up the arts, converted to Roman Catholicism, worked among the poor, and wrote a biography of his friend Hermann Hesse. But the Dada that went to Berlin inevitably became involved in its politics. Here was a city in which Dada could really react to events.

When Oberdada Baader made his speech at the Weimar city theatre, flyers were distributed with the message:

Dadaists against Weimar
On Thursday 6 February 1919 at 7.30 p.m.
in the Kaisersaal des Rheingold (Bellvue-Strasse), the OBERDADA
will be proclaimed as
PRESIDENT OF THE GLOBE . . .
We shall blow Weimar sky-high. Berlin is the place . . . da . . . da . . .
Nobody and nothing will be spared.
Turn out in masses!
The Dadaist Headquarters of World Revolution.

There were artists for whom Dada appealed to the heart – just as their intellects responded positively to Communism. George Grosz, who describes in his autobiography the hunger fantasies of the dispossessed in Berlin after the war, also tells of a dreamlike meeting with a cook who was a black-marketeer, and who took him to visit his great hoard of food, afterwards sending him on his way with two luxuries: a schnapps and a sandwich.[3] He then gives an example of what the poor had to eat:

Breakfast: turnip coffee, grey-green rolls, synthetic honey.
Lunch: turnip cutlets, mussel pudding.
Dinner: mussel *wurst*, grey-green rolls.

'In those days,' he adds, 'we were all Dadaists. If that word meant anything at all, it meant seething discontent, dissatisfaction and cynicism.'

Richard Hülsenbeck, who had returned to Berlin in 1917, defined the position concisely: 'Question: what is German culture? Answer: Shit. This culture should be attacked with all the weapons of satire, bluff, irony and, finally, violence. Beyond anything else, Dada is the artist's revolver.' At the first Berlin Dada evening, Grosz walked on stage and addressed the audience:

You sons-of-bitches, materialists,
Bread-eaters, flesh-eaters-vegetarians!!
Professors, butchers' apprentices, pimps!!
You bums!!

He then mimed urinating over a painting by the respectable Establishment painter Lovis Corinth, informing the outraged audience that urine made excellent varnish.

The Berlin group included the Herzfelde brothers, Wieland and Hellmuth. Wieland, known as Wiz, founded the left-wing Malik Verlag publishing house; Hellmuth, the inventor of photomontage, later changed his name to John Heartfield as an expression of his passion for the 'dreamland' of America. Grosz had also changed his name – he was born Georg Ehrenfried. Raoul Hausmann, polymath and philosopher, Walter Mehring, writer, and Kurt Schwitters, artist, were other principal Berlin Dadaists – and all were heavily involved with the political Left. They held Dadaist meetings, charged a few marks for admission and subjected their audiences to outright abuse: 'You old heap of shit – yes, you with the umbrella!' 'What's so funny, you dickhead?' 'If you don't shut up you'll get a kick up the arse!' Of course, news of these events spread quickly, they became fashionable, and the Sunday morning performances sold out. 'Things came to such a pass that we had to have the police in attendance all the time because of the fights that kept breaking out. Eventually we even had to apply for special police permits. We ridiculed everything, because that was what Dada was about. Dada was neither mysticism nor Communism nor anarchism, all of which had some sort of programme or other. We were complete, pure nihilists, and our symbol was the vacuum, the void.'[4]

They put on sketches: Mehring would sit at a typewriter and hammer away while reciting a poem, for example; but he was soon interrupted by Hausmann, or Heartfield, or one of the others, who might shout, 'Stop! You're not trying to fool that load of cretins out there, are you?' Sometimes things were planned, more often not. The performers were usually drunk, anyway. In the course of time they became more sophisticated, and gave concertos for car horns, typewriters and watering-cans. Races were held between typewriters and sewing-machines, to the accompaniment of a swearing competition. Kurt Schwitters recited his disjointed *Anna Blume* poems:

> Anna Blume . . .
> Who are you, beloved lady?
> Beef suet drips onto my naked back,
> You can even read you backwards
> The back of you's like the front,
> A-n-n-a . . .

And at the first Dada International Exhibition in Berlin,[5] Rudolf Schlichter contributed a life-sized pig-headed dummy dressed as a German general. It hung upside-down above the heads of the furious and nervous visitors. 'Hanged by the Revolution', read a placard attached to it. Kurt Schwitters filled his flat with junk – rusty nails, cigar butts, broken bicycle wheels, anything – from which he made what he called *Merz* collages, from the word *Kommerz* (commerce). They were nihilistic reflections on materialism, although art critics invented all sorts of other symbolism for them too. In the time of the great inflation, Schwitters and László Moholy-Nagy made collages of the

Weimar eagle out of billion-mark notes: in them, the eagle becomes a vulture.

Johannes Baader, the self-proclaimed 'President of the Republic', is a shadowy figure – he seems to have been genuinely, if harmlessly, mad, and would have appealed to the group as a leader. He too erected a monumental sculpture of rubbish, which he called *Germany's Greatness and Decline in Three Stages*. Baader was also the creator of the *Dadacon* – the greatest book ever written. It was made up of thousands of bits of newspaper stuck together in the manner of photomontage, and its purpose was to induce giddiness in the reader, through which he would come to eventual understanding. Baader later offered to sell the *Dadacon* to Ben Hecht of the Chicago *Daily News* for $25,000 – but only half that amount was offered. Baader later buried the book near his house in Lichterfelde-Ost.

Not all Dada artists were poor. Grosz remembers 'one who lived in a villa in Grunewald and had a fabulous wine-cellar criss-crossed by a network of lanes, each lined with barrels and cases of the choicest wines. These subterranean wine-lanes were named after his Dada companions (George Grosz Alley, for instance, ran between the sherry casks) and he would ride up and down on a motorcycle, headlights blazing. One giant vat was known as the Dada Barrel and contained a glorious Piesporter, which the connoisseurs among us called "a thoroughly Dadaistic little wine".'[6]

The Hotel Adlon bar was where the foreign press congregated in the spring of 1919, and there one day Grosz encountered Ben Hecht sitting, drunk, on top of a piano, playing *Everybody Shimmies Now* on a violin. No shortages here – the place was strewn with Havana cigars, bottles of Rhine wine, a bottle of Black & White whisky and another of cognac. At about 4 a.m. the party set off for a dance-hall, where Hecht taught the pianist ragtime. Hecht, in Berlin to relay to the American people 'the truth about the Germans', was made an honorary Dada and awarded the Dada charter – a beer *stein* half painted black, and half-filled with sand. This was broken in a mêlée soon afterwards, and could not be replaced – only one charter might be awarded per Dada every sixty-five years.

Harry Kessler befriended Grosz, and helped Wieland Herzfelde with his multifarious and often short-lived magazine publications – either they were seized by the police, or news vendors would refuse to distribute them. In one, *Every Man His Own Football*, a series by Grosz on 'The Lovely German Man' was projected. Soon enough, though, Dada itself faded as the interests of its creators became more personal; Grosz (the light tone of whose autobiography – written in the United States, where exile to all intents and purposes bereft him of his creativity – belies the passionate artist of the 1920s) was about embark on his withering damnation of German society, all society – the *Ecce Homo* cycle.

The Berlin public had treated the Dada 'happenings' as a kind of cabaret; cabaret itself appeared in the city a little later. In Germany it had its roots in Munich, but after the war the artistic focus of the country moved to Berlin. Everything was happening in Berlin. The revolution, though it had started in the provinces, was centred there; White Russians and Jews fleeing the Communist revolution in Russia brought a new cosmopolitanism to the capital; above all, the Weimar Republic ushered in a far more permissive age. That, the uncertainty of the times, and an aching need for enjoyment after long years of war, opened the floodgates. As Berlin slipped into the Twenties, theatres, dance-halls, bars and restaurants blossomed everywhere, as did newspapers and magazines of all kinds. Cinema was still in its infancy, but quickly caught up. Radio and television were only a few years away. And then there was cabaret.

Munich cabaret was an intellectual affair, artistic in the spirit of the Cabaret Voltaire. Literary cabaret went on in Berlin, too, but in the early Twenties, when the mark became worthless, life savings were wiped out, and middle-class values were scattered to the winds, most cabaret was *Amusierkabarett* of the kind shown in Bob Fosse's film *Cabaret*. The advantage of this form of entertainment is that it needs only a small space: a tiny stage, a spotlight or two, and five or six little tables where, in dim light, ten times the price of champagne can be charged for fizzy apple juice. The film sentimentalizes the times, and the Isherwood stories it was based on, but it does give a flavour of the desperate, frenzied enjoyment of the decade, and although set when the so-called Golden Twenties were coming to an end, it also reflects the early years of that decade, years of hyperinflation when you could live like a king in Berlin for just a few dollars and get the girl of your dreams for a pair of nylons or a packet of Camels. As the Weimar years wore on, cabaret became one of Berlin's major art forms.

Something else was starting, too: 'It is quite possible that there is no sphere of public life in which a series of factors – the emancipation of women, Freudian psychoanalysis, physical culture, the independence of youth – have brought about so complete a change within one generation as in the relationship between the sexes.'[7] Stefan Zweig was an Austrian who spent little time in Berlin and did not like the city, yet it is worth recording his apocalyptic but only slightly exaggerated impression – reminiscent of a poem by Walter Mehring:

The first American food
Is making revolution in the guts of the capitalists.
Berlin, your dancing partner's Death.[8]

Zweig wrote:

All values were changed, and not only the material ones; the laws of the State were flouted, no tradition, no moral code was respected, Berlin was transformed into the Babylon of the modern world. Bars, amusement parks, red-light houses sprang up like mushrooms . . . the Germans introduced all their vehemence and methodical organization into the perversion. Along the entire Kurfürstendamm[9] sauntered powdered and rouged young men, and they were not all professionals; every high school boy wanted to earn some money, and in the dimly-lit bars one might see government officials and men of the world of finance tenderly courting drunken sailors without any shame. Even the Rome of Suetonius had never known such orgies as the pervert balls of Berlin, where hundreds of men costumed as women and hundreds of women as men danced under the benevolent eyes of the police. In the collapse of all values a kind of madness gained hold, particularly in the bourgeois circles which until then had been unshakeable in their probity. Young girls bragged proudly of perversion; to be sixteen and still under suspicion of virginity would have been thought a disgrace at any school in Berlin at that time; every girl wanted to tell of her adventures, and the more exotic the better. But the most revolting thing about this pathetic eroticism was its spuriousness. At bottom, the orgiastic period which broke out in Germany simultaneously with the inflation was nothing more than feverish imitation. One could see that these girls of decent middle-class families would much rather have worn their hair in a simple arrangement than in a sleek man's haircut, that they would much rather have eaten apple pie with whipped cream than drink strong liquor. Everywhere it was unmistakable that this over-excitation, this being stretched daily on the rack of inflation, was unbearable for the people, and that the whole nation, tired of war, actually only longed for order, quiet, and a little security and bourgeois life. And, secretly, it hated the Republic, not because it suppressed this wild freedom, but on the contrary, because it held the reins too loosely.

An even darker note is struck in Erich Kästner's brilliant short novel, *Fabian*, published in 1926 when he was 27. It is a dry, bitter, young man's satire on the state of the nation, viewed through Berlin life. The scene is set by the couplet:

Love is just a passing show,
You give 'em one, then on you go.[10]

The hero of the book, which features cynically prosaic sex-clubs, world-weary journalists, and a host of down-trodden, two-faced characters from the underworld, is a 32-year-old war veteran. Indirectly, he explains one of the central reasons for Weimar nihilism:

My immediate future seemed to have nothing more in store for me than to have me turned into mincemeat. What should I do until then? Read books? Improve my character? Earn money? I sat in a huge waiting-room, and it was called Europe. Eight days later the train would leave. I knew that. But where it was going and what would happen to me – that no one knew. And now, today, we're back in that waiting-room, and once again it's called Europe! And once again we don't know what's going to happen. So we lead a provisional life: there's been no end to the crisis![11]

At the very successful Kabarett der Namenlosen a man named Elow put the stage-struck young on and let them, in their innocence, make fools of themselves. 'The Jägerstrasse audiences weren't mean with their ironic applause', recalls the journalist Paul Erich Marcus.[12] In Kästner's book the 'Cabaret of the Nameless' becomes the 'Cabaret of the Anonymous', where madmen perform to contemptuous audiences who need to look down on people more wretched than themselves. In a bitter exchange, Fabian asks Battenberg, the 'nice girl' in the novel,

'Why did you come to Berlin?'
  'One used to give oneself gladly to people, and then one was valued as a person would value a present. Nowadays one is paid, and there comes a time when, like all wares that are paid for and used up, one is thrown away. Men think paying is a better bet.'

And, a little later, as the pair walk along the Geisbergstrasse at night:

'Isn't it almost like being at home?' he asked. 'But then again, not really. The moonlight and the scent of flowers, the stillness and the small-city kiss under the gate's archway, are all illusions. Look, over there, there's a café, and in it Chinese sit with Berlin whores; just Chinese. And across there is a bar where perfumed homosexual boys dance with elegant actors and smart Englishmen and discuss their particular skills and what they'll cost; and in the end it's an old lady with dyed-blonde hair who pays, on condition that she'll be allowed to come along too. On the corner to the right there's a hotel in which only Japanese stay, and next to it is a restaurant where Russians and Hungarian Jews pump each other for information and rip each other off. In one of the side-streets nearby there's a *pension* where in the afternoons under-age grammar school girls sell themselves in order to boost their pocket money. Six months ago there was a scandal that was only very patchily hushed up; an older gentleman ordered a naked sixteen-year-old girl for his pleasure, and when he went up to the hotel bedroom, there she was, all right, but unfortunately it was his own daughter, which was one in the eye for him, rather . . .'[13]

But it was not all decay. The cinema was a burgeoning new area of artistic activity.

I remember frequently I would go to where my aunt worked and collect a ten-pfennig piece – they were made of zinc in those days, not aluminium - and go to a cinema in Neukölln called the Rollkrug. The screen in that cinema was in the middle of the auditorium; you sat on one side and paid twenty pfennigs, and on the other side you paid ten – for on that side you saw the film mirror-imaged. The reason for this arrangement was that the light from the projector wasn't powerful enough to project an image very far, so they used this method to maximize audience capacity – the mirror-image was fine for those who couldn't read, or who didn't mind about deciphering the captions back-to-front; of course we're talking about silent movies.[14]

Film arrived in Berlin in 1895 with the 'Bioskop' shown by the brothers Skladanowsky at the Wintergarten. The medium took off at once, and the First World War didn't stop the industry's development. As Stefan Zweig sadly pointed out, 'It should be remembered that the world conscience was still a courted power in the years from 1914 to 1918; the artistically productive, the moral elements of a nation, still represented a force in the war which was respected for its influence; the nations still struggled to obtain human sympathy instead of employing inhuman terror, as Germany did in 1939.'[15] Between 1913 and 1919 the number of film companies increased from 28 to 245. Not all their films had anything to do with conscience. Some early favourites featured English gentleman detectives: Stuart Webb, played by Ernst Reuter, was a copy of Sherlock Holmes – deerstalker, pipe and all. The dark, psycho-supernatural films of Paul Wegener looked forward to, and influenced, *The Cabinet of Dr Caligari, Nosferatu,* and a host of sinister-mystical films of the post-war years. On a less elevated level, underground pornographic films were circulating almost as soon as the medium was invented. Sex films came to be more broadly distributed after the war. There was a strong 'moral' reaction to them, even in Berlin, and blame was squarely placed on the Jews. Anti-Semitism was never very far from the surface, even during the best days of the Weimar Republic, and any excuse was good enough to attack Jews.

In November 1917, Universum Film-Aktiengesellschaft (UFA) was formed, at the suggestion of Ludendorff, by merging most of the existing companies under a national umbrella and investing heavily in them. The purpose was to counteract American war-film propaganda with some of Germany's own. UFA's majority shareholder after the collapse of the Imperial administration was the State Bank; later it fell into the hands of the right-wing plutocrat, Alfred Hugenberg. Although German films were banned in Allied countries, the Danish film star Asta Nielsen, who made her name in the German industry, became a pin-up of both French and German troops during the First World War. She was even lauded by Apollinaire. German film techniques and innovations were widely admired, and it was the pioneer German directors who made the boldest experiments with cross-cutting and close-ups, and explored the potential of film rather than using it as a device to record stage performances. Before Hollywood, Berlin was the centre of the film industry.

The first mainstream films, made towards the end of the war and in the early years of the Weimar Republic, were costume dramas. The best-known director of these was Ernst Lubitsch, who had started his dramatic career doing small comedy roles for Max Reinhardt at the Deutsches Theater. Before the war was over, the 25-year-old Lubitsch was engaged to make *The Eyes of the Mummy* with the even younger Pola Negri; it was followed by *Carmen* and a procession of swashbucklers with plenty of sex and violence but little sense of history. In November 1918 Lubitsch attended a gala press preview of *Carmen* with Pola Negri. In her memoirs Negri recalls that during the performance she could hear the sound of shooting in the street outside the theatre. When she asked Lubitsch if he did too, he replied, 'Yes, but there's nothing we can do. Just watch the film.' 'When the newspapers speak of disaster every day you soon stop listening to them,' the star remembered. At the end of the preview, people were reluctant to leave and face the dangers of the streets. Negri made her way to the underground, which was still running. As she picked her way through the deserted city, she kept stopping to listen, with her back pressed to the damp walls of the buildings. 'By the time I arrived at the station I was wringing wet.'[16] In 1922 she left with Lubitsch for Hollywood.

From very early on, the widespread popularity of some film stars sometimes enabled them to wield surprising influence. Henny Porten was unusual in that she went straight into films without stage experience; she had been a star from 1910. She was filming a dance sequence in a city-centre studio when the take was spoilt by people invading the stage to announce that the Kaiser had been toppled. Almost immediately the studio emptied and Henny was left alone with two lighting technicians, who offered to take her home – her usual driver having disappeared in order to get his horse and cab to safety. She changed out of her costume and, with one technician on either side of her, hurried into the street. There, hell had broken loose and the three of them had to shelter in an archway from a hail of bullets. But Henny Porten's face was known all over Germany; a lorry-load of revolutionary soldiers drove past, and one of them recognized her. Immediately they offered her a lift. The following day Henny was supposed to make a short public information film, designed to defuse the situation. At first she objected to the line 'Be calm! Be sensible! Think of your womenfolk and your children!', but the director convinced her that the purpose of the film was simply to establish order. 'Besides, only you can do it. You have such a serene personality.'

Immediately afterwards she was taken by government officials to speak to the sailors who were occupying the Schloss. She protested that there was absolutely no point in her speaking directly to them, and that in any case she didn't know what to say. 'Besides, I'm only an actress.' Her escorts turned deaf ears. At the Schloss she was not only greeted with enthusiasm by the sailors but invited inside, and once there, she had to speak: they were all waiting for her to say something.

'Be calm,' she said. 'Be sensible. Think of your womenfolk and your children.' They listened to her with adoration; but even she was unable to put a stop to the events now in motion.

The film industry continued to grow very fast and began to react to the demands of the public, both for entertainment and for more solid fare. The one- and two-reel comedies with which Lubitsch had begun were replaced by feature-length films. A large number of 'B' movies, almost all adventure films set in exotic places, provided for many people a welcome escape from the grey misery of life – though all were shot in Germany, since lack of hard currency ruled out foreign locations. Lubitsch also led the field in a number of light comedies; but the real strength of the German cinema industry lay in films of an altogether darker nature – films which dealt with the supernatural, with zombies, master criminals, mad inventors, and pacts with the Devil. The great period for these was the first half of the Twenties – the three or four years when the country was still on the edge of revolution, when Hitler began to build up his power, when demands for reparation were made which were impossible to meet, and inflation spiralled. There were films of unremitting social realism too, but the films that are remembered are mysteries. The first to be made after the war, and the one which really defined the form, was *The Cabinet of Dr Caligari*, produced by Erich Pommer.

The original story, by Hans Janowitz and Carl Mayer, tells of a mysterious elderly fairground huckster, Caligari, who is clearly far more than an ordinary entertainer. He keeps a 'somnambulist', Cesare – an equally ambivalent figure – who is in deep sleep but who can be 'brought round' to predict the future. That is the basis of his fairground act, but Caligari also uses Cesare to commit apparently random and motiveless murders. Two students, Alan and Francis, visit the show. Answering the question Alan poses about his future, 'How long will I live?', Cesare chillingly answers: 'Until dawn.' Alan is indeed murdered that night, and then Cesare abducts his girl-friend, Jane (English names were very modish). Chased by the surviving student and the girl's father, Cesare carries her over the roof-tops in a scene reminiscent of *King Kong*. He abandons her unharmed and wanders off to drop dead. Caligari is then trailed to a lunatic asylum where he turns out to be the director: the whole fairground act was a cover for his insane experiments in psychology. The villain is exposed, and bundled into a strait-jacket.

The rather anodyne final adaptation by the film-makers, which infuriated the writers, does not really diminish the force of a film which is principally remembered for its technical innovations. There are some telling episodes, too: only in a German film – possibly only in a Berlin-made film – would there be a scene where Caligari *feeds* Cesare. Admittedly it's a horrible-looking porage, but at least it is something to eat – *very* important in a city where people worry if they haven't had a bite of something for two hours or so.

The film has also become a landmark of period design. Its extraordinary sets were designed by three Expressionist painters, who also designed the stylized make-up of Caligari and Cesare. The sets are incredible: every room is cramped, and there are no right angles. Streets tilt and lean crazily. That the film is early is betrayed by the fact that the camera is static for every scene, each shot as if it were being performed on stage; but Cesare is the spiritual father of Frankenstein's monster, King Kong, and a host of other screen freaks and villains; he shares their vulnerability, although he is also more dangerous.[17]

The film's three stars – Werner Krauss, Conrad Veidt, and Lil Dagover – became among the greatest of the period; under the Nazis, Krauss notoriously played a range of Jewish caricatures in Veit Harlan's infamous anti-Semitic propaganda film, *Jew Süss*. After *Caligari*, Erich Pommer produced a string of celebrated Weimar movies, culminating with *The Blue Angel* and *The Congress Dances*. He was a shrewd businessman, a boon to this burgeoning industry which later grew so prosperous in Berlin. 'Art assured export, and export meant salvation. An ardent partisan of this doctrine, Pommer had moreover an incomparable flair for cinematic values and popular demands. Regardless of whether he grasped the significance of the strange story [of *Caligari*] . . . he certainly sensed its timely atmosphere . . . He was a born promoter . . . and, above all, excelled in stimulating the creative energies of directors and players. In 1928, UFA was to make him chief of its entire production.'[18] Pommer was then only 39 years old – the same age as Charlie Chaplin, Adolf Hitler, and Ludwig Wittgenstein.

Exports really mattered, because reparations were the next hurdle for the new republic. Harry Kessler's diary entry for Wednesday, 28 April 1919, is concise: 'This afternoon Rantzau and the peace delegation left for Versailles.'[19]

That there was no sense of war guilt among the Germans in 1919 was not entirely their fault. Propaganda had for years consistently indicated that the war had been forced on them by the policies of France and

Russia. Preoccupied with rebuilding their country, relieved that the war was over whatever the result, the German people hoped that reasonable terms would be negotiated with the Allies. The German Foreign Minister was not, however, the ideal man for that delicate job. There had been practical reservations about his appointment because of his homosexuality,[20] but there were other, more important factors which the new government might have taken into account, given complete freedom of choice. Ulrich, Graf von Brockdorff-Rantzau was 50 in 1919. He agreed to assume the office of Foreign Minister only under several clear conditions, chief among which was the power to decline the Allies' terms of peace should these deny the Germans the chance to lead reasonably decent lives. Although Rantzau accepted the new republic in principle, he remained at heart an old-school Prussian aristocrat, and he was also a snob. These character traits became all too apparent when he had been drinking, which was frequently.

Across the table was Georges Clemenceau, aged 78, and well aware of France's desire for revenge for 1870. Practically, he needed to ensure his country's security against a more industrialized neighbour with a larger population. France in 1919 was on its knees: the war had left 1.4 million French dead and 3.75 million wounded, and 20,000 French factories had been destroyed. Woodrow Wilson of the United States and Lloyd George of Great Britain (though he had run his election campaign on 'making the Germans pay to the last penny') took a milder line than France; Lloyd George had persuaded the French to let the blockade of German ports be lifted so that food could be imported for the starving population, but France was adamant that German reparations be such as to render her harmless for all time. This sowed the seeds of the repeat performance a mere twenty years later – but politicians are not clairvoyant. The imperative of the moment impelled Clemenceau.

France demanded Alsace-Lorraine; she would occupy Germany west of the Rhine for fifteen years, and take over the coalfields of the Saar, which itself was to be governed by the League of Nations. Poland's acquisition of Upper Silesia (an important industrial area) and West Prussia made a Polish corridor to the coast necessary, and this cut off East Prussia from the rest of the country. Germany's African colonies were to be taken over by the League of Nations. At home, the army was to be reduced to 100,000 men, and the General Staff disbanded. There were to be no military aeroplanes, fighting vehicles such as tanks, or ships above a certain size. The new republic was to accept responsibility for all damage done by the Imperial regime, and undertake payment of reparations to be decided by a commission – initial figures under consideration ran as high as $120 billion. The Kaiser and others designated as war criminals were to be handed over for trial.

The scene was set for this showdown – *l'heure du lourd règlement des comptes'*, as Clemenceau described it – by the train journey across France to which the German delegation was subjected. It was described by Walter Simons, then Ministerial Director of the German Foreign Office: 'Our journey was an overwhelming experience. The train deliberately went slowly through the desolate fields, once rich with fruit, now torn apart by bombs, past the ruins of former villages and towns, where no one was to be seen save those removing the rubble. We paused at stations amid hollow dwellings, gutted warehouses and exploded trains until we had seen all that we could stand.'[21] This did not move Rantzau, though. Nor did the choice of Versailles – where Bismarck had declared the Second Reich – seem to have struck him unduly. When on 7 May the Peace Treaty was handed to the Germans, he set it aside without looking at it. Worse, in replying to Clemenceau's speech, he did not do the assembly the courtesy of rising. An apologist later explained that his bad nerves had not permitted him to do so, but Rantzau never endorsed this explanation. The peace terms were received in Berlin with unanimous horror, but German protests left the Allies cold. An ultimatum was delivered: either agree by 19.00 hours on 23 June, or Germany would be invaded.

Frenetic and confused activity followed. Technically, the war was still in progress. The German army could still count – more or less – on 350,000 men, and there were also the Freikorps divisions. The ever-practical Gröner appealed to Hindenburg for a decision, in writing, on action to be taken. Hindenburg once again refused to commit himself – he knew that any military activity would be doomed; but he could not bring himself to condone the terms of peace. 'Shouldn't we appeal to the officer corps and the nation to sacrifice themselves for Germany's honour?' he asked. 'The significance of such a gesture would be lost on the people,' replied Gröner.

Finally, Hindenburg wrote that the army could not count on success-fully repelling a determined enemy attack – but added, 'as a soldier, I would rather perish honourably than sign a humiliating peace.' Gröner, mindful of his commander's iconographic importance and keen to preserve his reputation, allowed him off the hook. Hindenburg ensured that it was Gröner who broke the news to Ebert that military resistance was useless. After the necessary telephone call had been made, Hindenburg actually laid his hand on Göner's shoulder and said, 'The burden you have undertaken is a terrible one.'

On 17 June Harry Kessler noted in his diary: 'Tonight I suffered indescribable depression, as if life to the very depths of my soul were extinct.' His mood reflected that of the country. On 19 June Scheidemann resigned as Chancellor, unable to face responsibility for signing the

Peace. Rantzau also resigned. During a frantic twenty-four hours, Ebert cast around for a new government. He found a Chancellor in Gustav Bauer, a relatively minor SPD leader whose thankless task was now to preside over the inevitable. Bauer was aided – indeed, dominated – by Matthias Erzberger, who took on the Deputy Chancellorship and the Finance Ministry. The same day, the German fleet held by the British at Scapa Flow succeeded in scuttling fifty of its sixty-eight ships. This did not endear the Germans to the Allies.

The ultimatum was close to its deadline. As the final hours passed, Erzberger argued that if the Treaty were signed without more ado, there might be some hope of getting the Allies to drop at least the clauses dealing with war criminals and war guilt. He carried this through the Reichstag, with great difficulty, but the Allies rejected it out of hand. As a result, the government began to come apart again, and for a moment it looked as if General von Maercker was going to succeed in persuading Noske to take over as military dictator.

At the last moment Germany did bow to the inevitable. The peace terms were accepted eighty minutes before the expiry of the Armistice, and signed by the new Foreign Minister, Hermann Müller, on Saturday, 28 June in the Hall of Mirrors at Versailles. Germany had lost all her colonies. At home she had lost 6 million citizens and 70,000 square kilometres. In absolute terms, she had caused the Allies 500 billion marks' worth of damage, a sum which Germany would be able to repay only notionally, even over many decades, whatever her future economic performance. But while the harsh terms of the Treaty of Versailles laid the foundations for another war, it should not be forgotten that the peace treaties concluded by Germany on the eastern front – at Brest–Litovsk and Bucharest – were no more generous to the Russians. Meanwhile, Germany remained the second largest European power after Russia.

On Saturday, 10 January 1920, Kessler wrote: 'Today the peace treaty was ratified in Paris; the war is over. A terrible time is beginning for Europe, the kind of humid stillness before a thunderstorm, which will probably end in an even more appalling explosion than the world war. Here, everything points to a continuing growth of nationalism.'

In the meantime, the Russians had been busy in Berlin. Karl Radek, Lenin's special envoy, was there offering the nervous new government a military alliance against the Allies – an offer which, though it was refused, would have made the Allies anxious had they known about it. Born of Jewish parents in 1885 in Austrian-occupied Poland, Radek came to Marxism early, beginning his revolutionary career at fourteen. He was with Lenin in the train which left Berlin for Finland and Russia in 1917, and he was at the peace conference of Brest–Litovsk. His job in Berlin was no less than to organize a Communist uprising friendly to

Russia. His failure cost him his privileged position in the new USSR, and though for a period he was editor of *Pravda*, he compounded his misfortunes by siding with Trotsky, and subsequently disappeared into the Gulag.

Radek was imprisoned in Moabit after the Spartacist rising of March 1919 but, allowed visitors, he held court to German Communists and foreign journalists, and continued to promulgate the idea of a Russo-German alliance against the west. He was soon repatriated, as Germany had no desire either to ally with Russia or to offend her. In view of the alliance which was nevertheless subsequently forged, it is not without significance that one of Radek's visitors at Moabit was the future Minister of Reconstruction and Foreign Minister, Walther Rathenau.

As well as the Russians who came to Berlin with the approval of the new regime in Moscow, many hundreds also appeared there as refugees from it. In stark contrast to Radek was Fyodor Vinberg, a former Imperial Russian army officer who founded a small newspaper, *Prizyv* (The Call), one of many Russian-language newspapers and magazines that now sprang up in Berlin. There had always been anti-Semitism in Germany, but Vinberg's was a new and more violent strain. Unfortunately, the times encouraged such convictions. Many Communists in Germany were Jews, as were many of the founders of Soviet Russia. Jews began to be seen as an evil and subversive influence, working in secret unison for dark purposes of their own: the undermining of western civilization? The conquest of the world? Anything was possible, and no Jew was to be trusted.

Vinberg was among the first to argue publicly that Jews should be exterminated. He brought with him out of Russia a short work entitled *The Protocols of the Elders of Zion*. Concocted in 1895 on the orders of the Russian secret police, *The Protocols* were alleged to be the minutes of a series of meetings detailing the Jewish master-plan for world domination, including such implausible ideas as the construction of underground railway systems beneath cities, from which all Gentiles would be blown up. Despite its absurdity the book was taken seriously enough to sell 100,000 copies almost immediately. Henry Ford sponsored an American edition, which also sold widely. In Germany *The Protocols* was a major influence on future Nazi leaders seeking new meaning for their ravaged country in its semi-legendary past, in the Germany of Siegfried and the Nibelungen, and in nineteenth-century theories of racial purity. The newspaper *Prizyv* was short-lived, but the trend it fed was not.

Though many stayed, Berlin was a staging-post for the majority of Russians. Ludwig von Hammerstein[22] remembers that 'in the 1950s I was at a Four Powers conference in Paris and I went out to a Russian restaurant in the evening. I can't speak French but the waiter spoke to me in pure Berlinese: the Russian family had run a restaurant in Berlin from 1920 to 1937: "Berlin was great, but we could see what was coming, so we decided to move the business to Paris." '

Berlin saw many Russian enterprises open, from cafés to cabarets. The best of the cabarets was the Blue Bird, run by Jushnij. Non-political, its performances mingled Russian, French and German, borrowing from Russian folklore as well as from Constructivism and Cubism. The best restaurant was probably the Allaverdi, named after a folk-song and run by a Ukrainian family. At the Hotel Adlon, Boris Chaliapin and Maxim Gorky were tearfully reunited after a disagreement over the virtues of the new Russian regime had disrupted their friendship. Sergei Eisenstein came to Babelsberg to study film technique at UFA. Stanislavsky brought over the Moscow Art Theatre on a cultural visit. Vassily Kandinsky arrived to start a new life. Isadora Duncan appeared in Berlin in 1921 after a tour of Russia, trailing a new husband eleven years her junior – the alcoholic, half-mad poet Sergei Essenin. Dozens of Russian aristocrats arrived with nothing but their jewellery, to buy themselves uncertain futures.

Carl Zuckmayer recalls seeing Pavlova give an impromptu performance at the Allaverdi:

If you were known there and had a free spender with you, you could stay after the official closing hour. When the upstairs restaurant was closed, you descended a winding staircase behind the bar into the cellar, where, as in the speakeasies of New York during Prohibition, small tables and folding chairs had been set up among the racks of bottles and the kegs of beer. These tables were occupied until daylight. Drinks were mostly champagne, brandy and whisky, at high prices. To make these strong beverages go down more easily, platters of smoked salmon and sturgeon, Russian pickles and marinated mushrooms were handed around. A single gypsy violinist played softly to the accompaniment of a bass balalaika. One night, when we were there with a patron, a curiously excited whispering and buzzing arose among the Russians. It passed from table to table. Then there was a sudden silence, and many of the men stood to bow in the direction of a small sofa in one corner. There sat an inconspicuously dressed woman with a silk shawl over her head. It was Pavlova. She was obviously in no way annoyed by this classless homage. On the contrary, she suddenly rose and with an expressive gesture removed her shawl and the jacket of her suit, under which she was wearing a sleeveless white blouse. In a moment all the tables and chairs had been whisked into an adjacent cellar. Everyone crowded against the walls and bottle racks. Pavlova whispered briefly with the violinist, who began the melody of *The Dying Swan*, and for five minutes she floated about the narrow space like a phantom, then with a deep bow of her whole body sank to the stone floor. The cheers that burst out seemed on the point of shattering the vaulted ceiling, but she silenced them with another gesture of her lovely arms, then returned to the small sofa and her companions. Thereafter, no one looked in her direction.[23]

Thanks to the Russian influx, Berlin was on the way to becoming cosmopolitan. It was not long before people from the west, too, were drawn there – not as exiles, but as more or less innocent exploiters of Germany's economic situation. Meanwhile, the Russians continued to fascinate Berliners, though dissension between different factions among the 50,000-odd *émigrés* could lead to violence and tragedy. The editor of *Rul* (The Rudder), another Russian publication, was the father of the novelist Vladimir Nabokov. In 1921 Nabokov *père*, an active member of the mildly liberal Kadet Party, agreed to a public debate with a friend, another Kadet, Pavel Miliukov, concerning a difference of opinion which had split the Party: Miliukov proposed a return to Russia and accommodation with Lenin, which Nabokov opposed. News of the meeting, to be held in the Berlin Philharmonie, reached the ears of two right-wing *émigrés* in Munich, Shalbelsky and Taboritsky, who determined to make their way to Berlin and assassinate the compromise-seeking Miliukov. As the meeting opened at the Philharmonie they marched down the aisle, singing patriotic Russian songs and drawing their revolvers. Members of the audience shouted warnings, Nabokov thrust himself in front of his friend, and was hit. Taboritsky climbed onto the stage and fired three more bullets into him, thinking he was the target. Nabokov was dead by the time he reached hospital.[24]

Though the characters in this particular drama were Russian, the combination of theatricality, violence and error creates an image which could stand for much of Berlin at this time.

4 Comedy, Tragedy, Politics and Money

THE TREATY OF Versailles was a hard blow for nascent German democracy. However justified its conditions seemed to the Allies, it left out of account the new thinking in Germany. Instead of encouraging a change of heart and helping Germany to its feet, the Treaty's terms humiliated national dignity; the reparations demanded, together with the confiscation of territories, were designed to keep Germany on its knees. It thereby united the forces of reaction and left the liberal flank exposed. The price paid was the Second World War.

The first split to appear was between the government and the army. Germany traditionally looked east: the Quadriga on the Brandenburg Gate and the statue of Frederick the Great at the other end of Unter den Linden both face east. Now, provinces gained by Frederick were to be given to the despised and hated Poles. The French, enemies since Napoleon's programme of conquest not much more than a hundred years earlier, were to occupy (with the other Allies) valuable industrial territories to the west. The Germans had rid themselves of the regime which started the First World War, but Germany's enemies tarred the new government with the same brush. This, at least, was the army's understanding of the situation. The army was required to reduce its manpower by nearly three-quarters: the government it had supported, and defended against the Communist menace, had now betrayed it. Even Noske, given the chance to seize power, had wavered. 'Minister, for you both I and my troops would let ourselves be cut to pieces,' General von Maercker had said to him; but he had let the opportunity pass. No one can now say what Gröner would have thought of such a move, but it is likely that he was aware of the possibility: Gröner's loyalty was always to the army first, to the Republic second. Indeed, loyalty to the army had such deep roots that, even in 1944, those officers involved in the plot to bring down Hitler were concerned as much to protect the integrity of the army as to destroy the tyrant.

The government had now lost the trust of the army – but it was too late to consider replacing it with a real people's army based on soldiers' councils and the election of officers. There were two distinct centres of power and they were divided. Worse, the generals chose – to replace the Army Minister, Noske – a most unfortunate moral leader. General Freiherr Walther von Lüttwitz came from a long line of army men. Physically slight, in appearance neat, he was also a Prussian aristocrat and monarchist, from his monocle to the tips of his gleaming boots. His ambition without doubt was to stage a coup.

Right-wing politicians were also bent on seizing power from what they saw as an ineffective, weak, appeasing government; they had learnt none of the lessons of the First World War, and were as nationalistic and militaristic as ever. Ebert was still only provisionally President: a national election was needed to confirm the appointment. The right wing, under the leadership of Dr Karl Helfferich, a caustic nationalist (but also a financial wizard), placed their hopes in Hindenburg as a rival candidate. The nation would unify, they argued, under a familiar father figure who, as an aristocrat, soldier and landowner, would have at heart the same interests as the conservatives.

Helfferich was especially bitter in his professional jealousy of and enmity towards Erzberger. So vitriolic were their mutual denunciations in print that in January 1920 Helfferich finally forced Erzberger to take him to court for libel. Helfferich engaged the brilliant Jewish lawyer Max Alsberg to defend him and, after an action which lasted nearly three months, won. Erzberger was so hated by the Right that a young officer cadet who shot and wounded him on 26 January was given a negligible sentence by a sympathetic judge. After the libel action, Erzberger was ruined politically; and he was assassinated the following year. (Helfferich died in a train crash in 1924, and Alsberg, driven from Germany as a Jew, killed himself in 1933.)

Helfferich's group planned to use constitutional means to achieve their ends. Another group, still more extreme, took their lead from Ludendorff; in 1920 he was staying at the Adlon, free of charge, under the name of Karl Neumann. Since the Allied Disarmament Commission met in the same hotel, and since the Allies, at least theoretically, still wanted Ludendorff as a war criminal, the management thoughtfully provided the general with his own secret exit onto Wilhelmstrasse. Ludendorff too had dreams of political control: his *Nationale Vereinigung* called quite simply for a return to absolute monarchy, to be achieved by force if necessary. Ludendorff stood aloof, however, from the active members of the group, which included that Captain Waldemar Pabst who had interrogated Liebknecht and Luxemburg, now discharged from the army for breach of discipline. Other members were Count Westarp, former leader of the Conservatives in the Reichstag: and one Wolfgang Kapp.

Kapp was born in New York in 1868, the son of a veteran of the 1848 revolution who had emigrated as a political refugee after its failure. He inherited all his father's dedication, but replaced his liberalism with a fierce nationalism. When he returned to Germany, Kapp joined the Pan-German League and associated himself with such First World War policies as unrestricted U-boat warfare – of which his former adoptive country, the USA, was a principal victim. Ridiculously, Kapp even once challenged Chancellor Bethmann Hollweg to a duel, considering him a weakling. In the years immediately following the end of the war he found a ready ear in General von Lüttwitz. Like Kapp, Lüttwitz favoured a military coup; but the army was not united behind him. Lüttwitz had the Freikorps' support, but among the regular general staff, von Maercker, von Oven and von Hammerstein – the last his own son-in-law – argued 'that the army should seek its aims by constitutional means. 'As a result,' recalls Hammerstein's son, 'my grandfather relieved my father of his post, and family relations were very cool for a time.'[1] Sensing the threat from the Right, the SPD-dominated Reichstag ratified Ebert's election as President.[2] This had the effect of uniting the Right, though opinions within the army remained divided.

The government, in an attempt to soothe the Allies, set up a Commission of Enquiry into causes of and responsibilities for the war. Helfferich made a statement attacking the 'peacemongering' Erzberger, thereby winning himself great acclaim. Germany had been shamed: those who stood up for her rather than kowtowing to the people who had shamed her were quick to gain at least ephemeral popular support. Antipathy to Versailles was running high, and not all the feeling generated by the Treaty was short-lived – in his opposition to it, Adolf Hitler became (on 16 September 1919) a member – Number 7 – of the German Workers' Party in Munich, out of which the Nazi party grew.

The army brought Hindenburg to Berlin. With his reputation carefully preserved, he entered the city as a national hero. When he testified to the Commission, he had been well briefed by Helfferich, Ludendorff, and their associates. During the hearing, he announced to the German people that the army had been stabbed in the back by the new republic. Hindenburg actually said that the expression 'a stab in the back' had been used by a British general. No one on the Commission thought to ask him who that general was; if they had, the myth might not have become so well perpetuated. To the government's great relief, the *Reichsmarschall* left the capital after testifying. But in the corridors of power there was increased talk of a military coup and the restoration of monarchy. Harry Kessler noted that in the course of a railway journey an elderly, respectable gentleman in his compartment aired the view that someone should stick a couple of hand grenades under Erzberger's car. 'He spoke quite distinctly, in the crowded compartment, and no one raised the least objection to his view.'

Into this tinder-box the Allies now threw a spark in the form of a Note, dated 3 February 1920, demanding the surrender for trial as war criminals of almost nine hundred people; the list included virtually every leader of wartime Germany. The Allies also demanded that two Freikorps brigades be disbanded – the Marine Brigade, commanded by ex-Captain of Corvettes Hermann Ehrhardt, and the Baltikum Brigade, commanded by General Graf von der Goltz. The Marine Brigade had earlier been used by the government to such effect that it had been nicknamed 'Noske's Fire Brigade'. So far the German military had defied the Allies only in symbolic ways, such as by burning French trophy flags rather than returning them; it now seemed that they would not be content with such gestures. On 1 March General von Lüttwitz, taking the salute at a march-past (under the old Imperial flag) of the two Freikorps at their barracks at Döberitz, outside Berlin, declared that he would never allow the brigades to be dissolved. At the same time, Kapp's group was busy drawing up statements to the nation and plans for government, and preparing a cabinet. Among their number was a curious character, Ignatius Timothy Trebitsch-Lincoln, a Hungarian-born Jew and former British MP who was now wanted in Britain for fraud; he was to end his life as a holy man in Tibet.

As early as 2 March Noske had indications from a Security Police report of a coup in the making, but chose to take no action until a week later, when he ordered Ehrhardt's Marine Brigade to be transferred to the authority of Admiral von Trotha, as a first step towards disbandment. Battle lines were now drawn: warrants for the arrest of Kapp and his associates went out on 11 March. Tipped off, they escaped to Döberitz, from where their *putsch* would be launched. The Marine Brigade was spared; von Trotha had more sympathy with the *ancien régime* than with the government, and allowed Ehrhardt to march his troops towards Berlin. Noske had underestimated his enemies.

At a council of war the representatives of the regular army were divided, but Colonel-General Hans von Seeckt spoke for the majority when he told Noske that 'There can be no question of setting the Reichswehr to fight these people [the Freikorps]. Would you force a battle at the Brandenburg Gate between troops who eighteen months ago were fighting shoulder to shoulder against the common enemy?' Noske was appalled, but should not have been so surprised that in the

circumstances the army was not this time ready to stand by the government. Seeckt, and others more powerful behind him, may have hoped the
coup might provide them with a stepping-stone to power. Whatever the
case, the undefended government – Ebert, Bauer, and the Cabinet – was
forced to beat a hasty retreat from Berlin in a convoy of cars during the
early morning of 13 March. At 6 a.m. the Marine and Baltikum Brigades
marched to the Brandenburg Gate to the accompaniment of martial
music. On their helmets a new symbol was painted. This was the
Hakenkreuz (hooked cross), also known as the gammadion, fylfot, or
swastika. *Svasti* means, in Sanskrit, 'good fortune'. The Baltikum
Brigade had adopted this ancient symbol after service against the Communists in Finland, where it had been used as a distinguishing mark on
Finnish aeroplanes. Since it was already known in Germany as a symbol
of racial purity, Hitler was later quick to adopt it, with the hooks bending
to the right, as the sign of his Party.

The brigades were met by Ludendorff and Lüttwitz, in full uniform,
and by Kapp, with his associates. They marched down Wilhelmstrasse
and occupied the Chancellery and the government offices. Ehrhardt's
brigade sang its marching song: '*Hakenkreuz am Stahlhelm, Schwarz-
weissrotes Band . . .*' (Swastikas on our helmets, United by the black,
white and red . . .). Kapp was in power.

Unfortunately for the coup, events moved too quickly during the final
phase for adequate preparations to have been made. The established
right-wing parties had not been won over, nor were the proposed new
laws and Constitution ready to be proclaimed to the people – who,
incidentally, were rather bemused by the whole affair. Now an atmosphere of Ruritanian farce prevailed: Kapp's daughter, who was to have
typed the new regime's manifesto for distribution to the newspapers,
couldn't find a typewriter. By the time the job was done, the Sunday
papers had gone to press. By Monday morning the *putschists* had lost the
initiative. They encountered difficulties in the government offices as
well: the SPD delegate Alfringhaus swapped the door-signs on the
National Party and SPD committee rooms prior to leaving, 'to confuse
the vandals'; another senior official, Arnold Brecht, sent all the telephone
operators off for a week's holiday, and himself left the Chancellery with
all the official stamps and seals.

Kapp, the fearless fighter for the Right, was quite unequal to the
challenge of real power, having spent his life as a minor civil servant. No
arrangements for funding the coup had been made, and when State Bank
officials refused to release 100,000 marks to him on the strength of his
signature alone, Kapp proposed a bank raid. Ehrhardt expostulated that
he was no robber. Encountering blank incomprehension or downright
hostility where he had vaingloriously hoped for rapturous welcome

and a path magically smoothed, the wretched Kapp declared himself
Chancellor and immediately volunteered to cede the position to anyone
else who commanded popular support. Intemperately he issued edicts,
hours later he feebly withdrew them. Meanwhile, the Cabinet made its
way to Dresden, where General von Maercker held the command. Now
it was his turn to dither – perhaps he was hedging his bets, not knowing
how firm a grip on power Kapp had in Berlin. Mistrustfully, Ebert and
Bauer sped on to Stuttgart where they established a new seat of government, declared Kapp and Lüttwitz traitors, and called for a general
strike.

In Berlin, the call to strike was answered with immediate and universal
enthusiasm. (*Ja, jibt's denn sowat?! Na, det wird denen aber det Monokel
aus'm Ooge hau'n!* – Wot's 'e up to? Bleedin' 'eck! We'll knock 'is monocle
aht'v'is eye f'r 'm!) The city shut down. Kapp might have used the
Freikorps ruthlessly to break the strike and assert his authority, but he
was not up to it. As the National Government was out of his reach in
Stuttgart, he dissolved the Prussian State Parliament, but reconvened it
two days later; he arrested the members of the Prussian Cabinet, then
tried to get them to co-operate with him and was stumped when they
refused. At last he ordered the Freikorps to shoot all the strikers – a
manifestly impossible task, even if their officers had agreed to the
attempt. By now – Monday, 15 March – Maercker had swung back
behind Ebert and the National Government. Lord Kilmarnock, British
High Commissioner, denounced as a lie Kapp's claim that the British
would support him. The Nationalist Party and the National Association
of German Industry withdrew what reserved support they had offered.
Finally, on 17 March, the Security Police demanded Kapp's resignation.
In Berlin, violence was already breaking out between workers and
Freikorps, and the Security Police were crucial to any pretence of stable
government.

Kapp now issued a statement that as he had completed all his aims he
was resigning his authority to Lüttwitz. The man who, in top hat
and spats, had the previous Saturday headed a small army, now, on
Wednesday evening, in an overcoat and a soft trilby, bundled himself
and his weeping daughter into a taxi with some belongings and papers
wrapped in a sheet. From Tempelhof Airport he took flight to ever-
accommodating Sweden.

Lüttwitz was caught off-balance by the new turn in events. Like so
many soldiers, he found he was a bad swimmer in the murky waters of
politics. Before he had time to take charge, the more moderate elements
in the High Command had withdrawn their support. The army remained
whole at the expense of some of its more extreme leaders' careers.
Lüttwitz was obliged to resign his command, and left for exile in

Hungary. The army had learnt a lesson: to achieve its aim of military reconstruction, it must work with, not against, the new regime. Having been seen to serve its own interests rather than those of the nation, it was regarded with suspicion by the people – who, with their general strike, had seen Kapp off.

The government returned to Berlin. In the wake of the attempted *putsch* Noske was claimed by the left wing as their price for organizing the general strike so successfully. He was replaced as Minister of Defence by Otto Gessler. The liberal general Walter von Reinhardt resigned in consequence, and Hans von Seeckt became Commander-in-Chief of the army. He had learnt the army's lesson too; for the next six years he used his position skilfully to rebuild it.

The footnote to the Kapp farce is tragic: as Ehrhardt's Marine Brigade marched back to Döberitz in good order it passed through the Brandenburg Gate. There, someone in the watching crowd of workers passed a derogatory remark. Without waiting for an order from their officers, the Freikorps troops turned and fired into the crowd, killing twelve and critically wounding another thirty. Nevertheless, Ebert granted the Freikorps an amnesty, and also paid them a 16,000-mark bonus promised by Kapp. He still needed them, at least in reserve, as the threat of a Communist revolution was by no means yet over. During the Kapp interlude a force of 50,000 workers calling itself the Red Ruhr Army had arisen under cover of the general strike, and managed for a time to occupy Essen, Dortmund and Düsseldorf. In April an armed Communist band terrorized the Vogtland in Saxony. Unrest also drew the French Army of Occupation into Darmstadt, Frankfurt-am-Main, Hanau and Homburg – a move publicly much deplored by the British, and which fuelled German nationalism.

Gustav Bauer resigned as Chancellor on 27 March and in elections on 6 June Right and Left gained at the Centre's expense. The SPD and its allies remained dominant, but with a reduced majority. Gustav Stresemann's People's Party won sixty-two seats. There were also two Communists in the Reichstag, for the first time.

After Kapp's departure (he returned later and sued for clemency, but died in prison), Harry Kessler dined at Cornelie Richter's.[3] Among the guests was Hannah Wangenheim, wife of the former German Ambassador in Constantinople, whose lodger Kapp had been until the *putsch*. Later, when the Security Police searched his flat, they were clearly afraid of finding anything which would compromise him. 'Their leader said quite directly to Hannah: "I don't suppose he'd've left anything in his desk?" Upon which Hannah replied: "Probably not; the key's still in it." He had wrapped up the really compromising material carefully and given it to her, without telling her that it contained all the plans for the coup.'

The year 1920 passed uneasily. Another Communist uprising threatened, but cultural life flourished in Berlin. In July Kessler's barber was
whispering as he shaved him that 'in three months the Bolsheviks would
be in Warsaw, and then we'd join with them and march against France.
He'd go along with them. I mention this because even among the
ordinary people the mood against France and the desire for a new war
are spreading. The most unexpected people are speaking warmly of
both.'[4] On 4 February 1921 Kessler attended the première of Richard
Strauss' *Joseph*, for which he and Hugo von Hoffmansthal had written
the libretto. The next eighteen months, however, saw him more involved
with politics than the arts, as negotiations over the payment of reparations became acute and an intransigent France became the focus of ever-
increasing German enmity. These eighteen months saw the rise of a man
Kessler admired greatly, and whose biography he was to write – Walther
Rathenau.

According to the terms of the Treaty of Versailles, an instalment of 20
billion gold marks in war reparations was to be paid by 1 May 1921.
Meanwhile, the question of the reduction of the German army was still
on the table,[5] and the situation remained delicate. The prime minister
of Bavaria, Gustav von Kahr, at first refused to disband the 'home
armies', and in central Germany Communists were once again plotting
rebellion.

In the event, only 8 billion marks were paid on 1 May, the Germans
arguing that payments already made in goods, ships and coal were worth
more. But the Allies made no concessions. Now a new Chancellor
emerged. Joseph Wirth, previously Finance Minister, came to the post
with great zeal and some new ideas, the aim of which was to get Germany
on the road to recovery at last. He introduced a programme designed to
conciliate the Allies by settling demands rather than constantly
prevaricating. This programme, he hoped, would demonstrate Germany's willingness to co-operate, but also her limited ability to do so.

The appointment of Walther Rathenau as Minister of Reconstruction
caused a sensation, since he was known primarily as a philosophical
author and industrialist, not a politician. Like Gustav Stresemann, he
had been a hawk during the First World War but was now committed
to the cause of democracy and peaceful economic recovery, and also to
a new European economic and social community. He was an efficient
businessman and organizer, and an eclectic writer, covering economics,
philosophy, politics and religion; his complex thinking was occasionally
open to misinterpretation by less refined minds, a circumstance which
was to contribute to his downfall. Indeed, his intellect was almost *too*
finely-tuned: 'In a trope quite typical of him but not common in the
Reichstag, he illustrated his position with reference to the "difficult decision" of the last movement of Beethoven's Quartet in F Major, Opus

135: "It begins with faint tones and finishes with a decisive and powerful *It must be*. Whoever faces his task without this *It must be* will only produce a half-toned resolution." [6]

His temperament frequently made a glacial impression which belied the inner man. An assimilated Jew who considered himself pre-eminently a German and a patriot, he had not been baptized a Christian following the usual pattern of his class. Nevertheless, he could be ruthless and unfair in his condemnation of fellow Jews. Even though he was heir to the giant multinational AEG (Allgemeine Elektrizitätsgesellschaft), his Jewishness had restricted the momentum of his political career. Rathenau never married and, though wealthy beyond most people's dreams, led a relatively modest life, devoted to his work and his sense of duty, sharing a house with his mother in a west Berlin suburb. Despite his coolness, letters to an unnamed female friend quoted by Kessler in his biography reveal, if not passion, fine depths of extraordinarily complicated feeling, in which the influence of Nietzsche seems never far away. [7]

Rathenau was faced with a difficult task. Attempts to conciliate the Allies were hampered by the Germans themselves. First of all, there was the problem of a reactionary judiciary, a permanent thorn in the flesh of the Weimar Republic. Perpetrators of various crimes during the course of the war had been tried, but the sentences passed by the courts were lenient in the extreme (as they would be again, in the years immediately following 1945). For example, two U-boat officers had been responsible not only for sinking a British hospital ship, but for machine-gunning lifeboats filled with nurses and wounded. They were sentenced to four years' imprisonment – but escaped after a matter of weeks and were never recaptured.

The perennial political instability of the country was exacerbated by the killing of Erzberger who, for all his faults, had been a campaigner for peace from an early stage. He was shot dead in the Black Forest by two former Ehrhardt officers who then escaped safely to the sanctuary of Hungary. Worse than the murder itself was the jubilation it gave rise to in Germany. If they accepted Wirth's integrity, the Allies could nevertheless hardly be blamed for viewing his disorderly house with scepticism, and even fear. To make matters worse, fighting had broken out in Upper Silesia between Germans and Poles. [8] Though the crisis there was settled by October, it was clear to Wirth that a firmer line had to be taken.

The state of the German economy inevitably led to inflation, which rose steadily, then alarmingly. Most Germans firmly believed that the ruin of their economy was due to the reparations; the government had to borrow, though with increasing difficulty, the necessary foreign exchange. As the gold marks leached away, there was a rush to change marks for hard foreign currency – preferably dollars – by any means. And the economy slipped further into ruin. Until the First World War the rate for the mark against the dollar had been about 4.2 to 1. By November 1921 it was already 200. Expenditure began to overtake income from taxes.

The cabinet resigned and reformed. By now the Allies had grasped the fact that bleeding Germany white would be to no one's advantage, and Lloyd George, the only Allied leader present at the signing of the Versailles Treaty to be still in power, was very much in favour of a resolution. A conference was called at Cannes on 6 January 1922, at which Rathenau was chairman and chief spokesman for the German delegation. Briefly matters looked hopeful. The French Prime Minister, Aristide Briand, seemed amenable to compromise – but Briand was voted out of power. In these unfortunately-timed elections the French clearly displayed their fear of compromise: Briand was replaced by the conservative and inflexible Raymond Poincaré. However, at least some concessions and small deferments had been agreed during the initial stages, to Germany's advantage.

Rathenau returned to Berlin and was offered the unenviable post of Foreign Minister, an exacting job which would bring him into further direct contact, as an appeaser, with the hated Allies. As a Jew, and a man with very little popular appeal, especially to the Right, Rathenau knew that in accepting the job he was risking his life. As he wrote to his mysterious friend on 31 January 1922: 'It is late at night, and, heavy-hearted, I think of you. You will have heard from F of the decision I had to make this evening. What can one person alone do against an unfriendly world, with enemies at his back, aware of his limitations and weaknesses?'[9] Earlier that day, at lunch, his mother had reproached him: 'Walther, why have you done this to me?' He replied: 'Mama, I have to do it; they have found no one else.' But he did not fear death: his *Mechanics of the Spirit* contained a refutation of it.[10]

The first conference at which victors and vanquished sat down together on equal terms to discuss Germany's economic future took place at Genoa in April 1922. Germany sent four national government ministers, including Chancellor Wirth and Foreign Minister Rathenau. Lloyd George attended, but Poincaré did not. Significantly, the Russians were also there; at Rapallo near Genoa on 16 April, Germany concluded a private treaty with them. Ostensibly this merely renewed lapsed trade agreements and interests, but it actually paved the way for a secret collaboration in armaments development masterminded by General von Seeckt. In the autumn of 1922, Seeckt noted: 'Poland is the nub of our Eastern problem. Poland's existence is intolerable; it is incompatible with

the conditions of Germany's existence . . . Poland must disappear, and
it will disappear thanks to its own internal weakness and to Russia – with
our help. For Poland is even more intolerable to Russia than to us; no
Russian regime can abide a Polish State. Nor can Germany ever hope to
derive any advantage from Poland, neither economic, nor political, for
it is a vassal of France.'[11] Secret military collaboration with Russia was
against the terms of the Treaty of Versailles, but Seeckt and his aides
were prepared to violate it. Initial talks took place at the home of Kurt
von Schleicher, that master of military intrigue. Chancellor Wirth was
a party to these negotiations. It is more than probable that everyone
involved believed that their patriotism cancelled out the illegality of their
actions. The generals were convinced that a standing army of 100,000
was not enough to defend German interests; the loss of the Colonies had
been a blow; and Germany, as we have seen, traditionally looked east for
expansion. Furthermore, Poland had not existed as a country in its own
right between 1795 and 1918. Interestingly, none other than Harry
Kessler had been instrumental in getting Józef Piłsudski, the first leader
of an independent Poland for over a century, back to his country from
Berlin immediately after the end of the First World War.

Rathenau was pleased with the Rapallo Treaty; it became clear to him
that western leaders at Genoa were giving him no chance to talk con-
fidentially with them. Fearful of an Allied–Russian agreement which
would catch Germany in pincers, he courted the leader of the Russian
delegation, Grigorii Chicherin (whose French, records Kessler, was so
thickly accented that it took five minutes to realize that he was not talking
Russian, and then another five to attune to it). But the treaty was not in
reality a diplomatic triumph: it alienated the West, and was in itself of
little value. However, Rathenau's second appearance on the international
stage enhanced his personal reputation, and his personality reflected well
on his country; if Germany could produce such cultured, civilized,
immaculately-dressed people, perhaps it would after all be possible to
negotiate.

But respect for Rathenau abroad naturally upset the nationalists and
militarists at home. Very quickly a couplet, of the rhyming type so
beloved by Germans, became current:

> *Knallt ab den Walther Rathenau*
> *die gottverdammte Judensau.*[12]
> (Shoot down Walther Rathenau
> the goddamned slippery Jewish sow.)

Despite Rathenau's incontestable patriotism and even mild nationalism,
Karl Helfferich attacked him in the Reichstag as viciously as he had
previously attacked Erzberger. Helfferich claimed that Rathenau had not

stood up strongly enough for German interests, though in fact no one could have done more. Helfferich, actually a cultivated, educated economist from a liberal background, and no anti-Semite, was riding high on a nationalist political ticket. He returned to the attack again and again, appealing shamelessly to popular chimeras like French avarice and the threat of inflation. Perhaps he was unaware of the power of his own rhetoric; perhaps he was drunk on it.

Even before Genoa there had been death threats; Rathenau, a convinced fatalist, had refused police protection, only agreeing to carry a pistol. Kessler remembers, 'Shortly after his appointment as Foreign Minister, as I entered his office in Wilhelmstrasse for the first time with the usual greeting, "How's it going?", he reached into his pocket and pulled out a Browning, with the reply, "Like this!" It had already reached the point that he could only go out armed with this little tool.'[13]

In April, a 17-year-old schoolboy, Hans Stubenrauch, a general's son and, despite his youth, already a member of the extreme right-wing Band of the Righteous, disclosed to a student named Günther his intention to murder Walther Rathenau; Günther had already been fined for cursing the Republican flag, and was in contact with Helfferich and Ludendorff. The latter had escaped from Berlin after the Kapp *putsch* and was now in Munich, where sympathies had swung to the Right, and carrying on under a new assumed name – Lange.[14] Stubenrauch's decision was based on two sentences from one of Rathenau's works, quoted out of context by Ludendorff: 'The day will never come again, when the Kaiser will ride as a victor on a white horse through the Brandenburg Gate. On such a day, world history would lose its meaning.' Günther introduced Stubenrauch to Erwin Kern, an ex-naval officer and member of the right-wing underground terrorist Organisation Consul, formed by members of the Ehrhardt Marine Brigade after the collapse of the Kapp *putsch*.

Kern quickly took over the operation from Stubenrauch and involved a number of associates, chief of whom were Hermann Fischer, an engineer; Ernst Werner Techow and his brother Gerd; and another ex-naval officer, Ernst von Salomon. None was more than 25; Gerd Techow was sixteen. The plan was simple: to trail Rathenau's chauffeur-driven limousine from his home in Grunewald to his office, at a certain point to overtake and open fire at the Foreign Minister before speeding off. Naturally the operation needed, and got, financial backing; but where from has never been determined. The conspirators acquired a machine-pistol, and hand-grenades – they were certainly thorough – and a powerful six-seater open car.

Kern and the rest were convinced of their rightness, indoctrinated by *The Protocols of the Elders of Zion*, and by Houston Stewart Chamberlain's vast and turgid *Foundations of the Nineteenth Century*. An English adoptive German and Wagner's son-in-law, Chamberlain influenced not only these youths but the equally callow Adolf Hitler, who later paid personal homage as the old writer lay dying. In Kern's mind Rathenau was part of the same international Jewish conspiracy as Rosa Luxemburg, Karl Radek, Hugo Preuss and Karl Marx. Rathenau was working towards a betrayal of Germany – even though Rathenau had inveighed against the dress and the manner of Orthodox Jews, and declared himself to be 'a German of Jewish descent. My people is the German people, my fatherland is Germany, my religion that Germanic faith which is above all religions.'

On 24 June Rathenau left for his office marginally later than usual. His car was old and not very fast; the conspirators had decided to take him where Königsallee made a sharp curve at the corner of Wallotstrasse. The *Vossische Zeitung* immediately afterwards printed an eye-witness account of the attack from a man working on a building site at that corner:

> . . . In the first, slow-moving car . . . a gentleman was sitting on the back seat; . . . the car was quite open, it didn't even have a sunshade-roof! The second car was also open, a powerful six-seater tourer painted dark field-grey. There were two men in it, in caps that left their faces quite free . . . They didn't wear goggles, either . . . this [car] caught our attention because of the fine leather get-ups the boys were wearing. The big car overtook the smaller one . . . [Kern] leant forwards, drew a long pistol, and aimed at the man in the other car. He didn't need to aim. They were close enough for me to see him eye to eye, as it were . . . I took cover, because the bullets could have hit us too. The shots came quite fast – like a machine-gun. Then the other one [Fischer] lobbed a hand-grenade into the car, but the gentleman had already crumpled up on the seat and lay on his side . . .[15]

The shots were heard by the 16-year-old Dietrich Bonhoeffer, studying at a school nearby. The large car sped down Wallotstrasse, as Rathenau's chauffeur pulled over and shouted for help. Then the grenade went off, shaking the car and lifting Rathenau off his seat. Running over, the building workers found nine cartridge cases and the pin from the grenade. A young woman jumped into the car and supported Rathenau, while his chauffeur restarted the engine and drove back at full speed to a nearby police station. The girl who had climbed into the car was a nurse called Helene Kaiser. With the chauffeur, she took Rathenau home. He was unconscious and, apart from opening his eyes once, did not speak again. The bullets had shattered his spine and lower jaw.

The following day he lay in his coffin in his study, as Kessler remembers, 'his head turned slightly to the right, and wearing a peaceful expression, which nevertheless contained immeasurable tragedy, in the deeply furrowed, wounded, dead face, over whose smashed lower half a fine handkerchief had been spread.'[16]

That same Sunday, huge workers' demonstrations took place, the marchers parading under the black, red and gold flag of the Republic, and under the red flag, through the streets of west Berlin. They marched in their hundreds of thousands, four abreast. This was not the reaction the conspirators had been looking for. When Helfferich appeared at the Reichstag at 3 p.m. he was met by angry cries of 'Murderer! Murderer!' 'White as a sheet, with the mark of Cain on his forehead, but clutching a bouquet given him by an admirer of the murderers, he fled from the building.' Rathenau lay in state in the Reichstag building on Monday and Tuesday. They played the funeral music from *Siegfried* over him. The trade unions declared a national day of mourning: in Berlin alone the processions numbered a million people. Ebert and Wirth delivered sombre speeches. This might have been a turning point.

Most of the conspirators were rounded up. Von Salomon served five years, and ended up in Hamburg after the Second World War as a screen-writer. The older Techow, who had driven the conspirators' car, got fifteen years, which were commuted to four; he later became a lawyer, but died during the Second World War in a Russian prisoner-of-war camp. Kern and Fischer got away. They were on the run for a month in the deep forests of Thuringia, before being cornered at the deserted Saaleck Castle, near Kösen. Surrounded by a hundred policemen, the two climbed onto the battlements and shouted down to the crowd of onlookers, 'We live and die for our ideals'. They tried to throw down written messages weighted by stones, but a stormy wind tore at the paper as it fell. As the storm gathered, there was a shoot-out in which Kern was killed; Fischer laid out his friend's body as best he could and then shot himself.

Some of these misguided young men would doubtless have been hor-rified by what was to come, but they were part of a terrible process and made their contribution to it. On 17 July 1933 the National Socialists arranged a celebration of the eleventh anniversary of their deaths at the graves of Fischer and Kern. Heinrich Himmler laid a wreath, and in his oration Ernst Röhm, head of the brown-uniformed SA, addressed the dead killers: 'Your spirit is our spirit,' he declared. 'The bullets that hit Rathenau also destroyed Bismarck's work,' noted Kessler sadly at the end of his biography.

Rathenau's mother wrote to Ernst Werner Techow's mother: 'In unnameable pain I reach out my hand to you, most wretched of all women. Tell your son that I forgive him in the name and spirit of the man he murdered, and as I hope that God will forgive him, if he makes a full confession to the authorities on earth and sincerely repents before those in heaven. If he had known my son, the most noble creature on earth, he would rather have turned the murder weapon on himself, than upon him. May these words give peace to your soul – Mathilde Rathenau.'[17] And here is another footnote: 'Credible reports tell us that Gerd Techow sincerely repented of his deed and experienced a complete moral conversion. As a member of the French Foreign Legion he did all he could to assist Jewish victims of Nazi persecution.'[18]

On 4 July Harry Kessler reported an attempt on the life of the prominent liberal journalist Maximilian Harden; on the 12th he visited his friend in hospital: 'He told me of the unbelievable savagery of the killer, who went on beating him with an iron bar as he lay on the ground. "I can't live in this country any more!" ' On the 20th, Kessler noted furiously Ludendorff's interview with the *Daily Express* in which he claimed that Rathenau's murder was the work of the Bolsheviks – 'no true German would resort to underhand killing of this sort'. In fact, 376 political murders were committed in Germany between 1918 and 1922. Even the former Chancellor, Philipp Scheidemann, had acid thrown in his face.

On the day of Rathenau's murder, the mark stood at 300 to the dollar. By 6 July the rate was 450. The middle classes, those who had savings, trembled. Patriotic, though misguided, investment in War Loans during the First World War had cost many families their futures. Now, what remained seemed threatened with being wiped out – along with any faith in received values, ethical, material or moral. By the middle of January 1923 the mark stood at 10,000 against the dollar; by the end of the month, 50,000. At this point the State Bank intervened and forced the rate down, but it could not stem the tide for long. By May the mark was down again, to 70,000 to the dollar: by the end of June it was 150,000. By August the dollar stood at 1 million marks, and the banks were issuing 46 billion marks a day. By the end of September, the rate had risen to 160 million. The Ullstein newspaper presses were commandeered to print money. The figures on banknotes were overprinted as million mark notes became billion mark notes. Currency in circulation rose to 44 *trillion* marks. The government was accused of deliberately allowing inflation to skyrocket in order to avoid repaying foreign debts and reparations at par value.

Commerce fell into confusion; state business, from the issuing of tax demands to amending telephone bills and the cost of postage stamps, tottered. People were paid at midday and rushed immediately to buy food, or goods which could be bartered for food. As for shopkeepers, the art dealer Henni Handler, who now lives in London, remembers: 'They kept open late so that people had a chance to buy, then they'd grab their takings and rush out to buy produce immediately to restock with, to keep one jump ahead of rising prices themselves.'[19] Two examples indicate how inflation hit people in Berlin: on 16 July 1923 the price of a tram ticket was 3,000 marks; on the 30th, 6,000; on 6 August, 10,000; on the 14th, 50,000, and on the 20th, 100,000. And a cubic metre of gas cost 6,000 marks on 30 July; on 30 August, it cost 250,000. On 21 September, the first billion-mark note came into circulation. Strikes and civil unrest were the order of the day.

Foreigners moved in and bought up whole streets, whole Berlin apartment houses, for sums as risible as $500. The middle classes saw their life savings, and with them all hope of security, vanish; their formerly diligent support for a healthy state crumbled. Some turned for survival to crime. The most easily saleable commodity, which required no capital investment, was sex. In many once respectable apartments, sex clubs sprang up; the manager was the paterfamilias, the madam the mother, and the whores their daughters.

Some workers succeeded in keeping their wages more or less constant during this drastic devaluation, but it wasn't long before the trade unions' treasuries were empty. Even heavy industry, which still owned its plant and land, and could still earn some hard currency from export, faced the fact that the final débâcle could not be far away. If Poincaré had deliberately set out to bring ruin on Germany, he had succeeded with a vengeance thus far. But Poincaré was abetted by the other Allies.

How faded and forlorn the few remaining symbols of the Wilhelmine era looked now. A few grand shops, still signed 'By Royal Appointment', now depended for their survival on foreign custom. Profiteers – and the *nouveaux riches*, the so-called *Raffkes* – could still wine and dine their girl-friends in Borchardt's, Hiller's or Horcher's, paying the bill with a couple of dollars drawn with beringed fingers from heavy snakeskin wallets. The sound of jazz bands could be heard well into the night; warmth and light spilled onto the streets from bars and restaurants and dance-halls. In the streets crippled, half-forgotten war veterans begged or sold matches. *Bureaux de change* appeared on every corner, their blackboards noting the hourly decline of the mark. Big hotels like the Adlon and the Bristol stayed afloat on foreign exchange. The smartest shops were full of buyers; the perfumier Lohse kept going, as did the porcelain dealers Rosenthal; in Unter den Linden the jewellers Friedländer, Margraf and Wagner were open for business as usual. But in Neukölln and Wedding, stale bread and cabbage soup were at a premium. In middle class districts, in the prosperous suburbs in the west of the city, unfortunate householders trying to sell were driven to suicide as prospective buyers delayed payment for a week, rendering deals valueless to the vendors. Banknotes became literally not worth the paper they were printed on. Because they were printed on only one side, minor entrepreneurs set up *ad hoc* stalls bartering them as scrap paper. It was economic Armageddon. Inevitably, unemployment began to rise. In two months, the number registered as out of work in Berlin almost trebled. On the farms around Berlin country people with shotguns protected their crops from raiding parties. There were gun-battles over potato fields, and people were killed. In October 1923 a party of gleaners on stubble raided a nearby field that had not been harvested. The police intervened and shots were exchanged. One child died, and another was seriously injured.

Many *émigré* Russians remained in Berlin, and those who still had jewellery to sell, or foreign currency in their pockets, found themselves able to live in the grand style to which some of them had been accustomed in the days of Nicholas II. Dime-a-dozen princes and princesses could once again lord it on the back of unfair advantages. And they could make a Little Russia in Berlin. At Medjev's you could have borscht and kulibiaki, served on tables spread with white linen cloths – just like at home. At the Café Ruschko you could drink tea and vodka, listen to a balalaika trio, and lose yourself in the evocative, nostalgic smell of Balkan tobacco. What did it matter if reality was lurking in the barren streets outside? The buildings didn't look that bad. There weren't that many beggars. If you stayed in your own part of town, and you were rich, you could almost imagine that nothing was wrong.

One of the most symbolically powerful stories published at this time is Stefan Zweig's *The Invisible Collection*,[20] in which an antique dealer on the make visits an old collector of prints and manuscripts. The old man, now blind, proudly refuses to part with any of his priceless works. As he shows the dealer his portfolios, it becomes clear that his wife and daughter have, in desperation, sold nearly everything in order to buy food, substituting cheap reproductions or even blank paper for the prints. 'For sixty years,' the old man tells the appalled dealer proudly, 'I have had no beer, no wine, no tobacco, no travelling, no visits to the theatre, no books – all I have done is save and save for these portfolios.'

Inflation made people resourceful. When the great actress Tilla Durieux went to New York in 1921 with her husband, the modern art collector and publisher Paul Cassirer, they paid for their room at the Ritz with a picture, as the managing director was a fellow collector. Thus they avoided paying a fortune in marks. But tips could not be avoided and it became impossible for them to eat in the hotel restaurant, so with the director's connivance they cooked for themselves in their suite. This was strictly forbidden under the hotel rules, and food had to be smuggled in from a local deli in a flower basket.[21]

Lotte Laserstein, the painter, survived for a time in Berlin by spending her mornings drawing cadavers preserved in hydrochloroform for an anatomical textbook. She would take her pay and run to the shops before prices went up at 2 p.m. Berthold Goldschmidt's agent found him engagements to play the celeste in all concerts at the Philharmonie where the instrument was called for, and this provided bread-and-butter money. 'There were a lot of concerts because people from abroad with hard currency . . . would come to Berlin and engage the Philharmonic Orchestra for what to them was virtually nothing. You could buy yourself a concert for $100, and foreign conductors like Pierre Monteux profited from the opportunity. Inflation had a devastating effect on the population, but . . . it attracted an influx of very important artists . . . to Berlin because they could live cheaply there. Russians, Swedes, Poles – they all came and settled in Berlin.'[22]

The actress Steffie Spira's memories paint a less devastating picture of the fate of the middle classes – a useful corrective, and there *is* a danger of over-stating the case – but it is as well to remember that Steffie is a lifelong member of the Communist Party.

> In 1923 my father wasn't out of work. There was plenty of work for actors then. I was aware of the unemployment, of the strikes – and to some extent I was aware of their significance, though I was still only fifteen years old. But Wilmersdorf was very middle-class and really wasn't greatly affected – there weren't many workers living there, only bourgeois and petty-bourgeois. My family wasn't affected . . . There really were two worlds in Berlin. I remember one theatre had a sign up at the box office which pegged the price of seats to the going rate for goods: 'Orchestra stalls: the same price as half a pound of butter. Rear stalls: two eggs.' That was our new gold standard! Things like that were grotesque, but also funny, and it was still possible to laugh in those days.[23]

The film and theatre critic Arnold Bauer remembers:

> One was aware of great poverty on the streets. Money was distributed from lorries piled with huge laundry hampers full of the banknotes which came out of the State Bank in the mornings. Then people bought enough for one or at the most two days – that was as far ahead as they could afford to buy. There was a lot of bartering, too – big flea markets sprang up as people tried to make some money – or they became exchange places for goods, clothes, anything which there was no money left over to pay for in the normal way. There was also the tragedy of old people, despairing people, people on small fixed pensions . . . Poor, educated old people there were, who simply couldn't grasp what was going on.
>
> On the other hand there were people who could earn hard currency abroad . . . I knew a writer who got a fee of 500 Swedish kronor and it kept him for at least three months. And there were people who were lucky enough to have relatives abroad who would help them . . . Foreigners came here and lived like grandees – you could have a really good girl for a couple of dollars. Cigarettes and food did just as well. Like after the Second World War.[24]

The architect, architectural historian and teacher Julius Posener belonged to a comfortably-off family living in Lichterfelde:

> . . . we were fortunate because we owned the house. We rented out some of the rooms to make ends meet. I remember during the worst time my oldest brother and I went touring, on a tandem, the region around Berchtesgaden – this was before Hitler, of course. In the deep countryside luxuries like eggs and milk were available, and the people were charming, but we were on a tight budget. My father sent us a wire: 'Dear boys, I am sending you 10 million Reichsmarks, so that you may at least enjoy a glass each of true Bavarian beer!' But by the time the money arrived, it wouldn't have bought us a thimbleful . . . But we had no real distress during inflation. It was simply disagreeable. My mother's family fortune was not affected, as it was all in property or foreign investment . . . But one did notice the people in the streets in their threadbare clothes that never got changed because they only had one set.[25]

Not everybody lost. Another Berliner remembers an uncle who, marrying into a wealthy family, left banking and started his own business. 'He went into hire laundry and commissioned an artist to design him a company logo. During the inflation he got a contract with the underground train company for advertising space on a barter basis: he supplied the company with used-up laundry for use as rags in return . . . The free advertising gave him a flying start. He began with one horse-drawn cart. By the Thirties he had a modest fleet of vans. He went to London when the Nazis seized power and started his company up there. It still exists. It's called the London Linen Supply and still uses the logo he had designed in Berlin.'[26]

But it was Hugo Stinnes who really made a success out of inflation. His first fortune was made from coal, and as this earned him hard foreign currency, his credit was assured. From this foundation he was able to borrow vast sums in marks which he later repaid after their value had sunk. With the wealth thus amassed he bought on a stupendous scale, and ended up owning a bit of everything – from shipping lines to country houses, along with 2,000 companies. He headed the biggest industrial trust in Europe. Stinnes like to style himself – with 'pretentious simplicity'[27] – 'merchant in Mühlheim'. Like many successful businessmen before and since, he also fancied himself as a politician, and was for a time a People's Party delegate in the Reichstag. In his biography of Rathenau, Kessler describes Hugo Stinnes thus:

> . . . the most powerful man in Germany, a sort of secret emperor of finance: for the broad masses at home and overseas he was a figure of myth . . . a Cagliostro, an alchemist who could turn paper into gold . . . half prophet, half crafty businessman . . . impenetrable to friend and foe alike . . . southern-looking, black-bearded, with eyes that seem to look upon an inner

vision; dressed in peasant boots, in clothes that hang on him as if they'd been bought off the peg, always surrounded by his numerous family which he drags around with him everywhere; a cross between a patriarch, a commercial traveller, and the Flying Dutchman . . .

Stinnes's material success is beyond question, but from his photographs he looks crumpled and shifty, shabbily-dressed and hounded. Like many wealthy men, he seems meagre and unhappy; and, like those of many wealthy men, his empire crumbled to nothing at his death: greed and fantasy combined had led him to overstretch his resources.

Chancellor Wirth's second cabinet came to an end on 22 November 1922, and Wilhelm Cuno replaced him. Ebert was reconfirmed as President. Wirth had resigned because he couldn't get the SPD to collaborate with Stresemann's People's Party. The non-partisan Cuno was felt to be the right man to lead a more broadly-based cabinet. Although he had had a brilliant business career in shipping, Cuno was neither an experienced nor, as it turned out, a very gifted politician. The coming man was Gustav Stresemann.

At about this time the Nationalsozialistische Deutsche Arbeiterpartei (the National Socialist and Workers' Party of Germany – henceforward NSDAP or Nazi Party) made its first significant appearance. The consistently liberal Prussian State Government had banned the party and its motto 'Against Marxists and Jews,' and Karl Severing, then Prussian Minister of the Interior, forbade Hitler to speak in public. But Bavaria, which had recently swung right, welcomed the NSDAP leader. Although a Fascist dictator had seized power in Italy as recently as 30 October 1922, Munich seemed a long way from Berlin.

Meanwhile, Poincaré continued to resist German efforts towards a moratorium on reparations: the Germans must pay in full, in cash and in kind, according to the letter of the Treaty of Versailles. In the Reparations Committee Britain voted against Belgium, France and Italy in favour of Germany, but would not go so far as to sacrifice the Entente. A crisis was reached on 11 January 1923, when French and Belgian forces formally occupied the Ruhr in retaliation for German non-payment. From his Bürgerbräukeller base in Munich Hitler immediately attacked the 'appeasers' in government. Understandably, the reaction generally to the invasion was one of outrage. The occupation was a violation of the Treaty of Versailles, and the industrial Ruhr – as Poincaré well knew – was the principal source of the means of paying reparations money. There followed more prolonged and tortuous negotiations; passive resistance among the workers of the Ruhr added to the tension. The situation quickly deteriorated: mines were closed; there was enforced unemployment; and the occupying armies acted brutally.

Other Allied nations looked on and wrung their hands, but none intervened. The Franco-Belgian action was a gift to the NSDAP.

The German army could do nothing. Seeckt was carefully building up a semi-secret Schwarze Reichswehr (Black National Army – 'black' in German also means unauthorized), with 'temporary volunteers' – not, unfortunately, of high quality either ethically, morally or politically. It also drew upon the old Freikorps, quasi-military organizations such as Stahlhelm, and various 'sporting' clubs and societies. Captain Ehrhardt, imprisoned for anti-government activities but escaped, was in Bavaria organizing the private Oberland Bund army, aided by local gendarmes; his was one of many such units springing up, with names like Oberland, Oberland-Treu, Blücher. Of course, not all Germans were hawks; Harry Kessler was one of thirty speakers to address a 100,000-strong 'Never Again War' demonstration in the Lustgarten on 30 July 1922. But, as is usual in human society, the intemperate elements were the popular ones.

Seeckt was also involved in the foundation of a private Russo-German trading association, the Society for the Encouragement of Commercial Enterprises, or GEFU in its German acronym. GEFU had offices in Moscow and Berlin, a budget of 75 million marks at pre-inflation rates, and was headed by two trusted aides. Belying its innocent name, GEFU's first objectives were to set up a Junkers aircraft factory near Moscow to produce 600 all-metal aircraft and motors annually; and to establish a plant at Trotsk in Samara for the production of poison gas, and further plants for the production of artillery shells. In fact, GEFU barely got off the ground. The Junkers factory was closed owing to funding problems. As the whole project had been secret, Junkers could not sue for breach of contract; but they did circulate an account of the matter to every Reichstag deputy. A copy fell into the hands of the *Manchester Guardian*, which exposed GEFU in an exclusive story on 3 December 1926.

Although GEFU was wound up, secret German military reconstruction continued with the wary connivance of a government still treading a delicate path between betraying its principles and losing its power. 'Like many soldiers, Seeckt had an attitude of ambivalence towards war. "The soldier, having experience of war, fears it more than the doctrinaire, who being ignorant of war talks only of peace," he wrote before Hitler came to power. Yet after the rearmament of Germany – the foundations for which he had so ably laid – he said: "War is the highest summit of human achievement; it is the natural, the final stage in the historical development of humanity." It is not impossible that the fierce and savage beauty of war, as well as the professional pride of the soldier, may have been present in his mind, for he was artist as well as warrior.'[28]

Seeckt was a sensitive man, but also a product of his class and his training; he was a conservative and a patriot; and a quite adroit politician. His principal loyalty was to the army, and he saw his primary duty as preserving it and its traditions intact, in the face of the conditions imposed by Versailles. He developed secret rearmament links with Austria, Holland, Italy, Spain, Sweden and Switzerland, in addition to Russia, establishing a top-secret armament office in the War Department for the purpose. He successfully courted German heavy industry, which resented the enforced post-war demolition of much of its plant. In the end he overreached himself. A convinced monarchist, in 1926 he permitted the eldest son of the former Crown Prince to take part in the autumn manoeuvres. Such an appalling political solecism was bad enough – but that he committed it without consulting the Minister of Defence or the Supreme Commander sealed his fate. He resigned on 9 October. Thereafter, though he still played a role behind the scenes, his influence was never so great.

By the summer of 1923 Germany was not only reeling under inflation, but once again standing on the brink of civil war, as left- and right-wing elements polarized in the various states. Cuno's government fell in August; he was replaced as Chancellor by Gustav Stresemann, who was also Foreign Minister – a post he retained in seven successive cabinets, until his death. His chancellorship only lasted, through two cabinets, until 30 November, but he guided Germany with great skill between economic ruin and civil unrest. The founder and leader of the People's Party, he was an internationalist and a liberal – although he looked like the archetypal, square-headed 'Boche'.

Somehow, inflation had to be controlled. By now there was not enough gold to underpin the currency; Helfferich drew up a proposal for a National Mortgage Bank (the Rentenbank), which would receive an interest-bearing mortgage on all agricultural and industrial land in Germany, and would issue interest-bearing notes backed up by this mortgage. The new currency was not to be linked to gold, but to rye, hence its original name of *Roggenmark*. The 'rye mark' was pegged to the value of one pound of rye – chosen because it was the main product of German agriculture. After much wrangling, an enabling law was passed by decree on 15 October 1923, though the new Rentenmark, as it was now called, was after all pegged to gold, not rye. Helfferich thus redeemed something of the reputation he had lost by his intemperate politicking. The reformed currency was to be introduced on 15 November and Hjalmar Schacht was made National Currency Commissioner, to implement Helfferich's idea.

Meanwhile, Stresemann took the brave but unpopular step of calling off the passive resistance in the Ruhr which had been leaching away 40 million gold marks a day. This was all he could realistically do to salvage the economy, but it earned him the violent opprobrium of the Right. The hard-line French Premier Poincaré fell from office soon afterwards and the moderate Aristide Briand became Foreign Minister; Stresemann was consequently much freer to attempt to build a peace by diplomatic means. Had it not been for his early death and the irresistible rise of Adolf Hitler in the face of Germany's continuing economic problems, Stresemann's efforts might have kept the NSDAP from power, and even prevented the Second World War. Briand, like Stresemann, was an advocate of a United States of Europe; the two men became personal friends, and were jointly awarded the Nobel Peace Prize in 1926.

The Bavarians, infuriated by the cessation of resistance in the Ruhr, promptly declared a state of emergency, hoping to mobilize the Schwarze Reichswehr, and possibly to install Seeckt as military dictator. This forced Stresemann to declare a national state of emergency; executive power, however, went not to Seeckt but to his Defence Minister, the civilian Democrat Otto Gessler. There was an abortive coup attempt by the Schwarze Reichswehr under a retired major in charge of an Arbeits-kommando (Work Force division of the Black Army) at Küstrin. There is little doubt that the so-called *Küstriner Putsch* had the connivance of the regular army, but it was quashed and the government stayed afloat. It seemed nothing could be done, however, to stem the growing tide of private quasi-military organizations. The Bavarian State Government flatly refused a request by the National Government in Berlin to close down Hitler's hate-sheet, the *Völkische Beobachter*, a refusal which in turn led the SPD to withdraw in protest from Stresemann's coalition, leaving him with no majority. And Seeckt was still waiting in the wings.

It took a while for people to get used to the new Rentenmark. This was supposed to bear the same relation to the dollar as its pre-war predecessor – that is, 4.2:1. The paper mark had skyrocketed from a giddy 1290 billion to the dollar on 14 November to a stratospheric 4200 billion on 20 November; the exchange price, paper mark to Rentenmark, was fixed at 1 trillion:1, thus wiping out the face value of remaining paper marks.

On 8 November 1923 Hitler staged his abortive 'Beer-Hall *Putsch*'. The words 'Beer-Hall' conjure up the image of a ghastly drinking-pit, full of coarse, fat Germans swilling ale – but the Bürgerbräukeller was a fashionable and quite elegant place on the outskirts of Munich by the river Isar. The *putsch* failed because Hitler snatched too quickly at his opportunity, and because the Munich police and the regular army remained loyal to the legally elected authorities. Ludendorff, in abetting him, was finished as any kind of political force, although he went on to stand in the presidential elections of 1925. Editing the British Ambassador Viscount d'Abernon's diaries in 1929, Professor M. A. Gerothwohl

1. Scenes from the First World War. The 'Iron Hindenburg' statue below the Victory Column at its official opening; and Kaiser Wilhelm II, seen here striding forth to destiny.

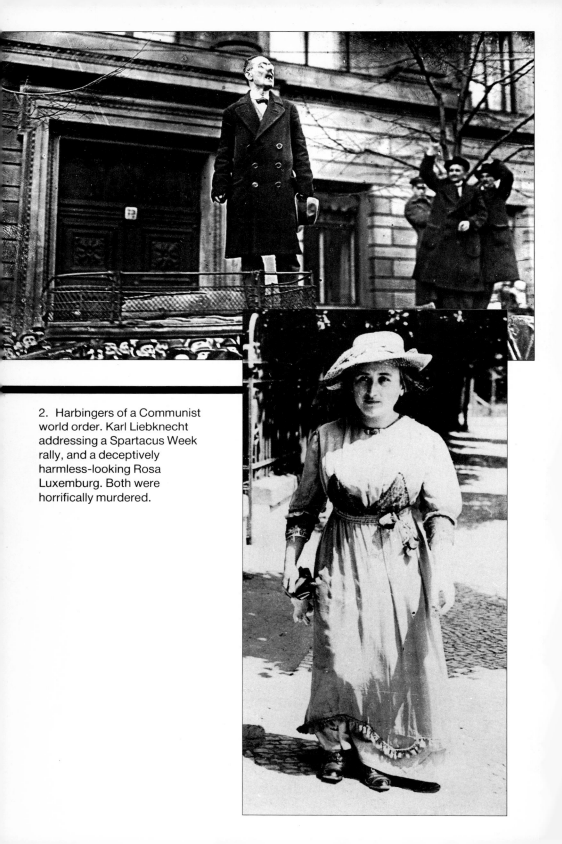

2. Harbingers of a Communist world order. Karl Liebknecht addressing a Spartacus Week rally, and a deceptively harmless-looking Rosa Luxemburg. Both were horrifically murdered.

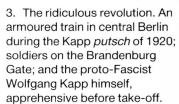

3. The ridiculous revolution. An armoured train in central Berlin during the Kapp *putsch* of 1920; soldiers on the Brandenburg Gate; and the proto-Fascist Wolfgang Kapp himself, apprehensive before take-off.

4. Contrasting figures in Weimar Berlin. Count Harry Kessler, diarist and man-about-town (painted by Munch); super-rich financier Hugo Stinnes with his wife; and Albert Einstein, on foot here. Einstein's difficulties with mental arithmetic were familiar to bus conductors.

5. Poor people's lives during the great inflation. The room shown here was for
seven people. In one year, the mark slipped from 10,000 to the $ to 160,000,000.

6. Hell or Heaven? Richard Ziegler's (*left*) and Lutz Ehrenberger's views of Berlin night-life in the Twenties.

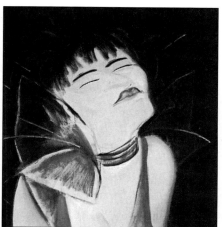

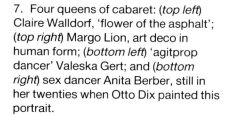

7. Four queens of cabaret: (*top left*)
Claire Walldorf, 'flower of the asphalt';
(*top right*) Margo Lion, art deco in
human form; (*bottom left*) 'agitprop
dancer' Valeska Gert; and (*bottom
right*) sex dancer Anita Berber, still in
her twenties when Otto Dix painted this
portrait.

8. The divine Josephine Baker, who stood Berlin its ears in the mid-Twenties and (*below*) Muguette at the Eldorado, Berlin's biggest gay men's club. Naturally, Muguette was a man.

9. The Tiller Girls on tour (with the Brandenburg Gate behind them), and the more *risqué* Haller Review, as advertised and on stage.

10. Two who might have stopped Hitler – had they lived. Gustav Stresemann (*above*), killed by overwork, and Walther Rathenau, brutally assassinated.

11. Dada comes to Berlin. At the first exhibition in 1919 are, standing, Raoul Hausmann, Otto Burchard, Johannes Baader, Wieland and Margarete Herzfelde, George Grosz and John Heartfield; sitting are Hannah Höch and Otto Schmalhausen.

12. Images of Berliners. Käthe Kollwitz's *German Mother*, Otto Dix's *Match-seller*, Heinrich Zille's *Woman Carrying a Bucket*, and a National Socialist Statue by Josef Thorak – widely known as 'Professor Thorax'.

13. Three Berlin artists. Käthe Kollwitz photographed by Hänse Herrmann, Max Liebermann in a woodcut by Conrad Felixmüller, and George Grosz painted by himself.

14. Two advanced buildings by Erich Mendelsohn. The Einstein Tower near Potsdam (1921; Einstein called it 'organic'), and the Columbushaus in Potsdamer Platz (1933). The traffic lights on the clock tower were Germany's first, and the crowds they drew initially worsened the jams.

15. Exotic developments in transport. A custom-built Mercedes (*top*) and a new approach to streamlining cars (both of 1934). Franz Kruckenberg's 'Zeppelin of the tracks' (*right*) reached 143 miles an hour in 1931.

IS-20611

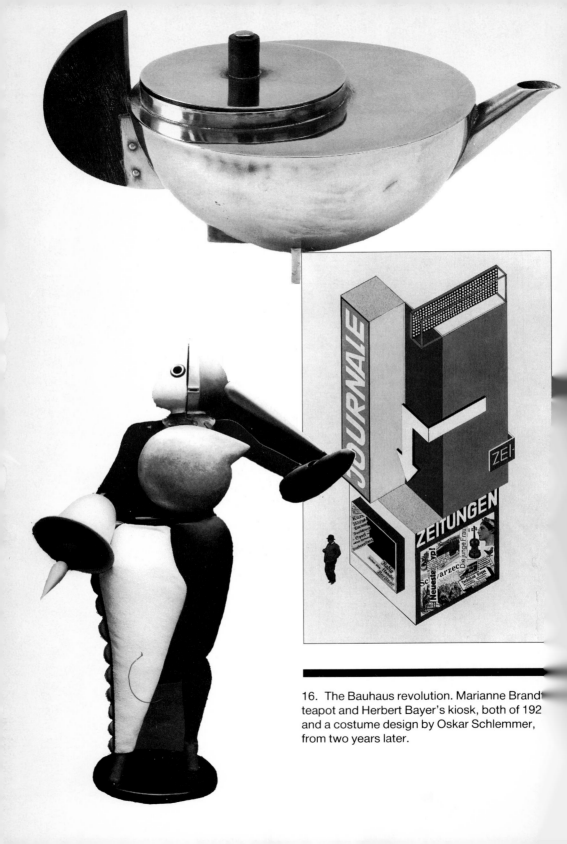

16. The Bauhaus revolution. Marianne Brandt's
teapot and Herbert Bayer's kiosk, both of 192~
and a costume design by Oskar Schlemmer,
from two years later.

noted, following the failure of the *putsch*, that Hitler 'was arrested and subsequently tried for high treason, receiving a sentence of five years in a fortress. He was finally released after six months [*sic*] and bound over for the rest of his sentence, thereafter fading into oblivion.'

Stresemann could not hold on as Chancellor after November 1923. The right-wing parties would not support him because of his Ruhr policy; the SPD, though they wanted him to remain as Chancellor, refused to join in a general vote of confidence because of their interests in the left-wing states of Saxony and Thuringia. Ebert, a clear-sighted member of the party, later remarked to them: 'Your reason for unseating the Chancellor will be forgotten in six weeks, but you will still be suffering the consequences of your stupidity in ten years' time.' The new chancellor was Wilhelm Marx, another Centrist; Hjalmar Schacht, who subsequently lent his support to Hitler, took over the presidency of the State Bank. He managed the currency reform skilfully, establishing friendly relations with leading British bankers. From new international committees set up at the beginning of 1924 to consider the problem of German reparations came two American-inspired and much more liberal repayment programmes: the Dawes Plan, and later the Young Plan.

In February a Munich municipal court tried the principal defendants in the matter of the Beer-Hall *putsch*, including Hitler, Ludendorff, and Ernst Röhm, the head of the notorious SA (the 'Storm Section' of the NSDAP); the trial was a shameful affair in which the defendants had the blatant support of the bench. Hitler served only twelve months of his sentence, in great comfort, dictating *Mein Kampf* to Rudolf Hess in the fortress of Landsberg. The law required the deportation of this treacherous foreigner (Hitler was Austrian); but Bavaria flouted national rulings. Almost as fecklessly, in Berlin the extreme Left refused to cooperate in the Reichstag with the government's plans to extract the country from debt and chaos. But the government was not entirely innocent: despite the onerous burden of reparations payments, Germany still spent billions on secret rearmament.

By the middle of the year, however, prospects were more hopeful. A loan of 800 million in gold to preserve the stability of the mark, raised principally in America, was to be administered by a board consisting half of Germans and half of foreign creditors. Plans were also agreed for French withdrawal from the Ruhr. But the Allies were well aware of Germany's rearmament programme, and the Cologne Zone remained occupied.

One firm to go to the wall was Barmat Enterprises. Julius Barmat was a Russian-born Jew who had moved to Holland in 1907 and subsequently established good relations with the leaders of the SPD. With his brothers Herschel, Solomon and Isaak, he exported large amounts of food to

Germany and later, having moved there, he used his SPD contacts to oil the wheels for huge loans on the Bank of Prussia and the German postal system. But the new enterprises started with these loans flopped, and the entire concern folded at the very end of 1924. The Barmat brothers and their associates were arrested, with debts in excess of 10 million marks. The trial of Julius Barmat lasted more than a year and the verdict, handed down on 30 March 1927, amounted to a 545-page history of the inflation period. Barmat was sent to prison for eleven months.

More significant than the financial scandal itself, apart from the unfortunate fact that the Barmats were Jews, was the number of prominent SPD members involved, among them Friedrich Ebert himself. The President, hated by the Left for betraying the revolution, by the Right for giving it respectability, and by the army for being a civilian (as President he was also Commander-in-Chief), was now so hounded by press and pulpit that he had to file almost 150 suits. The NSDAP joined the hue and cry, seizing any weapons that came to hand: their legal department dug up the fact of Ebert's participation in the strike of January 1918 – which made him, according to the letter of the law, a traitor. The right-wing courts quickly battened on this in the course of one of his libel actions. Ebert was already old beyond his years, and had never recovered from the loss of his two sons in the war. He had guided the country through a hellish six years conscientiously and well. He was bowed down with worry, work, and the weight of his responsibilities; in February 1925 he fatally deferred an operation for appendicitis.

Ebert was the first and last President of the Republic to go privately to a club – his was the non-political Deutsche Gesellschaft – for a beer and a cigar, like anyone else. He was the first and last whom anyone could telephone, informally, at his home. His wife Luise ran her own house and laid her own table. But he was spitefully pilloried: George Grosz spoke of 'Ebert, the former saddle-maker now President of the Republic [who] was occupied with having his moustache cut just so, so that he could look like the executive of a large corporation.'

National presidential elections were arranged, but as none of the candidates achieved the required majority there had to be a second round. The Right now had the idea of fielding Paul von Hindenburg as their candidate. The 'old gentleman', as he came to be known, was now 78 and living in retirement in Hanover. By training, background and even instinct he was a conservative, but he had no political experience and had shown no inclination for politics. He also considered himself completely unsuitable for the post, and only Alfred von Tirpitz's persuasiveness won his agreement to nomination. On 26 April 1925 he won the second round, by 14.6 million votes to Wilhelm Marx's 13.7 million. Stresemann, not pleased, consoled himself with the thought that the President could not determine the form or conduct of government. Although it was not widely known that Hindenburg had sought the exiled ex-Kaiser's permission to take office before doing so, it was clear that despite his links with the Weimar Republic, he had no loyalty to it. But the Germans had their father figure now. On 26 April Harry Kessler wrote in his diary: 'Voted at ten in Linkstrasse. A cold, rainy morning – a fine rain which emptied the streets. In Potsdamer Platz, just a few swastika-boys carrying heavy cudgels, blond and dumb like young bullocks. Very few flags in this district, and those few fairly evenly divided between Black-White-Red and Black-Red-Gold.' The following day he wrote: 'A new chapter in German and European history and politics begins with Hindenberg's election as *Reichspräsident* yesterday – a chapter which, without any doubt, will bring heavy blows and humiliations to the German people.'

5 Centre of the World

PEOPLE STILL TALK about the *Berliner Luft* – the light, dry, brisk air of Berlin. 'You're more efficient in Berlin; you can work harder, play harder, you need less sleep – it's like a dry white wine.' You can sense something of it even today – especially in the early spring, if you can get away from the exhaust-fume-laden boulevards and into the little streets, or to the quiet, elegant suburbs, or to the wooded parks which cover half the city's acreage and which are, with the lakes, the reason for the city's good air. The two colours of the city are green and grey. It is on a high plateau, which makes it a windy city. People always carry an umbrella, and tend also to carry a sandwich – a *Stulle* – in their briefcase (if nothing else), for Berliners live in constant fear of being separated from food.

In the Twenties there were certainly gangsters in Berlin, but even in 1900 Mark Twain was comparing the city to Chicago: 'It is a new city; the newest I have ever seen. Chicago would seem venerable beside it . . . The next feature that strikes one is the spaciousness, the roominess of the city. There is no other city, in my country, whose streets are so generally wide . . . Only parts of Chicago are stately and substantial, and [Berlin] is not merely in parts, but uniformly, beautiful.'

The city began as a fishing village, but as it was also a crossroads of trade and military routes to the north, south, east and west it quickly became strategically important. Nearby was the only fordable crossing of the river Spree for miles. The grid system of the city's streets was planned in the eighteenth century, and Friedrichstrasse was built early the same century by Friedrich-Wilhelm I, the so-called Soldier King, an otherwise resistible monarch devoted to the army, parsimony, and obsessive hand-washing. The Hohenzollerns had arrived – originally

from Nuremberg – much earlier, in 1448, when they conquered the free
city and forced it to leave the Hanseatic League. That it was once
independent still shows in Berlin's character today.

It is hard to typify the Berliner, but ideas about the *Berlinerin* are
pretty specific. 'Most of the womenfolk are blonde, with blue-grey eyes,
often with shades of yellow and green. The most usual dress size among
the girls is 14 – and they have the vital statistics of the Venus de Milo,
but later they become matronly,' says journalist and lifelong Berliner
Walter Kiaulehn. The ideal type of the *Berlinerin* was Marlene Dietrich,
the daughter of a rich watchmaker whose shop, Felsing's, was in Unter
den Linden. Long legs were then (but not, as far as I can see, now –
except for the high-quality prostitutes along the Kurfürstendamm) a
speciality of Berlin girls.

After the success of *The Blue Angel*, Dietrich left for America, Hollywood and stardom under the protection of Josef von Sternberg. Homesick, she returned in 1930, disembarking from her ship in Marseilles
where the German press was waiting to greet her. But she was wearing
trousers, and by 1930 the Nazis were gaining an ascendancy over the
liberal Weimar era. NO TRUE GERMAN WOMAN WEARS TROUSERS
blared the headlines. This cured her homesickness, and after a brief stay
in Paris she returned to the more relaxed USA.

One of Marlene's singing teachers was the cabarettist Claire Waldoff,
reputedly the first woman in Berlin to have her hair bobbed. Claire was
like a pendant to Marlene: instead of being tall, slim, leggy and blonde,
she was short, plump and redheaded – but she was just as thoroughly
Berlinisch. Berlin men were torn between the two types. The journalist
and cabarettist Kurt Tucholsky wrote:

> You get it all together in your thoughts –
> What you would really like: but do you ever get it?
> You're always after a tall, slim girl,
> And you always end up with a little fat girl –
> *Ssälawih!*

'*C'est la vie!*' Love in Berlin was a many-faceted thing, more so than in
other cities. Carl Zuckmayer remembered a party in 1924 held in rooms
with walls covered in maxims such as 'Love is the foolish overestimation
of the minimal difference between one sexual object and another'. 'The
girls hired to serve drinks went about naked except for transparent
panties embroidered with a silver fig-leaf. They were not, like the
"bunnies" in modern American night-clubs, there just for looks, but
could be freely handled. That'd been included in their pay.'[1] A popular
song of 1920, sung by Max Adalbert, Trude Hesterberg and Fritz Spira
(Steffie Spira's father), had as its refrain:

Wer wird denn weinen, wenn man ausseinander geht . . .

Who is going to cry, when we say goodbye,
When at the next street corner someone else is standing by!
You say 'So long' – but there's really no pain
When your secret thoughts are: 'Phew! there goes another spaniel-eyed
swain!'

Half a generation earlier, love had run a very different course. The best
shoemaker in Berlin was one Breitsprecher, who made shoes By Royal
Appointment and whose shop in Wilhelmstrasse was like a salon. At a
ball, his daughter fell in love with a bank executive named Jänecke. It
wasn't long before Jänecke was asking Breitsprecher for his daughter's
hand. 'On no account,' said the old man. 'She's my only daughter and
she'll marry a shoemaker like me.' Jänecke gave up his job and appren-
ticed himself in Vienna. Four years later, fully qualified, he asked for
Fraulein Breitsprecher's hand again, and this time his wish was granted.
Later, when Jänecke was measuring the Kaiser for a new pair of boots,
Wilhelm asked about his military background. 'When I was a bank
official, I belonged to the First Regiment of Foot as a reserve officer; but
as soon as they heard that I'd become a shoemaker, out I had to go!'

Berliners of Weimar days peppered their talk with '*Mensch*' and
'*notabene*' – '*Mensch*' means, roughly, 'man' (literally, 'person'); one might
easily overhear 'Notabene, Mensch, Mann . . .'. Yet while Münchners,
for example, *know* they speak a dialect and are proud of it, Berlin men,
at least, think they speak the purest form of German. (One is *born* a
Münchner, but one can *become* a Berliner.)

In Berlin today, you will notice that people move at an extraordinary
speed, even by London or New York standards; and they will walk you
down rather than walk around you. They also drive and cycle as if the
Devil were at their heels. Berliners had then, as now, a reputation for
excessive nervous activity, which they blamed on the brisk climate.
Going to work was a rush. Mostly, people used public transport. Even
by 1926 there were only 50,000 cars in Berlin, one for every hundred
people – in Paris, one in forty had a car, and in New York, one in six.
Nevertheless, there were traffic jams. To help relieve the congestion, the
world's first traffic lights were put up, in a kind of clock-tower at
Potsdamer Platz, but at first they only drew more crowds to see the
novelty. In the mid-Twenties, Opel and Hanomag produced little,
popular cars, forerunners of the 1938 *Kraft-durch-Freudewagen* – the
Strength-through-Joy Car, later renamed the Volkswagen, or People's
Car. (This was the brain-child of Hitler's friend, Dr Ferdinand Porsche,
but it never got into production during the Third Reich.) The little
Opels and Hanomags, nicknamed *Kommissbrot* (Army Bread) and

Laubfrosch (Tree Frog), were among a rash of new car designs, from the bizarre to the futuristic, which blossomed during the Weimar Republic. More expensive makes kept to traditional designs, though Mercedes would slinkily streamline custom-built orders. The 'best' cars were Mercedes or Horch, Austro-Daimler or Hansa-Lloyd. Brenabor made sports cars; Maybach, and Adler, limousines. In the south, the Bayerische Motorwerke (BMW) was in production, and by the Twenties Saurer and Deutsche Kraftwagen (DKW) were producing cars. Still the car was something for the rich, or the specialized. 'We always nicknamed any little car we saw a "doctor's car",' says the journalist Arnold Bauer. 'And that is what they generally were.'

Most people relied on the bus, tube or tram. Each had its advantages. The tramlines passed so close to the apartment houses that passengers could glimpse many aspects of their fellow Berliners' private lives:

> When on a tram you're travelling
> You see into the heart of things,

wrote Walter Mehring in one of his cabaret songs. The open-topped buses were fun in summer, especially if you took the Number 11 along Unter den Linden or the 12 along the Kurfürstendamm. And travelling by public transport greatly assisted the rise of newspapers. One of the Ullstein brothers went to Munich, thinking to start a paper there, but came back convinced that 'a city without a *U-Bahn* wouldn't support a popular paper'. So many of Berlin's hundreds of papers – the *Berliner Zeitung am Mittag* (or *BZ*), the *Achtuhrabendblatt* (Eight p.m. Paper), and the *Nachtausgabe* (Night Edition), for example – were precisely designed to be read in a hurry. If the papers weren't enough there were the *Litfasssäule* – the fat columns at street-corners, designed purely to have posters slapped on them, and invented by a nineteenth-century Berlin printer who now lies buried in a cemetery next to Bertolt Brecht's Berlin house.

Nowadays the unisex Berlin uniform, winter and summer, is a black leather blouson jacket and jeans. A man wearing a suit and tie is unusual enough to be stared at. In the Twenties Berlin men, at least, showed just as little regard for clothes – Harry Kessler was an exception – and it was only with difficulty that top tailors found a foothold. But in the Twenties Berlin did launch a new fashion for men: the *Stresemann*, consisting of a marengo cloth (pepper-and-salt) jacket with striped trousers. According to the time of day, you wore a light or a dark waistcoat with it, and it became standard Sunday wear for the more dignified male members of Berlin society, still occasionally to be seen even after 1945.

Before the First World War Berlin was not a city with any naturally developed bourgeois society. Instead of that it had a series of 'circles', from royal to criminal, all independent of one another until mixed in the melting-pot of the Weimar Republic. Apart from these more or less loosely-knit groups there were many clubs, which replaced the little parishes gradually being absorbed within the city. Berliners were fond of forming themselves into social organizations of all kinds – to go cycling, to wrestle, to play cards, to drink beer, to drink wine, to box, to do good among the poor, and so on – and wherever possible it was desirable to have a uniform, or at least a uniform hat. The exclusivity of these clubs was valued, as was the sense of belonging, in uncertain times. If Berliners were more reserved towards strangers than their fellow-Germans in the south, that may have been a legacy of the nineteenth century which, even before Bismarck, had seen a marked increase in the power of the Imperial Secret Police.

The predominant fear of the Berliner is that he may die of starvation at any moment. In the Twenties the best bulwark against this fear was the *kleine Helle*: a small glass of pale beer with an ice-cold corn-schnapps chaser, taken with a couple of *Hackepeterbrötchen* – open sandwiches or rolls spread with minced pork cut with onions and peppers, and maybe a gherkin or two on the side: this was consumed, for preference, standing in a café at one of the specially-designed limewood pillar-tables. These tables can still be seen, but today they are made of plastic and metal. Aschinger's was the first fast-food, fixed-price restaurant: pea-and-ham soup, say, a slice of *Bauernbrot* and a beer cost around 30 pfennigs before inflation. The Wurst Max Chain was also developed, to reduce the danger of Berliners falling dead on the streets, and there were several little snacks with which a Berliner could regale himself on the hoof: rollmops, meatballs, pickled eggs, and the ubiquitous gherkin. The gherkin 'godfather' was none other than Frederick the Great, who created a salt monopoly to finance his army. Every household was obliged to buy a fixed amount of salt, with the result that every household always had too much. The Spreewald was full of cucumbers, to be bought cheaply from the locals, and Berlin housewives took to salting the smaller ones. Another dish born of the salt monopoly was the *kasseler*, named after its inventor, the butcher Kassel: it is simply pork spare ribs, marinaded in salt.

Fish abounded in the Havel and Spree rivers and in the lakes, as did eel and crabs. Crabmeat was served with oysters for breakfast in the homes of the fortunate – and the oysters came from oyster farms which were another legacy of Friedrich-Wilhelm I.

If you were rich, you might eat at one of the great hotel restaurants. The Adlon was at first unpopular with Berliners because the beautiful Redern Mansion had been pulled down to make room for it. The Redern's owner had had to sell to pay off gambling debts – to King

Edward VII, among his other creditors. But the Adlon was favoured by
the Kaiser, Stresemann later took tea there, and the leading German
playwright Gerhart Hauptmann stayed whenever he was in Berlin. It was
the most expensive Berlin hotel, though the Bristol could claim to be the
most elegant and had the most titled, though not necessarily the most
interesting, guests. Top restaurants included Hiller's, where Harry
Kessler frequently ate, Borchardt's and Horcher's. A little further down
the scale was Kempinski's; the Kempinski family still has a hotel on the
Kurfürstendamm, though the original restaurant was in Leipziger
Strasse, and had a beautiful art nouveau façade. The Haus Vaterland contained a number of cafés, the decor of each determined by a different
region of Germany.

To the west of the city lies the Grunewald or Greenwood, with the
elegant suburbs of Dahlem and Zehlendorf on its eastern fringes,
together with the pretty little lakes, Schlachtensee and Krumme Lanke.
To the south are Nikolassee, and also Wannsee, where the policy of the
Final Solution was determined in 1942. To the north, beyond Charlottenburg, is the Berliner Forst or forest of Spandau, which spreads north-
east across Reinickendorf over the Havel and the Tegeler See. Across
town, to the south-east, following the Spree, are Köpenick, and Grosse
Muggelsee, and Treptower Park. The grey city alone on its plain has a
necklace of countryside and parkland. Even in the centre of town, the
Tiergarten and the Charlottenburg Palace park provide lungs for the
city.

'What I loved most as a girl was days out in the Tiergarten – the
playgrounds, the picnics, and visiting the Zoo, which used to be wonderful.' 'A friend of mine and I bought a canoe and went canoeing on the
Spree, down to the Muggelsee, and that's the best memory I have – along
with the firework displays . . .' 'Winters were colder and longer
then – there were three months when you could skate on all the Berlin
lakes. They would flood tennis courts and let them freeze as winter
rinks . . .' 'I loved cycling as an adolescent – school finished at 1 p.m.
daily and you went home for lunch. I skipped games, because gymnastics
were organized by the leading right-wingers in the school. A bunch of
us rode all over the Grunewald . . . And we used to make our own
fireworks on the quiet in chemistry lessons. I even made a little rocket
and compounded some nitro-cellulose to power it!'[2]

Seventy-five per cent of Berliners were Protestants, mainly Lutheran;
10 per cent were Catholic; 4.3 per cent, Jewish; 1.3 per cent, Eastern
Orthodox and Muslims – and there were also 310,000 atheists. Among
the foreigners who came to enrich this mixture during the Twenties – and among the half-million Christian and Jewish exiles from

Russia and Armenia who passed through on their way to France and the United States (though some never got further than this staging-post) – were the novelist Boris Pasternak, the journalist Ilya Ehrenburg, both from Russia; the writer Thomas Wolfe from the USA; the mathematician Hans von Neumann from Budapest, who went on to Los Alamos and pioneered computer construction during the Second World War; and the Dutch chemist Peter Deybe, who became director of the Kaiser-Wilhelm-Institut for Physics, and later received the Nobel Prize for chemistry. This is a mere handful. Berlin was known for its liberal views and left-wing sympathies; and for a decade became an artistic centre of such concentration that London and Paris paled beside it. And a high percentage of its leading lights were Jews.

In the theatre the king, Max Reinhardt, had his throne challenged after the war by Leopold Jessner; Victor Barnowsky ran two popular theatres. Actors of this time included the great Fritz Kortner, Elisabeth Bergner, Fritzi Massary, the princess of light opera, Max Pallenberg, Conrad Veidt (who played Cesare in *Caligari*, and later Major Strasser in *Casablanca*), Tilla Durieux, Rosa Valetti (who ran the Megalomania Cabaret and starred with Dietrich in *The Blue Angel*), Curt Bois (who celebrated his ninetieth birthday in Berlin in 1991), Lilli Palmer, Adolf Wohlbrück (who became a star in the USA as Anton Walbrook), and Peter Lorre. Richard Tauber was making his name. Rudolf Nelson, Friedrich Holländer and Mischa Spoliansky were the doyens of light music: the conductor Bruno Walter was a Berliner by birth, and directed the Charlottenburg Opera. Otto Klemperer was at the Staatsoper Unter den Linden; Hermann Göring wanted Leo Blech to stay as an 'honorary Aryan', but Blech preferred exile in Stockholm. The list goes on – Arnold Schönberg, Kurt Weill, Alban Berg, Hanns Eisler . . . In the world of film, as well as Fritz Lang, G. W. Pabst, Joe May and Ernst Lubitsch, there were directors in Berlin who went on to make their real reputations elsewhere: Billy Wilder, Max Ophüls, Alexander Korda, Paul Czinner, and Josef von Sternberg.

The mixture was very rich.

On 29 October 1923 Germany's first radio station opened in Berlin. In the same year,[3] Templehof was officially opened for civilian traffic, and for a long time it was the most advanced airport in the world. In 1926 Junkers Luftverkehr AG and Aero-Lloyd merged to form Deutsche Luft-Hansa; a year later, travellers could pick up a car from the airline's offices in Mauerstrasse half an hour before flights to fifteen European destinations.

Visitors came to Berlin for the night-life, the artistic life, the cheap goods, the sex, the pornography, the films, theatres, operas, concerts.

Some came for the museums. At the eastern end of Unter den Linden is the Museum Island, where some greyish-red, vaguely Palladian buildings house some of the world's great art treasures. The Hohenzollerns were not informed collectors – unlike the Electors of Saxony, whose acquisitions formed the basis for the Zwinger Gallery in Dresden. In the Napoleonic era, Friedrich-Wilhelm III had built museums and bought up existing collections to fill them 'instantly', but the results were unimpressive. In 1873 Wilhelm von Bode became the new assistant director of Berlin's National Gallery; when he died in 1929, aged 84, and was entombed in the basilica of an early sixteenth-century Florentine church which he had rescued and brought to Berlin, he was formally mourned by all the leaders of the Weimar Republic. Through the turmoil of the intervening years, he had quietly built Berlin's collections into some of the greatest in the world. Until 1990 his museums lay in what was for 45 years the Communist state of the German Democratic Republic; since then, they have once more become accessible to the rest of the world.

Bode's main inspiration was the Musée de Cluny in Paris, where objects are displayed in surroundings of their period (as they are also at the Cloisters Museum in Manhattan). Bode inspired fifty private collectors to help him, and he struck gold in his choice of an aide – the young banker and fledgling collector, Oscar Hainauer. Bode's plan was two-pronged: he would collect on behalf of the group he had gathered together, but they themselves would also lend, or contribute to, Bode's planned national collection from their private ones. In parallel, money generated from sales of works of art dealt in but not earmarked for the collections would provide capital from which to make further purchases. Hainauer's frequent business trips to Paris were especially useful, and Bode carefully trained his protégé's eye.

His other aides were the businessman Oscar Huldschinsky, and Eduard Simon, who realized for Bode the display of objects in their correct period settings. Paintings by the masters of the Italian Renaissance and of the Dutch seventeenth century were acquired, as well as artefacts from all ages – Ancient Egyptian, Greek, Roman, the Middle Ages – and from all the countries of Europe and Asia.

Inevitably there were black sheep in Bode's network – a certain Herr Gumprecht, for example. Bode offered Gumprecht a Frans Hals he had seen in London for £130, but Gumprecht was suspicious and wanted to see the picture before committing his money. The seller was not prepared to wait, so Bode bought it on the credit of the Berlin National Gallery. When he returned to Berlin with the picture, Gumprecht begged for it. Since Bode had bought it for the nation, Gumprecht offered to pay immediately, if Bode would let him have it for the original price, and undertook to leave the painting to the nation in his will. Bode agreed, then had the galling experience of seeing the Hals sold to Denmark for 270,000 gold marks in 1918.

Bode had cultivated a good relationship with the Kaiser, spiced with the Berlin humour which Wilhelm enjoyed so long as he wasn't its butt. With Royal approval, a museum to house the collection was built in the Kaiser's favourite neo-Baroque style. Remarkably, it took only six years, although Bode had very precise ideas about its form, and into it had to be built Dutch and Italian antique chimney-pieces, as well as sections of medieval cloisters and the great Florentine basilica where Bode now lies. Today, the museum is named after the man who created it.

Contemporary artists were not without their supporters. Herwarth Walden, the founder and editor of the magazine *Der Sturm* and at one time the husband of the playwright and symbolist poetess Else Lasker-Schüler, supported the work of the Expressionists, and also of Marc Chagall, who was in Berlin between 1914 and 1923. Walden was a creative artist himself, publishing three novels and ten plays. He had a habit of smoking his cigarettes in a little silver ring attached to his index finger.

The Düsseldorf art dealer Alfred Flechtheim also came to Berlin.

I knew my uncle Alfred quite well, although we didn't get on. He was a conservative and I a Communist, though earlier he had been in favour of the revolution, and in 1919 was a member of the Independent Socialist Party. He founded the *Querschnitt* [a liberal and very highbrow magazine]. As a person he was a madman – a funny type. He had a big imagination; he was volatile, like an artist himself. And he was interested in people – but to me he was never a sympathetic person. Later, when I met him in 1933, he told me he could get me out, to Italy, but the condition was that I should join the Italian Fascist Party! He went to London himself . . . a clairvoyant . . . foretold that he'd get an ulcer on his leg; that he'd neglect it, and die of it – and so it turned out. He was a stubborn man – though gifted in his way, and possibly even a genius. I also believe he was homosexual – he went for boxers especially . . . His great achievement was to introduce the Impressionists to Berlin, and he also had a very large private collection of Picassos, part of which was later taken over by his wife's children, though many fell into the hands of the Nazis and were lost. He started his gallery in Düsseldorf before the First World War and did business with new art among the locals, persuading them to buy paintings by the new groups for a couple of thousand marks with the promise that they'd soon be worth five. Now, of course, a Franz Marc is worth millions.

On his honeymoon, he spent much of his wife's dowry on pictures – which horrified the family, but he told them he'd made a good investment, and he had. He was alive at the right time – when a really new and important artistic renaissance was under way – and he had a brilliant eye.[4]

Flechtheim was known for the superb parties he gave in his luxurious apartment, generally beginning after midnight, when people had had time to go to the theatre and dine. The collector and publisher Paul Cassirer also gave lavish parties with his wife, Tilla Durieux: 'We arranged the buffet in the ground-floor rooms of our house in Grunewald, and on the first floor there was dancing. We made sure there were plenty of young people and pretty girls, and if a young artist didn't have a dinner-jacket, we insisted that he come along anyway . . .'

The marriage of Cassirer and Durieux ended tragically. 'He became impossible,' says Durieux in her memoirs.[5] 'My very presence became intolerable to him. Later, doctors explained to me that this form of illness would often direct itself in hatred against those nearest to the sufferer, but I did not know it then . . . I was overtired and longed to rest. No one helped me . . . So I decided to leave. But a life without him was unimaginable, so I decided to kill myself . . .' She moved out, shaking off the idea of suicide but determined on divorce. 'Unfortunately, Paul did the worst thing he could possibly have done. He started to send me things from home of which he knew I was fond. He had broken them. He also spread the most vile rumours about me . . . He asked for all the paintings back which he had given me instead of jewellery, and I returned them. He asked me for everything that had become dear to me in our long life together, and I gave them to him . . . Finally the day came when we had to go to the lawyer's office to sign the [divorce] papers. We all sat around a table. Suddenly, before we had signed, Paul murmured some excuse or other and left the room. Almost immediately we heard a shot next door . . .'

Harry Kessler reports the end of the affair:

Sunday 10 January 1926 Paul Cassirer's funeral. All of artistic Berlin present. The coffin on its bier in the middle of the great exhibition hall; beneath it a carpet of red roses. Max Liebermann [the artist] spoke first, I next. Although Ernst Cassirer [Paul's cousin, the philosopher] rang me last night at half-past eleven and tried to impress upon me *not* to mention Tilla Durieux (because there is such great animosity against her among Cassirer's friends and family), I naturally did mention her. She was there, heavily veiled (this, too, Ernst Cassirer . . . had tried to prevent). Afterwards I pressed her hand, and she thanked me . . .

Wednesday 13 January 1926 In the afternoon to visit Tilla Durieux at the Bristol. She was cold and bitter. None of [Paul's] relations took her hand at the funeral. She'd finished with Cassirer over some quite trivial incident. After twenty years she finally wanted to feel free for once. Perhaps after a time . . . she'd have gone back to him, but first she had to feel free, to breathe . . . Her sense of outrage is clearly suppressing a deep feeling of shock. But she is a cold, hard woman.[6]

In 1930 Tilla Durieux married her long-standing admirer, the brewer Ludwig Katzenellenbogen, who had been so much in love that he divorced his wife even before he knew Tilla Durieux would accept him.

It is curious that Kessler never mentions the cinema, so great was his interest in the arts, so wide his circle of artistic friends. The first cinema in Berlin had opened in 1910; between 1919 and 1925 the film industry enjoyed a golden age, which revived briefly at the end of the Twenties and the beginning of the Thirties. In the mid-Twenties, UFA – the film consortium assembled by Ludendorff for propaganda purposes – failed to take up a new invention offered to it: the sound film. This was the invention of three men, a physicist called Engel and two machine-builders, Massolle and Vogt, who set up a works not far from UFA's base at Tempelhof. They called their venture Tri-ergon, 'the work of three', and Stresemann had them use their new technique to film him as Chancellor in 1923. But, rejected by UFA, Tri-ergon turned instead to gramophone record production. Germany thus lost the chance to lead the world in sound film technology, and when in 1929 the matinée idol Hans Albers spoke the first words in a German sound film, *The Night Belongs to Us*, he was two years behind Al Jolson's *Jazz Singer*.

The little film companies had their offices crowded in Friedrichstrasse, Berlin's Wardour Street; there were film studios in Weissensee and Johannisthal and, after the First World War, in the old Zeppelin hangars in Staaken near Spandau. Only UFA had more glamorous offices, in Potsdamer Platz, and later in Kochstrasse and Dönhoffplatz, and separate studios in Babelsberg and Tempelhof.

In its beginnings after the First World War the film industry, *Caligari* and the historical epics of Lubitsch apart, took advantage of the new per-missiveness consciously promoted by the new democratic regime. A number of obliquely pornographic films emerged, more or less mas-querading as health-and-fitness documentaries; the master of the genre was the director Richard Oswald, who in 1917 had made a film called *Let there be Light*, warning of the perils of syphilis. Oswald could make a film in a few days, and engaged all sorts of talents, from serious actors like Conrad Veidt and Gussy Holl to the drug-addict sex-dancer Anita Berber. Some films had luridly suggestive titles – *Prostitution; Women Swallowed by the Abyss*; or *Lost Daughters*. There was a handful of films on homosexual themes, too, like *Scenes from a Man's Girlhood*, and *Dif-ferent from the Others*, starring Conrad Veidt. The journalist Alfred Fischer remembers:[7]

> Conrad was a charming and helpful man; but he was also mean – not that you could blame him for that: he had to pay alimony on so many broken mar-riages. He seemed to be addicted to marriage, despite the fact that he knew

it would lead to so much expense. He was also a very fine actor, and he was utterly convincing in everything he did. After he'd been in *Der ewige Jude* everyone thought he was a Jew; after *Different from the Others* they thought he was gay. How wrong they were!

Veidt's talent may explain Anita Loos' otherwise impenetrable statement that 'any Berlin lady of the evening might turn out to be a man [true enough]; the prettiest girl on the street was Conrad Veidt, who later became an international film star.'[8] Some of these films were of undeniable quality; some were genuinely informative and made with the best of intentions: the 'homosexual' films, in particular, were directed against the severe homosexuality laws in force at the time. The pioneer sex-therapist Magnus Hirschfeld collaborated on three of them.

Other films were outright sex-and-violence vehicles: 'I observed more than once,' wrote Ilya Ehrenburg, 'with what rapture pale, skinny adolescents watched the screen when rats gnawed a man to death, or a venomous snake bit a lovely girl.' Hard-core pornography was shown in private clubs or little cinemas at midnight. There was an attempt to protect minors: from 1925 no one under 12 could go to the cinema at all, and some films were forbidden to those under 18. Conservative reaction to sex films was strong; but like so much of Berlin's night-life they were a reflection of a new liberty, of release from the grey horror of unremitting war, and of social uncertainty. Sexual and moral barriers were cleared away, but so swiftly that there was no opportunity for people to adjust.

The technology of cinema developed so fast after 1920 that even as early as 1928 the programme note to the London Film Society's revival of Fritz Murnau's *Nosferatu* (made in 1921)[9] could refer to its special effects as so outmoded as to appear funny. The speeding stagecoach must have been one of them, and perhaps the vampire rising from his coffin. The films of the early Twenties preferred to keep to interiors, even shooting exterior scenes inside a studio, but *Nosferatu* featured genuine exteriors and, more importantly, also introduced a new, more optimistic element – the ultimate triumph of good: Nina destroys Nosferatu despite his apparent invincibility.[10] The film is based on, but developed beyond, Bram Stoker's original *Dracula*. Its primal plot has never been better handled – no improvement in special effects can compensate for dull artistic vision – and no remake has matched it.

The best-known film director of this period, Fritz Lang, was a monocled fanatic, remembers Alfred Fisher, who worked his actors and actresses so hard that actresses literally fainted on the set. He made his first mark with *Dr Mabuse, the Gambler* in 1922, which portrays a ruthless master criminal who ends insane. In the context of Berlin, its interest lies in 'the world it pictures [which] has fallen prey to lawlessness and depravity. A night-club dancer performs in a décor composed of outright sex-symbols. Orgies are an institution, homosexuals and prostitute children are everyday characters.'[11] A contemporary publicity brochure for the film reads: 'Mankind, swept about and trampled down in the wake of war and revolution, takes revenge for years of anguish by indulging in lusts . . .' *The Testament of Dr Mabuse*, the sequel made ten years later, is said to have been intended as a warning against Hitler – another mad criminal in pursuit of absolute power. But since Lang's collaborator was his wife, Thea von Harbou, a Nazi supporter, the Mabuse/Hitler parallels may have been merely coincidental.

Lang's two-part *Nibelungen* of 1922 and 1924 contains extraordinary special effects for its time – Siegfried's killing of the dragon Fafnir is particularly graphic. In terms of scene composition, cross-cutting, camera angles, and editing, film comes of age as an artistic form with this work.[12] Lang was another Jew offered 'honorary Aryan' status, by Goebbels – and indeed, *Nibelungen* contains many of the Germanic images and heroic set-pieces dear to the Nazi aesthetic. Lang turned down the dubious honour, but Leni Riefenstahl, the model-turned-actress-turned-director who was to be Hitler's most accomplished propaganda film-maker, later borrowed images from *Nibelungen* for her *Triumph of the Will* of 1934.

Lang's *Metropolis* is the subject of some interesting statistics. It was the first film to use extras in vast numbers – 35,000 of them – and it took 17 months to finish, costing two million marks, a vast sum for the time. For the Tower of Babel sequence a thousand people had their heads shaved. Lang used unemployed workers; crowd artists refused to have their heads shaved, as it would hamper their chances of further employment for weeks. The film has come in for some sharp criticism recently, being derided as sentimental and even vulgar. To some extent it is both, but it is also a triumph of art deco design (the robot especially); and if its criticism of man's tendency to enslave himself to machines is obvious, it is so in the tradition of Huxley, Orwell and Wells.

Hitler thought *Metropolis* an exemplary picture. Perhaps he identified with Young Fredersen, the hero, and saw himself as a liberator; perhaps he wholly missed the point of the film and thought it a *celebration* of man's enslavement to the machine; perhaps he approved of the ending, in which the tyrannical industrialist Fredersen scores a diplomatic triumph over the workers in the guise of a reconciliation. But in any case, Lang found Nazi approval oppressive. On the day that Goebbels asked him to stay in Germany and make films for the National Socialists, Lang packed his bags and left.

Running parallel with the films in the *Caligari* tradition were others dealing with the fates of ordinary people – more or less realistic, if tending to gloom. An exception was *The Last Laugh* (1925), written by Carl Mayer. Emil Jannings plays a hotel doorkeeper who, too old to continue in the post, is stripped of his resplendent uniform and downgraded to lavatory attendant. But an eccentric millionaire dies in his arms and, by the terms of his will, our hero inherits everything. At the time of its first appearance, critics rapturously compared this film to the Book of Job and Beethoven's Ninth.[13] In the same year, the Austrian Georg Pabst directed *The Joyless Street*. It was a story all too familiar to Berliners, of decline into poverty through inflation. Pabst's remorseless realism was so shocking that the film was actually banned in Britain; but it did provide Greta Garbo with her first major role.

Popular cinema specialized in costume-drama lightweights, and the more famous series of 'mountain' films, the brainchild of Arnold Fanck. Fanck relied on actors who were, or became, outstanding alpinists and skiers, including Leni Riefenstahl and Luis Trenker (my own father's old white corduroy mountaineering jacket is called a 'Trenker'). These films concentrated on taking the camera to real locations, and their plots were really just an excuse for natural history documentary footage.

A third popular genre was a series by itself – fictionalized biopics of the life of Frederick the Great, which people loved despite round condemnation by both the SPD and the Communists. 'Friedrich' films continued under the Third Reich, which used 'der alte Fritz', played, as in the Twenties, by Otto Gebühr, as an icon to legitimize itself. 'I went to the pictures a lot', remembers Illa Walter. 'And I saw all those Frederick the Great films, full of bombast about Germany's great past. The cinema was better than the theatre – especially after the Nazis came to power – if you were a Jew. It was dark, and nobody saw you.'

During the bad days of inflation, a film sold abroad could earn hard currency and repay its production costs many times over. And if a film were half-way decent, it stood a good chance of making money at home as well. Because there was no point in saving, everyone spent money on whatever pleasures they could find. Even after the mark had stabilized, people still turned to the cinema as an escape from their increasingly humdrum lives. But the German industry, despite its quality, now found it could not compete in quantity or allure with the foreign films flooding into the country, especially from the United States. UFA ran into deep financial difficulties, and the reactionary newspaper magnate Alfred Hugenberg was able to buy a majority shareholding in 1927. In the same year, a government skeleton fell out of the cupboard when the bankrupt Phoebus Film was revealed to have been funded by army money – invested in an unsuccessful attempt to help finance rearmament.

Between them, the lure of the dollar and the rise of the Nazi party emptied Berlin of its best artists, technicians and producers – to the benefit of Hollywood. Wilhelm Dieterle and F. W. Murnau went, and Conrad Veidt. So did Emil Jannings, Billy Wilder, and Erich Pommer, who had produced practically every famous film of the period: *Caligari; Dr Mabuse, the Gambler; Nibelungen; The Last Laugh; The Blue Angel*; and *The Congress Dances*. In leaving behind the unique stimulus of Berlin, though, many also left behind their best work.

The exodus did not, however, prevent a fresh spate of films from emerging. After 1924 there was a new run of sex films, again responding to public relief, this time from the stress of inflation. These were joined by a number of popular military films depicting jolly, rough-and-ready, honest-as-the-day-is-long soldiers. Sugary costume-dramas and operettas were still made as well.

In artistic film-making there was a new development. Partly for reasons of economy, UFA encouraged and produced a series of *Kulturfilme* – documentaries: the first of any significance appeared in 1925. *Ways to Strength and Beauty* was a largely nude celebration of healthy sporting and athletic activities, with reconstructions of the Periclean Games at Athens. Large numbers of very beautiful young people struck poses or paraded in front of the camera, or danced or performed callisthenics beside elegant pools or in lush meadows. The whole was very tastefully photographed, and only a few voices were raised in protest; a sex film it manifestly was not.

More substantial was *Berlin, Symphony of a Big City*. The idea was devised by Carl Mayer for Fox Europe. Mayer wanted to free himself from the studio *and* the storyline; his cameraman Karl Freund was equally on the lookout for fresh challenges, and inventive enough to sensitize stock film so he could shoot with it in poor light. The Germans had always admired Russian films, and *Symphony* was to have a score by Edmund Meisel, who had written the music for *Battleship Potemkin*. Unfortunately, Mayer had a disagreement about the concept with the film's editor, the abstract film-maker Walter Ruttmann, and withdrew from the project early. The film succeeds in its aim of presenting a panoramic vision of the life of a metropolis, though it lacks depth and focus. The location-shooting, documentary style was taken a stage further in *People on Sunday*, a 1929 collaboration as interesting for its collaborators as for its content: Eugen Shuftan, Robert Siodmak, Edgar Ullmer, Billy Wilder, Fred Zinnemann and the great encourager of young talent, Moritz Seeler, who had helped Brecht and Zuckmayer in their careers. Wilder went on to write the screenplay for *Emil and the Detectives* before the USA beckoned.

Some of the more grimly realistic films of the horrors of life among the poor and the working classes had been influenced by the Russian cinema, but a consciously left-wing film movement was slow to develop. The

most important left-wing theatre director, Erwin Piscator, had used film
by Walter Ruttmann as part of his stage productions – for example, in
Hurrah! We're Alive in 1927; and in 1928 the left-wing People's Union
for Cinematic Art was founded by Piscator, together with G. W. Pabst,
Karl Freund, Heinrich Mann, and others. Mainstream film directors
were not strongly political in their themes, nor indeed did they concen-
trate on any particular genre of film. 'We didn't go to the theatre or the
cinema much,' two old Communist Berliners told me. 'We might have
gone to the People's Theatre now and then, but we were students – the
mainstream places and the big cinemas like the Marmorhaus were just
too expensive. There was a little cinema in Unter den Linden called the
Kamera which showed Russian films, and you could get in for 50 pfennigs . . . But we lived in Neukölln. The Westend was another world for
us.'[14]

Cabaret, perhaps because it travels less easily, continued to flourish in
Berlin. The weakness of the government and the twin threats of
militarism and nationalism were favourite targets for satirical attack.
Erich Kästner, Walter Mehring, the poet Alfred Henschke (who wrote
under the name of 'Klabund'), Kurt Tucholsky – all wrote songs and
sketches for the cabaret, as did many others, including Brecht. Social
injustice, profiteering, the naked right-wing sympathies of the
judiciary – all were pilloried in the little clubs for people fed up with the
mess their country was in. The many-faceted Max Reinhardt had opened
the first Schall und Rauch ('Sound and Smoke' – the phrase is drawn
from Goethe) cabaret in 1901; his new cabaret opened in 1919 in the
cellar of the Zirkus Schumann, with a send-up of his own current production of the *Oresteia*. Agamemnon appeared as 'a general in his best years';
Aegisthus (his murderer) as 'a literary man and a professional moralist'.
This was a portrait of Ebert:

> Ladies and gentlemen, it's easy to sneer,
> But try to do better than I do here . . .
> In any case, have any of you governed before?
> Immediately, right and left try to settle their score.
>
> The morning papers' attacks draw blood,
> Caricaturists fling mud,
> One is shadowed, spied upon, mocked!
> The whole thing's lost its romance,
> The hero's pose, the grand gestures and stance.

Satire was good-natured, but at its best it was also sharp. It was so
uniquely successful in Berlin after the First World War because of the
capital's delight in its new freedom from censorship. Admittedly, this

had not been especially harsh before the war, but Wilhelm had been sensitive enough to Berliner *Schnauze* (an almost untranslatable word indicating a natural propensity for the ironic put-down or send-up) for the original Schall und Rauch to get into trouble with the police for mocking the Kaiser's favourite poets. Berliners are not natural respecters of authority.

Among the performers at the new Schall und Rauch was Paul Graetz, a native Berliner whose dialect songs and monologues had made him a local hero. He also appeared in a handful of films, including a 1929 short with Steffie Spira called *All About Making Waves in Hair and in Love*, which was one of the first sound films. After Schall und Rauch, Graetz went on to the KaDeKo – the Kabarett der Komiker. Later he was driven out by the Nazis, and died in exile in the USA in 1937 of a broken heart.

Gussy Holl, married first to Conrad Veidt and then to Emil Jannings, was a singer, *diseuse* and parodist of such talent that Kurt Tucholsky wrote, rather backhandedly, 'Frankfurt has produced two great men, Goethe and Gussy Holl'. One of her songs, by Tucholsky, mocks the trend for nudity on stage at all costs.

> Get 'em off, Petronella, get 'em off!
> For heaven's sake don't be a bore.
> If it's fame that you're after, and more,
> Lend an ear to the audience's roar
> And let your clothes slide to the floor.
> Get 'em off, Petronella, get 'em off![15]

From Munich, after a wartime spent travelling, the sailor cabarettist Joachim Ringelnatz came to the Schall und Rauch in the guise of the tough, boozy, nihilistic adventurer Kuttel-Daddeldu. The whole Establishment was mocked – and it enraged them – but the audience loved him.

The singer and actress Rosa Valetti, who appeared in a supporting role in *The Blue Angel*, was also a powerful political satirist. Her club, the Grössenwahn (Megalomania), in turn launched the career of Kate Kühl, whose gravelly voice was perfect for Brecht's songs. Valetti ran two other clubs, as inflation caught up with her and closed down the earlier ones; and she pioneered a peripatetic cabaret called the Larifari in the late Twenties, before being driven out of Germany by the Nazis. The beautiful Trude Hesterberg, daughter of a pharmacist and at one time Heinrich Mann's mistress, attracted Mehring, Tucholsky and Klabund to write sketches and songs for her Wild Stage club in the cellar of the Theater des Westens, and Valetti, Holl, Kühl and Graetz all performed there, as did the lathe-thin Margo Lion, art deco in human form, whose costumes accentuated her astonishing body. Her hoarse, mock-tragic voice gave extra edge to the songs she sang, sometimes in duets with Marlene Dietrich. Hesterberg also gave Brecht his first chance in Berlin:

> On the evening of the very day he had come to audition before her, Hesterberg had Brecht perform on the Wild Stage. That night it lived up to its name. Brecht appeared before the audience in an ill-fitting suit and carrying a banjo. He sang his *Legend of the Dead Soldier* in a shrill, aggressive monotone and by the end of the third stanza the audience, several [red-necked] *Junkers* among them, was in an uproar. *Sekt*-glasses were hurled on stage along with insults, and Hesterberg was forced to let the curtain fall. The *conférencier*,[16] Mehring ... took the stage and told the public a discreditable event had taken place that evening, not for the performer Brecht, but for them, the public. They would one day remember that they had been present on this occasion.[17]

Here are the first few stanzas of Brecht's song:[18]

> And when the war reached its fifth Spring
> with no hint of a pause for breath
> the soldier did the obvious thing
> and died a hero's death.
>
> The summer spread over the makeshift graves.
> The soldier lay ignored
> until one night there came an offi-
> cial army medical board.
>
> The board went out to the cemetery
> with consecrated spade
> and dug up what was left of him
> and put him on parade.
>
> The doctors sorted out what they'd found
> and kept what they thought would serve
> and made their report: 'He's physically sound.
> He's simply lost his nerve.'

This song so strongly recalls George Grosz's painting *The Faith Healers*, of 1916/17, in which an army medical board inspect a rotted corpse and pronounce it fit for duty, that one wonders if the picture might have been Brecht's inspiration. Certainly songs of this kind are a long way from *Tingeltangel* – the kind of nineteenth-century music-hall named after the comic Tange, whose gimmick was the triangle he played.

Künstlercafe (Artists' café) soirées were performed for left-wing intellectuals, and were often not so much acts in themselves as try-outs for ideas that might be developed later. The chief *conférencier* was Karl

Schnog, also an actor and radio broadcaster. Schnog managed to organize cabaret evenings of a sort even in the concentration camps to which he was later sent – Sachsenhausen, Dachau and Buchenwald. His *conférencier*'s patter was anything but light, though not without humour; he analysed what was going on in German society and politics, keeping his sharpest attacks for the gathering forces of the Right.

Ernst Busch appeared at the Küka and the KaDeKo. The songs he sang compromised no more than Brecht's. Robert Gilbert's *Stempellied*, or Rubber-Stamp Song, refers to the signing-on dole queues that shortened slightly in the late Twenties, when foreign investment created work, but then lengthened again with a vengeance after the Wall Street Crash of 1929. The song is reminiscent of 'Brother, Can You Spare a Dime?':

> Without a job, without a roof
> you're not worth a bean.
> You'll be flattened
> like a fly on a windowpane.
> Without work, without a penny
> you're not worth a damn;
> and the fat guy says 'By God,
> you keep your distance!'
> And society will chuck you
> out before you can say 'knife'.
> If you're hungry, if you're sick –
> Just keep your trap shut.

But the KaDeKo had a cabaret more broadly-based than left-wing agit-prop. The *parisienne* Yvette Guilbert, familiar from Lautrec's paintings and posters, sang here in the early days, and King Vidor's American wife Nina Mae McKinney performed here later. But the real strength of the KaDeKo was nonetheless its *conférenciers*. Among the best was Paul Nikolaus, whose scathing satirical monologues were extemporized from the day's papers, which he had delivered to him straight from the presses. The KaDeKo's revues were always highly topical – *Quo Vadis*, for example, was the first and only effort to satirize Fascism, when the movement was in its insignificant infancy. Nikolaus killed himself in Switzerland soon after the Nazis came to power. He left this letter:

For once there are no jokes. I am taking my life.

Farewell . . . Greet all those who liked me. Do not grieve. Laugh when you think of me: that is the greatest piety. I leave my comical body to Anatomy: I hope they'll accept it, even though the appendix is missing.

When I am on the other side I will not say hello to the Storm-trooper Horst Wessel . . .

The KaDeKo had been founded by the two *conférenciers* Kurt Robitschek and Paul Morgan, both from Vienna, and the popular *buffo*, Max Hansen. Robitschek ran the box-office personally, and not even film stars got in free. Steffie Spira remembers working at the KaDeKo.

> We did our cabaret acts late – after the theatre performances. We would leave the theatre and take a prearranged taxi to our cabaret date. Once . . . the cab broke down – or wouldn't start. I was on a tight schedule, and . . . there weren't any other taxis around. Of course I had my cabaret costume and make-up to put on . . . Finally I got a taxi – they were high cars, quite box-like. I said to the driver, 'Don't turn round and don't look in the mirror.' And I changed as he drove me along. People on the pavement gave us some funny looks but the cabbie was fine.

The last important cabaret to open in Berlin was the Katakombe, founded by the *conférencier* Werner Finck around 1929. 'Two thousand years ago, the catacombs provided a place of refuge for the first Christians; today, this is a place of refuge for the last!' A rash of small clubs opened during the closing years of the Weimar Republic, as satire was stimulated by the worsening political situation. The Katakombe concentrated on the horrors planned by the Nazis for their New Germany. As their power increased, so Finck kept up his attacks. Once, when a Nazi in the audience bellowed 'You dirty Jew!' he replied: 'You're mistaken, I'm afraid. I only look this intelligent.' Finck realized that informers were planted in the audience: he would single them out and say, 'Am I speaking too fast for you gentlemen? Are you following me? Or shall I follow you?' Goebbels permitted the little cellar club to continue for some time, but it was closed down in 1935 and many of those involved were sent to the concentration camps. Finck survived the war, and returned to cabaret in Hamburg after 1945. 'He always spoke softly,' Alfred Fischer remembers, 'he never declaimed. It gave everything much more force.'

The great period of German popular music began in the 1890s with Walter Kollo, Jean Gilbert, and Paul Lincke, who was so successful that he became known as the Johann Strauss of Berlin. After the war came competition from the United States. One of the songwriters of the time, Hermann Frey, found the song *Yes, We Have No Bananas* so annoying that he wrote a spoof with even more ludicrous lyrics: *Mein Papagei frisst keine harten Eier* – My Parrot Doesn't Eat Hard-boiled Eggs. Paul Lincke wrote the music. Walter Kiaulehn recalls: 'To his great chagrin, the song was an international hit. There was even a Berlin lady who took her chambermaid to court, because the girl had given the woman's ancient pet parrot hard-boiled eggs to eat, even though the song plainly

stated that parrots didn't eat them. The bird had died, and the lady was
incensed when the judge dismissed the case out of hand.'[19]

In 1927 there were over 900 dance bands in Berlin. Among the best
were those of Oscar Joost, Teddy Stauffer, and Bernhard Etté – who is
the violinist caricatured on the extreme left in the band in Otto Dix's
painting *Grossstadt*. Henry Hall was among the foreign band-leaders who
came over as guest performers, and hotter music was provided by Sam
Wooding, Lud Gluskin, Paul Whiteman and Sidney Bechet. Ninety per
cent of all the popular music composed in Germany between 1919 and
1929 was written in Berlin, about 2,600 tunes, of which a good hundred
became hits, even standards. There were songs about the Black Market,
about the revolution on the streets, about the increasing traffic, about the
telephone – now, in the early Twenties, being installed in every
household that could afford one. The new Voxhaus radio station spread
the music, and the Shimmy was followed by the Black Bottom, the
Tango and the Charleston.

Erik Charell turned revue theatre into big, spectacular shows, and his
production of the operetta *White Horse Inn* was a huge hit: people still
remember it. The queen of operetta was Fritzi Massary, whose husband
Max Pallenberg was the leading comic actor of his time. Following the
war there was a renaissance of popular music, musical revue, and popular
dance. Revue in particular, profiting from the absence of censorship, was
strongly satirical, and Erwin Piscator used the form for his epic 'Red'
revues of the mid-Twenties. His *Despite It All* was (amazing as it sounds)
a dramatic propaganda documentary tracing the history of the socialist
movement from 1914 to 1919. Revue producers drew on the same pool
of talent as the smaller, less escapist cabarets, but the genre also threw
up its own stars. Claire Waldoff was one. Joseph Roth described her as
'a flower from the asphalt'. For her act she wore an Eton collar and
tie – all that remained (together with a tartan scarf) of a full Eton suit
which the police had refused her permission to wear: at the time, it was
forbidden in Berlin for a woman to appear in public dressed as a man
after 11 p.m.[20] She became one of the most popular entertainers in the
city, but she is remembered now for a song which, as it unofficially reappeared on the streets, pilloried Hermann Göring.

> *Rechts Lametta, links Lametta,*
> *und der Bauch wird imma fetta.*
> *Un' in Preussen is er Meester.*
> *Hermann heesst er! Hermann heesst er!*
>
> (Tinsel right an' tinsel left
> An' his gut gets ever bigger.
> An' in Prussia 'e's the boss
> They call 'im 'Erman! German 'Erman!)

The unauthorized version became so popular that the Nazis tried to stop Waldoff from singing the original, but she refused.

Rudolf Nelson, cabarettist, composer, pianist, entrepreneur and gambler, let his theatre for a summer season to the Ballet Celly de Rheydt. The 'ballet' resulted in a fine for obscenity but thanks to inflation Celly's shady lover, Lieutenant (retd.) Saveloh was able to pay it out of his back pocket. Celly later performed in a blue show at the Black Cat. Sex and drugs were always fashionable, and clubs went in rival pairs in Berlin: at the White Mouse, Theo Oppermann and the Salome Ballet put on a similar show called *Opium*.

In the course of time Celly left Saveloh, married the director of the Ronachertheater in Vienna, and became a pillar of society. Saveloh replaced her with two dancing Scandinavian sisters, Iven and Karin Anderson. Göring fell for Iven, and they ran up credit together at Majowski's bar after the show each night, through Iven always found enough money to tip the waiter. Years later, when the relationship was long since over and Captain Göring had become *Reichsmarschall*, he gave Iven 1,000 marks – repayment for all the tips she'd given on his behalf when he was her penniless lover.

Paula Busch reopened the Zirkus Busch in 1919. The circus had been hugely popular in the nineteenth century and its traditions were continued in a modified form after the interruption of the war. People flocked on re-opening night:

Suddenly the drums began to beat. A tightrope was drawn from one end of the cupola to the other, leaving a chasm below. A Hungarian March was played and a man in a tail coat and shiny top hat began to dance to the rhythm of the music on the silvery rope. It was as if peace and elegance had returned, as if fashion had begun to dance again. A table was moved on to the rope from an elevated platform, then a chair. The table and the chair each had two legs, positioned centrally. A small stove was placed on the table. A frying pan was thrown up, a napkin was laid. The man sat down on the chair in a dangerous equilibrium. He balanced the table in front of him. The drums were now beating incessantly, the stove was lit, an omelette was prepared in the frying pan and the shells of the eggs smashed on the sand below. A bottle of champagne was thrown up to him, a glass was caught by an alert left hand while the right hand still stirred the omelette. The drums ceased, a waltz was struck up, and the top-hatted diner finished his meal on the tightrope at leisure. He emptied the glass unhurriedly and raised his hat. Everything was perhaps a little shaky, complicated and perverse. The table was caught in its fall by red-liveried attendants, the stove was cooled and the chair was thrown down deftly. The man on the tightrope now danced a foxtrot to the thunderous applause of the crowd below, then he himself came to earth, bowed to the right and to the left, and Berlin knew that it had discovered a fresh sensation.[21]

Berlin produced only one great clown, although Grock was a frequent
visitor – he returned and wept in the ruins of the Scala after the Second
World War. Erich Carow didn't work in the theatre, but had his own
cabaret in the unfashionable north of the town. His character was the
downtrodden little Berliner, and he drew his public from his own
district, though admirers came from further afield as well. One was a colleague, Charlie Chaplin. So successful was Erich Carow at his own club
that the Scala once decided to engage him. Carow agreed, but only for
the same fee as they would have paid Grock – and Grock, an international star, got the vast sum of 45,000 marks a month. Carow sold out
every matinée and evening of his run, and used the money to renovate
his old club, which he never left again. One night, driving home, he and
his wife thought they'd left the cash-box at their club. They drove back,
but found the box on the running-board of the car: it was so heavy that
it hadn't fallen off.

'I didn't go to cabaret much in the Twenties because I was a poor student then and cabaret was where you sat at a table and drank champagne,'
remembers Arnold Bauer. 'Even the people's cabarets were dear – only
Erich Carow's place on Weinbergsweg was relatively less expensive, and
even then not cheap . . . Frau Carow tried to introduce a few serious
items . . . but she had a large bosom and looked like a *diva*, and she
wasn't in her first youth – and I can remember hearing her sing "*Im
Opiumrauch, im Opiumrauch* . . ." – all meant very seriously indeed, but
of course killing.'

Carow celebrated twenty-five years in the business at his club on the
night of 27–28 February 1933. At 2 a.m. the *conférencier* for the evening,
Werner Finck, joked: 'I see the Reichstag's been lit up for the occasion.'
It was the night of the Reichstag fire.

There was no smoking in circuses or theatres, but according to Karl
Marx, 'it would be easier to wean the Chinese from opium than Germans
from tobacco'. Hence the popularity of smoking concerts, or smokers,
especially the summer garden theatres along Weinbergsweg and in
Hasenheide. But the best variety show of all was provided by the
Wintergarten of the Central Hotel at Friedrichstrasse Station. This was
a big theatre for its time – it held 3,500 – and the audience sat under a
soaring ceiling painted like a starry sky. Despite the proscenium stage the
show was very like a circus performance, with acrobats and clowns, and
plenty of brassy music, but the better wages here attracted a better class
of act. Big stars had performed there before the war: Otéro, the
Australian *chansonnière* Saharet and Cléo de Mérode, and also the exotic
dancer Mata Hari, who was shot by the British in Paris in 1917 after
being found guilty of spying for the Germans.

When the Wintergarten celebrated its fiftieth anniversary in the autumn of 1938, its director Ludwig Schuch received almost eight hundred telegrams, including one from the director of the KaDeKo, Willi Schaeffers, and one from the Nazi Commissioner of Berlin, Dr Julius Lippert. His theatre was renowned for originality; only seven years after its opening it had showed Berlin's, and the world's, first film – Max and Emil Skladanowsky pipped the Lumière brothers to the post by a couple of months. It was a pursuit film: a man runs out of a house and down the street, pursued by another. One after the other they fall into a canal. One emerges laughing, the other sadly. The End. But cinema-goers (and certainly film-makers) haven't tired of chase-sequences yet.

The years following the First World War were great ones for the entertainment industry. The eight-hour working day had been intro-duced in November 1918; as a *conférencier* put it, 'Now, you have two hours a day fewer to work, but you still get the same amount of money. Mark my words, it won't be long before people cotton on to the fact that there'll be two more hours of night-time to spend money in!'[22] Until the Crash of 1929, it was unusual not to see a 'House Full' sign outside either the Wintergarten or its rival house, the Scala.

In 1938 the Scala was only eighteen years old, but its reputation was such that its director Jules Marx could boast that a German artist could only make it to the international circuit via a four-week baptism of fire there, or at the Wintergarten. The Scala featured the 'Number Girls' – dancers whose job was to breeze across the stage carrying a number to indicate the next act on the programme. However these might be parodied in cabaret, Jules Marx and his successor, Eduard Duisberg, had always to be on the *qui vive* for replacements, as the girls picked up rich protectors, even husbands, very fast. Topless and nude shows were still tolerated as late as 1939 – in *Her or Nobody* at the Metropol that year, the girls wore only see-through Grecian dresses.

The variety stages saw tragedy, too – in 1934 the acrobat 'King Louis' lost his 12-year-old-son in a fall from the tightrope during their joint act at the Scala. The greatest scandal of contemporary variety life – and the inspiration for several feature films – involved the trapeze artistes The Three Codonas. Alfredo Codona was at that time the only man in the world who could perform a triple somersault in the air – and even now his act has never been bettered. His brother Lalo was the 'catcher', and the third member of the team was Vera Brux. They were wildly suc-cessful on the international circuit, and performed at the Wintergarten whenever they were in Berlin.

Alfredo was married to another acrobat, Lillian Leitzel, 'Queen of the Vertical Rope'. They rarely saw each other, for they were constantly and independently on tour. On 13 February 1931, after a performance in

Berlin, Alfredo was told that his wife had fallen fatally during her own act in Copenhagen the same evening. Determined not to let his own colleagues and public down, he managed the next evening's performance – but after that collapsed and could not work any more.

The Codonas took Lillian Leitzel's body to Long Beach, California and Alfredo erected a white marble monument in the grounds of their home. Only after a long time did he start to train again. Before setting off on tour he married his partner, and first love, Vera Brux. But the magic had gone. Alfredo could no longer always manage the 'triple' – he failed in Berlin in 1933, and again the following year, so badly that he spent five weeks in hospital. In 1935, a shoulder smash forced his retirement. The end was squalid, melodramatic, and sad. Alfredo took to drink; Vera was increasingly, and unhappily, unfaithful. Discussing their divorce in a New York lawyer's office in 1938, Alfredo pulled a gun and shot her six times before shooting himself as well. He died immediately, she hours later.

The two leading revue theatres – between which there existed a not always friendly rivalry – were the Apollo and the Metropol. The Apollo was in Friedrichstrasse, the Metropol less advantageously sited in the centre of the financial district. After a rocky start, the Metropol was taken over by a Berlin entrepreneur called Richard Schultz, who hit on the idea of the *Berliner Revue*, its own particular mixture of clowns, acrobats and musical. The evening usually started with a variety of circus acts, and following the interval a play – a mere confection of operetta and folk-tale, but with guest appearances by big-name comedians.

By the mid-Twenties the Metropol had another competitor, the nearby Haller Revue, which caused a sensation by importing twenty-four leggy girls from London – the Tiller Girls, 'all dancing together in exact tempo and step: an amazing mixture of Prussian precision, French sexiness, and English butter-wouldn't-melt.' The girls travelled with their own chaperone and clergyman.

There were other dancers from abroad – Tilly Losch and Isadora Duncan, for example; but naturalized Berliners could compete, too. La Jana (Jenny Hiebel) was not the greatest dancer ever, but she had the most beautiful body most Berliners had ever seen, and they saw most of it. She came to Berlin from Frankfurt via Vienna, and was an overnight success in a Charell revue in which she was carried onstage naked on a silver tray to dance. She was later to die, not inappropriately perhaps, of pneumonia. Then there was Anita Berber.

Anita Berber has again become a minor cult figure in Berlin.[23] She was astonishing. Her father was a well-known violinist in the Leipzig Gewandhaus Orchestra, and she showed great promise at ballet school. Making her way to Berlin, as did everyone who hoped to become a star, she first came to notice in a Rudolf Nelson revue, dancing the Shimmy dressed in a dinner-jacket, and she put her dancing partners, first Sebastian Droste, then the American–German 'Henry' (with whom she lived for the last few years of her life), in the shade. She could have reached the peak of her profession, but she went to the bad, and in Berlin in the Twenties you could do that very thoroughly. She attracted scandal wherever she went, ran through lovers of both sexes as if they were cigarettes, turned up at boxing matches and Six-Day Cycle Races at the Sportpalast attended by heavies of the nastiest kind, performed nude at the White Mouse, and by 29, marinaded in alcohol, cocaine and morphine, had contracted consumption.

> The last time I saw her was in front of Alfred Flechtheim's house during *Fasching*. He was giving a private masked party at his place, for company that was certainly a little too sophisticated for Anita, and she was not let in. She stood in the street and yelled so you could hear her all over Tiergarten . . . We didn't hear any more of her for a while after that. Then the rumour started to run around the theatre dressing rooms that she was fatally ill in the south. The south was Baghdad, and she was penniless. We got a collection together to bring her back, and so it was that she returned to Berlin to die.
> 'Henry' was late for her funeral. He'd stopped off to try and find some white roses for her.[24]

There were other dancers. Valeska Gert was a character dancer, her act very close to mime and clowning. Her work was a form of agit-prop, her dances little plays, little novels in themselves, in which a whole life, or one devastating human experience, was explored. Brecht admired her, and asked her to work at his own cabaret, the Red Grape. She became famous throughout Europe, and opened a cabaret of her own in Berlin, the Kohlkopp. Later, in exile in New York, she ran The Beggars' Bar. Her contribution to Berlin's artistic life was unique, but her style died with her. The *Börsen-Courier* journalist Hans Sahl remembers Valeska locking him in a Paris hotel room until he promised to write her memoirs.

In 1926 Josephine Baker made her appearance in Berlin. She was already a star in Paris, but the Berliners didn't know quite what had hit them. She was black, she danced nude to jazz – she was exciting and exotic beyond anyone's wildest dreams, with an aura of, at one and the same time, innocence and complete sexual abandon. The famous banana skirt caused more than a sensation – it passed into legend. Harry Kessler met her with Max Reinhardt at a party in the flat of Karl Vollmoeller, a wealthy businessman and *amateur* of the theatre, who had written Reinhardt's hit *The Miracle* (in which Diana Cooper starred when it transferred to New York). Kessler's entries for Saturday 13 February and the days following reveal a man in the grip of increasing excitement. On 28 February he even turned down dinner with Richard Strauss to see Miss Baker again.

> *Berlin, Saturday 13 February 1926* Miss Baker . . . wearing nothing but a diaphanous loincloth danced with sublime style and grotesquery, an Ancient Egyptian or archaic figure . . . like the dancers of Solomon or Tutankhamun. She dances for hours without the slightest trace of tiredness, always inventing new figures, and happy as a pleased child. She doesn't even become hot, but her skin remains fresh, cool and dry. A magical creature, but almost completely un-erotic. Eroticism enters one's mind as little, watching her, as if one were watching a beautiful beast of prey. The naked girls danced or lay among the five or six men in dinner-jackets, and little Landshoff [a niece of Sammy Fischer],[25] who really looks like a pretty boy [she too was wearing a dinner-jacket], danced to modern jazz on the gramophone.
>
> Vollmoeller wanted to write a ballet for Baker . . . As we talked, Baker and Landshoff lay entwined in each others' arms like a pair of lovers from a picture-book. I said that I would write a pantomime for her based on motifs from the *Song of Solomon* . . . Baker would wear period costume (or non-costume), Solomon would wear a dinner-jacket, quite deliberately mixing ancient and modern with music that would be half-jazz, half-oriental. Perhaps by Richard Strauss.
>
> Reinhardt was keen on the idea and so was Vollmoeller, and we made a date to dine at my place on the 24th with [Baker] and Landshoff . . .

In the days that followed, Kessler dined with Einstein, went to see Baker in Rudolf Nelson's *Black Revue,* and had tea at the Adlon with the adventuress and former spy Elsa Brandström, but it is clear that he could hardly wait for the 24th. Baker and Landshoff (in drag again) were the only female guests, and Baker danced for them in the specially-cleared library of Kessler's apartment. The pantomime idea was discussed enthusiastically.

On 28 February Kessler paid a quick visit to Strauss after the performance of *Die Frau ohne Schatten,* but didn't broach the subject of the pantomime and declined an invitation to dine; he was expected at Vollmoeller's to see Baker again. At Vollmoeller's after midnight:

> Extraordinary company there again, nobody knew each other, and only his very delightful lover [as we now discover], Miss Landshoff (in men's clothes again) shone at all. A classless atmosphere. He [Vollmoeller] . . . likes people who don't reveal their class . . . women in every stage of nakedness, whose names one doesn't catch and of whom one knows nothing – are they girl-friends, whores or ladies? Young Jewish men, who could be publishers or ballet-masters, actresses who have just been 'discovered' . . . Baker sat on the divan and instead of dancing ate one *Bockwurst* after another.

Sadly, the pantomime was never produced.

A pantomime of a different kind *was* produced by the 71-year-old mystic, Joseph Weissenberg.[26] He arrived in Berlin, from Silesia, at about the same time as Josephine Baker, and answered a different need: for something to believe in. The few years of relative material stability in the late Twenties were not nearly enough to eradicate the insecurity over work and identity which beset Berliners throughout the Weimar period. There was a readiness to believe in miracles, in faith healing, in fundamentalism, and Weissenberg's nostrum was easy to understand. He preached a programme of healing by laying on of hands or, when that failed, the administration of curd cheese. Known as the Curd Cheese Prophet, he was convinced his medicine had the power to raise the dead. So were his followers: he was adored by his disciples as a new saint.

Officially his sect was called The Evangelical Church of St John and of the Revelations of St John. Weissenberg himself was a fat, energetic, white-bearded man in a blue suit and a peaked cap. Seeing him at a meeting, one's first impression was of a little publican attending a reunion of wartime comrades; indeed, in the course of his life he had been by turns a shepherd, a bricklayer, a waiter, a hackney cab driver, *and* a publican. 'I had to give up the last job', he announced, 'because Jesus Christ ordered me to!' Towards the end of the Twenties he lived in north Berlin. A consultation cost only a mark, but in front of his poor-looking house stood an elegant car, in which the prophet would drive to the 'Peace City' he had founded in the Glauer Hills, an hour to the south of Berlin. Weissenberg had bought the land in 1919, for cash. His Church of St John didn't exist in those days, but as early as 1900 he had founded a Society for Serious Students of The Other Side, and Peace City had been planned as a pilgrimage centre and commune – a kind of *ashram* – for 1,500 people. By the end of the Twenties four hundred were living there, and two rows of houses had been built, together with a Hall of Meditation, an old people's home, an office building, a garage, a steam laundry, a waterworks, a dairy, and even a museum containing the miscellaneous objects presented to the Master by the Enlightened. The whole establishment was financed privately through collections and donations.

At Weissenberg's Awakening Meetings 'Sister Grete Müller', a thickset woman with a fleshy face, played the leading role. She could fall into a trance at will, and then voices from The Other Side would speak through her: Bismarck was especially keen. The Faithful sighed, screamed, and fell into trances themselves. Weissenberg would wander among them, laying on hands and conducting the Chosen to the stage, where they revealed themselves as various dignitaries, usually from the time of Wilhelm I – Moltke, for example, or Prince Friedrich Karl. Berlin had never seen such a mixture of savings bank, old soldiers' club, and fundamentalist Christian sect. Was it holy or sacrilegious? Should Weissenberg be allowed to carry on, or should the authorities be notified? In the end, the old man did stand trial on a charge of quackery: a child with inflamed eyes, who had been treated with prayers and curd cheese, had gone blind; and a diabetic pharmacist who had undergone the same treatment had died. Weissenberg was given six months, but the court of appeal quashed the sentence. Further trials and writs followed, but the law couldn't touch him. His followers were even more faithful than before, and he himself seemed not to understand what possible objection could be raised to his faith-healing. 'Where were you trained?' asked a magistrate. 'Holy Writ,' replied the prophet. 'There's nothing about curd cheese in the Bible!' objected another. 'If a man has no faith, how can I help him?'

The Church of St John still existed as late as the Sixties. The Nazis banned the sect in 1935, and took over Peace City – or New Jerusalem, as it was officially called – for SS barracks. Weissenberg himself died in 1941, full of years, in his native Silesia.

As an international centre, Berlin attracted other equally exotic but more respectable dignitaries, like King Feisal of Iraq, or the more flamboyant Fuad of Egypt, king, businessman, and self-declared friend of 'all revolutionaries – Masaryk, Piłsudski, Mussolini'. The most colourful visitor was King Amanullah of Afghanistan. A reforming king who wanted to modernize and westernize his country, he came to Europe in 1928 accompanied by his queen and a number of his viziers on a mind-broadening tour which included medical treatment as well. His was the only official visit of a monarch to Berlin after the First World War. 'I remember his visit,' says Gerda Bassenge.[27] 'It's one of my pleasantest memories, though at the time I just thought I was seeing some camel-driver from the Far East. My mother was determined that we children should see at least one king in the course of our lives. We took a tram up to Unter den Linden and there he was, in a carriage full of dusky ladies.' Amanullah attracted some pretty sharp, even racist, remarks from the press as well – Ernst Feder, the liberal editor of the *Berliner Tageblatt*, commented that he looked like 'a horse-thief in uniform'. But the press was kept at arm's-length, and Feder's asperity may have arisen from this. Doctors of the Medical Faculty of the University happily gave the Royal pair medical advice and care – but they waited in vain for their fees to be paid.[28]

Amanullah would not drink wine, but toasted the Republic in water at civic receptions. He sent the leader of the Reichstag, Paul Löbe, an Afghani Order; Löbe, as a socialist, refused it, earning censure from the right-wing press for lack of diplomacy, and from the Nazis the soubriquet

'Duke of Afghanistan'. A ceremonial robe was given to the State Secretary Dr Weissmann, known thenceforward as Weissmannullah. Unfortunately, Amanullah was deposed soon after his return to Afghanistan by more conservative elements who disliked the idea of too much literacy, or of abandoning the fez, or of being clean-shaven.

Among the more permanent guests in the city, those in the diplomatic community, the ambassadors of Britain and America stand out. Harry Kessler attended the masked balls which the d'Abernons gave, and Frederick Sackett, a colourful character with private means, was known for serving lobster at tea – an unheard-of luxury in Berlin. Also new to the Germans was Olive Sackett's having her own separate social calendar. On the Fourth of July five hundred guests were invited to the Embassy, the young in the afternoon and the middle-aged in the evening. The Sacketts also took an active part in Berlin's social life, and Mrs Sackett was much liked for her sense of humour and her friendly irony; she in turn sincerely loved the city, and encouraged the United States to help its struggling European neighbour. 'We prefer to see things solved over a green baize table than on the battlefield,' she insisted.

Inevitably all these people, and members of the international press corps, might be seen at one time or another at the Hotel Adlon.[29] The hotel was a palace, and opening-day reviews compared it to one. At his own request Wilhelm II was the first guest to enter the hotel, and was childishly impressed by what he saw. When he asked Lorenz Adlon the price of the carpets, imported from Constantinople, it became plain that Lorenz had managed to furnish the Adlon better and more cheaply than *Hofmarschall* Trützschler had Sanssouci; this earned Adlon the latter's enmity. Wilhelm was especially impressed that there were no service bells in the hotel – all call-signals were made by discreet electric lights.

The Chancellor at the time, von Bülow, asked Lorenz not to show the Kaiser his wine-cellar (which at the beginning housed only a modest quarter-of-a-million bottles): Wilhelm would immediately demand a wine-cellar of his own containing a million bottles, and that would give his *Hausminister* a heart-attack. Staff uniforms at the Adlon were impeccable, if vulgar: pale blue tunics with white gloves. They were (naturally) made by the very best outfitters in Berlin. The Adlons' private chauffeur, Carl Mirow, got his driving licence (List Three, Number One) in 1900; he was still driving in 1955, having completed his three-millionth kilometre.

Certainly the *brouhaha* caused by visiting foreign guests must have raised a few Republican eyebrows. Herzog Ernst Günther zu Schleswig-Holstein and his wife had to be moved from the third floor to a ground floor suite because the Tsar was to pay them a visit: Russian Court protocol (drawn up in the time of Catherine the Great) contained no guidance on behaviour in lifts, and the Tsar could scarcely be expected to climb the stairs to the third floor. On the other hand, such irritations must have been offset by the fact that Auguste Escoffier was the hotel's *chef de cuisine*. Among the untitled guests were Enrico Caruso and Carolina Otéro; among the titled was the Maharajah of Patiala, who during his stay bought three Mercedes cars and the entire contents of a lamp shop for his palace, and left a 40,000-mark tip on his departure.

Prominent on Pariser Platz, the Adlon was in the front line of fire during the revolution which succeeded the First World War. The windows facing the square were shattered by gun-fire from the Brandenburg Gate, and revolutionary guards demanded to know if any capitalists or officers were guests – given the hotel's prices, a somewhat unnecessary question. But in the event only a certain Rittmeister von Bergen qualified. He was in the hotel recovering from leg wounds. Lorenz Adlon's son Louis (who managed the hotel throughout the Weimar period) didn't betray him, but the revolutionaries decided to search the hotel anyway. Fräulein Hartmann, the housekeeper, hid with the Rittmeister in the laundry lift, in which the two rode up and down for the duration of the search. She left him only once, at his request, to fetch a bottle of cognac.

Pariser Platz continued to be the scene of fighting. One evening another squad of revolutionaries entered the hotel with an 'official' requisition note for its food. The Cellar-Master had the presence of mind to lock his doors (the cellar contained a million bottles of wine by now), and staff pushed large cupboards in front to hide them. It is odd that none of the revolutionaries should have thought of the wine-cellar, but possibly in such straitened times food was uppermost in their minds. The Spartacists went to the kitchens and the storerooms – but then a Freikorps unit arrived, with a similar requisition note. In this potentially lethal situation, Louis managed to persuade the two belligerent groups to split the goods down the middle.

As if such interruptions weren't enough, and as if it weren't enough (according to the delightfully snobbish Hedda Adlon, Louis' wife) to have to deal with the new post-war clientele, who were *nouveaux riches* and simply didn't have the *style* of the pre-war guests, the hotel had to cope with its first criminal. Shortly after Christmas 1918 a Baron Winterfeld checked into the hotel with an unusual item of luggage: a ship's trunk, big enough to hold a body. At about this time, anonymous letters were being sent to people known to be rich, urging them to transfer their money home, as Spartacists planned to seize all banks and freeze their assets on 4 January. Transfers like these would have involved the special postmen who handled letters of credit and financial papers, and the *Berliner Zeitung* published a warning that the letters could easily be the work of a gang planning an attack on these special postmen. But many preferred to take that chance and withdraw their money anyway.

On 2 January, following a bleak New Year celebration and the first fusillades of the morning, Special Postman Lange brought a letter for Baron Winterfeld, and insisted on delivering it personally to the baron as his last delivery had been rewarded with ham sandwiches and cigars. The hotel itself was never the object of attack (which perhaps bears out the old jibe that German revolutionaries always keep off the grass), but because of the gun-battles raging around it no one noticed that Postman Lange had disappeared until much later, when the alarm was raised by his office. He had been carrying 270,000 marks in cash and bearer bonds. The Police Praesidium had fallen into the hands of the Spartacists, which hampered the police enquiry, but on the morning of 3 January detectives broke into Baron Winterfeld's room to find the baron gone and Lange bound to a chair, strangled. The large trunk stood open and abandoned. Evidently Winterfeld had decided against concealing the body in it. The baron and the money had vanished. The mystery went unsolved until July 1922, when a man calling himself Blume was arrested in Dresden for the attempted murder of another special postman. Detective Chief Inspector Ernst Gennat, sent from Berlin to Dresden, found that Blume was indeed Baron Winterfeld. Oddly, he was also a playwright, one of whose works had dealt with the murder of a special postman, though it was set in New York. The career of the murderous playwright ended with his suicide in his cell.

Despite the bleakness and deprivation of 1919 the Adlon retained its style, even when food was in short supply. The hotel was built over its own well and had its own generator, so that even in the darkest moments of the civil war, even during the most efficient general strikes, there was always hot and cold running water and electric light. What is more, no light-bulbs were stolen, since the hotel had special ones for its 110 volt capacity – half that of the city grid. The Adlon was thus something of an oasis. It also provided neutral ground where, for example, dis-possessed White Russians might meet and talk with the new Communist masters of their country.

At about this time Berlin was plagued by a cat burglar. Though he robbed only the rich, and took care not to disturb sleeping women, he was apt to destroy priceless paintings and tapestries if he could find nothing easier to steal. This man was unfortunate enough to rob Hugo Stinnes, staying at the Adlon with his wife. A Swedish businessman disturbed him making his getaway, but did not immediately raise the alarm because he was in the hotel with his mistress and did not want his wife to find out. But in panic the burglar fell from a first-floor balcony and broke his leg. Happening to be rescued by two ladies passing in a rare taxi – the 'Red Countess' Hetta Treuberg and the Baroness Dosch – he claimed to be a victim of street violence, and was taken to the Charité Hospital. Casualty wards there were overflowing and no one checked his tale, but a gold watch he was carrying was noticed, together with some gold cuff-links and a good deal of diamond jewellery, and the police came to fetch him. He was a failed artist, Hugo Kessner, and hadn't realized that he had been robbing the great Stinnes.

All was restored to the couple except, as Frau Stinnes pointed out, for a dish containing goose pâté with chopped apple and onion that she herself had made. The police questioned the rescuing ladies; Baroness Dosch revealed she had been with the countess to the Widows' Ball – a working-class affair that took place regularly in a hall on the wrong side of Alexanderplatz. The baroness had been quite innocently slumming, but the police knew the countess's political affiliations. They set a watch and saw her pass an address to a known Spartacist agitator. There the police found Karl Radek, and on the table in front of him was the dish of goose pâté. The police now had the excuse they needed to arrest him. But they let him taste the pâté first, and he pronounced it excellent.[30]

The star of *The Blue Angel* owed her discovery, indirectly, to the Adlon's owners. At the première of a new play Hedda Adlon admired a young actress in a small role – Maria Magdalena von Losch. The girl was familiar to Hedda because she lived with her mother not far away at Unter den Linden 19. 'She became Marlene Dietrich, and was frequently a guest at the hotel – though she was extremely fussy about her food: absolutely no fat, and all meat had to be grilled.' During casting for *The Blue Angel*, Emil Jannings was consoling himself in the Adlon bar over the difficulty of finding a leading lady. Louis Adlon suggested that he go and see a new comedy called *Two Neckties*, in which Dietrich was acting with Hans Albers; Jannings did as he suggested.[31]

A handful of guests stayed at the Adlon free of charge – not entirely out of the goodness of Louis' heart: they sang for their suppers, and their presence attracted custom. One was Anton Kuh, a Berliner by adoption originally from Vienna. Kuh defies classification. He was a journalist, a columnist, a screenwriter and an impromptu cabarettist whose *ad hoc* performances were so brilliant that he could fill a theatre any Sunday morning at the drop of a hat. But he was also completely impecunious and his true profession, by his own admission, was sponging.

Kuh was on friendly terms with Richard Tauber and Erich von Stroheim. All three of them wore monocles. Kuh's was in a silver fame on a black silk ribbon. One evening he abandoned it in order to play a practical joke on the Soviet Ambassador to Oslo and Stockholm, Alexandra Kollontai. One of the first revolutionaries, she was by now devoted to the luxuries which her privileged and trusted position in the west brought her; she had also written a book about free love. She was a frequent guest at the Adlon, and it was here that Kuh decided to play his trick. He disguised himself as a beggar and lay in wait for the regal Kollontai; as she left the hotel for the opera with several other dignitaries, he accosted her and asked for money. As he had expected, she ignored him. So he shouted out, in full hearing of the press and the public: 'You wait 'til the Communists get in in Germany – you'll get your come-uppance then, madame!' Perhaps he had hoped to write up the incident himself for one of the papers, to earn some money; but for diplomatic reasons the whole affair was hushed up. At least Tauber and the normally forbidding von Stroheim were amused.

6 Berlin Alexanderplatz

███████ AT THE FAR end of Unter den Linden from the Adlon, across the Schlossbrücke, past the Schloss, the Lustgarten and the cathedral, along Kaiser-Wilhelm-Strasse, then right at the Zentral Markthalle, is Alexanderplatz Station. Beyond it is the square itself. Today it is a large, bleak, grey expanse, surrounded by hideous modern blocks. It has never been beautiful.

'I was born in Zehlendorf in 1915', an old *Berlinerin* told me, 'and, do you know, although I've lived all my life in Berlin, I have only been to Alexanderplatz once. It was always a hell of a place, and the buildings beyond it were never much better than the ones they've put up now. But in any case, there was never much point in going that far east in the city.' There were no theatres near it to speak of, and beyond it to the east and north the poor districts sprawled. The 'Golden Twenties' did not reach here; it would be a mistake to think of that short period of frenzied gaiety and creative activity in the big theatres as being available to other than the rich, or foreigners with hard currency. Nor did it spread beyond the very centre of town and the Westend. In the early Twenties the arts thrived because inflation pushed people into spending their money while it had value; in the late Twenties stability gave people more disposable income. But the limits of time and space hedged the 'Golden Twenties' in tightly, and most Berliners did not even know that they were there.

When Dickens was writing of London and Balzac of Paris, Berlin was still a provincial town. The first novel to feature Berlin appeared in 1929. Alfred Döblin's *Berlin Alexanderplatz* is a picaresque epic written by a doctor who worked among the poor, the dispossessed, and the petty criminal classes he describes. Attracting comparisons with *Ulysses*, which Döblin found mildly irritating, *Alexanderplatz* is a rambling book, sometimes stumbling, like its hero, confused but keeping hold of its own integrity, and concealing in its looseness an extraordinary constructive skill. The atmosphere evoked is intensified by the fact that it is written in Berlin dialect.[1]

Big city mercilessness is summed up by Carl Zuckmayer as he describes his arrival in Berlin as a penniless unknown of 24: 'It was a cold, nasty winter morning when I left Anhalter Station in Berlin, carrying my suitcase. The wet streets were filled with people with turned-up collars, hastening to their offices. I was bumped, pushed, snarled at: "Hey, watch your step or you'll need a car from Grieneisen." The full charm of this remark dawned on me only after I saw the name "Grieneisen" on billboards, along with pictures of a coffin. It was the largest Berlin funeral home.'[2]

The easiest way to survive in Berlin was through sex and drugs. Zuckmayer tried to keep afloat by working as a night-club tout and – once – as a coke-pusher.

> One night my boss suddenly transferred me . . . to Berlin's Westend. He . . . took me there in a cab and filled my pockets with . . . cigarettes and cigars, but above all with small, folded squares of white paper, like the ordinary headache powder packets . . . sold in chemists in those days.
>
> [My] . . . instructions . . . [were] to walk slowly up and down the street, just like a streetwalker, calling softly, 'Tssigars, tssigarettes' – with a sharp, hissing sound. That, he told me, was the signal for customers, who would identify themselves by sniffing loudly through their noses. When they did, and paid a considerable sum, I was to press one of the paper squares into their hands along with the cigars or cigarettes. When I asked what was in them, he said, 'Snow', but added reassuringly that in reality the stuff was only salt mixed with crushed aspirin, therefore hardly illegal – but all the same I should keep a sharp eye out for the police, and if necessary say that I had found the packets in a cab.

Miserably, and unsuccessfully, 'Zuck' tried his luck on the cold damp pavements around Wittenbergplatz and the KaDeWe (the Kaufhaus des Westens, a big department store), showing how green he was, and finally attracting the attention of a friendly Polish whore who pointed out that a plain-clothes cop was already on his tail. To save him, the girl told him to pretend to be one of her customers – there was nothing the policeman could do to her because she was legally registered and he knew it. Once they had given him the slip:

> 'Let's have a look at your stuff,' she commanded in an abrupt, matter-of-fact tone. Since I realized that she knew the whole story anyhow and that I was at her mercy if she wanted to inform on me, I took the little packets from my pocket – glad to get rid of them. She began counting them, her eyes assuming a greedy expression.

'How much is your boss asking for a shot?'

I told her.

'Wait here,' she said hastily. 'I won't run out on you; I have a connection over there in the Femina Café; he'll take the whole lot.'

I remained standing in the dark entry, and lit one of my 'tssigarettes'. Half an hour later she came back. She seemed in excellent humour and smelled of brandy.

'I bamboozled him,' she said. 'He was high already and didn't even count.' She pressed the money into my hand – more than I was supposed to deliver.

'Forget it,' she said when I started to thank her. I shook her hand.

'Where are you going now?' she asked. I shrugged. I really didn't know . . . 'You can come with me,' she said. 'I live in this house – it's got central heating. I've finished work for the night.' She saw me hesitating. 'Don't worry,' she said, laughing. 'It won't cost you a thing. I don't like staying alone.'

'I know how you feel,' I said.

The room was no better and no worse than all the others in this neighbourhood. Beat-up, once respectable furniture, a brass bed with lace coverlet, several wretched oil paintings on the walls . . .

'My name is Lyuba,' she said, tossing off her jacket. 'My family came from Warsaw, but I won't tell you they were Polish nobles.' She continued undressing . . . 'You don't have to come on all that fast,' she said when I sat down on a chair without going near her. 'Don't you like my looks?'

She had swiftly removed the paint from her face and I could see that she was quite pretty and far from old. 'I do,' I said. 'But I've got another girl on my mind.'

'And it's all over with her,' she said, taking something from her pocket. I saw that it was one of the packets she had evidently kept for herself 'Don't you coke?' she asked.

I shook my head.

She took a sniff, her eyes darkened. 'That's good stuff,' she said. 'Makes you forget everything. Try it.'

'I don't want to forget anything,' I said.

She took two glasses and a rectangular bottle from the closet. It was Polnischer Reiterschnapps, a strong, bitter herbal liqueur. I recall the picture of a cavalryman on the label. I tossed down one glass, then another . . . We drank the liqueur until she nodded off. I carried her to the bed, covered her up, and lay down on the tattered sofa.

Next day I sent her flowers. I thought that would give her a kick.

Zuckmayer stayed in Berlin and not only survived, but 'made it'. Wearily describing artistic parties a year or so later, he wrote: 'Artists in those days dressed very scantily. Even then – though only among intimate friends – ladies who had something to show went topless. Men sometimes appeared in bathing trunks – but with a formal bow-tie.'

Presiding over the sexual revolution was Magnus Hirschfeld, a sex therapist and researcher who was himself homosexual. He was a serious scientist, but his name was often taken in vain and he was later reviled as a pornographer by the Nazis, who destroyed his Institute and in 1933 tried to kill him. But the Institute for Sexual Research – the first of its kind in the world – did much good. Hirschfeld had founded it in 1918, and fought hard and sometimes successfully against laws restricting sexual freedom, though he failed to get the law banning homosexuality repealed. After his narrow escape from the Nazis he went to France, and died in Nice two years later. Alfred Fischer[3] remembers him well.

> He was far less elegant than I had imagined before I met him – in fact he looked rather shabby. But he was an amiable man, and highly knowledgeable. His dictum was always *Statt Hilfe Verbot heisst Steine statt Brot* ('To forbid rather than to help is to give stones instead of bread'). What I remember was rather nice and amusing about him was that although he was plump and tweedy like a professor, with crumbs of tobacco on his lapels, he had a high, piping, effeminate voice which didn't go with his looks at all. His nickname was 'Auntie Magnesia'.

It is curious that the homosexuality laws should have been so severe for so long, even if they were not observed. Another statute more honoured in the breach than the observance was that forbidding abortion. However, a couple who spent their youth in Berlin at the time told me that although 'there was a large degree of sexual freedom, and sexual advice centres to help, there wasn't all that much promiscuity. People had relationships without getting married, sure, but the relationships generally lasted – anything up to five years, and often of course led to lifelong partnerships. The sex advice centres weren't there specifically for the young, but young people could use them without fear of censure.'

But sexual liberation could be a double-edged sword for the young, as the affair of Paul Krantz, one of the sensations of the Twenties, demonstrated.[4] Paul Krantz and Günther Scheller were both 19 in 1927, and in their last year at school. They were good friends, and Krantz had fallen for Scheller's 16-year-old sister Hildegard, who was a good deal more sexually mature than either young man, as one of her poems, written to Krantz, shows:

> I fear that you still know little of the ways of love;
> Make haste, you have already missed much.
> What is the use of love if it is only in our thoughts?
> A girl will scarcely think she's beautiful
> If the fire of love is only expressed in poetry.

One evening in June, when the Scheller parents were away in Denmark and had left the children to fend for themselves, Paul and Hilde went to bed together at the Schellers' summer house in Mahlow. Later, at the trial, they both described what they had done with a kind of Victorian prurience. Hilde spoke of 'sinful kisses', and Paul of 'impure caresses'. However, it seems that Paul was more deeply affected by the experience than Hilde, who the following night went to bed at her parents' Steglitz apartment with another lover, an apprentice chef called Hans Stephan. A bizarre situation developed, in which Hilde and Hans were in a bedroom of the flat while Paul and Günther, who had arrived unexpectedly, sat in another room drinking fruit schnapps and liqueur, and discussing ways to punish the 'sinners'. The plan they evolved is not surprising, given the morbid romanticism that was fashionable then among German youth. Günther would kill Hans and then himself, and Paul would do the same with Hilde. The two friends then wrote a letter formally describing their pact. In the course of the evening a 16-year-old girl-friend of Hilde's, Ellinor Ratti, also dropped in. She was called as a witness later – but fortunately she does not complicate the story further.

By now the young men had worked themselves up into a state of great agitation, and the alcohol had not helped. Paul had a revolver, entrusted to him by a youth group of which he was a member, the Order of Young Germany. Günther fired a practice shot in the kitchen and nearly killed Paul, who then had second thoughts about the whole plan. Günther, though, remained determined to see it through. In the small hours Hilde joined them, fully dressed, and tried to cool the situation down. She had got Hans to hide in a curtained niche next to the wardrobe in the bedroom. She now appeared as if nothing untoward had happened, and told them she was preparing for school. She whispered to Paul that Hans had gone. Günther appeared to accept this, but he still had the gun. He wandered into the bedroom and moments later Hilde and Paul heard two shots. They found both Günther and Hans dead.

It emerged at the trial that Günther had founded a suicide society called 'Fehou'. Its twenty-odd members had sworn to kill themselves, each taking a 'rival' with him. The question then arose of what had motivated Günther in this case; Hans was hardly *his* rival. Had he done the deed, then, in some way to defend his sister's honour? Or was it a question of incestuous love? Or – a third possibility which emerged – were Günther and Hans rivals in a homosexual triangle? As if these convolutions weren't enough, Herr and Frau Scheller, returning from Denmark, accused Paul of both murders, *tout court*. However, the gun, the suicide pact letter and a pretty but corrupt teenage girl created a sensation. Both the Prussian and the National Parliaments raised questions. Reporters flocked from all over Europe, and a delegation of Japanese lawyers sat in on the trial.

Both Hilde Scheller and Ellinor Ratti were extremely pretty, which helped their presentation by the press – the crime reporter 'Sling' (Paul

Schlesinger) described Ellinor as 'an earthy beauty, an Italian half-caste', and Hilde, by contrast, as 'still half a child, with soft brown hair and black eyebrows and lashes, with dark blue eyes. Soft blushing cheeks in a finely-chiselled face, with a soft voice, clear and silvery.' Judge Dust, though, clearly regarded Hilde as the cause of the entire tragedy, and subjected her to the most detailed examination regarding her sex life. He was just as merciless with Ellinor. Hilde broke down, which outraged the public. They didn't mind the salacious aspects, but didn't like seeing the girl treated in this way, whatever the circumstances.

The Krantz family had engaged one of Berlin's top lawyers, the flamboyant Dr Dr Erich Frey, who wore an outsize monocle and a polka-dot bow-tie, and dabbled in writing operettas, and who cut the prosecution to ribbons. Magnus Hirschfeld was called as an expert witness, and so was the playwright Arnolt Bronnen, to analyse the writing of both the suicide letter and Hilde's poetry. Finally, the case was dismissed. Soon afterwards Paul Krantz left Berlin for Paris and the Sorbonne, changing his name. He became a novelist, emigrated to the United States, ended up as an academic under the name of Ernst Erich Noth, and wrote his own account of the case. Hilde became a librarian – the authorities vetoed a plan for her to play herself in a feature film. Ellinor Ratti became a court reporter.

The repercussions of the case were more important than the issue itself. Dust's interrogation drew such violent criticism from the press that judges were henceforward no longer allowed such freedom of intervention. The question of parental responsibility was also thrown open. It was ironic that the whole business had taken place in Steglitz, which had the lowest divorce rate in Berlin. Elsewhere in the city there were many one-parent families. Husbands and fathers had been killed in the war; mothers had to work, grandparents couldn't control adolescents growing up in an insecure, even paranoid society, where inflation had scattered bourgeois values to the winds. Paul Krantz himself had been largely brought up by his grandparents, as his parents, struggling musicians, had been too concerned with their careers to be bothered with him. 'Sling' wrote that Paul's parents didn't seem fully grown up themselves. Had the sexual revolution come too far, too fast? Here was a real-life *Spring Awakening*. The Krantz affair focused attention on such problems. From now on it wasn't just the handful of sexologists like Hirschfeld who would be concerned with them; others took note, too.

The Twenties saw a number of serial murder cases, on which the press battened with enthusiasm. What is striking about many of these cases is the practical way in which corpses and their effects were disposed of. It is not going too far to suggest that the expedients the murderers used were a result of the widespread poverty. Two of them involved innocent people in cannibalism.

In March 1921 the lame peddler Carl Grossmann turned up at Police Station 50 in Kleine Andreasstrasse near Schlesischer Station to report that his housekeeper had run away, having robbed him. Sergeant Karl Klähn knew the man well, for this wasn't the first time he had come in to report the disappearance of one of the little maids-of-all-work he habitually employed to look after his flat. People looking for this kind of servant would go to one of the big railway stations and watch the flood of wretched young people from the eastern provinces arriving in search of work. They could pick a likely one out without needing a labour exchange.

Several months later, Klähn was called to Grossmann's apartment block at Langestrasse 88. It was the night of 21 August, and neighbours had heard screams and cries coming from Grossmann's flat. In the kitchen a country girl called Marie Nitsche lay dead, badly cut up, and Grossmann, white as a sheet, stood over her. Under interrogation, Grossmann confessed to twenty-three similar murders, but he only did so on condition that the police agree to bring him his pet bird, Hänschen, to care for. He had sexually abused the girls before stabbing them, cutting them up and throwing bits of their corpses into the Spree, or the Luisenstäder Canal, or into the dark corners of rear courtyards. The police found a half-charred thorax in the kitchen, and several hands and fingers concealed about the flat. Why no one had reported screams before, remains a mystery, and nowhere is it explained why girls hadn't come across bits of their predecessors. On the eve of the hearing, Grossmann hanged himself in his cell. The case brought a new investigator, Detective Chief Inspector Gennat, into the public eye for the first time. He was one of the greatest investigators in police history. Between 1918 and his death in 1939 he solved 298 murder enquiries.[5]

A couple of years after the Grossmann case, neighbours went to the flat near Breslau of a local shopkeeper, Karl Denke, pillar of society and warden of the local Lutheran church. Drawn by the noise of a fight, they found Denke and a badly-wounded young workman. Denke claimed he had been attacked, but in his house the police found barrels of smoked human flesh, a crate of human bones, and jars of human lard. Germans had long since ceased to be pernickety about eating the odd cat or dog, and when Denke set up a modest business in cured pork, nobody thought twice about where his meat was coming from. Denke also committed suicide, leaving behind a notebook which neatly documented thirty victims, together with the weight and date of demise of each one.

In view of Germany's nakedly right-wing judiciary, which consistently punished left-wing agitators and let the right-wingers go free, Kurt

Tucholsky adapted Goethe's description of his country; instead of *Denker und Dichter* (Thinkers and Poets), for him it was a land of *Henker und Richter* (Hangmen and Judges). Now Brecht proposed that for *Denker*, Germans should read 'Denkes': '[Denke] killed people in order to use their corpses. He canned the meat and made soap from the fat, buttons from the bones, and purses from the skins. He placed his business on a scientific footing and was extremely surprised when, after his apprehension, he was sentenced to be executed . . . I contend that the people of Germany, those who condemned Denke, failed to recognize the qualities of true German genius which the fellow displayed: namely, method, conscientiousness, cold-bloodedness, and the ability to place one's every act on a firm philosophical foundation . . . They should have made him a Ph.D. with honours.'[6]

The most Gothick of the serial murderers was Georg Haarmann. Like Grossmann, Haarmann frequented railway stations in order to pick out his victims. Unlike Grossmann, Haarmann was interested in boys. Having picked up a victim he would offer him beer and sausage, and then take him home, promising to help him find work. But once the boy was safely bedded down, Haarmann (who, ironically, earned his living as a police informer) would overpower him, rape him, and then tear out his throat with his teeth. Haarmann later told his lawyer that he never remembered the attacks: he would feel a sense of rage, which grew, and then everything would go blank. Haarmann's career ended when some little boys discovered a skull on a river bank. A few days later a second skull was washed ashore, and when the police had the river dredged, they found enough bones amid the debris to constitute perhaps twenty-six bodies. By pure chance, the mother of one of the missing boys recognized her son's jacket being worn by the son of Haarmann's landlady: Haarmann, like Denke, was a practical man. He cleaned his victims' clothes and sold them. He also boiled down and potted their flesh for sale. It is almost inconceivable that he managed it without discovery.

Haarmann seemed untouched by his crimes. A psychiatrist argued that he was unfit to stand trial, but he was duly sentenced. The execution itself became an issue of national principle. In the early Thirties, even before their seizure of power, the Nazis controlled public opinion. Arthur Koestler, who had recently returned from Paris to become scientific editor on Ullstein's *BZ am Mittag*, describes the situation in his memoirs: 'For years the Ullstein Press had campaigned vigorously against capital punishment . . . As a consequence of the opposition of all progressive elements to the death penalty, it had not been used for several years. But in 1931 the case of the homosexual mass murderer Haarmann brought the controversy to a new peak; it became a trial of strength between the humanistic, liberal forces and the gathering power of reaction and barbarism.'[7] Koestler had become acting editor of the *BZ* and with the other chiefs was called in to a conference on policy regarding this issue. The meeting was important enough to be chaired by the Ullstein brothers personally. It was put to the meeting that as Haarmann was such an 'unsympathetic character', and as no one would wish to antagonize public opinion, the Ullstein papers should not support any request for clemency.

> As most of the editors already felt unsure of their jobs [because half of them were Jews], no one raised any objection. I remember that I murmured something about few murderers being sympathetic characters, but my words passed in polite silence. Thus without any fuss and in a few minutes a campaign which we had been waging for years and from the deepest conviction was abandoned. It was only one capitulation out of many, but it was the more significant for having no immediate political implications. We simply capitulated in the face of the rapidly-growing brutalization of the masses . . . That this was a question of basic ethics made me far angrier than if it had been a political question.

Haarmann was executed. Schoolchildren all over Germany had a little ditty about him. My father remembers it and can still sing it:

> *Warte, warte nur ein Weilchen,*
> *Bald kommt Haarmann auch zu dir.*
> *Mit dem kleinen Hackebeilchen*
> *Macht er Leberwurst aus dir.*

> (Just you wait a little while
> Soon Haarmann will pay you a visit.
> And with his little cleaver,
> He'll turn you into mincemeat.)

Among the cheaper amusements to be had in Berlin, away from the expensive hotel bars and restaurants, were the Lunapark, then and now a massive fairground, and the 'Resi' – a big café-bar with table telephones to enable single customers to get in touch with each other, or, via a waiter, to send a drink or a little present like a packet of cigarettes or chocolates to one another. 'We used to say that the "Resi" was the place where merry widows went to get picked up,' says Alfred Fischer. There was a telephone contact bar for younger people at the Turkish Café, and the Femina had one as well. The centre of the red-light district was the Oranienburger Strasse, which ran between Monbijou Platz and Oranienburger Tor.

> But there were plenty of other possibilities. For example, the club that Herr Wanselow ran in his flat, which was called the Aleifa (*Alles eine Familie –* All In The Family), which was a meeting place for every kind of sexual

contact – men with men, women with women, and women with men.[8]
Magnus Hirschfeld used to call Wanselow 'the father of beauty', after a
magazine Wanselow had once produced with that title. On National Boycott
Day (1 April 1933) an old Berliner friend of mine took an acquaintance to
the Aleifa, where he'd often been, but now Wanselow wouldn't let them in,
because they were Jews.

'But there were plenty of little clubs right up until the war which
catered to every possible taste,' another Berliner remembers. 'There was
one I used to go to where a woman danced with the men, having her but-
tocks naked. She had a specially-made dress. And if you couldn't find
what you wanted in the clubs, there were contact magazines, like *The
Grass Widow* and *Women Without Men*.'
Curt Riess recalls:

A frenzy for dancing seized the city. People made music everywhere, people
danced everywhere. And people were interested in spending, not saving:
inflation had taught them the futility of saving. *All* modern pop music was
called 'yats', which is how we pronounced 'jazz', and there was hardly a street
without its night-club, however small – six tables would be enough. Free
Love spiralled upwards. Cocaine became fashionable – all the hotel and
restaurant lavatory attendants sold it. And sexual perversion – albeit of a
mild kind – was equally chic. Homosexuality was so trendy that some pre-
tended to be, who were not. Walter Steinthal was the womanizing editor of
the *12-Uhr-Blatt* (similar to the British *Sun* newspaper). One day he was in
Schwannecke's bar boasting away to the actor Hans Heinrich von Twardowsky, who really was gay. Steinthal said he'd probably be able to sleep
with a boy, provided he was no older than 15, blond, and had a smooth body.
Von Twardowsky looked disgusted and retorted, 'You might as well sleep
with a woman!'

Guests at Magnus Hirschfeld's sixtieth birthday in 1928 included
Georg, Graf von Arco, who was Jewish on his mother's side. Arco, an
army officer, was a pioneer of wireless telegraphy and radio. Until 1930
he ran the multinational Telefunken; his wife presided over one of the
most distinguished salons in Berlin. The racist newspaper *Fridericus*
claimed that no Jew could have made the discoveries Arco had, and that
they had in fact been made by Robert von Lieben, a member of an old
German family. (If *Fridericus* had done its research, it would have found
out that Lieben was himself the son of a Jew, Leopold von Lieben, who
came from the Viennese 'new aristocracy' – so called – and was a banker
and the chairman of the stock-exchange.) Arco used to joke that
Hirschfeld would abandon his work if he were obliged to deal with
the sexual problems of women. He was a small man, but his wife was
Baroque. 'As the guests were presented at Hirschfeld's sixtieth,' writes

Alfred Fischer,[9] 'the Arcos were announced, to everyone's great amusement, as "Countess and Count".'

There was no formal law against lesbianism before the Third Reich, and despite Article 175 there were plenty of magazines catering for homosexual tastes on sale openly at every kiosk. The biggest and best gay club was the Eldorado, for men; the Oh La La catered for lesbians and prostitutes and for girls who were both. Bisexuals probably had the most fun of all. A young Viennese actor confessed happily, 'I'm a bit of a Don Juan in both directions'. Street prostitution grew as a direct result of unemployment and the economic crises at both ends of the Twenties. In the densely built-up newspaper district, women and girls used white handkerchiefs to wave invitations from their windows to men in the streets. Street-girls had all sorts of ways to indicate their specialities. 'Red shoes, for example, meant that you did discipline,' a *Berlinerin* told me. In 1933 there were 7,000 officially registered prostitutes in the city. The real total was nearer 25,000, including part-timers and amateurs. There were 8,000 pimps, of whom only a small proportion, about 15 per cent, belonged to organized criminal societies. Three thousand of the girls worked independently, but most of these had legitimate day-time jobs and worked as call-girls to supplement their incomes. The call-girl was a new variant of the oldest profession, made possible by the popular installation of the telephone after the First World War. There were girls in the windows in Markgrafenstrasse and Puttkamerstrasse. The pornographer Wilhelm Borngräber brought out his magazine *Reigen*, the title borrowed from Arthur Schnitzler's *succès de scandal*, his play *La Ronde*.

Massage parlours were notorious. Paul Morgan joked at the KaDeKo: 'Boys and girls, boys and girls, I thought I'd seen everything, but do you know what, the other day I went into a massage parlour and got – a *massage!*' The main haunt of transvestites was the Mikado Bar in Puttkamerstrasse, in Friedrichstadt South. As it was illegal to cross-dress on the streets, the police would lie in wait outside for a couple of quick arrests. It was in the nature of a joke: the next day, journalists would be bidden to the Alex to witness the 'girls'' release, still in their evening dresses, but with stubble growing through their make-up.

In September 1923 the Police President of Berlin tried to stem the moral ebb by introducing an order forbidding the presentation of nude dancing, or of female boxing and wrestling matches, 'insofar as these presentations have no artistic or sporting merit'.[10] But this order was no more enforceable than that forbidding dancing. Male transvestite prostitutes touted for custom quite openly, even along Unter den Linden, and those who could afford it would and did part with upwards of three-quarters of a *billion* marks for a bottle of champagne in one of the little private clubs where anything went.[11] That sum would have bought eight kilograms of butter on the official market.

Even Horst Wessel, at 21 the first Nazi 'martyr', and the writer of what became the National Socialist anthem, *Raise High the Flag*, was a pimp and a wastrel – built up into a national hero by Goebbels' propaganda. Wessel was the son of a Protestant army chaplain, but he had severed links with his family, abandoned his legal studies, and by 1929 was living with a prostitute called Erna Jännicke in a Friedrichshain tenement, from where he led the local SA unit. His value to Goebbels (once he was dead) was that he had broken with his bourgeois roots and committed himself to the 'great' National Socialist struggle. His 'martyrdom' came about like this: when Erna moved in with him, his landlady wanted to double the rent, but Wessel refused to pay. The landlady turned for help to a Communist cell she knew. One of their number, another pimp, Ali Höhler, went round to see Wessel and, in the course of a row, drew a revolver and shot him in the mouth.

Goebbels visited the hospital where for several days Wessel lay dying, in great agony. Issuing daily bulletins, he built up the credibility of this innocent victim, this courageous young *SA-Mann*, shot down in his prime by a ruthless Communist thug. When Wessel finally died, on 23 February 1930, the Nazis gave him a tremendous funeral. It was interrupted at the cemetery gates by a counter-demonstration of Communists bearing a banner reading 'A Last Heil Hitler to the Little Pimp Horst Wessel'.

In such an atmosphere, it is no wonder that people ceased to believe in anything. What is astonishing is that, in the midst of the chaos, the Prussian State Police and the Berlin Metropolitan Police maintained their integrity and behaved honourably, almost until the end. The Police Praesidium was known by various nicknames, from simply 'Alex', to 'The Red Villa' and 'Fat Maier'. In 1931, the Kriminalpolizei, the 'Kripo' (roughly, CID) numbered 1,810 officials, of whom 39 were women. In addition there were the uniformed Schutzpolizei, the 'Schupo', who numbered 10,600.

Ernst Gennat, whom we met over the Grossmann murders, had been promoted to Kriminalrat (Detective Chief Superintendent), and headed the Berliner Mordkommission. He owed his success to his pioneering work in forensic detection, and he is also remembered for forming the entire infrastructure of the Berlin police.[12] The 'crime car' he had built became one of the sights of Berlin. It was a six-seater Daimler-Benz; in the back was a mini-office, with two seats and a typewriter. The enormous, specially-adapted boot contained chemicals, searchlights, photographic equipment, tape-measures, town plans, large scale maps, and all sorts of tools, from diamond-cutters to pickaxes, as well as medical equipment for immediate, on-site forensic research. The boot was airtight. The car's springs were also modified: they had to be specially strengthened. Gennat habitually sat on the right rear passenger seat, and he weighed 170 kilograms (about 370 lbs). Even the driver was special: Patrolman Münchberg was the only man in Berlin at the time who could balance a car at speed on one side's wheels and keep it there. And this car – nicknamed 'Gennat's Toboggan' by the Berliners – was built like a tank.

Gennat achieved international fame, but two of his colleagues deserve recognition too. He could not have achieved what he did as Chief Superintendant without the support of his superior, the Police Vice-President of Berlin, Dr Bernhard Weiss. Weiss was a brilliant policeman, and a front-line veteran and reserve officer of the First World War, but he was also a Jew, and so was pilloried by Goebbels (who had not fought in the war because of his club foot). The other policeman was Arthur Nebe, whose complexity of character defies analysis. He joined the Nazi Party, as many did, from self-interest; he went on, however, not only to head the state criminal bureau and attain the rank of SS-*Obergruppen-führer*, but to command one of the infamous *Einsatztruppen* – special units which operated behind the front line in Poland and Russia, and were involved in the wholesale slaughter of Jews and intellectuals.[13] Notwithstanding this background, Nebe later became a prominent member of the Resistance to Hitler within German military and government circles. But that is another story.

Not all criminals presented quite such horrifying case histories as Grossmann and Haarmann. A more appealing character was Max Klante, who began his career soon after the end of the First World War. A neat little man with a carefully-trimmed moustache, white suit and boater, and flap ears, Max Klante understood what Berliners wanted: to thrive and survive. He started life as a broom-maker, then set up as a photographer, but finally found success betting on horses. Once he'd discovered this talent, he decided to buy a racing stables. To help him to this end, and to let others gain by his gift, he founded 'Max Klante Ltd' at the end of 1920. This company published a magazine, the *Meldereiter* (Racing News), in which Klante announced quite simply: 'Lend me a certain sum, whatever you can afford, on a regular monthly basis, and I will return it to you with 600 per cent interest.'

It may seem entirely fantastic, but Klante found plenty of customers, especially among blue-collar workers, who were happy to stake their life savings with him. He set himself up as their saviour: 'I will compensate those whom fate has handled roughly,' he announced. 'I will help all those whom the government has forgotten. They should have the same chances as the big capitalists . . . Fellow-countrymen, with your loans I will build factories and houses . . . together we will create a great co-operative of the people!'[14] At first everything went well. All that Klante had promised, he delivered. People showered him with their money. He took over an office building in Grosse Frankfurter Strasse, and queues of enthusiastic punters formed all day. His betting system seemed infallible. He opened a café next to his office block. A uniformed band played the *Max-Klante-March* and at mass meetings at the Zirkus Busch his supporters yelled '*Heil* Klante!'[15] At the beginning of 1921, when Hitler could count on about 900 supporters throughout Germany, Klante had 260,000 in Berlin alone.

Max's schemes brought him three cars, several villas, half-a-dozen mistresses, a string of jockeys in his blue and yellow livery, and a butler. But by the summer of 1921 he was having to borrow to fulfil his obligations – and that was the beginning of the end. He was arrested on 21 September: his creditors were owed about 92 million marks. It took them a year to gather all the evidence, and on 11 December 1922 his trial for fraud began. It was a sensation in itself: Max was brought into court borne on a litter; a lovelorn girl flung herself on him and had to be disentangled by force. As the public gallery was filled with his creditors, and inflation was already beginning to speed up, the tumult can be imagined. In the end he was sentenced to three years' imprisonment. The creditors had the small consolation of discovering during the following year that the financial hurricane would have wiped out their lost savings in any case.

Klante went back to being a broom-maker, and survived until 1955, when he committed suicide.

Berlin was a city of specialists – highly-trained skilled workers, tool-makers and mechanics. Some were safe-crackers. The Sass brothers were not only very good at this trade, but carried it on with a humour which rather endeared them to ordinary Berliners. Silence and no violence were their hallmarks, and they worked with such patience that many believed they earned what they took. One break-in was conducted from an unoccupied mezzanine room just above a night-watchman's lodge. The brothers took several nights to cut their way through to an adjoining strongroom, without once attracting the attention of the guard sitting immediately below. On another occasion they tunnelled under the pavement to gain entry to a bank, and when the police found the excavation later, they also discovered an empty cognac bottle, left behind but clean of any finger-prints. When the brothers appeared at the Grunewald race-track once, the band stopped playing and they were applauded by the crowd.

The Sass brothers kept one step ahead of the law, but when the Nazis came to power they moved to Denmark. There they undertook their boldest projects. They managed to involve themselves as craftsmen in the building of new banks and new bank security systems, adapting them so that when they chose to break in they could bypass without any trouble every technological obstacle placed in their path. They brought this off with particular *élan* at the new Copenhagen Girobank, and it was too much for the Danish police, who had them repatriated. The authorities in Moabit couldn't put together a case against them, but a rougher kind of justice prevailed in Germany by then and the brothers were 'shot while trying to escape'.

In the 1890s the Berlin underworld had begun to organize itself into 'clubs' which were more in the nature of unions, self-help or interest-protection groups. The first which appeared was dedicated to developing the physical fitness of its members, mainly through wrestling contests – hence the umbrella term for these societies, *Ringvereine*, or 'wrestling clubs'; their more or less formal 'cover' was as savings associations or social clubs. Originally there were about fifty, with a thousand members between them. The police had no objection; though the clubs protected the interests of certain areas of crime or certain areas of the city, they tended to be self-regulatory, and from the police point of view they also kept most of the black sheep under one easily identifiable roof. They were not as violent as the Chicago gangs during Prohibition, and would occasionally work with the police in bringing down a renegade outsider. The situation in Fritz Lang's film *M* is not far from reality.

Organization was good. You had to be over 21 to join, and be seconded by two members. Insurance was provided for families of members gaoled or killed; witnesses were drummed up to provide watertight alibis. Returning to freedom after a spell in prison, a club member could expect a formal reception at the prison gate, a welcome-back party and a lump sum to set him up in business again. Talismans were worn: after one year, a member received a 30-gram gold signet ring inscribed with the initials of the club; after two, he was given a gold fob watch; after five, a 10-carat diamond ring; and after eight, a 22-carat diamond. A member who died or was killed was given a most elaborate funeral by his comrades.

These clubs even had a press officer. This was Dr Artur Lansberger, a *literato* of good bourgeois Berlin stock and related to the newspaper-owning Ullstein family, who derived a healthy income from publishing pulp novels with Georg Müller in Munich. He was engaged at one time to Dolly Wertheim, the daughter of the department store giant; she wrote watery novels of Berlin society under the *nom de plume* 'Truth'. The engagement was broken off and Dolly threw herself from a window, but her fall was broken by a left-over Christmas tree. When the death of

Georg Müller brought an end to his pulp fiction income, Lansberger wrote a column about the underworld for the Ullsteins' *Berliner Zeitung am Mittag.*

The *Ringverein* also had their favourite *conférencier* – Harry Lamberts-Paulsen, who played the Weidenhof in Schiffbauerdamm and also commentated at the Sportpalast boxing-matches. As Harald Paulsen, he was the first Mack the Knife in Brecht's *Threepenny Opera.*

There is some disagreement, but the consensus is that the societies represented only 'respectable' areas of crime, and statistics about the make-up of their membership tend to bear this out. The élite were the safe-crackers (the head of the club in *M*, played by Gustav Gründgens, is a safe-cracker), the hierarchy descending through burglars to fraudsters and forgers, betting racketeers, loan sharks and protection agents. Pimps, like drug-pushers, formed only a small proportion of the total membership. Pushing drugs – especially *Koks* – was something everyone did, from tarts to war veterans; as often as not the pushers were also users, cocaine being the universal anodyne against the awfulness of life in Twenties Berlin, the poverty and the misery beneath the thin veneer of tinsel. The cry of the furtive hawker in his thin coat was *'Schnee? Navy Cut? Nackttänze gefällig?'* ('Wotcher after? Snow? Navy Cut? Nude dancing?'). Five marks would buy you a little packet of white powder, you'd snuff it up (*koksen*), and nine times out of ten nothing would happen, because you would have been sold powdered chalk.

The clubs and societies gave themselves high-falutin names: 'German Oak' had 1,600 members in 1929. Other examples were 'White Rose', 'Black Bear', 'Faith and Truth', 'Hand in Hand', and 'Forget-Me-Not'. Members aped bourgeois society, which many harboured an ambition to join one day as legitimate businessmen, or restaurateurs, or respectable night-club owners. The most distinguished club was 'German Strength', which always held its annual party at the Rheingold restaurant in Potsdamer Platz. Dress was formal, there was never any untoward behaviour, and guests of honour included such people as the Features Editor of the 'quality' *Berliner Tageblatt*, Fred Hildebrandt, or star defence lawyers like Max Alsberg and Erich Frey. As the high point of the evening a senior police officer, Superintendent Albert Dettmann perhaps, would conduct the band. But as the Twenties progressed, protection rackets based on Chicago methods grew out of some of these organizations, aimed at shop-keepers and, especially, bar-owners. Brecht drew on this development for his portrait of Hitler as a small-time hood who makes it big in *Arturo Ui*. One society formally sentenced two 'disloyal' members to death, informed them of the verdict in writing, and shot them down in the street. Inter-gang killings reached such a stage that a little street ditty became current, full of the usual black Berlin humour:

> There's a body in the Landwehr Canal
> Bring it here, bring it here!
> But don't hold it too tightly . . .
> (Because it'll fall apart!)

One group, the 'Friedrichshain Lottery Society', took matters beyond what the police could tolerate. In the late summer of 1928, two of its members mugged a cabinet-maker and robbed him of 2,000 marks. The men were soon picked up by the police; witnesses came forward to testify against them, but the society brought pressure to bear and they withdrew – all except one, who even took the anonymous death-threat letters he had received to the police. He was sent into hiding far from the headquarters of the society, and the police bided their time.

The Lottery Society left the centre of Berlin for a short visit to their summer headquarters at Schmöckwitz, a lakeside resort nineteen kilometres to the south-east of the city, where they were based at a pub called the Grosser Zug, accessible only by water. The police hit on the idea of sending a number of officers purporting to be an amateur male-voice choir from another society, the 'Solid As A Rock', to visit the Grosser Zug. Having sung a few numbers they folded up their song-sheets, whipped out their revolvers, and took their prisoners back to Berlin on board the steamer by which they'd arrived. But all the gangsters were let off for lack of evidence. The two muggers got three years each – but were looked after by their comrades. It was a very efficient freemasonry of crime.

Some relationships remained cordial. The two star lawyers, Alsberg and Frey, found themselves opposed to one another in court for the first time – another press sensation – defending two different criminal clubs in 1929. The clubs 'Forever True' and 'North' were in court following a drunken mêlée on 28 December 1928 at the Klosterkeller, between some Berlin workers and a group of Hamburg carpenters, in the course of which a member of the North club, an innocent bystander, was stabbed to death by one of the Hamburgers. Naturally this had to be avenged, and 'Muscles' Adolf of North's sister-club, Forever True, was engaged to mastermind the operation, which put seven badly-wounded Hamburgers into the Charité Hospital. One of them later died. In the course of the ensuing trial at the Moabit courts, Frey's fur coat was stolen. The coat was never recovered, and the thief was never discovered, but Forever True paid 2,500 marks for a replacement.[16] 'Muscles' Adolf and his associate, 'Beer' Albert, were acquitted, but the clubs were banned. Within a couple of months, however, Frey had had the ban lifted.

The clubs came to an end under the Nazis. Every former member was sent to the concentration camps with a 'green triangle' (denoting a criminal inmate – politicals wore red triangles, and Jews, yellow).[17] Ironically, during the period between May 1927 and March 1928, when the NSDAP and the SA were banned in Berlin, the SA set up all sorts of camouflaged clubs, after the manner of the criminal societies, to keep their organization together. There were the swimming clubs 'A Good Wetting' and 'The High Wave', and the bowling clubs 'Good Wood' and 'Nine at a Stroke', for example. At first the original societies thought they were in for some unpleasant competition, but quickly dismissed the new clubs as 'more crap from them crazy brownshirts'.

NOON

Berlin, the capital both of the German State and of Prussia,
lies at 13°23' longitude east of Greenwich, and at 52°30'
latitude north, on the navigable Spree, at 34–49 metres above
sea level. The community of Greater Berlin, which has been
in existence since 1st October 1920, embraces the eight towns
of Berlin, Charlottenburg, Köpenick, Lichtenberg, Neukölln,
Schöneberg, Spandau and Wilmersdorf, as well as 59 local
boroughs (Steglitz, Pankow, Lichterfelde, Weissensee,
Friedenau, etc.) and 28 districts. Including its lakes and
woods, Greater Berlin covers a total area of 878 square
kilometres. With (1925) 4,030,818 inhabitants, of whom
132,128 are foreigners, it is the third largest city in the world
after Greater New York (8 million) and Greater London (7.47
million). In 1910, 82.7% of the inhabitants were Protestant,
11.1% Roman Catholic, 3.8% Jewish.

Baedekers Berlin und Umgebung, Karl Baedeker,
Leipzig, 1927.

This city devoured talents and human energies with a
ravenous appetite, grinding them small, digesting them, or
rapidly spitting them out again. It sucked into itself with
hurricane force all the ambitious in Germany, the true and
the false, the nonentities and the prizewinners, and, after it
had swallowed them, ignored them. People discussed Berlin
only if its spheres of influence remained impregnable to their
advances, as if the city were a highly desirable woman whose
coldness and capriciousness were well known: the less chance
anyone had to win her, the more they decried her.

Carl Zuckmayer, *A Part of Myself*
(translated by Richard and Clara Winston)

7 In the Jungle of the Cities

IN HIS JOURNAL for 17 July 1925, Arnold Bennett quoted Rudolf Kommer, who was Max Reinhardt's manager for America. 'In Berlin,' he said, 'if you wanted to make a scandal in the theatre, you had to have a mother committing incest with *two sons*; one wasn't enough!' And indeed, the revolt of sons against fathers was a principal theme of the new Expressionist iconoclasts writing for the post-war theatre. A new kind of drama required new, non-naturalistic acting styles, which in turn demanded a new generation of directors, designers, actors and intendants. (An intendant was – and is – the overall director of a theatre: the job combines artistic and administrative roles. In Wilhelmine Germany such posts had frequently been given to senior army officers as civic appointments; their lack of experience or even of interest in the theatre had not mattered as long as it had remained essentially an amusement. Problems arose, though, when it became something more than that.) Avant-garde directors such as Berthold Brecht and Erwin Piscator worked with great designers: Brecht with Caspar Neher, Piscator with Traugott Müller.[1]

The man who raised the position of the director to one of power was Max Reinhardt. He transformed the role from that of organizer to that of artist. His sets were prodigious, extravagant cadenzas on reality; once he ordered a library to be built of real mahogany because cheaper wood stained in imitation didn't give the required sense of massiveness. He was a master of spectacle. His casts were huge and his crowd scenes a byword, influencing not only Ernst Lubitsch but even Fritz Lang. In 1919 he opened the Grosses Schauspielhaus (the former Zirkus Schumann) with a production of the *Oresteia*. It was practically a national event. Reinhardt's plan for his massive theatre-in-the-round was that it would become a centre – *the* centre – for new post-war drama. Fritz Engel wrote: 'Even the building itself offers tantalizing secrets and the expectancy of wonders . . . You could see fascination and admiration on every face, especially with the ceiling and the dome, which looked like the inside of an icicle cave.' Carl Zuckmayer gives an interesting glimpse of Reinhardt at work:

> Reinhardt staged Shaw's *St Joan* with Elisabeth Bergner – the German opening took place a few days earlier than the opening in London – and Pirandello's *Six Characters in Search of an Author*. Many of the great actors of Berlin were on the stage at that time, and I sat at rehearsals excited and fascinated, watching Reinhardt spin his magic. I took in every minute phase in the transformation from the first concept of a part or a scene to its full realization. All this was particularly instructive because Reinhardt . . . would dictate enormously comprehensive director's notes in which all the details of his production plan, down to the intonation and pantomime to accompany specific sentences, were entered in a language that sometimes sounded borrowed from trashy novels: 'A woeful twitch of sorrow appears on his face', or 'Her hand darts involuntarily to her heart', and so on.[2]

Zuckmayer and Berthold Brecht were, surprisingly, once engaged by Reinhardt as play-readers for his theatres, though they do not appear to have done much serious work: 'Brecht did not even make a pretence of working,' wrote Zuckmayer.

> Occasionally he turned up in the theatre and demanded dictatorial powers. Every so often I would actually read a play – I recall reading the manuscript of a comedy by Robert Musil. Since I was an admirer of Musil – sections of *The Man Without Qualities* had already been published in magazines – I started on the play with great respect, but found it involved and loquacious. I left the manuscript . . . for Brecht, asking him his opinion. Next day I found it; he had scrawled in pencil across the envelope, 'Shit'. That was one of our formidable attempts as play-readers.[3]

Reinhardt, unlike many of his colleagues, had no interest in politics. But he was a Jew. The Nazis called him 'the Jew Goldmann', because that was his family name, and he was to become one of their most prominent victims. Neither he nor his second wife Helene Thimig had at first any idea of what Hitler's rise would mean for them. Later, when they were obliged to leave Germany, they discovered Nazism's incompatibility with either art or loyalty. Helene Thimig recalled a last visit to one of Berlin's theatres, shortly before leaving to join Max in Florence. 'I walked into the auditorium and saw that they were rehearsing in great haste one of the first Nazi plays. At the centre of the stage was an enormous swastika flag, and it was surrounded by people on their knees, doing it reverence. Appalling. And appallingly *kitsch*. That was my last impression of Berlin.' Another betrayal was to follow. The Nazis persuaded the actor Werner Krauss publicly to denounce Max and his brother Edmund. Earlier, they had sent Krauss to Reinhardt, who had always been fond of him, with the offer of 'honorary Aryan' status; but this Reinhardt had refused. Forced into exile in 1933, he bequeathed his life's work to the German people in a long, dignified open letter. Reinhardt's theatres were confiscated. On a lecture tour abroad he wrote to Goebbels from Oxford: 'Not only do I lose . . . the fruits of 37 years of work, much more, I lose the very earth that has nurtured me all my life. I lose my homeland . . .'

Reinhardt settled in America but was never able to rebuild his life as an artist. He died in New York in 1943. In Vienna after the Second World War, Helene Thimig was reconciled to Werner Krauss.

Though it was politics that ended Reinhardt's career, his artistic domination had been challenged since immediately after the First World War. The man who definitively brought theatrical revolution to Berlin was Leopold Jessner. Jessner's work *was* political, and his politics were uncompromisingly Republican. The Jessner trademark was a flight of steps, always dominating and sometimes occupying the whole stage. The steps became a metaphor, and the relative position on them of characters to one another reinforced their spiritual and social relationships. Jessner also used powerful colour, especially in his early, Expressionist days when his powers were at their height. Green covered the stage for *William Tell*; for Shakespeare's *Richard III* it was soaked in red. Jessner was not much interested in individuals, or even in history; he was interested in bringing out a play's relevance to its audience, and its political message for his own time. *Tell* was a production in praise of righteous revolution, put on in the middle of what Jessner held to be one. His *Richard* was about power-mongering and career-building.

Jessner took up residence at the Staatstheater – the Theater am Gendarmenmarkt, the former Königliches Schauspielhaus. (Schinkel's great building still stands, on what is now called the Platz der Akademie.) His stewardship of so important a theatre was in itself a triumphant return after years deliberately spent, away from Reinhardt's 'kingdom', in Hamburg and Königsberg. His reputation was by then so great that Fritz Kortner, who was to become his leading man, went to unusual lengths to meet him.

I was still in Hamburg when I heard of his appointment and I set off immediately for Berlin, where I . . . learnt that he was leaving quite early the next morning for Königsberg . . . The next morning found me at the Königsberg platform. I had heard of his plans to produce the great classics and I had to tell him as positively as possible how much I wanted to act in them for him – so positively that even in the hurry of departure he would not be able to ignore me . . . He arrived a few minutes before departure, running the length of the train looking for his porter. I ran alongside him and, out of breath, told him my intentions. He was amused and without relaxing his pace told me I might have chosen a more suitable moment. Then he caught sight of his porter and hastily climbed aboard . . . He appeared at the window and the porter handed his luggage up to him at great speed . . . The train started to move slowly and I ran alongside it. Finally he leant forward and called: 'Go to the Dorotheenstrasse tomorrow. They'll give you a contract. I'll let them know by telegram.' Then he waved and gave me a warm, good-natured smile. I stood there and gazed after the already vanishing train.

William Tell was the production that made Kortner's name. It opened on 12 December 1919 and caused a storm. Schiller is one of Germany's classical writers, and here he was being treated in a way that had never been contemplated before. Detail and human psychology were swept away in favour of symbolism – of gesture, of set, of lighting and of colour. His patriotic lines on the 'fatherland' were cut, and the Austrian tyrant Gessler was portrayed as a uniformed, medal-clanking, red-faced *Junker*. As both Jessner and Kortner (who played Gessler) were Jews, anti-Semites tried to break up the evening by heckling, until they were quashed by an outburst from Albert Bassermann, playing Tell. '*Schmeisst doch die bezahlten Lümmel aus!*' he bellowed: 'Throw out these hired troublemakers!'

Within a year of Jessner's return, Reinhardt moved back for a time to Vienna, from where he had arrived a quarter of a century earlier. Recognizing that he was no longer king, he went consciously into exile. But just as Reinhardt was returning to Austria, many of the talents that went to form the backbone of theatre in the Twenties were travelling the other way – among them Kortner, the director Jürgen Fehling, and the critic Herbert Ihering.[4] Rivalry sprang up between Vienna and Berlin, just as there was rivalry between the theatre companies of Berlin itself. Rivalry provided a stimulus for creative activity, as did the insecurity of the post-war years. The main rivalry was that between the glittering 'stagey' productions of the Deutsches Theater, Max Reinhardt's earlier fief, whose traditions were continued by his lieutenant, Felix Holländer, and the Staatstheater, where the stress was on themes within plays, laid down by the director. This was a rivalry between the heart and the head. There were fifty theatres in Berlin and the turnover of plays was generally very fast. The energy produced by the competition between them led very quickly to the city's establishment after the First World War as the theatrical capital of Germany. Artists of great quality came from the good theatres in the provinces: from Frankfurt, Nuremberg, Munich, Dresden, and Hamburg. Actors could become stars overnight – Fritz Kortner, Gustav Gründgens and Käthe Dorsch all did –

and they knew that if they could make it in Berlin, they could make it anywhere.

As Expressionism began to lose its impetus in the early Twenties, new talents began to make themselves heard. Brecht's play *In the Jungle of the Cities* was put on in Munich, and soon afterwards he joined a group of young writers, including Carl Zuckmayer, gathered around Moritz Seeler in Berlin. Brecht for one eschewed the monocle-and-bow-tie image associated with the literary man, and made his clothes a form of rebellion too. He wore a flat cap, a leather blouson jacket, and steel-rimmed spectacles. He smoked cheap cigars and omitted to wash or shave regularly. He was also a good actor in his own right, and when he sang his songs in a reedy tenor, accompanying himself on the guitar, women were said to have fainted with pleasure. Since he was an inveterate womanizer all his life, he and his wife, Helene Weigel, agreed to live on separate floors of their house in Chausseestrasse.

New plays sought to overthrow old values with violence, and a theatre of brutality developed. Other groups appeared alongside Seeler's so-called Young Stage. The Troupe was founded by Bertold Viertel; The Actors' Theatre by Heinrich George and Karl-Heinz Martin. And though his headquarters remained in Vienna, within a short time Reinhardt was back with a series of productions of plays by foreign authors – Pirandello, O'Neill, O'Casey, Claudel; he directed the world première of George Bernard Shaw's *St Joan*. Shaw was popular in Germany – though the Nazis later condemned him, on account of his conscious intellectualism and his red hair, as a Jew. As the Twenties progressed, the spare stark plays of Brecht were tempered by Zuckmayer's wild successes – *The Merry Vineyard* of 1925, and *The Captain of Köpenick* of 1931.

Zuckmayer made his name with *The Merry Vineyard*, a folk-play *par excellence*. It was a sensational success, won the Kleist Prize for 1925, and ran in Berlin for two and a half years, besides spawning 500 further productions. Zuckmayer made a fortune out of the play, thanks to the acuity of his agent, Julius Elias; he had been in danger of selling all rights to the impresario Saltenburg for 20,000 marks.[5] Winning the Kleist Prize enabled him to take his wife for a celebration at his favourite restaurant, Hacker's, where he intended also to pay off his accumulated debts. When the time came to pay, though, Herr Hacker appeared personally at their table, tore up all 'Zuck's' bills, and said with a bow, 'A man who wins the Kleist Prize has no debts.'

Only the Nazis responded badly: 'The play has a quite unbelievably stupid plot, and it mocks Christian values, German customs, the German Woman, the German War Wounded, German Officialdom in the meanest way.' Certainly *The Merry Vineyard* was a breath of fresh air to the public. 'One laughed oneself healthy,' wrote the critic Arthur Eloesser. Another, the great Alfred Kerr, commented pithily, *'sic transit expressionismi'*.

The Captain of Köpenick satirizes a German weakness, blind obedience to a uniform. The story, suggested to Zuckmayer by Fritz Kortner and based on a real event of 1906, is this: the cobbler Wilhelm Voigt, released from prison, finds it impossible to re-establish himself in society without an identity document. He has the idea of raiding the town hall of the little town (now a suburb) of Köpenick on the south-east side of Berlin to get one. He obtains a military uniform from a pawnshop, takes over a detachment of soldiers, and puts his plan into effect. Everyone obeys him – or rather, the uniform – and he is only frustrated when it appears that Köpenick is too small to issue identity documents. (The real Voigt had attempted to abscond with the town hall's cashbox.) The play ends with the Kaiser's amusement at the story, and Voigt's pardon. Zuckmayer's delicacy made it the play of the decade. With a rapier he accomplished as much as Brecht ever did with a sabre.

The times were vigorous – there was no let-up. After the revolution came the Kapp *putsch*; the murders of Liebknecht and Luxemburg were followed by the murder of Rathenau and the Hitler *putsch*; underlying all were inflation, and, despite a liberal and democratic government, gross social injustice, murder and violence were never far away. Artistic influences ranged from *Battleship Potemkin*, which was so popular that the government trembled, to the films of Charlie Chaplin, whose Tramp took Berlin by storm in the 1920s.[6] Never was ground more fertile for the theatrical voice to be heard, or for theatrical experiment.

Brecht may have been a great ideological borrower, plagiarist and adapter of other people's ideas, but he was also the man to identify and give form to the new voice of the theatre, and he met a kindred political and artistic spirit in the Communist director Erwin Piscator. Piscator had returned from the war confused and shattered. Already in 1919, aged 26, he had founded a Proletarian Theatre, and made some contact with the Berlin Dadaists, but he had spent the winter season as an actor at Königsberg, where he had opened his first real theatre and done plays by Strindberg and Wedekind. When this venture failed, he returned to Berlin and, with financial support from the Communist Party and the Independent Socialists, he re-formed his Proletarian Theatre, which he ran until it was closed by the police in April 1921. He played various halls and assembly rooms in working-class districts, mainly with agit-prop and Left-orientated plays. 'You could describe him as a spontaneous Marxist,' says Walter Huder, the founder of the Berlin Akademie der Künste.

The First World War had driven him, like many others, towards Communism, because it represented the values of humanity over against the bankrupt and merciless values of imperialism. Returning, he saw that productions had been directed in a bourgeois idiom, and bourgeois values were represented. The classics – Schiller, Goethe, Shakespeare – needed to be reinterpreted; and there needed to be a whole new theatre technique to encompass this. He needed to take his theatre to the suburbs, to the workers' districts, to halls, and not stay in the centre, in conventional theatres, where police checked the content. He wanted to agitate. His production of Schiller's *The Robbers* was agitation against the bourgeoisie. It represented the struggle of a group of militant humanists: that was how he saw Schiller's robbers. He even gave the iconoclastic robber, Spiegelberg, the mask of Lenin. But the workers didn't take to his work; it didn't *look* like theatre. So he hit upon the idea of taking bed linen, stretching it like screens, and projecting images onto it – not romantic images, but symbolic ones. A crane, for example, or a locomotive. His work was reminiscent of the experiments of Maleevich, of the Futurists, who went back to simple forms to rebuild art afresh.

Piscator's pacifist views found their outlet in his famous production of Jaroslav Hašek's *The Good Soldier Schweik*. His concept of Schweik was as 'a profoundly asocial element . . . a great sceptic, who though always saying yes stubbornly to everything ends up by denying the lot.' Some of the inspiration for the role, in which the comic actor Max Pallenberg shone as never before, lay with Charlie Chaplin's Tramp, the little irrepressible man set against the world, who found great sympathy in Germany.

Piscator became very inventive in the matter of stage lighting and design as a result of having to solve practical problems of staging in the halls where he first worked, taking theatre to the people. Without question, many of Brecht's ideas on these followed his lead. Piscator could direct mass scenes as well as Reinhardt, and his conviction and innovatory power were unique. He introduced film sequences into his productions, and was the first to use a conveyor belt on-stage so that a static wheelchair (in *Schweik*) would appear to be moving along. George Grosz produced about three hundred satirical drawings to be used as slide projections for *Schweik* (they were later the subject of a blasphemy suit brought against Grosz by the state). But Piscator never quite had Jessner's sureness or subtlety of touch. And because of ideological differences, he and Brecht were never entirely easy collaborators. Though they enriched each other's creativity, and their principles were the same ('The theatre is not a mirror of the times,' said Piscator, 'but a means by which the times can be changed'), they did not work together often.

It is interesting to compare Piscator and Brecht as directors, since Brecht was of course a director as well as a playwright. This is the view of the actress Steffie Spira: 'Erwin was an inexorable director. I remember rehearsals for Grabbe's *Gewitter Über Gothland*. There's a scene where a soldier has to enter and say something like, "Here I stand, the first to set foot in Gothland". That's all. Piscator rehearsed the scene for two solid days. It was enough to drive everyone mad, and to have to work like that undermined one's confidence as an actor. I think warmth and friendliness in a director gets a lot more out of a performance. You could always talk to Brecht; he always had time for you, and if you had an idea for your character, he'd let you try it out, so you felt that you were contributing creatively to the production, instead of just being told what to do.' (Steffie scored such a notable hit as the dumb sister in the original production of *Mann ist Mann* that a jealous Helene Weigel had Brecht remove the part from the play!)

Walter Huder, who worked as Brecht's assistant at the Berliner Ensemble in the years following the Second World War, remembers: 'Brecht would always discuss ideas with the cast democratically. Of course he knew what he wanted, and how he wanted the scenes to develop, so he steered all discussions towards his goals, but subtly, so that the actors were encouraged, as it were, to think his thought for themselves, without knowing that they were being led.' He adds: 'Brecht was like this: you couldn't bother him when he was busy; you had to judge your moment to approach him. But when he wasn't busy, he would gladly and always make time to listen to you.'[7]

Although by 1922 Brecht had already made his mark, winning (at 23) the prestigious Kleist Prize for *Drums in the Night*, his greatest success had to wait until 1928. Ernst Josef Aufricht, a rich and successful actor who wished to produce, had taken over the Theater am Schiffbauerdamm and was casting around for a new play to open it with. What appeared, on 31 August 1928, after a nightmarish rehearsal period and unheard-of difficulties, was Brecht's reworking of John Gay's *The Beggar's Opera*, which he called *Riff-Raff*, a title he changed at the last minute to one suggested by his friend Lion Feuchtwanger: *The Threepenny Opera*.

There were last-minute problems with the cast. Peter Lorre and Helene Weigel fell ill and had to be replaced; Carola Neher dropped out when her husband, the poet Klabund, finally succumbed to the TB which had plagued him all his life. But the play, which introduced Brecht's new epic style with a forcefulness that belied the speed with which he had written and the difficulties which had beset him, was a triumph. Lotte Lenya, who played Honky-Tonk Jenny, wrote famously of the First Night: 'Up until the second scene it looked as if we had a failure on our hands. Then came the Cannon Song. There was an unbelievable storm from the auditorium. The public roared. From that moment on we couldn't go wrong . . .' The role made Lotte Lenya, despite the fact that owing to an oversight her name was left off the programme. A furious Kurt Weill (whose first – far from easy – collaboration with Brecht this was) had to see that a corrigendum was stuck into every copy before the curtain went up the next night. The famous 'Mack-the-Knife' song, the *Moritat*, was composed by Weill over-night and at the last moment, as Harald Paulsen, who played Mackie, had insisted on something right at the beginning to establish his character.

The Threepenny Opera became the rage of Berlin. The Nazi critic of the *Neue Preussische Kreuz-Zeitung* wrote the only unfavourable notice: 'An absolute nothing. To be recommended to chronic insomniacs as a cure.' Harry Kessler wrote on 27 September 1928: 'A gripping perform-ance, Piscator-ish and primitive and self-consciously proletarian in the Apache style. Weill's music is catchy and expressive, the actors (Harald Paulsen, Rosa Valetti, etc.) brilliant. It's the play of the moment, sold out solidly . . . "one simply has to have seen it".' A month later, on 30 October, Kessler met Brecht at Piscator's beautiful flat (decorated by Walter Gropius). 'Striking, decadent-looking man. Has almost the physiognomy of a crook, very dark, black hair, black eyes, dark skin, with a lowering expression: almost the typical villain. But when you talk to him he thaws, he's almost naïve.'

In the autumn of 1929, Nero-Film negotiated a movie of *The Three-penny Opera* and signed Brecht and Weill to write the screenplay and the score. G. W. Pabst was engaged to direct. Since writing the original piece, Brecht had moved significantly further Left, and his screenplay reflected the change. As in the later *Threepenny Novel*, Mack the Knife is transformed from gangster into banker, and the rest of the plot is adapted to fit a much more austere and Marxist critique. The film-makers wouldn't accept the changes, but Brecht dug in his heels. The matter came to a head in a court case in October 1930, which afforded Berlin another theatrical sensation. Brecht made his firmness of purpose plain, but finally gave in when Nero offered him and Weill a generous settlement on condition that they would not block the film. Alfred Fischer interviewed him at the time.[8]

Brecht used to write all his appointments on a vast blackboard in his flat. I remember seeing my name up there when I went to interview him about the *Threepenny Opera* affair. This was before Nero had offered the settlement, and he told me very passionately that 'No money in the world would ever persuade Weill and myself to allow this scandalous work to appear on the screen!' In the end, though, Nero paid off Brecht and Weill with 100,000 marks between them. In those days Brecht came across as an ascetic, womanizer though he was. He was increasingly left-wing, but he knew exactly what course he was on and how to steer it. He and Weill could be forgiven for relenting when they heard about Nero's offer, because 100,000 marks was a huge amount of money in those days. Jarres, the *Oberbürgermeister* of Düsseldorf, who was once a candidate for the presidency, claimed that he was entirely incorruptible precisely because his salary was 100,000.

Because of its much greater political commitment there, theatre has in the past been a more potent force for change in Germany than in the United States or Britain. Georg Kaiser's two *Gas* plays and Peter Martin Lampel's *Giftgas Über Berlin* (Poison Gas over Berlin) are visions of a bleak, mechanized and depersonalized big city, and its effect on its inhabitants. Hans Rehfisch's *Skandal in Amerika* and Lion Feuchtwanger's *Petrol Island* deal with the power of oil in world economics and politics. Arnolt Bronnen's life was itself a curious reflection of his times and of Germany. He was born in Vienna in 1895, and came to Berlin as a young man. It was of his early work and not Brecht's that the term 'epic theatre' was first used. His play *Patricide*, written in 1915, caused a riot when it was produced in Berlin in 1922. It takes Hasenclever's *The Son* a stage further – the son sleeps with his mother, kills his father, rejects his mother. By the time he wrote *Rheinische Rebellen* (Rheinland Rebels) in 1925, as a reaction to the French occupation of the Rheinland, Bronnen was moving towards the Right, and later he became an active supporter of the NSDAP. After the Second World War he swung left again, however, and ended his days as a theatre critic in East Berlin.

Many of the leaders of German theatre during the Weimar Republic were Jews – Jessner, Reinhardt, the Rotter brothers (who ran a chain of rather reviled popular theatres), Kortner, and Bergner. The NSDAP declared war on them at a very early stage, and they were among the first to depart once the Nazis had come to power. Actors married to Jews, like Max Pallenberg and Tilla Durieux, also chose to leave, though their status might have protected their spouses. Many other artists joined the Jews in exile; but some stayed behind and, if they did not support the Nazis, came to terms with them. The pros and cons of their moral position are still hotly debated. Arnolt Bronnen continued to write under the Nazis, and Hanns Johst became a kind of unofficial playwright-laureate.

The critic Herbert Ihering also stayed. His arch-rival, Alfred Kerr, the Grand Old Man of Berlin theatre criticism, was a Jew, and left for London soon after Hitler had become Chancellor. Unpleasant cartoons followed his departure. Ihering and Kerr disagreed over Brecht's plays, which Ihering enthusiastically supported and Kerr more or less consistently damned. Ihering's columns were serious, often proselytizing; Kerr's were quirky, telegraphic, often arrogant, usually fair. The Berlin press took the theatre very seriously. A newspaper might print a review, and then print revised versions in the light of later performances. Kerr had great power: he could make or break an actor, director, or playwright. He would arrive well before curtain up, taking his habitual third-row seat, and survey the auditorium like a king his realm. He dressed in an old-fashioned morning coat and high-necked waistcoat, and tilted his huge chin arrogantly upwards. Unfortunately, Kerr used German in so original and individual a way that he is almost impossible to translate without a loss of *brio*: for this defect in what follows, I apologize.

I.
The evening belonged to: Dorsch.
   Germany's theatres have one more recruit. One more strength. One more force.
One more plant. One more big number. One more soul.

'Ihering was a Savonarola of theatre criticism,' remembers Hans Sahl. 'But Kerr was an Escoffier.' Kessler, though, had no time for him. When Kerr referred to Hölderlin as a 'melody in trousers' (the phrase is just as infelicitous in German), Kessler remarked drily that it was a pity Le Pétomane was no longer alive – 'otherwise he could have greeted Hölderlin as a colleague'. For all Kessler's scorn, actors certainly cared what Kerr wrote. Roma Bahn, who played Polly in the first *Threepenny Opera*, remembered not infrequently waiting up all night after a première, in Schwannecke's bar with her colleagues, for his review to appear when the *Berliner Tageblatt* came out at 6 a.m. Others even went to the stations at 3 a.m., when the *BT* was being loaded onto trains bound for the provinces, and bribed the porters to give them an advance copy.
   Alfred Fischer remembers Kerr as

> . . . not as majestic personally as he is so often depicted. I met him when I interviewed his children and he sat by and was tremendously pleased and proud. He talked to me afterwards and, as was his nature, very generously offered to give me all the help he could if ever I needed it. And just before he left Germany in 1933, he made two very brave broadcasts against the NSDAP. But he could also be extremely aloof. He kept himself apart from actors as much as possible, partly out of snobbery and partly for professional reasons . . .

Kerr spent the war in London, where he became president of German PEN in exile. Returning to Hamburg in 1947, he immediately went to the theatre to see a production of *Romeo and Juliet*, in the course of which he suffered a stroke. ('I've never seen the play done so badly,' he joked later.) The attack left him half paralysed, and on 12 October 1948, aged 81, he took an overdose of Veronal in Berlin. 'I loved life greatly,' he had written to his son Michael, 'but I ended it when it became a torture.'[9]

'Ihering was quick and sly like a fox,' remembers Hans Sahl. 'He didn't have such a good seat as Kerr, and would observe the play through opera glasses, like a general watching a battle from a redoubt.' Ihering and Kerr led a field of excellent theatre critics. It was not unusual for a critic to become a director, or vice-versa. The theatre critic on a Berlin paper enjoyed a position of far greater importance than he does (or did) on a British one. Emil Faktor, the theatre critic of the best of the Berlin papers, the *Börsen-Courier*, was also its editor-in-chief.

The Berlin of our period was a star-struck city, and was entertained by some of the most memorable actors and actresses Germany has produced. 'My best memories of the theatre all have to do with Elisabeth Bergner,' remembers the journalist and theatre critic Arnold Bauer.[10] 'We used to hang around her house for hours in the hope of an interview. I even rang her up to ask for her autograph, but she hung up on me!' His admiration was shared by Boleslaw Barlog, then a stage-struck young man, but after the Second World War intendant of the Schiller Theater. 'My God, she was beautiful! I saw her as Rosalind in *As You Like It* at the Lessing Theater, directed by Barnowsky; and I fell so hopelessly in love with her that I saw the production a dozen times with a standing-room ticket.' Barlog, now the most charming and ebullient 85-year-old, was a great romantic. On another occasion, when he was 23, he lay down in the street in front of Carola Neher's car in order to oblige her to hear his declaration of love before she could drive off.

Arnold Bauer also remembers the 'great performances' of Heinrich George as Peer Gynt, and Gustav Gründgens as Mephisto.

I think Gründgens is much maligned. Sure, he made his name under the Nazis, but he did what he could within his company to keep real artistic intergrity alive, and he was able to protect the Jews and half-Jews in the theatre too, because he had the ear of Emmy Sonnemann. She ended up married to Göring – and the *Reichmarschall* was quite able to pick and choose which Jews could be spared the fate devised for them, though it became more difficult after 1942, when the Final Solution had been formalized. As for Emmy Sonnemann, she was a simple provincial actress; she'd been the juvenile lead in Weimar, and she had a middling talent. I'd say she was quite a good-hearted woman, not terribly bright. She had lots of sympathy for Gründgens.[11]

Steffie Spira, whose parents were both 'in the business', appeared as Hymen in Viktor Barnowsky's *As You Like It*. 'I was the beginner, the newcomer, and my dressing-room was up on the third floor . . . On the First Night Elisabeth Bergner came up to my dressing-room to do my make-up for me. It was a tradition in the theatre then – that the star did the newcomer's make-up on the First Night.'[12] Viktor Barnowsky

himself had had a different way of welcoming her when she first joined
his company: 'I remember my costume was a heavy velvet dress which
was very low-cut. I was seventeen, very excited and rather nervous. I
wasn't on until the second act but I went down to the stage and stood
at the back by the cyclorama to listen. Barnowsky was there too, pacing
up and down in soft-soled shoes. Suddenly he appeared to notice me for
the first time, came over, and without more ado plunged his hand into
my bosom. I gave him a slap, which luckily didn't make too much noise.
He grinned, and said: "Just like your mother!" '

In 1929 Georg Kaiser's play *Two Neckties* was produced at the Berliner
Theater. It was an enormous popular success, with Hans Albers in the
leading role, supported by, among others, a rather plump and unsophisticated Marlene Dietrich. Steffie Spira was also in it.

> This comedy hinged upon a waiter swapping his black tie with a guest in a
> fashionable restaurant in order to save the latter's bacon: the theme was a
> variation on the uniform joke – only waiters wear black tie with tails, so the
> guest to escape his pursuers dons a black tie and that's disguise enough for
> him to be overlooked. Hans Albers played the waiter. Also in the cast in a
> minor role was the spoilt and empty-headed son of the Tomaselli coffee
> family. As a joke the rest of the company – unknown to Albers – told young
> Tomaselli that it was the latest fashion to wear black tie with tails, and he
> should do so. Well, he did so without a thought – and Albers was, as
> expected, furious – he should have been the only one on stage in a black tie!
> In the end we had to explain the whole thing to him because the poor
> wardrobe-master nearly got the sack on account of it.

Steffie joined the Communist Party in 1931, in response to the conditions of the time – unemployment was rising at about the same speed as
the influence of the NSDAP. 'There was no such thing as the "Golden
Twenties". It was something dreamt up by journalists for foreigners.
There was glitter and there was fun – but only in tiny pockets, and
twenty metres away there was reality. Not that we didn't enjoy ourselves;
we had great dances at home with the gramophone. We went to the
theatre and to cabaret when we were working there, but not as
customers – it was too expensive.'

She joined *Truppe 31* and played in the Communist revue, *The
Mousetrap*, at the Kleines Theater in Unter den Linden, where Max
Reinhardt had had his first Schall und Rauch cabaret in 1901. 'The
theatre was owned by the Swedish match millionaire, Ivan Kreuger, who
told us how pleased he was that was it was being used for proper theatre;
that he was a little tired of seeing it just rented out to sex-shows!'[13] The
revue was a success all over Europe, wherever they toured it, but 'We had
fights, real fights, with the Nazis. We weren't intimidated. We'd play
to workers in their canteens, and we'd go out at night to stick up

Communist propaganda notices, going out in twos and pretending to be lovers in order not to arouse suspicion. After 1930 the SA were to be seen everywhere. It was very bitter.'

Walter Huder knew Lotte Lenya, of whom he remembers that 'she was a natural talent. She couldn't read a note, but she had perfect pitch. And she was a lovely person, with great politeness and delicacy. After the war, she came to stay with us, and we took her to the airport at the end of her visit. By the time we returned home there was a telegram from her thanking us for her stay. She'd sent it from the airport. That was what she was like. She was fantastic . . .'

> She was a great friend of Margarete Kaiser – the wife of Georg Kaiser. Lotte got to know Kurt Weill in the Kaisers' flat. There used to be an informal literary club there in the evenings, which Brecht also attended. At that time Kurt Weill was living in a small furnished room and played the piano at night in a bar in the Friedrichstrasse to earn some extra cash. There was a piano at the Kaisers' flat which was never used, and their friend the conductor Fritz Spiegel also knew Weill, and knew that he was in need of a piano to sit and compose at. He got Kaiser to let Weill use the piano in his flat during the daytime, and that's where he composed *The Threepenny Opera*.

The story goes that Lotte and Kurt Weill fell in love at the Kaisers' summer house at Grünheide – and that is certainly where they spent their honeymoon.

The end of the Twenties saw the appearance of the film which everyone associates with Berlin: Josef von Sternberg's *Der blaue Engel*. It was produced in 1929, and based on a much earlier novel by Heinrich Mann, *Professor Unrat*. The male lead was the veteran silent film actor Emil Jannings (who in 1929 received the very first 'Oscar'), and *The Blue Angel* was his first talkie. He was nervous about it, but at least his principal problem (not his voice, but his female lead) was solved with a vengeance. 'Sound film has been saved by Dietrich's legs', proclaimed the *BZ am Mittag*. Only Dr Goebbels' *Der Angriff* gave *The Blue Angel* a mealy-mouthed, disapproving review. Marlene became *the* star. All girls imitated her voice and looks. Suddenly all girls were wearing trousers and nail-varnish. 'Falling in Love Again' became the hit of the year. At the première at the Gloria-Palast, she totally eclipsed Jannings. Immediately – she couldn't even attend the première party – Sternberg took her off to Hollywood with him on the *Bremen*, at the time the fastest, biggest, most beautiful liner on the high seas.

Whatever one might have forgotten about *The Blue Angel*, one can never forget Marlene's theme song. In his autobiography, *Von Kopf bis Fuss*, Friedrich Holländer describes how it came to be written. He had composed the melody without great difficulty, but he was stuck over the words. Sternberg came to listen to what he had done, and Holländer, having played it, finished by saying apologetically *'und sonst gar nichts – and that's all'*. The phrase gave him his lyric:

> *Ich bin von Kopf bis Fuss auf Liebe eingestellt*
> *Denn das ist meine Welt, und sonst gar nichts.*
> *Das ist – was soll ich machen? – meine Natur;*
> *Ich kann halt lieben nur; und sonst gar nichts.*
> *Männer umschwirren mich wie Motten um das Licht,*
> *Und Wenn sie verbrennen, dafür kann ich nicht.*
> *Ich bin von Kopf bis Fuss auf Liebe eingestellt*
> *Denn das ist meine Welt, und sonst gar nichts.*

The year 1929 had already seen fresh Communist revolts on the streets of Berlin, and there had been bloody clashes on May Day. As the depression deepened in 1931, a German–Austrian customs union was disallowed by the International Court at The Hague, and the banks closed. Unemployment rose to 5.7 million and the NSDAP and the German Nationalists withdrew from the Reichstag, forming the Harzburger Front. Street fighting increased, the Kroll Opera closed on account of inflation and the Schiller Theater was threatened with closure as well. Unemployed actors formed their own companies, and those more fortunate held benefits and fund-raising events for their disadvantaged colleagues. As the political situation plunged further into ruin, many artists not hitherto strongly politicized felt compelled to make a stand. Weill, Hindemith, Grosz and Tucholsky all embraced political responsibility and tried to reach the population, especially through schools, the trade union movement, and the political parties. Brecht and the left-wing composer Hanns Eisler, as well as Ernst Busch, took their work directly to factory canteens and school assembly-halls. Out of this Brecht evolved the *Lehrstück* or parable play.

The Sayer-Yes is based on a *Nōh* play by Zenchiku, called *Taniko*. In Brecht's version, a boy joins a holy expedition in search of counsel and medication against a plague. He falls ill on the way and, 'according to custom', consents to be thrown into an abyss rather than hold up the journey. When the play was performed in front of students at the progressive Karl-Marx-Schule in Neukölln, it met vigorous criticism. Why couldn't the boy's companions have saved him? Was such a cruel and extreme decision necessary? Was the success of the expedition worth the sacrifice of the boy's life? Brecht's response to this was to write *The Sayer-No*, in which the boy refuses to be abandoned to death and questions the wisdom of 'custom'. However, in this second play, the purpose of the expedition is exploration, not the salvation of a community. The moral question is therefore much more simply answered. Whatever the value of these plays today, their importance then was that they questioned the necessity for blind obedience. Brecht insisted that henceforward they should always be performed together.

But Brecht left Berlin in 1932, and German theatre was in any case moving in a very different direction. The play of 1933 was Hanns Johst's *Schlageter*. Johst had started life as an Expressionist, but became increasingly right-wing and narrow-minded. The play was about a recent German resistance hero of the Ruhr, Leo Schlageter. He was an ex-officer engaged in sabotage, captured and executed by the French in May 1923. He promptly became a hero to the Nationalists. The play was reviewed in muted tones by Paul Fechter, a good critic who didn't initially have the courage to leave. Describing the audience, as he always did, Fechter wrote: 'In the auditorium there is a quite new public: the old First Night spectators of the former Staatstheater have almost all disappeared.' That was written on 22 April 1933, when it was still possible to get away with vaguely disapproving comments. There was no adverse criticism of the play. 'The play points the way to a supra-individual unity, from which we may expect everything possible,' wrote the critic of the *Tägliche Rundschau*. From that moment, genuine criticism was at an end. Reviews might as well have been written by machines, and the theatre entered an ice-age from which it did not emerge until after 1945.

For the sake of completeness, this chapter must close with a mention of Max Epstein, 'the cloakroom king'. Epstein was second only to Reinhardt as a great entrepreneur who actually made money out of the theatre. His success rate was more consistent than Reinhardt's, for Epstein took on all the cloakroom, bar and lavatory franchises he could lay his hands on – and he never lost money! He wrote two books: *Theatre as Business*, and *Business as Theatre,* in which he revealed that his takings at comedies were higher than at tragedies, and that he could expect little when the house was 'papered' with complimentary ticket-holders. On the back of his proceeds, he built himself a theatre in Nürnberger Strasse, and got Gerhart Hauptmann to guest-direct in it.

8 House of Bricks, House of Straw

BERLIN'S BEST KNOWN mayor was Gustav Böss, an energetic and conscientious Democrat given to unconventional ways of getting things done. He took over the city in 1921, when its infrastructure had all but collapsed. Berlin had ploughed 614 million marks into the war effort and was heavily in debt. In 1913 the rolling deficit had been 80 million; by 1919 it was 875 million. Special taxes were imposed on beer and cinema tickets to help reduce it, but there were other problems. Although Böss broadened the base of the council by making room for more representatives from working-class districts, he had a narrow path to tread between the various rival factions in the newly united Greater Berlin. The old districts jealously protected their services and amenities. When the Sarotti Works in Tempelhof burned down, it was probably because the Tempelhof fire brigade was too proud to call the Old Berlin fire brigade to its aid until it was too late. Rationalization was essential.[1] Before the incorporation of Greater Berlin, the area it covered had seventeen separate waterworks, forty-three gasworks and fifteen electricity stations. Ludicrous situations had arisen, such as Schöneberg having to spend millions building its own sewage farm instead of tapping into neighbouring Old Berlin's more than adequate system.

Disorder was a constant fear. Strikes, especially by electrical workers, frequently disrupted the efficient running of the city; inflated gas prices in 1923 led to riots in the streets; and the population was swollen by the large numbers migrating to Berlin after the end of the First World War. Unemployment remained high, since Berlin's large industrial base attracted more people to the city than it could offer jobs, and inflation destroyed many businesses. The biggest employers were the metal-

working industry, electro-technology, the clothing industry, shoe manufacture and leatherware, furniture manufacture and film. Three-quarters
of the total of 11 billion marks in German joint stock were held in the
seven major Berlin banks. Trade fairs and motor shows, particularly
between 1924 and 1928, attracted millions of visitors and provided some
stimulus to employment.

Berlin's ordinary people continued steadfastly left-wing; the city voted
differently from the country in the 1925 presidential elections, not liking
Hindenburg's association with the old monarchy. Hindenburg gained an
absolute majority in only three, bourgeois, districts. He was well aware
of the low esteem he enjoyed in the capital, and delayed his first official
visit there for eighteen months after his election, which did nothing to
increase his popularity. In June 1926, Berlin's inhabitants voted by 96
per cent against the restoration of the monarchy. Again, the tendency by
district was revealing, if not surprising: for example, right-wing Zehlendorf was only 27.9 per cent against, while 'Red' Wedding was 79 per cent
against.

One of Böss's main concerns was to provide Berliners with amenities
of all kinds, particularly cultural and sporting ones. He had the right
instincts, but was neither a natural Maecenas, nor a connoisseur. As the
city lawyer C. A. Lange records in his memoirs,[2] 'His methods of
acquisition of paintings were sometimes a little odd. When in 1927 he
personally delivered the letter according Honorary Citizenship to Max
Liebermann [the Grand Old Man of the modern art movement], he took
a small oil-painting by the Master from the wall and stowed it away in
his brief case. This was his rather crude way of indicating to Liebermann
that in return for Honorary Citizenship he might like to give the City
a little present himself. The artist did not display the expected sense of
humour on this occasion, and immediately sent the City a bill for 8,000
marks.' To raise money for a pension for the writer Arno Holz, who was
living in straitened circumstances, Böss hit on the idea of commissioning
a fine Collected Edition of his work, to sell for 600 marks. Visitors to
Böss's office found themselves more or less obliged to subscribe for a set.
His ventures were not always happy ones, and sometimes as a patron of
the arts he overstretched himself. He bought Liebermann's *The Siblings*
from Paul Cassirer for 50,000 marks, hoping to recoup the money by
public subscription from city worthies. But he was told roundly by Franz
Ullstein, who declined to contribute, that art experts were agreed on a
value of about half what he had paid.

Though not himself musical, Böss, aware of Germany's musical reputation, started a series of Town Hall concerts in 1924 to encourage young
players and composers. He took over the Charlottenburg Opera House
in Bismarckstrasse in rivalry to the Prussian State Opera House in Unter

den Linden, and chaired its board himself. To retain Bruno Walter, he
agreed to pay him 60,000 marks a year for just forty evening appearances,
with time off for the London Season. He organized a higher subsidy for
the Berlin Philharmonic to dissuade Wilhelm Furtwängler from leaving
for Vienna; he was also behind the founding of the Berliner Philhar-
monische Orchester GmbH, which was run as a limited company, owned
75 per cent by the City of Berlin and 25 per cent by the Prussian State;
and in 1929 the Berlin Festival Weeks were inaugurated under his
auspices.

In 1928, Siemens completed the electrification of all city and suburban
railway lines, and in November of that year the city council decided to
found the Berliner Verkehrsgesellschaft (Berlin Transport Company –
BVG: it still exists). Inaugurated on 1 January 1929, BVG was the biggest community transport system in the world, and probably Germany's
largest industrial concern except for the State Railway and the massive
chemical conglomerate I. G. Farben. Its inception was surrounded by the
usual political jockeyings in pursuit of plums and plum jobs. Ernst
Reuter, then 37, was chairman of the supervising board; he became the
first mayor of Berlin after 1945. A prisoner-of-war in Russia during the
First World War, he had become a Bolshevik, rising to the rank of
People's Commissar among the Volga Germans. On his return to
Germany he rose to senior rank in the Communist Party there, but broke
with them in 1921 and joined the SPD.

The underground railway system was frustrated in its development by
economic problems. Reuter argued hard for expansion to ease traffic congestion in central Berlin, but the public preferred the cheaper over-
ground *S-Bahn* and, still more, the trams. There were ninety lines and
643 kilometres of track by 1929.

Demand for flats following the First World War far outstripped
capacity. Wartime disruption and inflation prevented new building, but
from 1918 on, 80,000 people a year flooded into Berlin. Overcrowding
was appalling. People lived even in the dampest cellars, and there were
tenements and hostels with up to thirteen inhabitants in every heatable
room. A public building programme was introduced after 1923, funded
by money raised through the imposition of a House Rent Tax. From the
humble beginnings of public housing in 1919, when wooden barracks
were erected, progress accelerated to, for example, Bruno Taut's
showpiece, the Hufeisen-Siedlung (Horseshoe Development) in Berlin-
Britz. Critics from the Right claimed the new flats were 'too opulent' for
'simple people' (they all had gas, electric light, and bathrooms), but Böss
countered, 'We want to bring the lower levels of society higher: that is
not only a moral, but an ethical undertaking.'

The housing programme was accompanied by a general city clean-up and restoration plan. It brought the city fathers into contact with leading modern architects such as Otto Bartning, Walter Gropius, Erich Mendelsohn, Ludwig Mies van der Rohe, Hans Poelzig, Hans Scharoun, and Bruno and Max Taut. They all built for industry, administration and residence in the city centre. In the outer suburbs, model residential quarters sprang up, along with garden suburbs like Siemensstadt and Onkel-Toms-Hütte (Uncle Tom's Cabin – named after an inn) in Zehlendorf. Planners towards the end of the nineteenth century, like James Hobrecht and I. W. Carstenn, had been able to develop canalization and garden city ideas to a limited extent. The Kurfürstendamm, an idea of Carstenn's inspired by the Champs-Elysées, was actually laid out by James Booth, a Scottish tree-nursery specialist. The new architects could take advantage of these achievements.

The building programmes created opportunities for the unemployed: there were also road-building projects, together with canal excavation, and construction of sports- and recreation-grounds. For those who could not work, unemployment benefit was increased, and city aid was made available to the disadvantaged: the deaf, the blind, even ex-prisoners, the *demi-monde*, and delinquents. There was an increase in crêches and kindergartens as women took advantage of their new liberation and worked in all manner of professions and trades alongside men. For children, the city organized holidays. Every year 65,000 children were sent for six weeks to more than 80 homes on the North Sea and the Baltic. For all these projects Böss worked tirelessly, drumming up contributions from industry and charitable trusts.

Unfortunately, the war against unemployment and poverty was one of attrition. At the end of the Twenties, large tent settlements grew up by the shores of the Berlin lakes, housing the homeless and the jobless. The organization of these camps was impressive. The numbered tents were erected in neat rows, and the rows even had names as if they were streets. The camps were clean and free of violence, friction and vandalism. They even had 'town councils' and 'mayors'. There were playgrounds for the children and special areas for the communal kitchens. The best-known of the settlements, Kuhle Wampe, was the setting for a film in 1932, scripted by Brecht and starring Herta Thiele, who a year earlier had come to stardom through her role in *Girls in Uniform*. *Kuhle Wampe* was the first and last overtly Communist film to be made, and it was banned because it criticized Hindenburg, the administration of justice, and religion. It is not a great film, but it portrayed honestly and sympathetically the confusion and despair caused by the mass unemployment of the early Thirties, which resisted the efforts of Böss and his colleagues.

Böss was ahead of his time in appreciating the social and health advantages of exercise. He ran into difficulties with the Right over the arts, but had no problem in persuading his council to fund sports facilities. Sports Weeks were introduced, and by the time he left office in 1930 Böss had seen 4 million square metres of land designated for public sports use.[3]

Like President Ebert, and equally unfairly, Gustav Böss was brought down by innocent involvement in a financial scandal. The firm of Sklarek near the Spittelmarkt was run by three brothers of Russo-Polish descent, Leo, Max and Willi. That they were also Jews was unfortunate, given the rising tide of anti-Semitism.[4] The Sklarek company was based on textiles. By suborning officials and making false claims to the council, the brothers cornered the market in supplying textiles and uniforms to the city. They extracted large loans from the council for expansion and, by presenting false business papers, had run up 10.5 million marks' worth of credit at the Berlin City Bank by 1929. Since they appeared to be easing the management burden for the council, their operation was not looked into too deeply; as a matter of routine, Böss had signed some of the authorizing documents.

The brothers lived well on the rewards of their fraud. Their villa in Ahornstrasse was the scene of enormous parties, they maintained a hunting lodge in Mecklenburg, and a racing stables. In the end they overreached themselves. Officials at the bank started to analyse their affairs with real attention, and the bubble burst. Leo and Willi were arrested (Max was unfit to plead, on grounds of 'diminished responsibility'), and one of the trials of the century began. The first surprise was the sheer number of people involved. The Sklareks had provided clothing, free or at greatly reduced prices, to city officials and politicians at all levels – a revelation which in those impoverished times led to great popular hatred and bitterness. The Sklareks' chief book-keeper had turned state's evidence to mitigate his own sentence, and the names kept rolling off his tongue. Finally he revealed that Böss had bought a fur coat for his wife at Sklareks', for an advantageous price.

Böss had certainly bought a fur jacket. After several reminders from Böss a bill was sent to him, but for only 375 marks. Böss knew this was an absurdly low price, and that the Sklareks were trying to oil him; but instead of sending the jacket back, or finding out the correct price, he sent with his cheque a stiff letter announcing his intention of spending the difference between the price asked and what he assumed to be the real price on an acquisition for the city. He put aside 1,000 marks of his own money, bought a Max Pechstein painting for the city art gallery with 800, and divided the 200 left over between two needy relatives of his own. With that, he thought the matter was honourably settled. But it transpired in court that the true value of the jacket was 4,950 marks.

At the time of the trial, Böss was away on business in California. If he had had any idea of the seriousness of what was going on in Berlin, he

might have hurried back immediately to refute the charges the newspapers now made against him; but he felt secure in the knowledge of his
own innocence. Unfortunately, despite his exemplary record as mayor,
it looked to the ordinary Berliner as if Böss were a corrupt grafter too
bare-faced even to care when his corruption was revealed. On his return
in November 1929, he was vilified by an angry mob threatening physical
violence. Appalled and deeply hurt, he immediately instituted an official
enquiry into his own actions, and withdrew from city business. The
right-wing committee of enquiry took its time, and in May 1930 found
that Böss should be dismissed – the harshest sentence possible. This was
quashed on appeal; a fine of one month's salary was imposed instead, and
his honour was publicly vindicated. But Böss himself was finished. The
mayor of Berlin for its most glittering and most unruly decade now sadly
resigned.

The trial of the Sklareks took over two years to prepare and lasted eight
months. The brothers were sentenced to four years' imprisonment each.

Those with money had no difficulty finding ways to spend it. The great
temples of Mammon in Berlin were the department stores, and the
greatest of these was Wertheim's in Leipziger Platz. It was the apotheosis
of the department store, a palace of temptation with a 330-metre frontage
and covering a site twice as large as the Reichstag. Brilliantly lit by
100,000 bulbs, it had 83 lifts, 1,000 telephone extensions, and a lavish-
ness equal to the marble halls of the Adlon: there was an Onyx Room,
Bohemian chandeliers, a Fountain Hall in Istrian limestone, and a carpet
department with walls of Italian walnut.

At the other end of Leipziger Platz was Tietz' department store with
its vast food hall, topped by a great glass globe illuminated at night. Tietz
pioneered the tomato in Berlin, selling it at 10 pfennigs a kilo in 1908
and so conjuring a market from the utmost initial suspicion. In the
Twenties Karstadt founded its first store, in Neukölln, with a huge roof
garden and magnificent staircases. As an opening publicity stunt,
Karstadt got the *equestrienne* Cilly Feindt to ride her white horse up these
opulent stairs, from the ground floor to the roof garden. Window-
dressing became a new art form, and the florists of Potsdamer Platz were
its masters. In Leipziger Strasse, Erich Mendelsohn built a new store for
Herpich, the furriers. At first Böss regarded the building as such a blot
on the landscape that he did everything possible to prevent it, but two
years later it had protected status. In the Twenties, artistic taste developed fast in Berlin.

Of course, not everyone lived at this level. The working classes had no
access to such luxury. 'We ate simple food,' Erna Nelki remembers.
'Lunch might be pea-soup with sausage, or new potatoes with herring,

and we could even make a meal of rice pudding with sugar and cinnamon. Real meat was very rare: bacon and lentils was as near as we got to it. It was always a question of money, money, money . . . !'[5] The middle classes, if they were fortunate, could live comfortably and stylishly, though without pretension. The Hammersteins had the advantages attached to an army family. 'I was born in Charlottenburg when it was still a separate town,' remembers Ludwig von Hammerstein, whose grandfather was the General von Lüttwitz who had supported the Kapp *putsch*.

Charlottenburg was a much greater city than Old Berlin, though the richest town of all was Schöneberg because it was a banking and industrial district. We weren't in Berlin during the inflation period. My father was posted to Magdeburg then. We returned to Berlin in 1924. My father wasn't a general yet. He became an *Oberstleutnant* [Lieutenant-Colonel] and Chief of Staff of the Third Army Division when we returned to Berlin. He had already sent the family out of Berlin before, in 1920, during the Kapp *putsch*, because he said it was too dangerous to stay. My father disagreed with the Kapp *putsch* and would have nothing to do with it, whereupon my grandfather, his father-in-law, relieved him of his post, and for a time family relations were broken off.

We were seven brothers and sisters, four girls and three boys; but we were lucky enough to have our family home at Hardenbergstrasse 32. I went to an ordinary school; we weren't rich – army officers weren't that well paid and we were a large family. Half our class were Jewish boys. My great friend was called Samuel, and our favourite sport was to ride on trams without paying! And we used to nick an apple from the greengrocer's display on the way to school. There was no sense of anti-Semitism in our school, and certainly not in our class. I don't think we were aware of a difference at all. After all, the Jewish boys were just as cunning, lazy, clever, naughty – as we were. They had their ears boxed neither harder nor more softly than us.

But we never had much money as children. I remember taking my little sister, Puppe, from the house to Zoo Station – a distance of about 15 metres. At the station I parked Puppe in her pram and held taxi doors open for arriving travellers, making a deep bow, and collecting tips. When I'd got enough, I'd wheel Puppe down to the end of the street – to the corner of Hardenberg and Fasanenstrasse – where there was an ice-cream waggon, and I would buy both of us an ice! Another thing I used to do was help out with a cigarette stall – standing in for the man when he wanted to pop round the corner for a beer, or to pee, or place a bet.

It's hard to imagine the unity the city had, because now it's hard to imagine how it ever possessed such a thing, or ever will again. One lived generally within one's own district, going out specifically – to the theatre, for example, or to shop at Wertheim's, or to the Tiergarten. From 1931 until the beginning of 1934 we lived in Bendlerstrasse and that was very central: everything was walkable – Wertheim's, the Reichstag, the Brandenberg Gate. We used to go riding in the Tiergarten, and there made friends with the British Ambassador's children.[6]

'I went to lots of concerts by the Philharmonie,' says Helga Russow, another of Hammerstein's sisters. 'The concert hall was near Potsdamer Station. You could get cheap seats for a mark, where your view was impaired by a column but you could still hear perfectly. And I liked going to the theatre. It was possible to get one-mark seats there too, and I went to everything I could. There were hundreds of plays to choose from. Theatre-going could have been a full-time job, and very demanding at that.'[7]
Hammerstein family life had a certain practicality.

> Outside school hours [continues Ludwig von Hammerstein] a lady taught us wood-carving at home. In the garden of our house we grew vegetables under the direction of our mother, and when we had a chance we would scrump a few apples from the neighbours' trees. At the bottom of the garden were the stables and the garage for our father's car, and that is where his chauffeur, a soldier, also had a flat. I was always down there, and he taught me mechanics. I also liked to clean the car, which was either a Mercedes-Benz, or a Horch. There was certainly one of each at one time or another. And we would take apples to the horses, and learnt from the ostlers how to look after a horse and groom it. Once a month there was a great event: the rat hunt. There were dozens of rats in the stables and the ostlers would smoke them out. As they appeared, some of the boys would drive them down to the other end of the stables where their mates would be waiting with shovels and pitchforks.
>
> From the stables you could ride directly out into the Tiergarten. The two horses allocated to the general by the army for his personal use were massive things, and we learnt to ride on them. It was great fun, though rather a long way to fall! Later on, at Bendlerstrasse, a branch of Tattersall's opened,[8] where you could hire horses; and behind the zoo there was the *Hippodrome*, where you could do jumping – though we weren't good enough for that.

Berlin offered an extraordinary cultural richness to those alert enough to take advantage. A Jewish Berliner who stayed until 1939 remembers the music especially:

> I had a number of jobs. I worked for Electrola Records, and it was there that I met the 15-year-old Yehudi Menuhin, who was doing a recording for us. I must have been about 23 then. His parents escorted him, and I remember how proud they were to say that he was able to lead a more or less normal life. He was not allowed to read his own reviews. I went to one of his concerts – it was his Berlin début – and I think he played like an angel. He was still wearing short trousers, and he was a little bit plump; but he was utterly charming and his playing was so fresh. I saw Chaliapin, too, who came with his whole company to do *Boris Godunov*. It was sold out months in advance.

I went on the night and queued in vain for a return, but in the end I got a ticket that wasn't collected by a reviewer, for next to nothing, and of course it was one of the best seats!

I also heard Beniamino Gigli, and I saw Pavlova dance *The Dying Swan*, which was sublime. I didn't know that the laws of gravity could be so completely defied. And I went to the First Night of *The Threepenny Opera*. At first we in the audience were confused, but as soon as the actors got to the Cannon Song we all went wild, and the enthusiasm reached riot proportions by the time the performance ended. The play was absolutely new – it broke every rule! But it wasn't only the play, the music was just as iconoclastic!

Despite the efforts of the liberal Berlin administration, and despite the great influence and creativity of the Berlin artistic world, the shadows that had surrounded the city since the end of the war refused to be dispelled. There may have been greater financial stability during the later Twenties, but it did little to ensure political stability. 'I remember that my stepfather always used to take Swiss newspapers,' says Ed Rosenstiel. 'Especially the *Basler Nationalzeitung*, right up until 1925, because he felt that the German papers weren't to be trusted. After that he relaxed, but within five years he said, "I think it's time to get the *Basler* again", and so we did, until the Nazis stopped the sale of foreign papers altogether.'[9]

The political outlook was bleak. By mid-1925, diplomatic jockeying among the Allies, with the sympathetic collaboration of the British Foreign Minister Austen Chamberlain, and Aristide Briand, had brought about broad acceptance of Stresemann's moves towards a genuine *rapprochement* between France and Germany.[10] At home, however, Stresemann was facing the customary opposition from the Right. They were fearful that he would sell Germany short, and even agree that borders should be negotiated rather than determined by might. The new eastern frontier was an especially sore point. Showing an irresponsible disregard for long-term tensions between German and Pole, the Versailles Treaty had set it to Germany's punitive disadvantage. Hans von Seeckt was still in charge of the army in 1925, and his comment was: 'We must acquire power, and as soon as we have power, we will naturally retake all that we have lost.'[11] Seeckt, like his successor Schleicher, had too high an opinion of his own powers as a political thinker, and underestimated the turbulence that would be created even by discussion of realignment, either in the east or the west.

Stresemann's conciliatory line was attacked by the Communists, too. Ruth Fischer[12] stood in the Reichstag and accused: '. . . you have offered German soil and German workers for a future war against Russia as the price of reconciliation with England and France. Your foreign policy is attempting to turn Germany into a village of timorous vassals who seek union with the great British robber baron in order to share in future spoils.' The ancient President, Hindenburg – a landowner, a soldier and a conservative – was also against him. Stresemann later said that the hardest moments of his political life were those which preceded an interview with Hindenburg, as he prepared the approach most likely to convince the Old Gentleman. The toughest battles were fought before the signing of the Locarno Pact, which confirmed the inviolability of Germany's frontiers and the demilitarization of the Rhineland, and before Germany's entry into the League of Nations.[13] Alongside Hindenburg was the owlish right-wing businessman Alfred Hugenberg, whose powerful press interests and control of the UFA film corporation could sway public opinion.

Stresemann and his chancellor, Hans Luther, had a majority in the Reichstag and were able to push through what for them, and for their like-minded allies Chamberlain and Briand, were diplomatic triumphs. Locarno should have guaranteed European harmony and peace;[14] in view of the events of the following two decades, Briand's words spoken at the time now seem sadly ironic:

> If a new spirit does not accompany this gesture, if our act does not mark the beginning of an era of mutual trust, then our deeds will not have the effect for which we hope. Between our two nations [France and Germany] there are still areas of friction and points of pain. May the pact which we have just signed serve as a balsam to these wounds . . . Then we shall be able to work together towards the realization in every area of life of the ideal we all bear in our hearts: a Europe that will fulfil its destiny by remaining true to its tradition of civilized and generous spirits.[15]

In Germany the right-wing press bellowed that at Locarno the government had sold Germany out to her 'enemies'. When Stresemann and Luther arrived at the Anhalter Station they needed a police cordon to protect them. The silent majority may have wanted peace and a quiet life as much as their fellow-Europeans, but mob demonstrations did nothing to dispel fears that intemperate militarism and nationalism were once again building up in Germany. The liberal voice was simply not loud enough.

Following Locarno, the Allies continued their withdrawal from the Rhineland, despite the fact that Germany was not only not disarming, but was *re*arming. It was almost as open a secret as Seeckt's contempt for the Allies. Luther, however, could not maintain his shaky coalition, and resigned. Unable to find an effective alternative, Hindenburg was obliged to turn to him again, to form the next coalition. It proved just possible, but democracy – so young in Germany – was not enhanced by

Luther's difficulties. Throughout the Weimar Republic, government was hampered by proportional representation, which led to a proliferation of parties, and unstable majorities. The result at this time was an increase in Hindenburg's prestige as a father figure. He assumed the position of National Leader in the popular imagination.

Despite further attacks from the Right, Stresemann (once again Foreign Secretary in Luther's new government) continued with his efforts to make Germany part of the international fellowship, and by February 1926 he was seeking admission to the League of Nations. His endeavours were scarcely helped by Luther's agreement to an extraordinary move by Hindenburg, who determined that the merchant marine flag, featuring the old Imperial colours in a corner of the Republican flag, was henceforth to be used at German embassies and consulates abroad. The diplomatic furore resulting from this arrogant reference to German imperialism was only to be expected; it brought about the fall of Luther, although Hindenburg, as usual, emerged unscathed. Wilhelm Marx succeeded Luther, but the offensive flag remained.

Despite the flag, and even despite an attempted right-wing coup, Germany was admitted to the League as a permanent member in September 1926. It was ironic that Germany, on the brink of ruin in 1923, had now so successfully recovered that Stresemann could be generous to France over reparation repayments, while France was hard-pressed to meet commitments to its own war-time creditors, the United States and Great Britain. German industry and municipalities were attracting enormous credit, especially from American banks. Despite the spectre of German militarism, the Allies seem to have been rather trusting about the use to which economic expansion fuelled in this way might in the end be put.

The attempted coup was Seeckt's. He sought to install himself as military dictator but, lacking Hindenburg's support, was forced to draw back. Hindenburg was no admirer of Seeckt, and complained that he was 'ruining the character of the officer corps' with his vanity. Truly of the old school, Seeckt had even sanctioned the reintroduction of duelling and the cult of scars. He was now disgraced – not for his coup attempt, but for a diplomatic blunder in allowing the young Prince Wilhelm, grandson of the Kaiser, to take part in military exercises. The magnanimity of the Republic in permitting Prince Wilhelm's return from exile did not, incidentally, prevent another returned Hohenzollern, the Kaiser's son Prince Oskar, from openly sending fifty cigarettes with a letter of support to a youth in gaol charged with an attempt to murder Stresemann.[16]

Still the Allies had sufficient confidence in Stresemann to exercise forbearance. Perhaps they underestimated the instability of the situation. Even when the *Manchester Guardian* leaked the Junkers memorandum revealing the existence of secret factories in Russia,[17] the Allies continued to wind down military control; and after the end of January 1927 the Inter-Allied Military Control Commission which had been in place since the war was withdrawn. Meanwhile the German government ruled that any revelation of violations of the Treaty of Versailles would henceforth be regarded as an act of High Treason – regardless of international law.

Whatever the forbearance of the Allied governments, there was certainly concern in France over German militarism, and signals emanating from Germany did nothing to reduce it. In the summer of 1927, while the League of Nations was still in session at Geneva, Hindenburg once again behaved insensitively, attending the unveiling of the Tannenberg National Memorial in East Prussia. To compound his unfortunate timing, the Old Gentleman made a speech exonerating Germany from any blame for the First World War. He may have been a hidebound old man, but he was neither foolish nor senile, and his conduct cannot be excused on the grounds of artlessness. The best that can be said for him is that he was conscientious and consistent. That a man so much of the past should have been in a position of such power was, however, a major contribution to the tragedy that followed.

Otto Gessler, the one Democrat in the cabinet, was forced to resign following the scandal which arose over revelations of army investments in Phoebus Films and other private-sector organizations. At Hindenburg's suggestion Gessler was replaced by an equally durable figure on the Weimar military and political scene, General Wilhelm Gröner – he was a Democrat, but he was also a soldier. More than once (over the Kaiser's abdication, and Ebert's signing of the Treaty of Versailles) Gröner had accepted responsibility for unpopular decisions made by Hindenburg; as he admitted, aridly: 'I deliberately sought to glorify Hindenburg's name for political reasons.' The cabinet he joined was on its last legs. He remained in the next cabinet, as did Stresemann, that other survivor. His tasks were to overhaul the war ministry and disband the discredited Schwarze Reichswehr.[18]

Elections in May 1928 brought a polarization to Right and Left and a decline in the moderate parties, including Stresemann's People's Party. Though only 50, Stresemann had undergone more than his share of nervous strain, and his health was wrecked. His doctors having ordered him to Bühlehöhe, near Baden-Baden, for rest, he was not in Berlin when the SPD Chancellor, Hermann Müller, was composing his new cabinet. Despite the fact that both Stresemann and his colleague Julius Curtius, the Economics Minister, were members of the People's Party, Müller managed to retain them in the cabinet on account of their long experience; he was sensible enough to see that Stresemann's contacts with foreign powers should not be interrupted at this stage.

Alfred Hugenberg now took over the chairmanship of the far-right Nationalist Party and stepped up his campaign against Stresemann. The Nationalists had moved away from a monarchist stance by now; it was no longer relevant to far-right ambitions. The Kaiser himself, in exile in Doorn, had not. He presented a visitor, the comedy writer Rudolf Presber, with a photograph of himself inscribed: 'I hereby proclaim everything all of you have done in Germany to be null and void.'

The extremists of the Right were infuriated to see an SPD Chancellor in office again. 'We hate the present form of the German state with all our hearts because it denies to us the hope of freeing our enslaved Fatherland, of cleansing the German people of the war-guilt lie, [and] of gaining necessary *Lebensraum* in Eastern Europe . . .' Such views were supported by the Stahlhelm Society, with Hindenburg among its members. Meanwhile, enmity between the SPD and the Communists also grew – the SPD was not hard Left enough for the Communists, who dubbed them 'social Fascists'. To the extent that they succeeded in merging the SPD with the far right in the public mind, the Communists must take responsibility for hiding the growth of the genuine threat.

Stresemann, perhaps the one man who might, with support, have pulled Germany back from the precipice, was now uniformly vilified and Goebbels, who in the emerging NSDAP power-structure was now *Gauleiter* of Berlin, published an attack on him in his new magazine *Der Angriff* (The Attack):

> From a confidential source close to the Jewish – we observe in passing – Professor Zondek [one of Stresemann's physicians] we learn that the Foreign Minister's health is much worse than the public assumes and that it has given cause for some concern . . . There are only two likely sources of [this] kind of kidney trouble: either a severe inflammation of the throat or the excessive consumption of alcohol and heavy, indigestible foods. To the best of public knowledge, the Foreign Minister has not suffered from an inflammation of the throat in recent years.

In fact, Stresemann was suffering from a serious paratyphoid infection of the kidneys.

He also had a Jewish wife. 'When the headmaster said in a history lesson one day, "Today we are going to learn about Gustav Stresemann", I was just about to put up my hand and say that he was my uncle when Herr Waldeck continued: "The only bad thing that can be said about Stresemann is that he had a Jewish wife." I was glad that I had kept my mouth shut.'[19]

The Allied Reparations Agent, Parker Gilbert, reached broad agreement with Hjalmar Schacht, President of the State Bank, over a final method of repayment, but Schacht's arrogance almost caused the breakdown of a reparations conference in Paris in 1929, which would have been disastrous for the German economy. The mere rumour that the conference was in danger led to a run on the State Bank; yet Schacht's own position was unaffected. The liberals were not powerful enough to muzzle intemperates on either Right or Left; Schacht, moving steadily towards the Right, had presidential ambitions. Wickham Steed, a former editor of *The Times*, told François Poincaré that 'university professors in Berlin had told him that they intended to indoctrinate German youth with the aim of regaining Alsace-Lorraine. Confronted with this in conversation, Stresemann found his task of re-establishing German probity abroad increasingly an uphill one.'[20]

The Young Plan, a re-drafted reparations repayment deal more lenient to the Germans which superseded the Dawes Plan, was at once denounced by the Right to gain political advantage. In a speech to students at Marburg, the Nationalist Hugenberg said: 'It is better for all Germans to live together as proletarians until the hour of freedom strikes, than for some of us to exploit our own people by becoming agents and beneficiaries of foreign capital.' Students and workers swallowed such stuff whole. In the early Thirties Hugenberg started to make overt political use of UFA, which controlled film distribution to 120 cinemas; Hitler took it over in 1936. Hugenberg was one of many whose vanity helped pave the way for Nazi dictatorship.

A continuing row between Right and Left centred on the Allied occupation of the Rhineland; despite more important economic and social issues, the moderates were forced to confront the problem in order to stay in power, as it was a constant election issue. At a conference in The Hague in August 1929 Stresemann managed to achieve Allied agreement that no new concessions would be exacted from Germany in exchange for total Allied withdrawal of the Rhineland. Effectively he achieved what the Right was demanding: a return to German dignity and autonomy. In the event, he received no public recognition, and Hindenburg exploited the occasion to wring from the Prussian State Government a revocation of a ban on the Stahlhelm in Rhineland-Westphalia. That organization promptly held a rally in Coblenz which led to ugly confrontations with the last departing French troops.

In the first elections following the withdrawal, the Nazis polled 6.5 million votes. The new British Ambassador, Sir Horace Rumbold, remarked – apropos Hitler's paper celebrating the evacuation – that ingratitude was an unpleasant characteristic of the Germans. The Right immediately began to issue demands for further concessions from the Allies.

Although public recognition was denied him, Stresemann did receive a letter of congratulation from Theodor Wolff, the influential and distinguished editor of the *Berliner Tageblatt* between 1906 and 1933. If only the liberal element had been stronger – but it was not. Wolff was a Jew. Forced to flee Germany, he was later arrested by the Germans in the south of France; following brutal treatment in the Sachsenhausen-Oranienburg concentration camp just north of the city, he was transferred to the Jewish Hospital in Berlin where he died, in 1943, in his 76th year.

Had Stresemann recovered his health, it is possible that he might have turned the tide against the Nazis. But, worn out both physically and mentally, he died on 3 October 1929. He was 51.

It only needed the Wall Street Crash, which undermined German economic recovery, to set the stage for Hitler. He had luck – and he had setbacks; but from 1930 onward Hitler's own ruthlessness, devouring ambition, reckless opportunism, and ability to sway a mob did the rest.

Hitler had started to write *Mein Kampf* (the title was suggested by his publisher, Max Amann) during the twelve months he served, in Landsberg Fortress, of his five-year sentence for his leading role in the Beer Hall *putsch* of 1923. He was released on 20 December 1924, and the first volume went on sale the following June. It sold 9,000 copies and netted its author 20,000 marks. The second volume had less success, but by 1930 the complete book had sold 50,000 copies, and after 1933 its yearly sales reached 850,000. By then it was compulsory reading. By 1940, 5,950,000 copies had been sold, and *Mein Kampf* had become the world's most widely read book after the Bible. But 'the miserably low intellectual and literary value of the book explains ... why Hitler's political opponents failed to pay it much attention. For they simply couldn't imagine that such shoddy scribbling could make an impression on any reasonable man and thus rob them of their voters. How wrong they were!'[21]

The future of the Nazis was not always assured. The early days of the party were times of small and fluctuating support. Nazi fortunes improved when Hitler recognised Goebbels' value as a propagandist, and wooed him away from Gregor Strasser, his chief political rival. His diaries reveal Goebbels to have been intelligent, clever, amoral, cynical, unscrupulous and envious, but slavishly loyal to Hitler. His descriptions of the Führer are so disgustingly adulatory that, were it not for his known philandering with women, one might suspect a sexual passion for his leader. He put all his energy into promoting the Nazi cause and the cult of Hitler's personality, but the NSDAP was none the less defeated heavily in the 1928 elections. By doing deals with like-minded parties, however, they managed to claw twelve seats together, of which Goebbels, Göring and Strasser each held one. A Reichstag delegate could say what he liked in the House without fear of prosecution – and he was also entitled to a free rail pass. These were almost as advantageous as Hugenberg's financial backing, for the NSDAP's finances were low. The *Sturm-Abteilung* (Storm Division) or SA, the Nazis' paramilitary wing, had brown uniforms because brown was the colour of the cheapest cloth available: only later was the symbolic association with the earth trumped up. The Stahlhelm lent further support; they gave the SA a hint of respectability by parading publicly with them.[22] Under Ernst Röhm the SA began to see itself as the forerunner of a People's Army which would supersede the regular army, but Hitler had no desire to see his lieutenants wield such power, and broke with Röhm in 1925. During the five years of the rift, Röhm found military employment in Bolivia. Meanwhile Hitler, after reorganizing the SA's leadership, created his own élite corps, the *Schutz-Staffel* (Defence Brigade), or SS.

Hitler may have been failing at the polls, but he was gaining in strength. Between 1926 and 1927, NSDAP membership rose from 17,000 to 40,000. In the summer of 1929 the party had 120,000 members; after the Wall Street Crash membership rose to 250,000, and by autumn 1930 to a million. Hugenberg continued to back Hitler. The Nationalists had the money, and Hugenberg the propaganda vehicles, but the Nazis had the popular support.

Hermann Müller managed to steer his cabinet through the white waters of the winter of 1929/30. After Stresemann's death Julius Curtius took over as Foreign Minister, and the Young Plan was finally ratified. Schacht, after attempting to interfere in politics once too often, finally resigned as President of the State Bank in March 1930. But by now unemployment was rising fast again and the disaffected and dispossessed were turning to the extremes of Right and Left; a repeat of 1919 threatened, but with higher stakes. Müller was tired and ill (he was to die in 1931, aged 55) and his government found it impossible to agree on means either to counter unemployment, or to provide for the unemployed, in an economy which see-sawed between volatility and depression. Müller's government collapsed amid disagreement over an incremental increase from workers and employers to the National Unemployment Service. The *Berliner Tageblatt* lamented a 'crisis over 0.25 per cent'. The collapse was a disaster. Not for the first time the SPD, failing to reach agreement among themselves, fuelled the forces of the Right.

Naturally, civilized life went on, unaware of approaching Nemesis. On Tuesday 22 January 1929 Harry Kessler gave tea in his Berlin apartment to Vita Sackville-West (Mrs Harold Nicolson), and Virginia and Leonard Woolf:

Virginia Woolf is no longer young and somewhat dried-up, rather decadent-looking and quite large, but she has the pleasant manners of English polite society. Leonard Woolf is very highly-strung and stammers, but he's clever and profound. We discussed Mrs Nicolson's translation of Rilke and the possibility of publishing it with the Cranach Press [Kessler's high-quality printing works in Weimar]. Virginia Woolf is very typically *upper middle class*,[23] the best sort of *upper middle class* English professor's daughter, and Mrs Nicolson is just as typical of the English aristocrat, a big woman, tall, thin, big-boned, but she holds herself lightly and there is great style in her every movement; a person who has never known any embarrassment or social inhibition.

Harold Nicolson, whom he met later, he liked less. 'An amusing man, but who comes across to me as somehow unsympathetic; though in what way I cannot decide.'

On 23 April Kessler went to hear Yehudi Menuhin play: 'The boy is a real prodigy. His playing has the godlike inspiration of genius and the purity of childhood. A fantastic virtuosity seemed secondary, as if it were a thing unto itself. A wonderful sense of style, without the slightest vulgarity or sentimentality, but informed with pure, deep feeling.'

May and June saw a cultural orgy for Kessler, with visits to see Toscanini, in Berlin to conduct *Falstaff* and *Rigoletto*, a performance of Hindemith's *Neues vom Tage*, Reinhardt's gala production of *Die Fleder-maus*, and Stroheim's film *The Wedding March*. But the second half of the year was marked by a series of deaths – that of the Austrian writer and Richard Strauss's librettist, Hugo von Hofmannsthal, tragically following the suicide of his son; that of Serge Diaghilev, who had been a friend of Kessler's; and finally that of Stresemann. Kessler returned from Paris for Stresemann's funeral on 6 October 1929. He at once noticed the many black-white-and-red flags and commented that the colours of the Republic, black-red-and-gold, seemed apologetically displayed. 'I fear that the first political consequences of [his] death will be the movement of the People's Party towards the Right, the break-up of the coalition, and an easing of the way for those who would wish a dictatorship on us.'[24]

9 The Crystallizing Arts

THE STABILIZATION OF the mark in 1923 slowed the giddy tempo of Berlin. For a short while people could think once more about a real future. Artistic movements also settled down after the upheavals between 1918 and 1923. But Berlin had only a scant five years before the Wall Street Crash of 1929 started the ten-year descent into a new war.

When the court painter Adolph von Menzel died, laden with honours, in 1905, the Kaiser walked behind his coffin in the cortège. No painter had been so honoured by his king since Velázquez. Menzel was followed by the renegades of the Secession. One of the leaders of that movement, Max Liebermann, also lived to a great age, and saw two new art movements supersede the one he had started. He died aged 87 in 1934. He might, like Menzel, have reached 90, had not the horror of Hitler's regime broken his spirit. On 30 January 1933 he lowered the blinds in the flat in Pariser Platz he had inherited from his parents, to shut out the SA torchlight parades celebrating Hitler's appointment as Chancellor, and never raised them again. Interviewed shortly before his death, the old Berliner gave vent to this comment: '[Nowadays], one can't eat as much as one would like to throw up.'

Growing out of the Secession and succeeding it, Expressionism in turn gave way about 1924 to *Neue Sachlichkeit* (New Objectivity). It stemmed from 'the general contemporary feeling in Germany of resignation and cynicism after a period of exuberant hopes'.[1] The exuberant hopes had found their outlet in Expressionism, but an apolitical art movement was no longer possible. Most Expressionists moved to one side or the other – mainly to the Left, though a few, like Emil Nolde, briefly supported the NSDAP. The cynical strain in the art of New Objectivity could be construed as healthy, as perhaps could also a new enthusiasm for reality, stripped of the trappings of symbolism – though it was not so simple: 'reality' applied as much to the *manner* of its observation. Nor was *Neue Sachlichkeit* confined to painting. Thomas Mann's *The Magic Mountain* can be seen, on one of its many levels, as the story of Hans Castorp's moving from the darkness of German Romanticism and a love affair with death, to a more rational and positive attitude to life. Brecht's rise to fame as a playwright directly coincided with the abandonment of the old symbolism.

In the mid-Twenties, Berlin became the definitive artistic mecca of Germany. 'Centralization is inevitable,' Heinrich Mann wrote in 1923.[2] Perhaps an element of self-disgust which had entered the souls of many sensitive Germans, including artists, in the years immediately following the war as the country plunged into revolution and self-doubt, began to lift. None the less, some writers continued to prefer living abroad. Many thought France was now the artistic heart of Europe, and Paris its core. Like Heine before him, and perhaps for not very different reasons, Kurt Tucholsky adored that city. As he wrote in his poem, *Parc Monceau*,

> It is pretty here,
> Here I can dream quietly.
> Here I am a person, not just a citizen.

In Berlin, *Neue Sachlichkeit* gathered to it a vigorous body of artists. In painting its basic tenets were realism in execution, lack of comment, concentration on everyday objects (a still life might easily be of a dustpan and brush), and a certain coldness of approach. Giorgio de Chirico, in his *pittura metafisica* period, was its chief influence. Everything is in focus, everything has equal importance. People are part of the scene more than individuals within it. People, in fact, are not often necessary at all. The natural and bitter compassion of two of its chief exponents, Otto Dix and George Grosz, made them exceptions to this rule: even their harshest depictions could not be described as dehumanized. Max Beckmann, arguably the greatest German artist of the period, was too interested in the people he painted to be strictly a *Neue Sachlichkeit* painter at all; he defies categorization. At the other end of the scale, Carl Grossberg banished human beings altogether: in his work bats and apes take their place as servants of perfect, immobile machines.[3]

Later, after 1933, Otto Dix embraced *innere Emigration* – he did not leave the country, but went into self-imposed internal exile, living on the shores of Lake Constance and painting what appear to be innocuous landscapes. 'Emil Nolde's name was used to frighten naughty children before 1914: "If you don't behave," their mothers said, "I'll tell Nolde. He'll come and wipe you all over one of his pictures." '[4] George Grosz's teacher, Richard Müller, had this to say about him: 'That lout just sticks his finger up his arse and smears it all over the paper.'[5] As I have mentioned, Nolde, one of the best-known and, in our own day, most popular of the Expressionists, had a flirtation with the NSDAP, but it didn't last long. His early, deliberately primitive paintings appealed to certain back-to-Nordic instincts in the Nazis. Perhaps the life of a hermit that he lived in his north-coast fastness appealed to them too. Certainly Goebbels hung his office with Noldes in the early days and declared, 'We are all Noldes now.' But Goebbels had some genuine artistic perception, too.

If Nolde thought his acceptance by the Nazis might give him a long-term respectability, he was quickly disabused. By the mid-Thirties his work – with that of all the other Expressionists – was rejected in favour of a sentimental or muscle-bound 'realism', the child of Socialist Realism and late nineteenth-century academicism. Nolde withdrew, like Dix; throughout the war years he executed a series of 'unpainted pictures', owing something to the Fauves, but far more melancholy. They are all watercolours (oil paint has a giveaway smell), and they are small (thus easy to hide). Nolde was indulging in a hollow defiance.[6]

Another notable figure was the polymath Ernst Barlach, a sculptor who was also a master of the woodcut, a playwright and a novelist. He was greatly admired by Käthe Kollwitz, and I think there are affinities between his work and hers. He wrote no fewer than seven Expressionist plays between 1912 and 1929, many of which explore the relationship between father and son and some of which – unusually for plays of this period – are still performed today. He was made a member of the Berlin Academy in 1919, and was awarded both the Kleist Prize and the *Pour le Mérite*. But his work was deemed 'degenerate' by the Nazis. Perhaps his greatest achievement, his war memorial at Güstrow Cathedral, a great bronze Angel of Death, was ordered to be removed by Hitler as 'subversive'. He was hounded by the Nazis until his death in 1938.

George Grosz was one of the first to leave Germany. At Hamburg on 12 January 1933 he boarded the *Bremerhaven* for New York. He was not quite 40, but his best work was behind him. Like so many artists in exile, he could not find a new seam of inspiration away from his homeland. America had always been the land of his dreams and perhaps, even when he got there, it never really entered his waking consciousness. Like Dix he turned to innocuous landscapes, in which it is impossible to recognize the wiry energy of his Berlin work. His socialism mellowed. There is no doubt that he was homesick. Carl Zuckmayer remembers him in New York City, alcoholic, drinking *sazerac* – a cocktail of absinthe and bourbon. Grosz was not alone in his wretchedness. He writes in his autobiography of the death of Ernst Toller, who hanged himself in a Manhattan hotel room on 22 May 1939. There were other suicides, but it is impossible to know how far they were the result of homesickness, and how far of despair at what was happening in Germany.

Grosz survived the war, however, and returned to Berlin in 1956. His friend Walter Huder remembers:

> When he came back I booked a room for him and his wife in the Hilton and had a present put there of seven bottles of red champagne – red to reflect his socialist leanings, and champagne because of his inclination towards capitalism. He saw the joke and laughed ringingly. There was a big reunion in the Akademie der Künste, with people like Herbert Ihering, John Heartfield, Wiz [Wieland Herzfelde], and Hans Langhoff . . . One bottle of whisky after another was drunk. By three in the morning no one could stand upright except for George, who knew how to drink, and how much he could take, and me, because I know too . . . He was invited to return to Berlin [permanently], and three years later he did so. I managed to organize the old studio of Arno Breker [the Nazi artist] for him. It seemed fitting that George should get such a place, to exorcise it . . .
>
> . . . He wanted first to visit Neukölln, to breathe again the air of the Berlin proletariat. We went on a pub-crawl around Neukölln and he drank *Molle mit Korn*. A *Molle* is a small beer, and *Korn* is the workers' schnapps.[7] I kept throwing my *Korn* away when he wasn't looking because it's hard to take, but he drank one after the other . . . Then he wanted to go on to Wedding, where he'd painted in the Twenties . . . We took the *S-Bahn*, not a taxi, because he wanted to be with ordinary people, to feel them around him. On the journey, we discussed Kafka, and especially his fragment *Amerika*; and I have never had such an enlightening conversation with anyone about Kafka before or since. George himself was Kafkaesque – he knew Kafka's characters as if they were his own.
>
> We got to Wedding about 3 p.m. when the Berliner *Müttchens* [little mothers] take off their aprons and come up from their basements after lunch to chat while the sun still shines. Wedding is the old Huguenot quarter – people's names and traces of French in the local dialect bear this out: look at the name-plates on houses in Müllerstrasse, for example. A Weddinger will say *trottoir*, not *Gehsteig*, and *apartement*, not *Wohnung*. These *Müttchens* were talking in their *Berlinerisch*; and when George heard them, he cried, because he recognized his Berlin again.[8]

Grosz did not enjoy his homecoming for long. He died the same year:

> There have been several versions of George's death given out – that he was drunk, that he drank himself unconscious and died . . . But the truth is this: he met friends in the evening and went on a pub-crawl. At dawn they made their separate ways home – one of the friends even accompanied George as far as Savigny-Platz, where he lived. It was an old Berlin building in *Bürgerbarock*, with a spiral staircase. They'd added a lift later, which went up the inside of the spiral. George was making for the lift when he slipped on a banana skin and hit the back of his head on the newel-post of the staircase.

He was found by the *Morgenpost* delivery boy at 7 a.m. and died on the way to hospital.

Grosz was steeped in the spirit of his times. Even the contradiction of wanting to travel by *S-Bahn* to be with the workers, yet on it discussing Kafka with a fellow-intellectual, devalues neither the situation, nor the goodwill.

His wedding to his fellow art student Eva Peter in May 1920 had been a full-blooded Dada event, celebrated in a painting by John Heartfield. On an earlier occasion, the photographer Erwin Blumenfeld had managed to obtain sixty bottles of wine from his family's cellar, and invited Erwin Piscator, Richard Hülsenbeck, Wieland Herzfelde, John Heartfield, Grosz, and half a dozen others to help him drink them. Grosz then made a poster which read:

WELL-BUILT SOCIETY GIRLS
WITH FILM TALENTS
INVITED
TO A STUDIO PARTY
STUDIO GROSZ
8 PM
EVENING DRESS

This was then fixed to a pole and Grosz and Blumenfeld paraded with it up and down one of the main streets of Berlin. After more than fifty would-be film stars arrived on the night, the door was closed, and the 'orgy' (to use Blumenfeld's term) got under way. The master–servant relationship between the men and the women, implicit in the advertisement, was made explicit. Someone suggested that everyone should strip, but in the event only the women did. It was a wild evening. Two days later Blumenfeld awoke, freezing cold, in Grosz's bathtub. Someone had stolen his new blue suit.[9]

Like those of art, the bounds of architecture had been broken before the First World War, but rationalization of the new movements followed in the mid-Twenties. Architecture in Berlin takes many forms. The western suburbs contain beautiful examples of late nineteenth- and early twentieth-century domestic building, including the only Jugendstil station in Berlin – the one in Zehlendorf built by Hart and Lesser. In Klopstockstrasse the house at Number 19 is by a Scots architect called Campbell, and there are several by the great German architect Hermann Muthesius, a disciple of Frank Lloyd Wright whose splendid family houses are to be found throughout this delightful area.[10] Muthesius was also influenced by Ebenezer Howard's *Garden Cities of Tomorrow*, published in 1900, and with the Kaiser's blessing spent time in England studying English architecture and planning. As for Campbell:

17. Typewriter heroes. (*clockwise from top left*) Bertolt Brecht, Erich Kästner, Carl Zuckmayer and Kurt Tucholsky.

18. Leading ladies. (*clockwise from left*) Fritzi Massary, Tilla Durieux, Elisabeth Bergner and Greta Garbo.

19. Kings of the theatre. (*top left*) Max Reinhardt (and the interior of his Grosses Schauspielhaus); Leopold Jessner (*bottom left*) who toppled him; and the powerful critic, Alfred Kerr, with Bello.

20. German cinema reached its apogee against a background of revolution and rising Nazism. Scenes here from *The Cabinet of Dr Caligari*, *Nosferatu*, and Fritz Lang's *Metropolis*.

21. (*above*) Fritz Lang himself with monocle and Brigitte Helm; (*below*) Hans Albers in Georg Kaiser's *Two Neckties*, with Rosa Valetti and a slightly dumpy Marlene Dietrich.

22. The image that launched the Dietrich legend: the original poster for *The Blue Angel*.

23. Scenes from Berlin's musical life.
(*top*) Wilhelm Furtwängler on the slopes,
(*right*) Otto Klemperer with Paul
Hindemith, (*bottom*) Lotte Lenya with her
husband Kurt Weill.

24. Berlin's less edifying aspects. (*top*) Sexologist Magnus Hirschfeld, (*centre*) 30-stone ace detective Ernst Gennat, and (*bottom*) a *Ringverein* or criminals' mutual society with its mascot – a puppet policeman.

25. Less edifying still. Hilde Scheller (*top*), the centre of a celebrated sex and murder scandal; Georg Haarmann (*right*), serial murderer (Hitler's face reminded Klaus Mann of Haarmann's); Max Klante (*bottom*) whose genius for gambling swept him to a vast fortune, then to fraud and ruin.

26. Sport. The great boxer Max Schmeling, the start of
one of Berlin's six-day cycle races at the Sportpalast, and
Sir Malcolm Campbell at the Avus racetrack. Did he race
in that suit?

27. The 1936 Olympics. Racially pure German women at the opening ceremony. Leni Riefenstahl (*on the right*) directs a shot for her film *Olympiade*. A javelin thrower from the film.

28. Berliners had a weakness for clubs. (*above*) The Club of Seventh-month Children, proudly wearing beer bellies not easily achieved in their day. (*below*) A thoroughly serious women's wrestling club.

29. More clubs: (*above*) A Berlin cycling club goes through its paces; note the uniform. (*below*) A fitness club in the Grunewald, in uniform of another sort.

30. Unity Mitford, dedicated Nazi and
friend of Hitler, chats with an SS officer
outside the Brown House in Munich. (*inset*)
SA men on National Boycott Day, 1 April
1933. Why their placards are in English is
not explained.

31. The beginning of the end. (*above*) Seen from the Brandenburg Gate, a torchlit SA procession on 30 January 1933 celebrates Hitler's seizure of power. (*below*) On 10 May the same year, torches are applied to books.

Triumph des Willens

32. The finale. In this scene from Leni Riefenstahl's *The Triumph of the Will*, massed ranks of the SA march past as Hitler (*top left*) salutes. For all his megalomaniac plans, Hitler's victory ended Berlin's greatness for half a century.

Campbell was active in Berlin from about 1910 to 1925. What he did during the First World War I don't know, but he was in partnership with a German colleague. I recently received three fine pictures executed before the First World War of the first houses by Campbell and others in this part of Berlin. They were done by Le Corbusier – he was still Charles Edouard Jeanneret then – when he was studying with Peter Behrens. He spent his spare time going round sketching modern houses. They were all here together. There is a famous photograph of Le Corbusier, Mies van der Rohe, Gropius and Hannes Meyer, all in one picture together. Behrens moulded the whole of the younger generation, and no one else could have done it at that time.[11]

The neighbouring suburb of Dahlem also contains examples of work by Bauhaus architects, especially Walter Gropius, whose Haus Sonnefeld (with Hannes Meyer) is his tribute to Expressionism – a stupendous art deco log cabin built in 1921. Along what is now Argentinische Allee is a handful of small, fussy and self-consciously rustic villas which typify Nazi domestic architecture. Away to the north-eastern edge of Dahlem is Breitenbachplatz, where stands a block of workers' flats by Max Taut. 'It's a beautiful building,' says Julius Posener. 'Uncomplicated, consistent, sound, noble, workmanlike: incredibly good.'

A leader of the modern movement based in Berlin was Erich Mendelsohn, whose most famous building stands near the city. It is the Einstein Tower on the outskirts of Potsdam – an astrophysical laboratory and observatory which still forms part of a scientific institution. He was 33, and unknown, when he took on the commission for the building; and designed it, he later said, out of 'some unknown urge', letting it 'emerge from the mystique surrounding Einstein's universe'. When Einstein inspected the building, he approved of it much less garrulously: 'It is organic,' he said. Mendelsohn also built the astonishing, and alas now vanished, Mosse Building for the eponymous newspaper group, in the city centre. A large model of it in the Berlin Museum gives some impression of what it must have been like. He was also responsible for the Columbushaus office block which was erected on one side of Potsdamer Platz in 1931 – another revolutionary building now lost to us (and not to be confused, as it was by many Berliners at the time, with the Columbiahaus, a military convalescent home in Columbiastrasse in Templehof, later turned into a temporary concentration camp by Hitler). Mendelsohn's great colleague Hans Poelzig, who transformed the Zirkus Schumann into the Grosses Schauspielhaus for Max Reinhardt, was also a theatre and film designer, working for example on Paul Wegener's *The Golem* with his wife Marlene.

As a young architectural student, Julius Posener worked as an unpaid assistant for both Poelzig and Mendelsohn.

Mendelsohn's office struck me as a little Prussian. The pencils were stamped with the name of the firm – I imagine to prevent any from being 'lifted'. Mendelsohn, a disciplined worker himself, valued discipline highly. The Columbushaus was his last major project in Germany [in exile he designed the Hebrew University in Jerusalem], but working in the office was dull because you just sat at your desk and did a bit of detailing. I enjoyed myself much more when I was appointed assistant clerk of the works on site – then I was able to watch the building grow . . . Poelzig, on the other hand, was a very great teacher; the greatest influence of my life.

The Bauhaus was not a Berlin institution, but its influence during the Twenties and Thirties and beyond was mighty, and it ended its days in Berlin. (Today, there is probably no better place to see a concentration of domestic Bauhaus architecture than at the Weissenhofsiedlung in Stuttgart, where there are houses by Frank, Mies van der Rohe, Le Corbusier, Behrens, Oud, Scharoun, and others, all part of a 'model development'.)

The Bauhaus was founded in 1919 in Weimar. It drew its inspiration from the work of – among others – Gottfried Semper, Joseph Paxton (who designed the Crystal Palace), William Morris and, latterly, Peter Behrens. The school spent the years between 1926 and 1932 in a building designed by Walter Gropius in Dessau. In 1933 the Nazis closed it.

Born in 1883, Gropius had a grim war, and at the time of the Bauhaus' foundation was coming to terms with the collapse of his marriage to Gustav Mahler's widow, Alma. She went on to an affair with Kandinsky and a third marriage, to Franz Werfel. Gropius, who was involved with Bruno Taut in the Bauhaus' immediate forerunner, the Arbeitsrat für Kunst, set out its aims in the famous manifesto of April 1919: 'The goal of all creative activity is building . . .' As with the Arts and Crafts movement, its function was to produce a practical synthesis of all the arts and to mould a systematic style related to and inspired by industry; and to use machinery in the service of art. Artists and craftsmen and women of great standing representing every field were connected with the school as teachers and associates. People came and went, there was disagreement, but there was also a consistency in the output of the Bauhaus which perhaps helps to account for its far-reaching influence. It comes as a shock to learn that Marcel Breuer's 'Vassily' chair, the first tubular steel chair ever to be designed, dates from 1925, when Breuer was only 23. Put into production in 1926 by Standard Furniture of Berlin, it is still being made. Virtually all subsequent design owes something to the aesthetic principles of the Bauhaus, which perhaps accounts for the perennial modernity of Breuer's chair.

In 1922 one of the painters in the school, Paul Klee, drew a schematic diagram of a star within a circle. Around the circle were inscribed the basic materials used – glass, stone, wood, metal; and the courses to be followed in colour, composition, and construction. At the heart of the star was a smaller circle in which the fundamental aims of the Bauhaus were shown: *Bau und Bühne* – building and stage.

Surely few other schools can ever have boasted as distinguished a list of teachers. Besides Klee, painters included Lyonel Feininger, Johannes Itten, who originally directed the six-month foundation course, Oskar Schlemmer, Vassily Kandinsky, Piet Mondrian, and László Moholy-Nagy. The painter Gerhard Marcks was also a potter and sculptor. Christian Dell was in charge of metalwork, with Marianne Brandt – and both designed teapots and wine jugs; the painter Josef Albers joined the Bauhaus at Dessau, and he also designed tea-glasses and fruit-bowls. Marcel Breuer was in charge of cabinet-making. The Bauhaus was also involved in theatre. Gropius was engaged in a grandiose plan for a theatre for Piscator, and Oskar Schlemmer created a series of design dances. He was himself a brilliant dancer and mime and, inspired by Expressionism, designed for the *Bühnen-Werkstatt/Bauhausbühne* a series of costumes which defy description. Several of them are preserved in the Stuttgart Art Gallery.

When it became too 'progressive' for Weimar, the Bauhaus moved to Dessau, and it was in Dessau that the department of architecture was founded. The very left-wing Hannes Meyer was its first director, and when Gropius left in March 1928, succeeded him as principal. Kandinsky and Klee, who wanted to follow a freer kind of painting than that defined by the Bauhaus' philosophy, left at the same time. Meyer was not a successful principal, and was succeeded in 1930 by Mies van der Rohe. But the power of the NSDAP was waxing, and within two years the school was driven out of Dessau by the Nazi majority on the town council, inspired by the architect and art-theorist Schultze-Naumberg, who called the Bauhaus degenerate and 'Jewish–Marxist' (though in fact none of the members at that time were Jews). Only one or two voices were raised in protest.

The Bauhaus had a short life in Berlin as a private institute. Mies worked fast and hard, and it opened its doors in October, in a disused telephone factory near Steglitz. Unfortunately it soon attracted the attention of the Nazi press, which called it a 'breeding-ground of Bolshevism', singling out Mies, Albers and Kandinsky (who had returned as a teacher) for special attack. On 11 April 1933 the police and the SA occupied and searched the building. Mies spent several weeks negotiating with the Nazis for the school's survival, but in vain. The staff dissolved the institute on 19 July, two days before the Gestapo issued the harsh conditions under which it might remain open. Most soon left for America.[12]

As a footnote, this very short history of the Bauhaus returns to its origins. The original Weimar Bauhaus took root in a design school there run by the Belgian, Henry van der Velde, a champion of Jugendstil, who made his reputation by designing, in 1900, the interior of a large apartment in Köthnerstrasse in Berlin – which belonged to Harry, Graf Kessler.

In her diary on 26 February 1927, Käthe Kollwitz wrote: 'The last Schnabel concert today. For finale he played the Beethoven Sonata in C minor, Opus 111 ... The strange, glittering tones shot flames – a translation into the spheres; the heavens opened almost as in the Ninth. Then a return. But a return after Heaven has been assured. Clear – consoling – good – that is what this music is. Thank you, Schnabel!'

To mark 1927, the centenary year of the death of Beethoven, Artur Schnabel became the first pianist ever to play the complete cycle of thirty-two sonatas in one sequence, over seven Sundays at the People's Theatre.

Serious music has always been Germany's greatest artistic strength, and enthusiasm for serious music in Berlin in the Twenties was as high as it is for popular music in any big city today. Rudolf Serkin studied there, Georg Szell made his conducting debut there in 1914; Claudio Arrau, Vladimir Horowitz, and Wilhelm Backhaus all worked in the city. Composers and performers arrived as exiles from Russia, among them the cellist Gregor Piatigorsky. Pablo Casals performed in Berlin; Stravinsky and Toscanini conducted, as did Richard Strauss. In his autobiography *Theme and Variations*, Bruno Walter writes of unprecedented artistic sensitivity and passionate concentration.

There were three principal opera houses: Erich Kleiber ran the State Opera in Unter den Linden; Bruno Walter the Municipal Opera in Bismarckstrasse; and Otto Klemperer the Kroll Opera on the edge of the Tiergarten – where after his modern-dress *Flying Dutchman*, Wagner's son Siegfried accused him of *Kulturbolshewismus*. Klemperer also premièred Paul Hindemith's opera *Neues vom Tage* at the Kroll. 'A blazing success,' declared Harry Kessler. Hindemith must have felt himself vindicated by this success. Eight years earlier Richard Strauss had said to the then 26-year-old: 'Why do you write this atonal stuff? You have talent!' Hindemith had replied: 'Herr Professor, you make your music, and I'll make mine.'

At the Philharmonic, Artur Nikisch was principal conductor until his death in 1922, when his place was taken by the 38-year-old Wilhelm Furtwängler. The tall, angular Furtwängler was slow to show his talent, and for some time only his teacher, Max von Schillings, had any faith in him. When he conducted, he flailed his arms like the sails of a windmill. To rid himself of this habit, he practised with books clamped under his armpits.

The dominant figure of the first half of the Twenties was the composer and pianist Ferrucio Busoni. Born in 1866, he first came to Berlin in 1894, and in 1920 settled there for the last four years of his life. Following his death, Arnold Schönberg arrived to succeed him as director of the composition class at the *Hochschule*, the Berlin Conservatoire. He came from Vienna, a thin, asthmatic, embittered 51-year-old, sustained, in the face of years of opposition, by the belief that he had created a completely new grammar for music. In his early years he had supported himself by orchestrating operettas – as did his even more austere pupil, Anton Webern – and his first important work, the *Gurrelieder* (Songs of the Dove), waited twelve years from composition to performance. But then, surprisingly in view of its title, the *Gurrelieder* requires a 200-piece orchestra, four choruses and five soloists.[13]

Schönberg's pupils included Serkin, the Englishman Alan Bush, and the Americans Marc Blitzstein and Henry Cowell, but his most important students were Webern and his fellow-Viennese Alban Berg. Schönberg was a passable painter, and his portrait of Berg shows a dark, tall, stooped, graceful figure with large and beautiful eyes. Prosaically, Berg began his career as a government accountant, dealing with alcohol tax and pig-farming statistics. His major opera, *Wozzeck*, published by Berg himself with financial backing from Alma Mahler (then still married to Gropius), had its première at the State Opera in the face of stiff resistance from the Establishment, and was conducted by Erich Kleiber.

At the First Night, on 14 December 1925, the audience reacted violently.

'There were fist fights,' said Hans Heinsheimer, who was there, 'angry challenges shouted across the orchestra seats and from the boxes, deriding laughter, boos, and hostile whistles that threatened for some time to over-power the small but, at last, vigorous group of believers. As the tall, noble figure of the composer appeared before the curtain, the riots increased, the bravos and the boos, the waves of enthusiastic excitement and outraged hostility. Berg seemed a little taken aback by it, perhaps a shade paler than usual, but quite unaffected, calm, very sure of his work.'[14]

Critics were beside themselves with indignation; but time, and his welding of Schönberg's difficult and austere twelve-tone system to traditional and folk music forms, have helped Berg achieve greater popular accessibility than either his master or his fellow-student, Webern.

Because Schönberg was a Jew, even his non-Jewish pupils suffered from Nazi censorship. Though baptized and assimilated, in exile in Paris

Schönberg returned to the religion of his birth. From Paris he went to America, and ended his days there.

Wilhelm Furtwängler was among those who elected to stay on in Germany during the Third Reich and, like all his colleagues who made the same decision, had to bear public opprobrium for a few uncomfortable years following 1945. Opinion about him varies. Boleslaw Barlog, a struggling young theatrical befriended by Furtwängler in the Thirties, has no doubts where his loyalty lies.[15] 'Once Franz Jastrau, the orchestra's factotum, asked the Master [Furtwängler] and me to come and have a look at his pigeon loft ... once we were there, he selected a pigeon, wrung its neck, and stuffed it into Furtwängler's jacket pocket. Then he did the same for me. "That'll make a good stew for yer, gennulmun," he said. In such romantic circumstances did I have my first real meeting with Furtwängler.' A few months later, Barlog found himself at work in Furtwängler's apartment, sorting out his musical scores under the eye of his devoted housekeeper Lenchen Matschenz. Lenchen was from the Spreewald, with an accent as thick as pea-soup. Barlog maintains that Furtwängler was consistently and loudly anti-Nazi, and throughout the war did his best to protect the interests of victims of the regime.[16]

Shortly after the end of the Second World War, Barlog and others were sitting at the American Club at Waldsee in Zehlendorf with Otto Klemperer who, as a Jew, had been obliged to leave Germany in 1933. Klemperer and Furtwängler had been great rivals before the war, though they stood on different pinnacles. Furtwängler was Dionysian, Barlog says, and Klemperer, Apollonian:

> We were having an exhilarating conversation, and Furtwängler's name cropped up. Klemperer immediately became furious and shouted, 'That Furtwängler! That ghastly old Nazi!' There was an awkward silence ... One of us then said quietly: 'Herr Klemperer, you really shouldn't say that Furtwängler was a Nazi. You really shouldn't say that.' There was a pause. Klemperer brushed some glowing pipe-tobacco ash from a pullover, already full of holes from similar minor accidents, and finally replied, equally quietly: 'Well, there you are! He couldn't even be a Nazi!'[17]

Herbert von Karajan, then a young conductor from Aachen, posed a threat to Furtwängler's crown after his very first Berlin concert in 1938, and aroused the older man's envy. Karajan, incidentally, was the first in Berlin to conduct without the music in front of him.[18] 'Furtwängler was the greatest conductor of his day,' says Grete von Zieritz,[19]

> although Karajan was the *enfant terrible*, the great innovator. Göring brought him from Aachen to Berlin, and I remember seeing him conduct when he was 26 – and I was 35. He wasn't afraid of extremes: pianissimo

really was pianissimo, and to conduct without a score was a piece of bravura then. As for [Furtwängler's] staying – many of us stayed. I have been in this flat since 1926 and in 1945 it was one of the few buildings left standing in the street. Karl Böhm stayed in Dresden and tried to keep the flame of internationalism alight even during the worst times of the Third Reich. Furtwängler helped many people, and managed to get his Jewish secretary over to London to work for Sir Thomas Beecham. Böhm didn't give a damn about the Nazis when he did *Die schweigsame Frau*, which had a libretto by Stefan Zweig, who was a Jew. And Richard Strauss stayed, and Hauptmann – though he called himself a coward for doing so.

Grete von Zieritz has devoted her life to musical composition, supporting herself also by working as a pianist and teaching. Born in Vienna, she has become a *Berlinerin* by long adoption. In 1932 she ran into trouble with her *Die Passion im Urwald* (The Passion in the Primeval Jungle).

I wrote the words and the music, and I sat for the first performance with my teacher, Franz Schreker, and Erich Kleiber. The following day – and this was still before the *Machtergreifung* (seizure of power) – an SS *Sturmbannführer* came to the apartment. I remember everything on his uniform jingled all the time – medals, spurs, I don't know what, the idiot, and he came in and he said, 'Herr Dr Goebbels was at your concert, and he was appalled! How can a blonde German woman write a piece of work in which the negroes are honoured?' I replied, '*Herr Sturmbannführer*, tell Dr Goebbels that he has totally misunderstood the piece. It's about a German couple who are doing research in the jungle and they are ambushed by negroes who kill the husband and imprison the wife in a negro *kraal*. Thereupon I combined the woman's fear of death with the colours of the jungle.' The interview was at an end. The *Sturmbannführer* stood up, his sabre clattering, and left the apartment. He had no choice. I'd have thrown him out otherwise. And that was the last I heard of the matter. I continued to write honestly and I wrote what I wanted to write. But I have to say that my work was very melodic, and part at least was inspired by the German landscape, by Luneberg Heath; so that it was essentially German music – of a kind that only a German could write, and I expect that it was as a result of this I got very good reviews in the Thirties.

In 1936 her *Vögellieder* (Songs of the Birds) had its première in Dresden under Böhm to tremendous acclaim, with the soprano Erna Sack, who had a particularly high upper range.

Furtwängler originally planned to do the *Vögellieder*. I was summoned to his apartment . . . Furtwängler asked if I had a singer in mind. I said that Erna Berger was prepared to do it provided we found the right conductor! He replied, 'You're a charming Viennese. I have to go to Vienna tomorrow. Will you come with me?' I said, 'Dr Furtwängler, I'm very sorry, but at the moment I have no business in Vienna.' He handed me back my score, and I left. But shortly afterwards I met the heroic tenor of the Dresden Opera, who told me Böhm was looking for something for Erna Sack. So virtue prevailed! Furtwängler couldn't keep his hands off women, from little ballerinas to society hostesses. But I never furthered my career by means of the bedroom.

As a Jew, the composer Berthold Goldschmidt had to leave Germany. Born in 1903, his extraordinary career includes a break in composing work between 1958 and 1983, but he is now the subject of major rediscovery. The day he arrived in Berlin, Goldschmidt went to a concert at the *Hochschule* of Schönberg's *Pierrot Lunaire*. 'There was a scandal afterwards – people even came to blows in the audience; but that wasn't unusual. People could get very passionate about art. One point of etiquette: you didn't show your disapproval by booing, but by whistling.' Three years later, Schönberg attended the première of Goldschmidt's First String Quartet.

> [Schönberg] came round to congratulate me afterwards. 'You've had a success; I'm glad for you,' he said. But he didn't say that he liked my piece. He shook my hand and he was clearly expecting me to ask him, 'Herr Professor, may I please continue my studies with you?' . . . I didn't. He didn't react at all then, but 25 years later a friend of mine was conducting a piece by me in Los Angeles. Schönberg was present, and, noticing my name on the programme, said: 'Goldschmidt! Goldschmidt! There's another one who never had any faith in me!' So he had not forgotten what he had read as a snub. Which I had certainly not meant it to be. Schönberg came across as a very nervous, strict man. I was aware that he was a great genius and a great teacher – so great that I didn't want to join his students, because they all stood in his shadow and lost their independence.

Goldschmidt got to know Klemperer while working as his assistant in 1924.

> At end of the following year I won the Mendelssohn Prize for composition, and the fact was published in the Berlin press. A day or so later I went along to the music agents Wolff and Sachs, who managed all the important concerts in Berlin and who effectively controlled the Philharmonic at the time. I'd studied under Luise Wolff's – Queen Luise, as she was called – son in Hamburg, and so had a marvellous introduction to her. I was going to show her the score of the piece that had won the prize when I met Klemperer. 'Herr Goldschmidt, I see you've won a prize.' 'Yes.' 'Do you have the score?' 'Yes – I'm taking it to Frau Wolff.' 'Let me see it.' And he took it and glanced at it. 'Has it been performed?' 'No – but Kleiber is going to conduct it.' He was furious. 'I see. *So!*' he snapped.
>
> He was a vain and terribly jealous man. He couldn't bear Furtwängler – he thought him an exhibitionist, and over-indulgent of personal feelings, not letting the music speak for itself. And as far as he was concerned, Kleiber was a capricious experimenter. Bruno Walter was sentimental . . . But I got on

with him and we remained in touch all his life. He was furious with me when I did my work on Mahler's Tenth. 'Such a sketch should have been burnt! That was what Mahler wanted!' 'Not at all,' I replied. 'Anyway, you were the first to conduct the first two movements at the Philharmonic in Berlin in 1924 – I was there!' 'Yes, but I wouldn't do it again!'

Goldschmidt worked with all the great conductors active in Berlin between the wars.

The only one who didn't suffer from vanity and jealousy to a degree and who genuinely appreciated other people's work was Erich Kleiber. And everything he touched turned to gold. Unfortunately he isn't very well represented on record, but his interpretation of Mozart, for example, was masterly. Oddly, he was just as much at home with Wagner. But where some conductors used a whip, Kleiber used a magic wand. Walter was delicate and lyrical, Klemperer stylish and stern. You could tell who was conducting within the first eight or nine bars of a given piece. Walter had a gentle personality, yet was rather an unapproachable man.

I never knew Strauss personally, though I did play under him. He was Jupiter-like; above everything. He was neither condescending, nor friendly, nor cold. He simply expected the orchestra to do as he said and it did, out of reverence. His style was concise.

And Furtwängler adopted a deliberately diffuse style because he wanted a nebulous, Brahmsian sound from the orchestra. He stayed on under the Third Reich because he was vain, and that is something I will never forgive him for, because he could easily have left. But then he was unchallenged in Berlin after 1933 – until Karajan came along, which he didn't like one bit.[20]

University education in the Weimar era was in general regimented and classical, with an emphasis on militarism and nationalism. Jewish students and teachers were not encouraged, often actively discouraged, which cut universities off from what at the time was Germany's richest intellectual vein.[21]

The number of students increased: in 1925 there were 80,000, and in 1930 125,000. But student opinion of the time presents a contrast with our own period, perhaps with most periods. The young were traditionally conservatively minded in any case, and the difficulties of student life and problems in getting a job after it attracted the young to the simple solutions offered by the Right. The NSDAP was weak in the big cities but strong in provincial towns, and many provincial towns had universities. Not all universities were hotbeds of Nazism; but they were lukewarm about the Republic. Staff viewed republican ideas with conservative suspicion, and this was reflected in their teaching. Not surprisingly, anti-Semitism was strongest in universities like Rostock and Erlangen, where there were very few Jewish students or staff; but it is interesting that Heidelberg – with which one associates student clubs and duelling – was liberal in its outlook. By and large academia was hide-bound in a way that bordered on caricature. Harry Kessler angrily reported the celebration to mark the sixtieth birthday of Gerhart Hauptmann at Berlin University (which was then Friedrich-Wilhelms-Universität, and is now Humboldt), on 15 November 1922:

> Hauptmann sat between Ebert and [Dr Paul] Löbe . . . Some professor of literature, I think his name was Petersen, gave a boring, colourless speech . . . [We witnessed the] grotesquely narrow-minded behaviour of the students and the professors. The students' union had voted with, I believe, a four-to-two majority, not to take part in the Hauptmann celebration, because Haupt-mann, having made his Republican sympathies known, could no longer be considered a German of sound character! And I heard from Sam Fischer the publisher that this Petersen . . . had been to him two days earlier to ask him to withdraw the invitation to Ebert, because it would not be pleasing to the university to have the head of the Republic in its midst. And when Fischer refused, Petersen asked him at least to see about preventing Löbe from com-ing, as two Social Democrats at once would be a bit much![22]

Not all right-wing academics were so stupid, of course; nor was academia in general bereft of thought or culture. There were Republican intellectuals, like Johannes Ziekursch, neither a socialist nor a Jew but a committed Republican none the less, who between 1925 and 1930 published a major critical history of the Second Reich. Various left-wing intellectual and philosophical groups sprang up, with a large Jewish membership: the Deutsche Hochschule für Politik excluded only Com-munists and Nazis; the Institut für Sozialforschung (Institute for Social Research) in Frankfurt was 'a centre for left-wing Hegelians persuaded that Weimar was only a way-station to socialism',[23] and it was not closed down by the Nazis when they came to power (possibly because they hadn't any idea what the 'Frankfurt school' represented, so obscurely were its ideas expressed). One member, Herbert Marcuse, went on to become a thinker greatly admired by students in western Europe and America during the Sixties.

In Berlin, Freud's thinking was taught and developed at the Psycho-analytical Institute. This began as a branch of the International Associa-tion in 1910, and achieved independence in 1920. It was headed by Max Eitingon, assisted by Hans Sachs and Karl Abraham.[24] Abraham was one of the members of the Committee of the Seven Rings, and thus a chief disciple of Freud. The rings had been distributed by Freud himself, as 'a token of their solidarity'[25] in the quest to uncover the function and malfunction of the psyche.

Germany was so advanced in the field of physics that at the end of the Second World War all its principal scientists were gathered together and interrogated about their knowledge of nuclear weapons. They were taken to Farm Hall, twenty-five miles from Cambridge, and left there for observation. In the evenings their conversations were secretly taped. Friedrich von Weizsäcker looked after the roses, Max von Laue walked around the property fifty times a day (six miles of exercise), Werner Heisenberg read all of Anthony Trollope. On 6 August 1945 they heard the news about Hiroshima on the wireless. Otto Hahn was reduced to a state of suicidal depression. Seven years earlier he had read a report of experiments by Frédéric and Irène Joliot-Curie, and had repeated them in Berlin. When Hahn reported his findings to his close associate Lise Meitner (with whom he had worked for years in a Berlin University basement, as it was against the rules for a woman to enter the laboratories) she realized the significance of what he had achieved. He had split the atom. Meitner had later been hounded from Germany as a Jew.

Hahn had been working within a strong scientific tradition. Not long before, Einstein had developed Max Planck's Quantum Theory relating to light and energy into the Theory of Relativity, and observations of the solar eclipse in 1919 were used to test it. Einstein was a combination of many things of which the Right and the Nationalists disapproved: he was a Jew, a liberal, an internationalist, an innovator, a sceptic, and a physicist of suspiciously abstract intellectualism. A group called The Working Committee of German Natural Philosophers delivered a series of lectures against the 'Einstein hoax' – some of which Einstein attended, greeting their attacks with ironic laughter. But he was also abused directly at his own lectures, and the Jew-baiting abraded his spirit.

In 1927 a young scientist, then 18 years old and still a student, was involved in practical experiments in Reinickendorf in north Berlin. He and a group of associates interested in rocket research founded the Society for Space Travel, but they were also interested in developing the rocket as a weapon. They conducted experiments in a large rented field which they named Rocket Airport. The young scientist was Wernher von Braun. Later he was put in charge of the Nazi programme to develop a rocket-delivered warhead and, using facilities and slave labour provided at the concentration camp of Dora, saw both V1 and V2 rockets in use before the end of the Second World War. At the end of the war, he was snapped up by the Americans. Preparing for the Cold War, they were fearful of letting such men fall into Russian hands. By October 1945, von Braun was ensconced in El Paso, Texas, enjoying a handsome salary.

Gustav Stresemann's description of Berlin as a 'metropolis of brain-power' was not one of his more inspired, but the ugly image was true. Between 1918 and 1944, only two of the twenty-five Germans who won Nobel Prizes were not associated with Berlin. The presence of Planck and Einstein guaranteed that scientists would be attracted to the city, and the strong science facilities of the university outweighed its conservative reputation. The Kaiser-Wilhelm-Society had been founded in 1911 for scientific research, and Berlin had a long academic tradition. The philosophers Hegel and Fichte had studied and taught there, as had the philologists, the brothers Grimm. Alexander von Humboldt, the naturalist and geographer, had worked there also.

The fact that so few could understand Einstein's Theory of Relativity gave rise to some comedy. Roda Roda, the Viennese writer and *conférencier*, decided to do some research on behalf of his readers in the *BZ am Mittag*. First of all he went to see Planck, who of course knew exactly what his friend and colleague Einstein was getting at, but couldn't explain it – 'It's too hard!' Roda Roda therefore saw Einstein himself.

> 'I can't tell you about my theory,' said Einstein.
> 'Is that because I'm too stupid to understand it?'
> 'No, it's because *I'm* too stupid to *explain* it!'

'Relatively' became a catch-word in Berlin: he slept relatively well; her new boy friend is relatively good-looking; times are relatively hard. Ordinary Berliners took Einstein to their hearts. Perhaps they felt sorry for him. When he tried to explain his thoughts, his face took on the good-natured expression of a man who knew he would never make himself understood. His difficulty with mental arithmetic was also endearingly familiar, especially since he didn't drive, to the occasional Berlin bus conductor.

Einstein was lecturing in America when Hitler came to power, and decided to stay there. He became an American citizen in 1940.

Max Planck's personal life was a tragic one. Having lost his elder son in the First World War, his two daughters in childbirth, and his wife, he lived to see his second son, Erwin, executed in 1945 for his part in the German resistance to Hitler. Like Otto Hahn, he was hounded by the Nazis for his protective attitude towards the Jews. He died in Göttingen in 1947. The Kaiser-Wilhelm-Society became the Max Planck Institute in his honour.

During the first thirty years of the century, Berlin's Charité Hospital was acknowledged to be one of the world's leading medical research centres, and when they travelled abroad its professors carried diplomatic passports so that they and their valuable instruments should not be disturbed. The head of the surgical department from 1927 was Dr Ferdinand Sauerbruch. In the mid-Thirties Lord Dawson, the Physician Royal, sent his nephew to be Sauerbruch's assistant and to study with him. Sauerbruch operated on many German and other European leaders. Although Goebbels lay in bed at the Charité for ten days with appendicitis, refusing an operation, which filled him with fear, Fate must have been on his side: Sauerbruch pulled him through, despite receiving two anonymous telegrams reminding him of his duty *not* to help. Sauerbruch, who remained in Berlin throughout the Second World War and survived it, also operated on the infamous Dr Robert Ley, head of the German Workers' Front (a Nazi organization designed to replace trades unions) and of the *Kraft durch Freude* (Strength Through Joy) organization. Ley suffered from piles; but he was less scared of the operation than of the anaesthetic, preferring to dose himself with two bottles of brandy.

It fell to Professor Carl von Eicken to operate on Hitler himself. Hitler had a panicky fear of cancer of the larynx and wanted an examination. Eicken, the head of the Charité's ear, nose and throat department, diagnosed a polyp on the vocal cords resulting from overuse, and operated on 22 May 1935. Hitler's anxiety was neither the operation nor the anaesthetic, but that anyone should know he was unwell. The operation took place in deepest secrecy. Sauerbruch and his colleagues may have had cause to reflect on the relative morality – in their case – of strict adherence to a physician's duty.

10 Stopping a Catastrophe with a Typewriter

BERLIN CAFÉ SOCIETY was – so far as such a thing is possible – informally regimented. There were cafés for the old, cafés for the middle-aged, and cafés for the young. There were cafés for all classes. And there were particular cafés for particular professions. In the civilized society of mainland Europe, the café is the club, debating society and workroom of the artist. In 1929, Berlin was blessed with 16,000 bars, coffee shops and dance-halls.

In Rankestrasse was the Weinstube von Schwannecke. The proprietor, Viktor Schwannecke, from Saxony, was a former actor who had been intendant of the Bayerischer Staatstheater in Munich after the First World War. His was an actors' dive, and a place to show off, for the steeper your slate the higher your standing. The actors Fritz Kortner, Rudolf Forster and Ernst Deutsch drank here, along with Leopold Jessner and the famous dancer Gret Palucca. To stay 'in', it was essential to be seen at Schwannecke's at least once a month. Then there was Anna Maenze's in Augsburgerstrasse. This place was discovered by Ernst Lubitsch. It wasn't at all grand, like Schwannecke's. In fact, it was quite shabby, but comfortable. Outside, the paper-seller Papa Duff (Adalbert Duffner) had his pitch. He also worked as an extra in dozens of films. Anna's was for film people.

More sophisticated establishments were the bars to be found in the grand hotels. The Eden Bar provided a haven for Kortner, for Max Pallenberg and Fritzi Massary, for the writer Erich Maria Remarque, and for Albert Bassermann. 'Gossip and tittle-tattle, and very little politics,' remembered Kortner. The Adlon Bar was the rendezvous for the foreign press, taking refuge from the natives, and the Café Adler in Nollendorfplatz was used by doctors and writers – and people like Alfred

Döblin and Gottfried Benn, who were both – and by the *Berliner Tageblatt* critic, Ludwig Marcuse. The Austrian playwright Joseph Roth (who wrote *The Radetzky March*) was a regular at Mampe's Gute Stube in Kurfürstendamm, and Erich Kästner wrote poetry at a table in the Café Leon. Further west, the Westend-Klause was the place where people who lived on Sachsenpark and nearby met: they included Paul Wegener, Henny Porten, Max Schmeling, Joachim Ringelnatz and Kate Kühl, who sang songs by Ringelnatz, Brecht and Tucholsky with an intensity that became legendary. Die Kleine Scala, opposite the Scala Variety Theatre, was run by 'Mutta' Schwanebeck, fat and jolly but also a shrewd businesswoman. The walls were hidden beneath signed photographs of her clientele – all international stars – and a gilded bust of Grock presided over the drinking. Among those who frequented Freddy Kaufmann's bar, The Jockey, were Max Slevogt, Max Liebermann, Jean Cocteau, Anthony Asquith, Ernest Hemingway, Marlene Dietrich, Vicki Baum, Richard Tauber and Alfred Kerr.

But the café of cafés, the Athenaeum of Berlin literary society but also 'an asylum for the homeless in spirit',[1] was the Romanisches Café. The Romanisches building itself, destroyed during the final pitiless bombardment of Berlin at the end of the Second World War, was a horrible, inhospitable neo-Romantic pile; the harshly lit interior was divided into two rooms and a gallery. Its atmosphere was provided – in return for not being nagged to buy more than one cup of coffee every ten hours – by a very mixed collection of artists and writers. Apart from the genuine ones, there were many who merely dressed the part, and a lot of tourists, too; their spending subsidized the bearded men in tweed jackets and bow-ties and the plump or slinky women with bobbed hair, smoking cheroots and waving long fingers heavy with rings, who would lean towards each other across bare tables, sketching ephemeral masterpieces on paper napkins, or sit over the traditional artist's 'breakfast' (sometimes their only meal of the day) – two eggs in a glass.

Until the débâcle of 1933 there were 800 dramatists and other authors living in Berlin (excluding journalists), of whom perhaps a quarter are still known today. The concentration of hopefuls in the capital was not surprising: Berlin was also the base of all the big publishers, from established companies like Ullstein to firms new then but which today have entered the pantheon of great international publishing, such as Fischer, Rowohlt and Kiepenheuer. Altogether there were 1,200 publishing concerns in Berlin, though some did no more than produce poetry magazines with a circulation of perhaps one hundred. The Romanisches Café – whose doors were open especially to writers – stood across from the Gedächtniskirche in Auguste-Viktoria-Platz; its portals were presided over by the tall, blond doorman, Nietz, and inside, a house hierarchy obtained. There was the 'swimming pool', the meeting place for regulars like George Grosz, Max Slevogt (who had a *Stammtisch* – a permanent table), Emil Orlik and Leo von König, as well as for visitors like Luigi Pirandello. From here a staircase led to the gallery, where the chess tables were. Emanuel Lasker, the brother-in-law of another regular, the poetess Else Lasker-Schüler, and a world grandmaster for three decades, played here. He was 'a mathematician with a lowering, reptilian gaze when he played'; and there were humbler though no less passionate *aficionados* of the game, like the actor Oskar Homolka.

In the 'paddling pool' the writers and poets met – Erich Mühsam, Roda Roda, Ernst Toller, Bertolt Brecht, Heinrich Mann, Walter Mehring, Carl Zuckmayer, Billy Wilder, Egon Erwin Kisch, Anton Kuh (managing to get by without paying a penny, as he always did), Joseph Roth and Walter Hasenclever. Kisch was a globe-trotting Czech reporter who had made his reputation by breaking the Redl spy scandal in Karlsbad before the First World War. 'He was great,' remembers Steffie Spira. 'And so was his girl-friend for all the time I knew him, Gisl Liner. If anyone ever asked him why he didn't marry Gisl, he'd say with his slightly twisted mouth, between whose lips a cigarette always dangled, "I know her too well; she's not a sympathetic person", and he'd smile at her with all his considerable charm.'

'Kisch used the Romanisches like you or I would use a hotel,' remembers Alfred Fischer. 'We Jews nicknamed the Romanisches the *Rachmonisches* – from the Hebrew *rachmones*, mercy.' Minor luminaries, hopefuls and poseurs would sit in the café all day, teasing out a cup of coffee, arguing, declaiming, sorting out the world's problems. The Berlin critic Herbert Pfeiffer noted that there were 'people who were only capable of reading and doing their writing in the Romanisches Café'. Alfred Fischer remembers Johann (or John) Höxter, a talented cartoonist rumoured to write beautiful poems on lavatory paper.

> He looked terrible, though. He had a mouthful of black teeth, and he was certainly a drug-addict. He was a bit of sponger, too, like Anton Kuh, but unlike Kuh he'd be happy with 50 pfennigs. Kuh wasn't just a sponger, but a talented writer – he wrote the screenplay for Lubitsch's *Maria Stuart*, for example. I remember being quite offended that Kuh never touched me for money, but he selected his targets with care, and I wasn't rich enough to be a good prospect. He had to leave when the Nazis came to power, and he made his way to New York. He came up with a famous line when he left: 'Spongers are needed everywhere.' He died in New York in 1941. I don't think he was more than fifty.

The Romanisches was a magnet for visiting artists, from T. S. Eliot to Robert Musil (who lived in Berlin for two years, composing the bulk of his massive *The Man Without Qualities*); from Sinclair Lewis and Thomas Wolfe to André Gide. It was also the first stop for hopefuls arriving in Berlin. Billy Wilder, fresh from Vienna,[2] used the café network as effectively as anyone. He was a good journalist, but once or twice, when the flow of money from articles dried up, he worked as an *Eintänzer*. 'He had three qualities essential to a gigolo: he was a good dancer, he had his own dinner-jacket, and he spoke English.' He first came into contact with show business people by dancing at the Eden Hotel with Carola Neher; her husband, the poet Klabund, couldn't dance because of his TB. She set Wilder to write a series of articles on life as an *Eintänzer*, which he sold to the *Berliner Zeitung am Mittag*. He also wrote an article on Erich von Stroheim called 'The Man You Love to Hate'. Stroheim, already an established Hollywood director, was moderately furious. Twenty years later, in 1943, he played the lead in a Wilder film about Rommel, called *Five Graves to Cairo*. When they met on the set in Hollywood Wilder said to him, 'Even when I wrote that article, I knew you were ten years ahead of your time.' Stroheim fixed him with a monocled eye and said coldly: 'What do you mean, ten years? I was at least *twenty* years ahead of my time, Herr Wilder!'

Journalists were simply writers who lived less leisurely lives. In 1930 Berlin had more newspapers than any other city in the world. There were 149, from the big quality dailies like the *Vossische Zeitung* and the *Berliner Tageblatt*, though the yellow press *Berliner Morgenpost* and *Berliner Lokal-Anzeiger* to local weeklies like the *Dahlemer Nachrichten*. About twenty dailies ran to two editions, and *Tempo* ran to three, so that on any day a new edition of one or the other was on the streets every ten minutes. Apart from the papers, nearly 400 specialist and monthly magazines were compiled and published, from the *Berliner Illustrirte* to the *Grüne Post*, the *Koralle*, the *Dame*, and the *Woche*. There were literary and politically critical magazines such as the *Weltbühne*, the *Querschnitt*, and the *Literarische Welt*. There were comic and satirical magazines like *Uhu* and *Ulk*. Most papers had Sunday colour supplements.

The whole empire was shared between three kings: the newspaper and publishing houses of Mosse, Scherl and Ullstein. 'Radio was just learning to walk; television wasn't out of nappies: the word still reigned supreme. Anyone with a gram of ambition could sell articles in Berlin in those days,' an old Kochstrasse journalist told me when I was last in the city.

Rudolf Mosse was the first to arrive. He had made his money as an advertising agent; the only newspaper not to give him work was the rather stately *Vossische Zeitung* (founded in 1705 by the bookseller Christian Friedrich Voss), which did not take classified advertisements. Mosse decided to produce a rival newspaper to 'Auntie Voss', and in 1872 he started the *Berliner Tageblatt*. In 1876 the Ullstein family, already established in the printing and paper supply trades, followed with the *Berliner Zeitung*. In the course of time they took over the *Voss*, which under Georg Bernhard became such a distinguished voice of democracy that the Nazis closed it in 1933. August Scherl founded the *Berliner Lokal-Anzeiger*. This paper was the first to make imaginative journalistic use of the telephone. When Friedrich III lay dying and Wilhelm sealed the palace at Potsdam so that no one could get in or out, news of the emperor's condition was frozen. But when Friedrich died and the secret police had completed their search, the state of siege was lifted, and the castellan rang to tell the Potsdam laundry that 'the laundry could be picked up'. The laundry telephoned this news through to the *Lokal-Anzeiger*, which correctly inferred from it that Friedrich was dead, and broke the news accordingly.

The editors employed by Mosse and Ullstein, especially Bernhard at the *Voss* and Wolff at the *Tageblatt*, remained guardians of the Republic until the end. But after Scherl's death, his publishing concerns were bought by a syndicate led by Alfred Hugenberg, and their focus shifted sharply to the Right. For all his political ambition and business acumen, Hugenberg earned little respect. His nickname was The Silver Fox – but Goebbels called him 'Hugenzwerg'. *Berg* is German for mountain, *Zwerg* for dwarf.

By virtue of the people who read them, small-circulation papers might also be influential, so that to this short tally of important editors may be added the names of Siegfried Jacobsohn of the *Weltbühne*, and Emil Faktor of the *Börsen-Courier*.[3] Drama critics held positions of special power, partly because of the value placed on drama by Berliners, but also, particularly in the Wilhelmine era, because the drama critic was one of the few journalists who could write his mind. Political journalism in any critical sense of the job scarcely existed; but within the context of reviewing a play, the drama critic could by implication extend his findings and opinions beyond the stage.

The Dada and Expressionist movements drew in their train a number of left-wing publications. Malik was the most famous left-wing publishing house, founded by the Herzfelde brothers and run by Wieland, who took the business to Prague after the Nazis came to power. The Communist magazine *Linkskurve* clung so rigidly to Party lines that it was too busy criticizing left-wing deviants to notice the rise of the real enemy – the Nazis. It was hardly alone in that; *Die Weltbühne* (The World Stage) at first made the same mistake, and it was a far more significant and more broadly-based left-wing magazine. It acquired a sharp political focus under its last editor, Carl von Ossietzky, when its star was

Kurt Tucholsky, writing under four pseudonyms; and it also managed to attract contributions from such intellectuals as Ernst Bloch and Walter Benjamin.

Paradoxically, what hamstrung intellectual influence in politics was probably the very thing which gave it its quality – Jewish domination. Jews were in the majority in most branches of artistic and intellectual activity, and this was resented. Giving vent to his disgust at the permissiveness of Berlin, the press and theatre, and at left-wing thinking and internationalism, the journalist Friedrich Hussong wrote (in his book *Kurfürstendamm*, published shortly after Hitler's accession to power):

> A miracle has taken place. They are no longer here . . . They claimed they were the German *Geist*, German culture, the German present and future. They represented Germany to the world, they spoke in its name . . . Everything else was mistaken, inferior, regrettable kitsch, odious philistinism . . . They always sat in the front row. They awarded knighthoods of the spirit and of Europeanism. What they did not permit did not exist . . . Whoever served them was sure to succeed. He appeared on their stages, wrote in their journals, was advertised all over the world; his commodity was recommended whether it was cheese or relativity, powder or *Zeittheater*, patent medicines or human rights, democracy or Bolshevism, propaganda for abortion or against the legal system, rotten Negro music or dancing in the nude. In brief, there was never a more shameless dictatorship than that of the democratic intelligentsia and the *Zivilsationsliteraten*.[4]

This was the authentic voice of the right-wing backlash. The respectable silent majority had seen its savings destroyed in the inflation, its moral sensibilities scattered to the four winds, and even the sacrifices it made in the First World War devalued. The pendulum now swung too far in the direction of reaction. The new-found freedom of expression used by an articulate minority to express itself after years of repression was misinterpreted and overestimated by the Right; but the politicians of the Right also used public reaction as a tool to regain power.[5]

Party newspapers were already entrenched in their attitudes. The KPD's newspaper, *Die Rote Fahne*, interpreted events only from a Marxist-Leninist viewpoint, and the SPD's *Vorwärts* was no less partisan, though its articles were more temperate. At the other extreme was the ill-written and rabid *Völkische Beobachter*, the NSDAP's organ, which after the Nazi seizure of power became Germany's only national newspapers; other newspapers continued to operate only under severely restricted reporting conditions.

Die Weltbühne was a still, small voice of opposition to the Right, a small-format weekly magazine, whose circulation hovered around 20,000 but whose readers were the cream of intellectual society. It attracted writers of the calibre of Arnold Zweig, Walter Mehring, Ernst Toller and, above all, Tucholsky, who for a short time was its editor. His successor was Carl von Ossietzky.

Ossietzky was a staunch Republican who did not hesitate to publish an article by the aircraft designer Walter Kreiser about the armed forces' secret research and development into military aircraft, though he thereby exposed official contravention of the Treaty of Versailles. The armed forces bayed for his blood. Kreiser fled to Paris but Ossietzky preferred prison, as a means of drawing attention to militarism and embarrassing the government. In 1931 he was tried, and sentenced to eighteen months' gaol. A few years earlier this might have caused a furore, but by the early Thirties it was no longer possible for a liberal voice to be raised and heeded. When Hitler came to power Ossietzky was sent to Sachsenhausen-Oranienburg concentration camp, where he had the low (and therefore early) prisoner number 562. He was released in 1935, and in the same year was awarded the Nobel Peace Prize on the recommendation of, among others, Thomas Mann. Hitler was so infuriated by this that he forbade Germans to accept Nobel accolades in any field for the future, and Ossietzky was refused permission to travel to Stockholm. He died three years later, aged 39, of sickness picked up in the camp. (In opposition to the Nobel Prize, the Nazi Party instituted a German National Prize for Art and Science, among whose recipients were the Party ideologue Alfred Rosenberg, and the surgeons August Bier and Ferdinand Sauerbruch. A branch of science known as Aryan Physics, which sought to refute Einsteinian theory, was also inaugurated.)

While Thomas Mann, in Switzerland since February 1933, was censured *in absentia* for his support of Ossietsky, his eldest son Klaus recorded a striking insight. He was in the Carlton Tea Rooms in Munich one afternoon in the early Thirties. Sitting at a nearby table was Hitler, eating strawberry tart and discussing a musical with a couple of his henchmen . . . 'I suddenly remembered whom Herr Hitler resembled. It was that sex-murderer in Hannover, whose case had made such huge headlines . . . his name was Haarmann . . . The likeness between him and Hitler was striking. The sightless eyes, the moustache, the brutal and nervous mouth, even the unspeakable vulgarity of the fleshy nose; it was, indeed, precisely the same physiognomy . . .'[6]

As early as 1923 Carl Zuckmayer, then also in Munich, had noted a personal impression of Hitler.

During this period I frequently attended Adolf Hitler's beer-hall meetings. I wanted to know just what the situation was. Once I succeeded in getting a seat so close to the speakers' platform that I could see the spittle spraying from under his moustache. For people like us the man was a howling dervish; but he knew how to whip up those crowds jammed closely in a dense cloud of cigarette smoke and *Wurst* vapours – not by arguments but by the fanaticism of his manner, the roaring and the screeching, interlarded with middle-class oratory, and especially by the hypnotic power of his repetitions, delivered in a certain infectious rhythm. This was a technique he had developed himself, and it had a frightening, primitive force.[7]

Liberal writers watched the rise of Hitler with acuity and increasing panic. Most knew that they could not stay if he came to power; but that outside the German-speaking world they would have no livelihoods. Few spoke or wrote English or French well enough to express themselves in those languages, and besides, their country and their intimate knowledge of it provided their raw material. For Jewish writers and artists, the agony was even more intense.

Through Annemarie Seidel, an actress in *Der fröhliche Weinberg*, Carl Zuckmayer made the acquaintance of a wide group of artists, including many writers. Among them was Walter Mehring: 'Born and brought up in Berlin, he epitomized in his early writing the *élan vital* of the city, and its highly-charged intellectualism. His cabaret songs – sung by him in a sharp, somewhat nasal voice – [were] the quintessence of Berlin, dealing with all aspects of city life.'[8] Mehring was a highly cultivated man and an internationalist. He edited the humorous magazine *Ulk*, and translated French and American poetry into German, as well as writing poetry and plays, and cabaret songs. Like Tucholsky he was a major contributor to the *Weltbühne*, and like Tucholsky he spent more and more time in France from the mid-Twenties on.

When Zuckmayer won the Kleist Prize, three of the five Ullstein brothers turned up to the reception to celebrate, and he was able to draw on his publishers almost limitlessly. But within a year he already felt that 'time was running out for the German Republic. The evil tide was already rising ... It was all the more urgent, therefore, to do well whatever we did now, and to find a firm place to stand before the ground was washed from under our feet.'

At this time of increasing uncertainty and flux (for those perceptive enough to be aware of it) Zuckmayer made the acquaintance of another *Urberliner* – a Berliner to his fingertips – Max Liebermann, who at 80 designed the sets for Zuckmayer's play *Schinderhannes* in 1927.

My meetings and conferences with the great man, sometimes in his country home at Wannsee, sometimes in his city apartment in Pariser Platz, are among my gayest memories. His Berlin wit and his bluntness of speech were proverbial. I was given some astonishing examples of it. Once, when I visited him in the morning, he offered me a bottle of heavy Burgundy and a giant Partagas cigar. 'You see,' he said in his thickest Berlin dialect, pouring me glass after glass without drinking a drop himself, 'I can't any more. I used to love to drink and smoke in the morning. But when you cross the 80 line,

that's over. The only thing that still does its job right' – he slapped his
trousers loudly – 'is the old peter.' I may have looked at him in some perplex-
ity, for he added, 'Would you believe it? – only yesterday in the studio.
There was one of these women who are crazy about art . . .'

But there was little to relieve the gathering sense of doom. Returning
to Berlin in mid-July 1931 from his country retreat near Salzburg,
Zuckmayer found the banks closed, and their buildings surrounded by
angry, fearful people. It hardly seemed possible that financial disaster
could cost people their savings a second time in eight years. 'The average
German felt himself abandoned by all sides. No wonder he mistook the
lust for power of the Nazi leaders for something healthy and vigorous,
promising a gleam of hope for better things to come. He did not realize
that instead of honest though feeble efforts to deal with the crisis, all
would be staked on a vicious gamble.'[9]

Meanwhile, life had to go on; Zuckmayer was not as politically engaged
as many, at least not in his writing. He had come back to Berlin to work
on an adaptation of Ernest Hemingway's *A Farewell to Arms*, a vehicle
for Käthe Dorsch, who badly wanted to play Catherine. His collaborator
was Heinz Hilpert, the director who had taken charge of the Deutsches
Theater, and one of the artists who elected to stay on under Hitler.

Hemingway came to the opening from Paris, where he was then staying. He
was drunk by the time he arrived. He had a hip-flask of whisky in his coat
pocket, and from time to time would raise it to his mouth, screwing up his
eyes as if taking aim: then he would look around, half absently, half daringly.
Hilpert took him to the Hotel Eden, where he promptly went to the bar and
ordered champagne. He brought the hip-flask to the performance, and
whenever he was not taking a nip from it he seemed to be dozing. He
understood no German, and it was not clear whether the scenes he saw on
the stage reminded him of anything in his book, or of anything at all. During
the intermission he was taken to the dressing-room to see Käthe Dorsch. He
squeezed her hand and asked loudly and clearly how much 'this girl' charged
for a night. Since she understood no English, she thought he had paid her
a compliment on her performance. She smiled and gave him a gracious nod.
Thereupon he offered her a swallow from his flask, which she refused by sign
language. We managed to persuade him to leave the dressing-room after he
had made a firm offer of 'a hundred dollars and not a cent more'. Fortunately
she did not understand that, either. Hemingway was well aware, of course,
that you cannot buy an actress for a night, but was having fun playing the
American hillbilly. At the end of the evening, which proved a great theatrical
hit, the hip-flask was empty and Hemingway had to be taken home in a cab.
He spent the rest of the night drinking at the Eden Hotel, then took the train
back to Paris in the same state in which he had arrived.[10]

Before the night of Nazism fell, it was still perfectly possible for writers to indulge their fantasies, have fun, and even play political practical jokes.

> Edith Tietz, the department store heiress, was in love with Ernst Toller when he was still a young playwright. The Villa Tietz, which no longer exists, was a copy of the Wartburg, and had a large statue of Bismarck outside it. At the time of the romance, Toller lived two streets away in a furnished flat, so that when the family went away to Italy on holiday, Edith rang Ernst and suggested that he move in for three weeks to make use of the house, the servants and the grounds. So he did, but living alone in the great building he quickly became bored, so he invited Walter Hasenclever – who at the time lived in nearby Dahlem – to join him. They both became bored together. As an antidote, they decided to throw a big society party. They sent out invitations on Tietz letter-head but in their own names, requesting formal dress – white tie. It was a typical Berlin joke that two proletarian poets should hold a levée in the home of one of the local princes of capitalism. The guests were offered potato cakes – workers' grub – but they were served with Henkell Trocken, which is the best local champagne. Everyone thought this was a very chic idea; but the potato cakes had been fried in castor oil and this had a lightning effect on people's bowels. Worse, in all the huge villa there were only two lavatories – so that the guests were forced to rush out into the grounds to look for bushes to crouch behind. The whole thing was a fiasco, and later Edith's father bought up the entire edition of *Die Rote Fahne* which carried the story, to cover up the practical joke.[11]

As I have mentioned, the mainstay of the *Weltbühne* throughout his and its career was Kurt Tucholsky. He was a Jew, born in Berlin in 1890, and his weapon was satire. He wrote two short romantic novellas, one at the beginning and one at the end of his career, and with Walter Hasenclever he penned a not wholly successful play; but the body of his work was journalism. He left 2,500 articles and poems behind him. With a kind of consciously cultivated cultural schizophrenia, he gave each *nom de plume* he used a distinct personality. Theobald Tiger wrote bitter-sweet poems and cabaret songs; Peter Panter was the creator of the crisp satirical aphorisms for which Tucholsky is still known and admired:

> The reader is fortunate; he can choose his own writer.

> The Danes are stingier than the Italians. Spanish women indulge in illicit sex more readily than German women. All Latvians are thieves. Bulgarians stink. Romanians are braver than Frenchmen. Russians embezzle money. (None of this may be true – but you will see it in print in the next war.)

> On account of bad weather, the German revolution took place in music.

> This continent is proud of itself and has a right to be. What they are proud of in Europe: Of being a German. Of being a Frenchman. Of being an Englishman. Of not being a German. Of not being a Frenchman. Of not being an Englishman.[12]

Kaspar Hauser was reflective; Ignaz Wrobel was angry, direct, and not afraid to be bitter. It was no secret to Tucholsky's readership who was behind these various personae. He was much loved, and Erich Kästner described him pithily as a 'fat little Berliner trying to stop a catastrophe with a typewriter'. How sadly apt the remark was.

The impossibility of the task was borne out in Tucho's own life. Had he opted for story-writing he might have been happier; his *Rheinsberg – ein Bilderbuch für Verliebte* (Rheinsberg: A Picturebook for Lovers), published in 1912, which was 'a charming and unconventional love story acclaimed by both the critics and a wide readership',[13] had sold fifty copies by 1921 – and 100,000 a decade later. Unfortunately, Tucholsky had sold his rights in it to the publisher Alex Juncker for 125 marks.

Like many others, Tucholsky had been politicized by the events of 1918/19; despite *Welbühne's* popularity, even its influence, he was pursued by the thought that all he wrote against the ills of society was futile, and from 1923 on he suffered increasingly from the failure of his work to make the desired impact. 'What worries me is the problem of effectiveness,' he wrote in 1931. 'Does my work have any? (I don't mean success: that leaves me cold) . . . I write and write – but what effect does it have on the conduct of my country?' Reproached by the Establishment for taking too negative an attitude to his own society, Tucholsky replied in the *Weltbühne* that it was impossible to be anything but sharply critical in a country where genuine revolution had failed and where the forces of reaction still had the whip hand. The freedom to express oneself on paper had been achieved, but not the freedom to *do* anything. Sensitive and complex through Tucholsky was, a satirist with a romantic streak, his personal attitude to women was certainly sexist by today's standards. He paid his second wife the 'compliment' of using the masculine pronoun for her, and in his 'Essay on Man' he wrote: 'Man breaks down into two parts: a male part which doesn't want to think and a female one which is unable to.' This apart, his work (and nature) was informed with an intense humanity. And his urgent fear that militarism and nationalism would lead, as night follows day, to another destructive and pointless war was all too prophetic. His despair increased with the rise of Nazism. 'Satire has a limit at the top,' he wrote. 'Buddha is above it. It also has a limit at the bottom: the Fascist forms in Germany . . . One cannot shoot that low.' And a hint of the decision he was heading towards may be found in another of his aphorisms, 'He who has seen much of this world smiles, folds his hands on his stomach, and is silent.' He could never, though, absolutely give up writing; nor did he – at least privately.

He left for Paris in 1924, returned briefly two years later as editor of the *Weltbühne*, left again and drifted away from the paper and his friends on it. Tucholsky never lived in Berlin again after 1927, though he returned on frequent visits. He allied himself with the Communists, in the face of the Nazi's escalating power, but became disillusioned with them after the slump of 1929, and felt isolated. In a letter of 18 January 1931 to his younger brother Fritz, he explains why he does not wish to become directly involved with the *Weltbühne* again: 'Don't tell anyone else, but the whole thing doesn't interest me any more. I am fed up with it . . . I don't have the intention to become a Catholic any more than I have the intention to go to Goebbels or to do anything fantastic at all – I am fed up with it all. You have no idea what the country looks like from the outside: a bunch of neurasthenic madmen, who are all wrong, separately and together.' At the end of the same year he wrote to a friend, the author Rudolf Leonhard: 'Never forget: it was gentlemen like Theodor Wolff, Georg Bernhard and the *Frankfurter Zeitung*, hand in glove with the SPD, who gave so much power to those shits like Gessler and Gröner, the representatives of evil *eminences grises* whom they can barely control.'

Tucholsky moved to Sweden to live by the sea at Hinda near Göteborg. He published his last article on 8 November 1932: 'What we are proud of in Europe'. His self-imposed retirement was both an admission of defeat, and a protest. He was contemptuous of what Germany was doing to itself, and regarded its descent into darkness as inevitable; unlike two other literary exiles, Thomas Mann and Alfred Döblin, he was unable to believe in the continuing existence of decent Germans. Anyone who hadn't left by 1933, he said, was *de facto* a Nazi.

When the Nazis came to power, Tucholsky's books were among those proscribed and burned, and on 28 August 1933 he was formally stripped of his nationality, along with Alfred Kerr, Lion Feuchtwanger, Heinrich Mann and Ernst Toller. Their property was confiscated and the Nazis threatened punitive action against their relatives. To protect his estranged wife Mary Gerhold, Tucholsky had divorced her – in the nick of time – on 21 August. He was now stateless, without income, subject to the whims of Swedish bureaucracy, living on lottery winnings and the kindness of his friend, the Swiss physician Hedwig Müller. He had eight operations to attempt to clear his sinusitis. Refused Swedish citizenship, he was unable to travel to Switzerland with Müller. After twenty-five years of non-stop writing, his own voice had ceased to be heard – and the writer he had most admired, Knut Hamsen, espoused the National Socialist cause. Lonely, humiliated, and depressed, he took an overdose of Veronal in 1935. He was 45. Shortly before his death he wrote: 'If I had to die now, I would say: "That was all?" – And: "I didn't quite understand it." And: "It was rather noisy."'

This is Tucholsky's impression of Hitler – whose name he would never use, referring to him as 'Adof' (*sic*) or 'Edgar'. He heard Hitler broadcast on the radio in 1933 and wrote of it to Walter Hasenclever:

Göring spoke first, an evil, bloodthirsty old woman who shrieked away and really whipped the people up into a murderous mood. Shocking and disgusting. Then Göbbeles [*sic*] . . . then lots of Heils and roaring, marching and music, and a big pause. It was time for the Führer . . . I walked a couple of metres away from the set and stood. I listened with my whole body. And then something quite odd happened. That is, nothing happened. The voice isn't half as unsympathetic as you'd think – it smells a bit of the seat of the pants, of man, unappetizing, but nothing more. Sometimes he yelled himself hoarse, sometimes he retched. But otherwise: nothing, nothing, nothing. No tension, no heights; he didn't grab me, and in the end I'm too much of an artist not to admire any artistry even in yobs like him – but there was nothing there. Nothing. No humour, no warmth, no fire. Nothing. He didn't say anything, either, beyond the stupidest banalities . . . *Ceterum censeo*: it's all got nothing to do with me.

Erich Kästner was just as aware of the futility of the fight, but unlike his friend Tucho he never expected writing to have any effect on society. 'The people of Thinkers and Writers has never taken its Thinkers and Writers seriously,' he said in 1950. But that didn't mean the voice of protest and criticism should not continually be raised. Kästner was born in Dresden, the son of a saddler, Emil, who gave his name to the hero of Kästner's most famous book. His parents were not close; his mother Amalia aspired to a higher social level, taught herself hairdressing, and from it earned enough to indulge in middle-class pursuits for herself and her son. She took him to lectures, to the theatre and the opera; he had piano lessons, and was taken on regular summer holidays and cycling tours. He responded to this gratefully, and his own first ambition was to be a teacher. He was called up in 1917 and his terrible experiences at the Front during the last two years of the war made him a convinced pacifist and republican. Becoming a journalist instead of a teacher, he got a job on the *Neue Leipziger Zeitung*, but was fired after two years for publishing an erotic poem. He then made his way to Berlin.

There, he quickly found work with leading papers and periodicals, including the *Weltbühne*, the *Vossische Zeitung*, and the *Berliner Tageblatt*. Within three years he had conquered the city and could be regarded, in the words of his contemporary, the influential Jewish–Marxist literary critic Walter Benjamin, as 'the embodiment of the left-oriented trend of New Objectivity'.[14] He was a poet, a playwright, a novelist, a children's writer and cabaret song writer, all with equal facility, and his output was prolific. Though he made his name with *Emil and the Detectives*, published in 1928 and filmed and also staged soon after, his other works should not be forgotten. The collection of poetry, *Noise in the Mirror*, of the following year, introduced his idea of 'practical poetry', which certainly bears out Benjamin's remark and is defined by Kästner as follows:

There are poems from which even the literarily innocent person gets palpitations and bursts out laughing in an empty room. There are poets who feel like normal human beings, and express these feelings (and views and desires) by proxy. And because they do not write just for their own benefit and to show off their twopenny originality, they get across to people . . . Poets have their function again. Their occupation is once more a profession. They are probably not as indispensable as bakers and dentists; but only because rumbling stomachs and toothaches more obviously call for relief than non-physical ailments.[15]

'Berlin was the most important city in the world in those days,' he said; and the capital became his spiritual home until the outbreak of war. He earned well and had no family ties, so he travelled extensively. He was to be seen in the chic, arty cafés, like Schwannecke's, the Carlton, and the Café Leon. His association with the *Weltbühne* brought him into contact not only with Tucholsky and Ossietzky, but with Jacobsohn's widow Edith, the magazine's publisher, who also encouraged him to write for children, and through her with a host of film people, critics and journalists. Among them were the cartoonist Erich Ohlser (also known as e. o. plauen), the illustrator Walter Trier, the parodist Robert Neumann, and the critics Alfred Polgar and Hermann Kesten. (When Kesten and Kästner met again after the Second World War, they picked up a conversation which had been interrupted in 1933 'as if nothing had happened in between'.)[16]

Kästner was politically left of centre, an anti-militarist and against Fascism, but he was never a Marxist. When he visited Moscow with Erich Ohlser in 1929 he was not impressed with the way of life there. 'We only saw what they wanted us to see . . . We preferred the freedom of Berlin, and the ability to live life at one's own risk.'[17] But much as he loved Berlin, he saw early on the danger threatened by the NSDAP, and identified the risk posed to the Republic by an alliance between industry and the extreme Right. Here is one stanza from a bitter poem published in the *Weltbühne* on 1 October 1930:

> We don't need bread; what we do desire
> Is protection of National Honour!
> Once again it's the hero's death we require,
> And heavy machine-guns to fire.[18]

And yet, when Hitler came to power, Kästner stayed. He maintained it was a writer's duty not to abandon his country in time of national crisis; however, his post-war work does not significantly reflect the Nazi period. During the war, most of which he spent in his native Dresden, he was tolerated by the authorities, and though his books were proscribed within Germany, he was allowed to continue to earn income from foreign sales. In this the Nazis achieved a double purpose – Kästner was a world best-selling author, and he brought in needed foreign currency; the continued sale of his books abroad would also, they hoped, indicate a liberal attitude towards artists.

On 10 May 1933 there was a general burning of books written by 'decadent' writers. This 'spontaneous' gesture had been organized in advance by the Nazis, who encouraged students to 'cleanse' public and private libraries. Lists provided as a guide were also circulated to bookshops, and broadcast on the radio. The burning took place in university towns throughout Germany from 6 p.m. on the appointed day. Newspapers described the event as a 'street festival'. 'They even nailed offensive books to pillories,' Stefan Zweig wrote as he contemplated the destruction of his world. 'I regarded it more as an honour than a disgrace to be permitted to share the fate of the complete destruction of literary existence in Germany with such eminent contemporaries as Thomas Mann, Heinrich Mann, Werfel, Freud, Einstein, and many others whose work I consider incomparably more important than my own . . .'[19]

'So extraordinary was the revival of brutal medieval practice', remembers Berthold Goldschmidt, 'that one wondered if they might start putting pigs and donkeys on trial next; as for getting rid of the proscribed books from your own shelves – it wasn't easy. What to do with them? You couldn't burn them because there was no fireplace in a centrally-heated flat; you couldn't take them to the dustbins for fear of being caught by a snooper – and most of the concierges were Nazi stool-pigeons. You couldn't smuggle bulky books out under your coat and throw them into the canal. These seemingly little problems ramified the terror.'[20]

In Berlin, Erich Kästner stood in the street by the bonfire – the only author present whose books were going on to it – and heard Goebbels yell: 'In the fight against decadence and moral corruption! In the name of breeding and rectitude in State and Family! I consign to the flames the writings of Heinrich Mann, Ernst Glaeser and Erich Kästner!'[21] There would be no more of the little book-vans which used to crowd the university quarter, selling literature of every sort, from engineering to sociology, each with its speciality. Students in brown uniforms hurled bundles of books onto the fires, and the little doctor made a viperish speech over each lot. One pyre was topped by a bronze bust of Magnus Hirschfeld, whose Sexual Research Institute had been gutted. At first, the flames refused to catch the thick books, but then petrol was poured over them, and the rest of the evening went swimmingly.

As he watched this act of vandalism, Kästner cannot have been the only one to recall Heine's line: 'Where they burn books, sooner or later they will also burn people.'

Later, the Nazis tried to win Kästner over to their side – without success, though he did some screenwriting under the pseudonym of Bertold Bürger. Indeed, he approached Boleslaw Barlog at the UFA studios in Babelsberg for work in this capacity.[22] 'He was one of the team which did the script for the film of Fallada's *Little Man, What Now?* Viktor de Kowa played the lead and opposite him was a charming young girl. She wasn't a great actress, but she looked fabulous. She was Kästner's girlfriend, and she also wrote terrific children's stories, with which no doubt she was helped by her experienced boyfriend.'[23]

Kästner's chief wartime contribution to Nazi propaganda – still controversial – was the screenplay for the film of *Baron Münchhausen*. The film's subject was Kästner's own suggestion, and it was made in 1942 with Hans Albers in the lead. It celebrated UFA's 25th anniversary, and the spectacular special effects required by the story gave Goebbels a platform to show the world that German film technique could compete with American. In fact, the film was made with a Hungarian director, Josef von Baky. A Russian cameraman, Irmen Tschet, was in charge of special effects, and the two Germans principally involved – Albers and Kästner – were tolerated under the regime only because of their great popularity. Writing as 'Bertold Bürger', Kästner included nothing overtly subversive in the film's dialogue, except for one line, delivered by Casanova and noted by Kästner's mistress: 'The state inquisition has ten thousand eyes and arms. And it has the power to do good and evil according to its whim.' This line is not in the current version of the film. But subversiveness was implicit in such scenes as those set in the despotic sultan's palace, and audiences whose sensibilities were heightened by oppression would have noted it. When Hitler found out who 'Bertold Bürger' was, he was seized by a fit of rage, and Kästner was placed under a total ban.

'I was born in Schöneberg in 1917, in the district known as Jüdische Schweiz', remembers Emil Faktor's daughter.

> This was the area around Bayerischer Platz, where all the streets were named after towns in Franconia: Bamberger Strasse, Nürnberger Strasse, and so on – towns in the Fränkische Schweiz. Hence the nickname, since there was a very high percentage of Jews living there. I went to a mixed school – that is, Jews and Gentiles together – and I remember that after Hitler came to power the Aryan girls wore brown jackets, which seemed a bit odd to the rest of us. Despite them going on about superiority I was always top of our class, and my friend Sybille Ortmann was second. I remember that we had a fervent Nazi in our class who wasn't very bright academically – she was in the League of German Girls, of course. Her name was Ulrike, but we all nicknamed her Hitlerike.[24]

Emil Faktor's daughter saw little of her father when he was editor of the

Börsen-Courier in the Twenties, because his first love was the theatre and he would attend seven First Nights a week, if not all of plays, then of films. However, he did bring his world home.

> During the winter my parents held open house every other Monday, sending out a general invitation at the beginning of the season to about two hundred people from the cultural milieu. The only people who weren't invited were actors, because my father was sensitive about compromising his position as a critic; but the publisher Ernst Rowholt was often there – he was a huge man who loved to eat and drink, and who used to shout 'Long Live Anarchy' when he was in his cups. Then there were Joachim Ringelnatz, and Klabund – whose play about the chalk circle was copied by Brecht much later. Leopold Jessner came, and Erwin and Maria Piscator (whom we called the *Piss-Katze*!). Some of them arrived at lunch-time and stayed until breakfast the next day – that was what it was like in those days. Herbert Ihering, who took over as theatre critic from my father, was there, and the crime writer 'Sling', and some of our star writers, Hans Sahl and Fritz Walter. But I remember that my father sacked Billy Wilder for sloppy writing!

'The *Berliner Börsen-Courier* was probably the best, liveliest paper in the capital,' remembers Hans Sahl.[25] 'Its editor was the little, attractive Emil Faktor, and its features editor was a young man from the Rhineland, Fritz Walter . . . He had blood-red lips in an otherwise strikingly white face, and he polished his articles with all the care of a jeweller working on a royal coronet.'

'The *Börsen-Courier* was like a club,' recalls Fritz Walter's widow.[26]

> There were tiny, untidy offices at Beuthstrasse 8, run in apparent chaos, but containing a delightful group of people. They were all pure intellectuals, highly civilized and cultured, more interested in the content of their work than in making money. It was idyllic, and even a man with Fritz's sad temperament was happy there. After Hitler came to power he had to leave quickly, and for a time earned a living in a lavatory factory in France, before coming to England. He'd known Marlene Dietrich in Berlin, and once when she was staying in Hampstead, doing a concert at the Golders Green Hippodrome after the war, Fritz stood next to her in the delicatessen queue. She didn't recognize him and he didn't dare speak to her. But afterwards, he sent some flowers to the theatre. He was very unhappy that she never wrote to thank him.

Herbert Ihering, once his position as a major drama critic had been confirmed, held open house much as the Faktors did. Sahl describes one visit he made with Walter when they were both young journalists.

> The Iherings loved to invite guests to their house in Zehlendorf on Sunday afternoons . . . As we opened the garden gate, I saw all the élite of the German theatre a short distance away on the terrace . . . They were holding

glasses and talking to each other. 'Oh God,' Fritz Walter whispered to me. 'There they are.' 'Who?' I asked. 'All of them,' he said flatly . . . Frau Ihering introduced us to the guests. 'Lotte Lenya,' she said. 'Pleased to meet you,' we said in unison, and I knocked over a glass from sheer embarrassment. 'Kurt Weill,' said Frau Ihering. 'How do you do,' we said; and so it went on, with introductions, bows, timid handshakes and beating hearts on our side, from Erwin Piscator to Helene Weigel, from Fritz Kortner to Ernst Busch to Gustav Gründgens. 'Pleased to meet you; pleased to meet you.' Someone gave me a glass, but there was nowhere left to sit, and as I went to a corner of the terrace to fetch a chair I saw two men there sitting on dustbins, their legs dangling. 'Brecht,' said one, 'Bronnen,' said the other. I fled. I got as far a glass door, but as I opened it, a vast bird, I thought an eagle at first, with a sharp beak, descended on me. It was just a crow, however. Frau Ihering later told me smilingly that she'd got it for the amusement and diversion of her guests. It was said that it had plucked Bronnen's monocle out of his eye. 'Sorry,' I said to the crow. There was no one else in the kitchen. I made my way back to the garden and joined a group of people busy making dramatic gestures and rolling their 'rs' a good deal, who were welcoming a new arrival called Müller . . . 'And what do you do, Herr Müller?' I asked after we had stared at each other in silence for a while. 'I?' replied Herr Müller in astonishment. He had a round moon of a face and wore a red roll-neck. 'I am Traugott Müller. I am Erwin Piscator's set designer. I design theatre sets, that's what I do. And what do *you* do?' Later on we went into the house for an improvised dinner in a Biedermeier room that smelt strongly of cats. The whole house smelt of cats, especially in Frau Ihering's bedroom, where there were twenty of them . . .

Arthur Koestler arrived in Berlin early in 1927 as General Secretary of his Zionist group (though that was a post in name only) and shortly afterwards joined the Ullstein newspaper group as a journalist. To work for the Ullsteins in those days was to become part of the aristocracy of European journalism. Their motto was political liberalism and modern culture; and they were against militarism and chauvinism. They were European in the best sense, lending their support to the Franco-German friendship nurtured by Briand and Stresemann. Ullsteins embodied the progressive and cosmopolitan spirit of Weimar Germany. In 1930 Koestler became Scientific Editor of the *Vossische Zeitung*, and a year later Foreign Editor of the *BZ am Mittag*.

Hiding his shyness under a cloak of arrogance, Koestler didn't make many friends. His patron was Franz Ullstein, the oldest of the five brothers and the firm's senior partner, and at about this time the four younger brothers were attempting to oust Franz from power, to the extent of accusing his young wife of spying for a foreign state. This led to a long, dirtily-fought legal battle to clear her name, in the course of which Georg Bernhard, editor of the *Voss* for a decade, lost his job and was replaced by a Nationalist.[27] Meanwhile, the elections of September 1930 had produced ominous results: the NSDAP representation in the Reichstag had leapt from 12 seats to 107. Ullsteins – a Jewish company whose staff were nearly 50 per cent Jewish – attempted to keep afloat by 'aryanizing' their operation as far as possible. Most who lost their jobs were left-wing, or Jewish, or both, as Koestler points out bitterly in his autobiography.[28] But in the end their last-ditch operation availed the Ullstein brothers nothing.

'The two great editors of the day . . . Theodor Wolff and Georg Bernhard . . . were as different as chalk and cheese', remembers Alfred Fischer.[29] 'Wolff was a sensitive, literary man. Bernhard was more of a doer, more practical, realistic and political. He even became a Reichstag representative. After they'd left Berlin, they both worked on the *Pariser Tageblatt*, which Wolff founded in exile, but it didn't last long because there wasn't much money to run it, and most of the exiles didn't stay put in Paris but gradually moved on. America was the goal for most of them, and perhaps even in the early Thirties they thought that Paris was too close for comfort.' Fischer suggests that Bernhard may have been sacked from the *Voss* because he became emotionally involved with one of the Ullstein sisters. There were five, as well as the five Ullstein brothers. All were assimilated and baptized. In Berlin they were known as 'the collective of geniuses'. It was almost impossible to *get* fired from Ullsteins – the harpist-turned-popular-novelist Vicki Baum recalls drily that 'stealing the silver wouldn't have been enough; you'd've had to go after the gold.' The Ullstein group spread over thirteen buildings, not including the new Tempelhof Printing Works by Erich Mendelsohn, with its 77-metre-high tower. The main Ullstein building was such a labyrinth that eminent visitors were usually given a guide to take them around. It was the greatest newspaper concern in Europe at the time, yet all its power could not save it.

'The two papers which were allowed a semblance of independence after the [Nazi] seizure of power were the *Vossische Zeitung* and the *Frankfurter Zeitung*,' says Arnold Bauer.[30]

But even that didn't last long. The *Voss* was closed down in 1934, and the other Ullstein papers, like the *BZ* and the *Morgenpost*, were rationalized – *gleichgeschaltet*, as the Nazi term for it was. All the socialist and Communist papers were shut down immediately after 30 January 1933 . . . The entire press became 'brown' – not all as dark brown as the *Völkische Beobachter*, but still only reflections of the party line. Occasionally people would be brave enough to slip in some criticism between the lines, but it didn't happen often. The stakes were too high, and Gestapo informers jumped at shadows. Most of the journalists were replaced, though the magazine sections and the colour supplements, which had no political content, were spared quite such purging, and in the early days of the Third Reich the magazine section editors were always looking for young writers to do articles (under assumed names) that were aimed against the NSDAP . . . But there was a whole new Nazi press, run by Max Amann, from nationals to local rags, and it was set up in competition with the established papers. In the event, though, all that happened was that people who used to belong to the SPD and the left, now turned to the former Weimar conservative press, like the *FZ*, as the lesser of two evils, and the NSDAP papers never got a very big readership despite the huge print runs, and the obligation of all party members to subscribe. The *Angriff* and the *Völkische Beobachter* didn't sell well on the stalls at all, especially here in Berlin. You really noticed when you saw someone on the tube reading the *VB*; it was exceptional.

Bauer smiles. He spent more time than he cares to remember in Gestapo custody. 'Even so, when night fell, it fell fast.'

11 Sportpalast, Speedway and Ring

'THE SPORTPALAST IS located at Potsdamer Strasse 72, with an area of some 2,600 square metres for large-scale events (ice skating, six-day races, boxing matches and so forth). It was opened in 1910 and restructured by O. Kaufmann in 1925.' These few dry lines from Baedeker's 1927 *Berlin* introduce a world that was, to its *aficionados*, as exciting as film or theatre, concert or opera. The Palast was originally built as an ice-rink, and at its opening on 11 December 1910 Richard Strauss conducted the orchestra of the Imperial Opera and a massive choir in a performance of Beethoven's Ninth Symphony. The pomp of the occasion was not appreciated by the Berlin press. The orchestra had to perform on a podium erected on the ice, and many musicians slipped and fell on their way to it, to the unsympathetic amusement of the crowd.

Figure skating attracted a public of 100,000 a day during 1910, and though the six-day bicycle races which began in 1911 became the core of the Sportpalast programme for the next two decades, the ice-rink was not completely overshadowed: stars such as Sonja Henie, and the Berliners' enjoyment of ice-hockey, saw to that. The music of course became slightly less elevated: the Sportpalast Waltz – officially Siegfried Translateur's *Praterleben* – was played by the Otto Kermbach orchestra. The 'soloist' was Krücke, the lame newsvendor, who whistled the melody.

The six-day races were not new, and not peculiar to Berlin. They had begun in New York City in the 1890s when the bicycle was the fastest-moving machine, and it is hard to say why their popularity endured for so long after the advent of motor-racing. They combined sport and entertainment and, as in modern professional wrestling, there were clear-cut heroes and villains for the public to cheer and whistle at. The Dutchman Piet van Kempen and the American Reggie Macnamara ('The Iron Man') were regarded as demigods by their fans.

'I used to go all the time as a young man,' remembers Ludwig von Hammerstein.[1]

> There was always a great press of people. The cyclists competed in two-man teams, and each had a little cabin – called a *koje* – by the side of the track in which the off-shift team member could rest. In a way the six-day races were where sport and folk festival met. The idea was that they raced for six days continuously, but my guess is that between, say, 2 a.m. and 9 a.m., when very few spectators would normally be there, there might have been a general pause . . . As for the Sportpalast Waltz, you can still hear old Berliners whistling it on the streets.

The theatre director Boleslaw Barlog, such an enthusiastic sportsman that his first ambition had been to teach PT, as a youth earned money opening car doors for visitors to the Sportpalast – 'though sometimes instead of the hoped-for 50 pfennigs you got a box on the ears for your trouble'. He made friends with Krücke, through whose influence he got a steady job as a *koje* attendant. 'Which meant that I could watch the races as much as I liked for free, and had money to spend on books from the little book-waggons, which in those days were as plentiful as the street-walkers in Bülowstrasse!'[2]

'There were always twelve or fourteen two-man teams,' remembers Curt Riess.[3] 'Of course some dropped out in the course of the competition, and progress was hard to follow. Even the cyclists lost track of where they stood in the race at times, and the whole thing was won or lost on the basis of a complicated system of points gained through a series of sprints . . . the tension was kept up day and night. There was always the chance of a crash in one of the steep curves, and broken arms and legs.'

As in Paris, the Berlin six-day races were entertainment for the not-so-well-off. 'They could get a place in the gallery or standing-room by the curves for a few marks and they used to raise the roof. But the races also provided an opportunity for the great and the good to show themselves off: they sat in the boxes or the centre stalls and had themselves served champagne – everyone from film-stars and politicians to fashionable doctors and lawyers.' In the middle of the arena the racers' wives and girl-friends took up their stations, ready to provide their men with coffee from Thermoses, or gherkins and thickly-filled *Stullen* (sandwiches) as required. After the evening's performances were over, actors and singers from the Berlin theatres would join the *Haute Volaute* (high-flyers). Some, like Richard Tauber, would give the public a song.

When he came to power, Hitler banned the six-day races as 'unsporting'. The Sportpalast was used for Nazi rallies after that.

Boxing vied with cycle-racing as Berlin's most popular sport. It had been forbidden in Germany before the First World War, and matches had taken place only in secret, private clubs. Its first official home was the Zirkus Busch, where both competition and challenge bouts were held. All the early boxers were former prisoners-of-war of the British; they had learnt to box in the camp on the Isle of Man.[4] The middleweight Curt Prentzel, Hans Breitensträter and Adolf Weigert were the most successful. Prentzel in particular (like Mohammed Ali 50 years later) developed a style which turned the new sport into something of an art form. Hans Breitensträter was the special darling of Berlin, and remained so even after his resounding defeat by the gigantic Englishman, Tom Cowler.

Black boxers like The Dixie Kid were especially sought-after to begin with, not only because Africans were fashionable – 'but also because when you got a bout with a black guy versus a white one you could tell the difference more easily!' The Kid, with his flashing gold teeth, became a local hero; even after his addiction to cocaine forced him to retire from the ring and turn to training, his lightness of foot was still legendary. So popular was boxing that the baritone Michael Bohen turned manager and for a while looked after Prentzel, who however soon transferred his allegiance to the more professional Hermann Wulff, one of the great pre-war bookmakers and by 1920 Germany's leading sporting agent. Prentzel continued to be boxing's most attractive ambassador and his wife, the silent film star Fern Andra, brought her sophisticated friends to matches. So boxing became fashionable as well as new, and in the Twenties had the added attraction of being disapproved of by the older generation. Many artists liked to be seen in the company of boxers. Brecht even set *Mahagonny* in a boxing ring.

The promoter Theo C. Buss, who started life as a circus strong-man in the Rhineland, put up posters advertising:

SABRI MAHIR
THE TERRIBLE TURK
COMING SOON!

This boxer would, the publicity promised, take on four opponents in a row at the Zirkus Busch.

On the evening of the bout the place was full up. At the last minute a couple of dozen Turks with fezzes and Korans and prayer beads filled the first two rows closest to the ring. Then Sabri made his appearance – a broad-shouldered man – and addressed the audience in immaculate German . . . he despatched the first three fighters elegantly, quickly and mercilessly. The fourth was a tougher customer. After going four rounds with him, Sabri stopped the bout and, good showman that he was, announced to the public: 'Ladies and Gentlemen! My opponent is too brave a fighter for me to wish to destroy him with my terrible knock-out punch. I have decided instead to take him under my wing and teach him all I can.'[5]

The fourth man was Adolf Weigert, who soon afterwards became Germany's middleweight champion. But his career foundered, he ended up scraping a living in fairgrounds, and died young.

Mahir was knocked out in the second round of a bout with a Dane, Eckeroth. His explanation that he was not on form because of the death of his dear old mother led his fans to throw at him the hardest things they could lay their hands on. He retired from the ring, revealed himself to be one Sally (Samuel) Meyer, from Cologne, and set up a fashionable gymnasium near Tauentzienstrasse. He was a natural showman, and got far better publicity than the much better trainer, Billy Smith. Meyer's gym filled up with film-stars, bankers and businessmen, paying well in the war of attrition against obesity.

The boxer of his age, however, was Max Schmeling, who became World Champion in 1931. An intelligent man and an elegant boxer, he was welcomed into Berlin society with open arms; but despite his social popularity he was too much of a professional to neglect his training. He lunched with Gustav Böss, and became a great friend of Fritz Kortner and Hans Albers. He made a film in 1930, married the popular actress Anny Ondra, and retired to become a successful businessman. 'I met him often at my brother's place. He was charming and shrewd. He invested his money from boxing wisely, and although he stayed on under the Third Reich, he did a lot to help those who were persecuted – my brother left it very late to get out – 1939 – and he might not have done so without Max's help and support.'[6]

Berliners were keen equestrians. Show-jumping and dressage had always been smart, and racing became popular when the Hamburg Derby took place in the capital (Hamburg's track being out of commission at the time) in 1919 and was won by Gibraltar from the Graditz Stables. The Derby was run at Berlin's principal track, the Grunewald-Rennbahn, but there were several other flat-race and steeple-chase tracks around the city, notably the flat course at Hoppegarten, which was also a training centre for jockeys. The Berliners' obsession with speed – *Tempo, Tempo* – gave their most popular jockey, Otto Schmidt, his nickname 'Otto-Otto'; his rivalry with the long-bodied American, Everett Haynes, kept punters happy throughout the mid-Twenties. The four big stables were Graditz, Oppenheim, Weinberg and Haniel, but other ventures came and went on the tide of inflation and speculation – those of Max Klante and Willi Sklarek, to name but two.

Motor-racing started early. The Avus speedway, in the south-west of the city, was a 9.8-kilometre proto-Autobahn built by Hugo Stinnes between 1913 and 1919 to connect the Westend and Wannsee; its two ends curved together to make an ellipsoidal track reminiscent of the Circus Maximus in Rome, and the 'Avus' (*Auto-Verkehrs-und-Übungsstrasse*) provided mass entertainment in a similar way. The north curve was the sharpest in the world at the time (44°), and the track drew international competition, including Sir Malcolm Campbell from England, Earl Howe, and Prince Lobkowicz of Czechoslovakia, who was killed on the track in 1932 when he crashed his Bugatti. The stars of the Avus, however, were Hans Stuck, Bernd Rosemeier, and above all Rudolf Caracciola, who drove for Mercedes.[7] The first races were run early in 1920 though work on the Avus was not finally completed until 1921, which was also the year of the first post-war Berlin motor-show. International races were held for the first time on 24 September 1922, when 500,000 people watched Fritz von Opel win in a car made by his father's engineering firm. Four years later, Caracciola won in an eight-cylinder Mercedes, and in 1928 von Opel drove the first rocket-powered car down the track. It accelerated from 0 to 100 kph in eight seconds. In 1931 Ernst Henne established a new world motor-cycle record on a BMW: 220 kph. 'Time drives a car and no one knows how to steer it,' wrote Erich Kästner in a contemporary poem. In 1918 there were fewer than 100,000 cars in Germany; by 1928 there were 1.2 million.

As early as 1911 the Ullsteins had inaugurated the '*BZ* Prize of the Skies'. Aeroplane developers and pilots competed for it above Berlin. But flying in Germany in the Twenties was dominated by another kind of craft – the airship. The Zeppelin first appeared in 1914, and represented to the ordinary German the apogee of technological achievement. The military application of those 'flying gherkins' hadn't been terribly successful; they were slow and unmanoeuverable, hence vulnerable to attack by enemy fighters,[8] but as civilian craft they seemed unbeatable. They had a safety record infinitely better than winged aircraft (the much-publicized airship disasters were the *only* ones), and they were economical. The Allies demanded that the big airships be handed over as part of the post-war reparation demands; but the Germans destroyed all that had survived the conflict. Production was then officially banned until 1925. However, in 1924 *LZ 126*, constructed by Hugo von Eckener (Ferdinand, Graf von Zeppelin's spiritual heir) under contract to the US Navy, flew non-stop from Friedrichshafen to Lakehurst, New York, in 81 hours and 17 minutes, landing to a ticker-tape welcome. Zeppelin (who had died in 1917, aged 79) would have been proud. *LZ 127*, a bigger craft, built by Eckener from public subscriptions and twice the length of a football pitch,[9] flew to the United States in 1926, around the world in

1929, and across the North Pole in 1931. The 1926 and 1929 flights carried payloads: the former twenty passengers and 66,000 letters and
parcels, and the latter a full complement of passengers, a grand piano,
a consignment of canaries, and a gorilla called Suzi. Eckener's circum-
navigational flight averaged 100 kph and was completed in three weeks.
On board the 1931 flight, reporting for Ullsteins, was the 26-year-old
Arthur Koestler.[10]

The Zeppelin was fast enough for its time. If German and world
technology had not been so preoccupied with speed, the airship might
have had a better future. In retrospect, it seems unfortunate that neither
the airship nor its cousin, the massive flying boat, were further
developed. The *Dornier X* had twelve engines powering six propellers,
and could carry 169 passengers; but it, too, was relatively slow; worse,
it needed a great stretch of calm water on which to land and take off. But
there was one sense in which such considerations did not matter: German
technology was leading the world, and awareness of it soothed the
national psyche. Pride reached new heights in 1928 when the new liner
Bremen won the Blue Riband on her maiden voyage. Speed was the
thing. When Charles Lindbergh crossed the Atlantic in 1927 in *The
Spirit of St Louis*, Brecht was inspired to write a radio play about
the event, with music by Hindemith and Weill. When the *Hindenburg*
crashed at Lakehurst in 1937, public reaction to the disaster was out of
all proportion to its actual size; it was enough to put paid to the airship
industry.

Interest in sport, in travel, even in exploring their own country, was
new for ordinary people all over the world, but it was most marked in
Germany. The change came about gradually, its turning-point the First
World War. The revolution of 1918–19, the twin influences of liberal
government and tremendous social instability, the dramatic liberation of
women, and the breaking-down of much of the class structure, all
encouraged a desire for exploration and self-discovery.

Nude bathing became fashionable. In Frankfurt in 1930 with his friend
the 70-year-old French sculptor Aristide Maillol (whose biography he
was to write, and who at the time was enjoying a respite with a young
model from his preternaturally jealous wife), Harry Kessler wrote:
'Maillol was delighted with the uninhibited nakedness [at the swimming
pool]. He kept drawing my attention to the beautiful bodies of the girls
and the young men and boys. *Si j'habitais à Francfort, je passerais mes
journées ici à dessiner* . . . I explained to him that this was only part of
a new feeling for life and a new approach to it, which has grown up in
Germany since the war. People want to really *live*. To enjoy the light,
the sun, happiness, their own bodies . . . [it is] a popular movement
which has taken hold of all the young people of Germany.'[11]

Just as organizations such as the Boy Scouts grew up in Great Britain and the United States, so in Germany youth groups of all kinds appeared – of both military and non-military inspiration. They represented different religions, sects, political parties and aims, but were united in an aspiration to maintain physical fitness and broaden horizons. The roots of the movement in Germany are to be found in the *Wandervögel* groups which originated almost by chance in Berlin-Steglitz in 1896 when a group of students banded together to take hikes in Grunewald. There were uniforms, there were songs, there were oaths to be taken and principles to be adhered to. There was a strong streak of anti-Semitism in the right-wing youth groups, which led Jews to form similar organizations for their own people. Even though this was not yet the anti-Semitism of the Hitler Youth and the League of German Girls, early ideas of racial purity were already at large. Heinrich Himmler was a minor figure in the Artaman group, which provided labour for the farms of Eastern Germany to prevent them from being 'polluted' by Polish farm-workers.

Whereas in 1914 the youth of Germany had gone blithely and idealistically to the slaughter, that of half a generation later was faced with national shame, social insecurity, unemployment, and a future apparently so bleak that only extreme measures seemed appropriate for salvation. In such circumstances, the youth movement provided a breeding-ground for a new spirit of nationalism and militarism. There was great loyalty within groups, and to groups, whatever their philosophy. People needed a sense of belonging.[12] But a sense of belonging can become a pack instinct and the pursuit of health, by extension, a preoccupation with purity. It is only a short step from here to the idea that anyone who doesn't belong to the pack is impure.

Tellingly, in a statement made in 1933 (eleven years after the event), Ernst-Werner Techow, one of Walther Rathenau's assassins, said: 'The younger generation was striving for something new, hardly dreamed-of. They smelt the morning air. They gathered in themselves an energy charged with the myth of the Prussian-German past, the pressure of the present, and the expectation of an unknown future.'[13] Muddled, quasi-mystical, quasi-romantic thinking of the most insidious kind entered the minds of frustrated young people, encouraged by such books as Hans Grimm's right-wing novel *People Without Room*, which was published in 1926 and had huge success, or Hans Freyer's *Revolution of the Right* or the anti-Semitic Ludwig Klage's *The Spirit as Adversary of the Soul*. Vague terms were seized upon, misunderstood, misused – as, for example, was Nietzsche's concept of the *Übermensch*. The technically difficult work of the right-wing philosopher Martin Heidegger, Rector of Freiburg University under the Third Reich, was hailed as giving respectability to Nazi ideas; the professor himself, with his conscious provincialism and his hatred of big cities – especially Berlin – and his equation of sophistication with vice, popularly personified the ideal NSDAP thinker. The stage was set for an even greater European disaster than that of 1914.

NIGHT

That is the miracle of our age, that you have found me, that
you have found me among so many millions! And that I have
found you, that is Germany's good fortune!

> – Adolf Hitler (translated by Michael Bullock)

Today all my household goods and furniture go up for
auction in Weimar. This is the end of the chief epoch of my
life, and of a home I built up with much love.

> – Harry, Graf Kessler, diary entry, Paris,
> Saturday 20 July 1935

12 House of Cards

■■■■■■■ AT ABOUT THE time Josephine Baker was conquering Berlin's *beau monde*, a small, neat man arrived in Berlin at the Postdamer station. Josef Goebbels was 29 years old, stood about 5 ft (1.5 m) tall, and weighed barely 8 stone (45 kg). His left leg was 4 inches shorter than his right, as result of infantile paralysis. He never allowed himself to be filmed in movement, or standing close to a group of people. Photographers generally had to stand lower than he did, or far enough away for perspective to deceive the eye. Goebbels was the maker of his own myth as well as of the Nazi Party's.

When Hitler sent him to be *Gauleiter* (District Leader) of Berlin, he knew what he would be up against in the traditionally free-thinking and liberal capital. In fact he was paying Goebbels a compliment in giving him such a post. Goebbels hated the city – 'a monster of stone and asphalt' – while admiring its hard-working inhabitants. He had reservations about their 'fanaticism' and 'ruthlessness', however, attributing them to the 'rootless international Jews' and the Jewish-owned press, which 'spews Jewish poison throughout the capital'.

Goebbels is the most fascinating of the Nazi leaders. A devoted and inventive lieutenant, he would have made an unhappy leader; an intellectual with good artistic taste and literary leanings, he was also the slave of envy and probably of self-loathing. A sexual profligate, he could and did sacrifice his feelings to the interests of his career. Of his many conquests, the one who seems to have genuinely captured his heart was the beautiful Czech actress, Lida Baarova, who was born in 1914 and now lives in seclusion in Salzburg. Already a star in Czechoslovakia, she came to Germany in 1934 to make *Barcarole* for UFA, and became Goebbels' mistress two years later. When Magda Goebbels complained to Hitler of the affair, Goebbels obeyed his Führer's command to drop her, and she returned to Czechoslovakia. Today, Miss Baarova still speaks adoringly of the little doctor, saying that his influence made her a better actress; but it is equally clear that his attitude to her was entirely selfish. He wouldn't permit her to travel to the United States or, for fear of a scandal, to have children; today she is a dignified, misguided, and rather sad old lady.

Goebbels' attitude to Hitler was slavish to such a degree that it seems he must have wanted to 'lose' his own personality within that of the Führer; but he may also have made his diary entries with half an eye to the possibility of them becoming public one day. Rejected by the academic world he longed to join, rejected by the army as unfit to serve, he was also rejected in his first choice of career as a journalist. He was a brilliant orator, advertiser and propagandist, but he would never have made a writer. His one novel, *Michael*, is, not surprisingly, full of bombast and wish-fulfilment; what is striking is the virulence of his anti-Semitism, even at this early stage in his career: 'Jews make me physically sick; the mere sight of them does this. I cannot even hate the Jew. I can merely despise him. He has raped our people, soiled our ideals, weakened the strength of the nation, corrupted morals. He is the poisonous eczema on the body of our sick nation. That has nothing to do with religion. Either he destroys us, or we destroy him.'[1] One has to remember that it was Jews in the fields of academia and journalism who rejected Goebbels. All that was needed to turn the mixture into poison was a warped nature with nationalist and militaristic leanings, and the political climate of the time.

Goebbels arrived in the capital in November 1926. The local SA group was small and demoralized, and their headquarters was a cellar. Reluctant as he had been to accept the post, the new Gauleiter set about the task of reorganizing and revivifying his group with tireless devotion and application. He was on more favourable ground than he had suspected, for he stood on the left of the NSDAP and he was a convinced anti-capitalist. He knew his chief rivals were the Communists, and as soon as he felt strong enough he deliberately provoked them: in February 1927 he held a meeting at the Pharus Assembly Rooms in Müllerstrasse in Wedding – in the Communist heartland. The Pharus Rooms were traditionally a Communist meeting place. The provocation had its effect, and the 'Pharus Battle' – a brawl between Nazis and 'Kozis' – was inflated to Norse Myth status by Goebbels and used to good propaganda effect. From now on, in working-class districts street fights of one kind and another constantly recurred between Communists and SA men, until the KPD was banned soon after Hitler came to power. Goebbels followed up this first success by launching his magazine *Der Angriff*. It was a drop in the ocean of Berlin's journalism, but its readership grew (as did party membership), slowly but steadily. It carried, for a magazine of its type, a relatively strong news section, and drew finance from advertising, which filled a quarter of its ten pages. From February 1931, it was strong enough to publish daily; Goebbels used its pages to target prominent Jews.

By the time Heinrich Brüning took over as Chancellor in 1930, the forces of the Right were already in a position of strength. On 15 September Harry Kessler recorded: 'A black day for Germany . . . The Nazis have increased their representation almost tenfold, rising from twelve seats to 107. The impression made abroad must be catastrophic . . .' Brüning, a conservative at heart but not a reactionary, supported the Republic, but did not move against the NSDAP until it was too late. He was also fatally in awe of Hindenburg. By the time he left office at the end of May 1932, the Weimar regime existed only in name. Already Wilhelm Frick, an NSDAP delegate and Minister of the Interior in Thuringia, which had now swung to the right, was promoting NSDAP protégés in education and the police; when the Federal Minister of the Interior, Karl Severing, resigned and was succeeded by the softer Joseph Wirth, Frick went so far as to introduce a daily anti-Semitic 'prayer' into Thuringia's schools.[2] This was stopped, but the danger signs were there.

Brüning presided over a fragile coalition. Its internal conflicts prevented agreement on sensible measures to raise revenue, such as increased taxation on tobacco and beer, although the government badly needed to increase its income following the withdrawal of foreign investment after the Wall Street Crash. Confidence was further undermined when Ludendorff, in whom jealousy had now turned to hatred of his former commanding officer, broke the scandal surrounding Hindenburg's acquisition of his estate at Neudeck. This had been given him by a syndicate of German industrialists as an eightieth birthday present in 1927. Neudeck had formerly been a Hindenburg family possession, and returning it to the family was a ploy to encourage him to support the interests of East Prussia: landowners there were worried by a government scheme to raise money by increasing cereal crop prices – a plan which Hindenburg had originally supported. The ensuing political skirmish[3] further strengthened the position of the Right, and helped secure NSDAP triumph at the polls. The rising number of unemployed, 3 million at the time, also divided their vote between the extremes, the Communists and the NSDAP. Germany was suffering no more than other countries from the international slump, but had already endured several debilitating years. People born since 1910 had known nothing else. Middle-class prosperity had collapsed, and with it the moderate parties. The young were disaffected and disillusioned. The NSDAP appeared to have much to recommend it. Its campaigning was positive and aggressive; it was new; it traded on pride in nationality; and it offered to guarantee a German resurgence. Hitler was heavily funded by such tycoons as Fritz von Thyssen and Emil Kirdorf, but in fact ordinary people also paid admission to his rallies. Hitler could show extraordinary energy and charisma, however lazy and indecisive he may have been privately.

Abroad, the French were appalled by the NSDAP's success; the British played down any threat, and even mildly approved.[4] But Nazi ranting had a disastrous effect on the most sensitive barometer – the international market. Domestic securities plummeted, the government could not sell its Treasury bills, and September and October 1930 saw 633 million marks of gold and foreign exchange withdrawn. Ironically, these disasters further fuelled the success of the NSDAP.

Hitler turned his attention to wooing the army. The veteran General Gröner had always maintained a neutral political role for the Wehrmacht, but the NSDAP now turned its blandishments on the officer corps. When three young army officers were tried at Ulm for attempting to suborn their fellow officers to the Nazi cause, the NSDAP made tremendous political capital out of the trial: here were more martyrs. The Stahlhelm organization staged a huge rally at Coblenz, in the recently-evacuated Rhineland, and 100,000 men marched past such luminaries as the retired General von Seeckt and the former Crown Prince. The bellicose message of the demonstration was unmistakable at home and abroad.

Brüning attempted to recapture the initiative by pandering to the popular spirit of nationalism, and sought to reverse Stresemann's foreign policy strategy; he instructed Stresemann's successor, Julius Curtius, then in the middle of negotiations with the League of Nations at Geneva, to go onto the offensive – though he did not say how. Curtius refused to obey such an irresponsible request, but Brüning was now hopelessly caught: he could not take a stand against the NSDAP, nor could he side with it.[5]

To compound matters, the Allies were panicked by a proposed customs union between Germany and Austria. The French withdrew short-term loans to Austria, whose economy had been in a better state than Germany's, and major Viennese banks had to be bailed out by the government as a result. Briand in Geneva desperately fought to avoid what now appeared to be an inevitable slide into war, and in June 1931 President Hoover in the United States announced a moratorium for one year on all reparation repayments. Brüning survived, but the German right-wing press howled, and Goebbels in *Der Angriff* wrote furiously under the headline 'GERMANY AGAIN VICTIM OF AMERICAN BLUFF!' The French, Germany's biggest creditors, refused to accede to Hoover's moratorium; meanwhile, the Germans refused to stop spending on military development: a second cruiser was under construction. Hindenburg would not allow the military budget to be touched, and Brüning could not or would not stand up to him.

Germany's domestic economy had long been a house of cards. In July 1931 the huge Bremen textile concern Northern Wool collapsed and took the Darmstadt National Bank (Danatbank) with it. To avert a general panic, and to prevent a domino effect, the stunned government guaranteed Danatbank's deposits, but too late to stop a run on the other banks. After 1923 and 1929, this was the last straw for the German saver. *All* banks had to be closed, as did the Stock Exchange. The banks did not reopen until 5 August, the Exchange until 3 September.

Meanwhile, General Kurt von Schleicher, a master of intrigue who had sat at the centre of the politico-military web for years, began to make his own moves on the political chessboard. On 10 October he introduced Hitler to Hindenburg. Neither was impressed with the other. Hindenburg saw only a common-looking 'Bohemian corporal' with an ugly accent; Hitler saw a dinosaur. But a key connection had been made. A month later a massive right-wing rally took place at Bad Harzburg, involving Alfred Hugenberg's National Party, the Stahlhelm, and the NSDAP. They pledged 'to preserve our country from the chaos of Bolshevism'. Among other speakers was Hjalmar Schacht, Director of the State Bank, who had allied himself to Hitler as well. The Allies' discomfort increased. Since the death of Stresemann, there seemed no one in Germany with whom they could talk reasonably.

Within the country, there were to be few more setbacks for the Right; Hitler's strength was that his rivals for power on the Right underestimated both his cunning and his ruthlessness. The unsophisticated little corporal from Linz with a chip on his shoulder was soon to enjoy his finest hour. One event might have stopped him. At Boxheim at the end of November a number of papers were discovered containing details of secret NSDAP proposals for administration when they came to power. They had been drawn up by Judge Werner Best, later Nazi Commissioner for Denmark; among other things they advocated that the sentence for virtually every offence against the state should be death, and that Jews should be deprived of food. Prima facie, the documents were treasonable, but the state took no action.

By 1932, Hindenburg had been President for seven stormy years. He was 84 years old. His sense of duty kept him at work, but he was tired, confused and irritated by the increasing disorder which surrounded him, and beginning to lose his grip. Presidential elections were due in 1932, and at a rally at the Sportpalast in February Goebbels announced the candidacy of Hitler, who had been hastily naturalized a German citizen for the occasion. The Communists put up Ernst Thälmann (who later died in Buchenwald); the Nationalists, by now estranged from the NSDAP, fielded Theodor Düsterberg (who, the NSDAP maliciously revealed, had a Jewish grandfather): the serious money in Germany was on Hitler. The Nazis made their headquarters at the Kaiserhof Hotel in Wilhelmplatz, close to the centres of power. They were helped by former crown Prince Friedrich-Wilhelm's announcement that he would be backing their candidate. By making such a statement he broke the chief condition of his permit to stay in Germany (to abstain from political life) and also, as the NSDAP had no plans to restore the Royal family, alienated himself from the pro-monarchy Nationalists. In the event Hindenburg won, but only just, and only after a second round. Hitler increased his share of the vote by 85 per cent beyond what had been achieved in the September 1930 Reichstag election.

On 13 April 1932 Hindenburg, by presidential decree and under pressure from Gröner, dissolved and banned the SA and the SS. Many private armies with political affiliations had grown up since the Versailles limitation on the Wehrmacht, including the SPD Reichsbanner, but none were as well-organized or as menacing as the Nazi groups. The army was finding itself in an increasingly difficult position. Schleicher, from his position of supreme power as head of the office of the Minister of Defence, allowed his dislike of the Left to blind him to the power of the Right. He thought he could easily remove Hitler's private armies from the scene and with them Hitler himself. In reality, the reverse was true; Hitler would soon dispose of Schleicher. General Gröner, still Minister of Defence, was himself growing increasingly mistrustful of Schleicher, his subordinate and protégé, and he was right: Gröner's moderate stance was about to cause his downfall. Attacked in the Reichstag by the Nazi delegate Göring, deserted by Schleicher and his Ministry on account of Schleicher's personal ambitions, and unfairly castigated by Hindenburg because of his recent second marriage to a much younger woman who bore him a child less than nine months later, he ended his long career by resigning on 13 May 1932.[6] As for Schleicher, the historian John Wheeler-Bennett remembers seeing him dining with friends at the Königin Restaurant in Berlin in the spring of 1932, 'resplendent in full uniform': 'Suddenly the dance-band stopped with the abruptness of syncopation and von Schleicher, whose voice had been raised to be heard by his friends above the music, was overheard declaiming: "What Germany needs now is a strong man"; and he tapped himself significantly upon the chest.' He was, of course, not without supporters. Ludwig von Hammerstein, whose father and Schleicher were friends, remembers the private man affectionately: '. . . We drove down to see the Schleichers at Babelsberg in our new Adler – my mother had just learnt to drive – and I remember that Schleicher took us all out in his little motor boat. He was a very approachable, friendly man . . . As for von Papen, my father wouldn't have his name mentioned in the house. In his view, von Papen was a traitor and a villain. And my father didn't want to hear Hindenburg's name either – Hindenburg had betrayed the army, if not the country. He tore up the picture of Hindenburg which the President had given him as a retirement present.'

The next head to roll, a fortnight after the departure of Gröner, was that of Brüning. The East Prussian landlords were a contributory factor in the Chancellor's fall – they viewed askance a plan of his to turn over 'wasted' agricultural land in their province to resettlement areas for the unemployed; and there is little doubt that Schleicher was also involved in the collapse of Brüning's government. After many years in the corridors of power, it seemed to him that now was the propitious moment for his move.[7] However, few ordinary people can have regretted the disappearance of 'the Hunger-Chancellor' whose attempts to save the economy had squeezed the Germans so harshly. But he was the last truly Republican leader; and the man to benefit most from the Byzantine machinations which ended the Weimar Republic was Adolf Hitler.

Brüning's successor, and Hindenburg's nominee, was Major Franz von Papen. His political 'form' consisted of having once been military attaché in Washington, DC, where he had lost some secret papers. He was a devout Catholic, an aristocrat, a cavalry officer, and a scion of the *Herrenklub* (League of Gentlemen) – an exclusive society whose president was Bodo von Alversleben and whose members included Schleicher and Hindenburg's son Oskar. Hindenburg himself, gradually descending into senility, adored him as a representative of past values; he was also a great friend of Schleicher's – they called each other Fränzchen and Kürtchen. His limited talent was offset by the size of his ambition, and Erich Eyck, the historian of Weimar politics and himself involved in them, has written the following trenchant critique:

> If it is true that those who denied him political advancement did so because they doubted his political capabilities and expertise, von Papen can be said to have gone out of his way in his memoirs to show how right these people were. Seldom have political ignorance and superficiality been displayed with such self-satisfaction as in his autobiography, while the author forfeited any claim to gentle treatment by his critics when he gave the German edition of the book the arrogant title *Der Wahrheit eine Gasse* (Make Way For Truth!). In point of fact, Herr von Papen's memoirs do not have much more claim to this title than do the tales of that other noble narrator, the notorious Baron Münchhausen.[8]

Probably Kürtchen wanted Fränzchen in office as his own puppet. The appointment outraged the Left, and caused dismay abroad. Rule by presidential decree, permitted under Article 48 of the Constitution and invoked increasingly by Brüning, had been an evil necessary to cut through the stalemate of endless bickering coalitions, but now the tendency seemed to be leading towards dictatorship. Von Papen formed a cabinet of 'gentlemen' – all upper-class ex-army officers (five of whom, including von Papen himself, went on to serve under Hitler). The cabinet neither represented the national interest, nor was it unified. Sir Horace Rumbold, the British Ambassador, commented: 'The present Cabinet is a Cabinet of mutual deception. Herr von Papen thinks that he has scored off General von Schleicher and Hitler, General Schleicher thinks he has scored off Hitler, and Hitler, for his part, thinks he has scored off both.'[9] The ban on the SA was lifted on 16 June 1932; uniform-wearing was permitted again from 28 June. 'The republic is cracking up,' observed Harry Kessler in his diary entry for 25 June; from that date, his entries became grimmer and grimmer. He left for Paris on 8 March the next year, and did not return to Germany. Von Papen's conduct at the International Reparations Conference at Lausanne in 1932 drew this whispered comment from the French Finance Minister, Edouard Herriot, to his British counterpart, Sir John Simon, as they sat across the table from the Chancellor: 'The more I study the face of a German cavalry officer, the more I admire his horse.'[10]

In Berlin the decay of political procedure is indicated by Goebbels' remarks in his diary for 28 May 1932. He is writing not of the German national government, here, but of the Prussian Landtag, or state government, also based in Berlin. It had an SPD majority and was headed by the SPD's Otto Braun as prime minister. Goebbels describes a debate: 'In three minutes we were masters of the hall . . . Our group sang the Horst Wessel song. Eight badly wounded from various political parties. This was a warning example. It is the only possible way you can create respect. The assembly hall was one great shambles. We stood as victors in the ruins.'[11] Not many months later, Göring, who by then had become the new master of Prussia, would say at an assembly: 'The measures I intend to take will not be constricted by any legal considerations. I do not have any truck with the niceties of the law! What I have to do is weed out and destroy, no more and no less than that!'[12] No less contemptuous of democracy was the conduct of von Papen and Schleicher, the veritable *Max und Moritz* of German politics, who moved against the SPD state government of Prussia. The suspicion of a planned Communist coup was planted, and Hindenburg persuaded to dismiss the Prussian government from office and make von Papen National Commissioner for Prussia by decree. When Karl Severing, then the Prussian

Interior Minister (Otto Braun was absent on sick leave), refused to give way except to force, a state of emergency was declared in Greater Berlin and Brandenburg. The Prussian government yielded to a small force of no more than half a dozen federal police – oddly, considering that the Prussian police were not only loyal but 90,000 strong. Perhaps Severing did not want to trigger a civil war – violence on the streets, escalated by the Nazis under Goebbels' direction, was beginning to reach the levels of twelve or thirteen years earlier. Perhaps Severing still believed that negotiation was possible, that the democratic process still existed. In fact, like the Weimar Republic, it was already dead. Otto Braun escaped on Saturday 4 March 1933. 'He was driven across the border into Switzerland by Hermann Badt. Badt was a senior civil servant and a devout Jew, but he was able to break the Sabbath because it was a matter of saving a man's life.' [13]

Under von Papen's limp-wristed control, the political situation degenerated fast. There were five elections in the course of eight months during 1932, and outside Berlin, where the left-wing parties still had more popular support, the first four each saw the NSDAP grow stronger. In the autumn a strike against the threat of decreased wages (resulting from the depression) was called by the Berlin Transport Company. Communists and Nazis combined; and this time the fighting was between strikers and strike-breakers. Goebbels exulted in the chaos, observing: 'Naturally, our people have seized the direction of the strike in all parts of the city. That's the only way. If you're going to hit them, hit them hard!' Who 'they' are he does not say, but he probably meant von Papen's tottering cabinet of 'gentlemen'. Already new martyrs to the Nazi cause had been found: SA thugs in Potempa were sentenced to execution for kicking a Communist to death in front of his mother.

In the final elections of 1932, on 6 November, the Nazi vote dropped by two million. But the party still had 196 Reichstag seats, and von Papen could rely on only 62. It was the end of his career as Chancellor, though later he was Hitler's Vice-Chancellor, and finally Ambassador to Vienna. Hindenburg saw him go with undisguised regret, his hand forced by Schleicher, who now proposed to take over as Chancellor himself and defeat the Nazi threat by dividing the NSDAP against itself: those of its members who supported Hitler against those who stood with Gregor Strasser. At the time he stepped in, the auguries seemed reasonable: the NSDAP's finances were in a disastrous state and their popularity was waning fast. Hitler was promising his faithful either a speedy victory, or his own death by suicide. There is little doubt that he intended the latter if he failed to achieve the former. But the gods were with him once more. On 8 December, Gregor Strasser resigned all his party posts, and no one followed him into the wilderness. Schleicher's hopes of splitting the Nazis were dashed: the party filed in behind Hitler. Göring was already President of the Reichstag. The opening address to a new government was by tradition made by the oldest delegate. In September, the 75-year-old Communist Clara Zetkin had expressed her hopes of a Soviet *Reich*; in December, the 82-year-old NSDAP delegate, General Karl Litzmann, spoke of Hitler as 'the people's saviour'. It was a role Hitler relished. In time, and once he had dealt with the Jews, he would elbow Christ out of His part.

Schleicher had intrigued his way to the top, but his timing was bad, and despite his belief in his own strength, he lacked both the force of personality to rule, and attractive, original policies to bind the people to him. Without the support of the SPD, who did not understand that Hitler could only be stopped by supporting the new Chancellor against him, his position was weak. To make the situation worse, von Papen by no means considered himself out of the game, and now started to intrigue with Hitler against Schleicher. Bankers and industrialists were again approached for their support, and Hitler's fortunes took another upward turn. They needed all possible help. Goebbels had spent a fortune on the presidential election campaign. He owed money everywhere, not least a personal 400,000 marks to the tax inspectorate – a debt that would be wiped out if he came to power. The Reichstag was due to reconvene on 31 January 1933, and throughout the winter recess secret meetings went on, as Schleicher found himself increasingly isolated. He lacked even Hindenburg's support, as Fränzchen was still the President's blue-eyed boy. After only a few months in office, and without ever having enjoyed its power, Schleicher resigned. Von Papen, Oskar von Hindenburg and State Secretary Otto Meissner now importuned Hindenburg to appoint Hitler Chancellor. Their plan was to isolate Hitler in cabinet, and there politically disarm him. Once again the Right made the mistake of thinking they could use Nazism to further their own ends; that they could get rid of the upstart Austrian, contemptuously nicknamed 'Emil' by many of the generals, when he had served their purpose.

On 27 January Hindenburg refused to make the appointment. On 29 January he changed his mind. Neatly dressed in a morning coat, Hitler called on the President. On Monday, 30 January, he became Chancellor. The SA celebrated that night with vast torch-lit processions along Wilhelmstrasse, Unter den Linden, and beneath the Brandenburg Gate.

'Come to Berlin. Berlin means boys,'[14] Christopher Isherwood telegraphed W. H. Auden in London in the early Thirties. Isherwood, tradition has it, had been so strongly advised never to go to Berlin that he determined to do so at all costs. Auden joined him, and married Thomas Mann's daughter Erika. Auden was a great friend of Erika's brother,

Klaus, and by giving Erika British citizenship the marriage enabled her to escape the Nazis. It was a marriage of convenience, since both partners were homosexual. The wedding took place in 1935, and from 1936 onwards Erika lived mainly in the USA, working as a journalist, though she also wrote children's stories. Auden took American citizenship in 1946, and the marriage lasted until Erika's death in Zurich in 1969.

Isherwood's own accounts of life in Berlin between 1930 and 1933, the collection of stories and vignettes in *Goodbye to Berlin* and the novel *Mr Norris Changes Trains* (published in the USA as *The Last of Mr Norris*), provide a superb picture of that city in decay. George Grosz wrote to Isherwood after the war: 'You are the first really to capture Berlin's atmosphere . . . Forgive me for sending you my compliments: I just wanted to say that you are a great story-teller, a fine observer, and also a poet.'[15] Isherwood accurately and atmospherically traces the rise of the Red Front and the Nazis, the economic crisis of the end of the Twenties and its effect on Berliners (his landlady Fräulein Thurau was the original for Fräulein Schroeder), the collapse of order in 1932, and so on to Hitler's accession and the Reichstag fire of 1933.[16] There are splendid details of Berlin life, and the reactions of locals to epoch-making events. His Berliners take on a variety of jobs to beat economic depression, and hold down several at the same time, just as they do, for the same reasons, in present-day Budapest; the term *Kaiserwetter*, for good weather, is transformed into *Hitlerwetter*, and Fräulein Schroeder reacts characteristically to the Reichstag fire and the half-daft youth, Marinus van der Lubbe, convicted of causing it: 'Such a nice-looking boy . . . However could he go and do a dreadful thing like that?' Here is a description, from 'Sally Bowles' in *Goodbye to Berlin*,[17] of the day the banks closed:

Next morning, Frl. Schroeder woke me in great excitement:

'Herr Issyvoo, what do you think! They've shut the Darmstädter and National! There'll be thousands ruined, I shouldn't wonder! The milkman says we'll have civil war in a fortnight! Whatever do you say to that!'

As soon as I'd got dressed, I went down into the street. Sure enough, there was a crowd outside the branch bank on the Nollendorfplatz corner, a lot of men with leather satchels and women with string-bags – women like Frl. Schroeder herself. The iron lattices were drawn down over the bank windows. Most of the people were staring intently and rather stupidly at the locked door. In the middle of the door was fixed a small notice, beautifully printed in Gothic type, like a page from a classic author. The notice said that the Reichs-president had guaranteed the deposits. Everything was quite all right. Only the bank wasn't going to open.

A little boy was playing with a hoop amongst the crowd. The hoop ran against a woman's legs. She flew out at him at once: '*Du, sei bloss nicht so frech*! Cheeky little brat! What do you want here?' Another woman joined in, attacking the scared boy: 'Get out! You can't understand it, can you?' And another asked, in furious sarcasm: 'Have you got your money in the bank too, perhaps?' The boy fled before their pent-up, exploding rage.[18]

The section of Stephen Spender's autobiography dealing with his Berlin sojourn[19] is as revealing about the city as it is about Isherwood, though Spender views both with a jaundiced eye. His descriptions of crumbling streets, disgusting food, and Isherwood surrounded by his 'originals', act as a useful corrective to anyone under the illusion that after 1929 there was anything 'golden' about life for any but the very rich. Spender writes:

> A peculiar all-pervading smell of hopeless decay (rather like the smell of the inside of an old cardboard box) came out of the interiors of these grandiose houses now converted into pretentious slums . . . The streets were straight, long, grey, uniform, and all their ornaments expressed the ideal of Prussian domination. There were a good many squares, but these had little positive character. They were just places where several streets halted and had a rest before going on with their uniformed march, at the exact opposite side of the square from where they had left off . . . nothing expressed the cynical relationship between the grim architecture and the feckless population more than the belief of the Berlin population that one of the stone lions outside the palace at the end of Unter den Linden roared whenever a virgin walked by . . . In this Berlin, the poverty, the agitation, the propaganda, witnessed by us in the streets and cafés, seemed more and more to represent the whole life of the town, as though there were almost no privacy behind doors. Berlin was the tension, the poverty, the anger, the prostitution, the hope and despair thrown on the streets. It was the blatant rich at the smart restaurants, the prostitutes in army top boots at corners, the grim, submerged-looking Communists in processions, and the violent youths who suddenly emerged from nowhere into the Wittenbergplatz and shouted '*Deutschland Erwache!*'

During 1931 George Grosz wrote a series of letters and cards from his flat at Trautenaustrasse 12 to his friend the journalist Mark Neven du Mont in London.[20] On 3 January, he says that the Nazis are perpetrating a political murder 'almost every third day'; in a letter decorated with cartoons, dated 24 August, he begs Neven du Mont to send him some tobacco. On 28 September: 'I'm sitting here . . . with a pipe of your generous tobacco, but I'm smoking it sparingly, for the times are really covered in shit . . . no one buys paintings any more, and the future looks bleak enough.' On 23 December he writes, 'Everything's bankrupt. Covered in shit from A to Z! . . . Be glad, little Mark, that you grew up in England . . .' Shortly after, he reports that New Year's Eve with the Brechts was not as much fun as it had been in the old days: 'We were home by 5.15 a.m.!'

But, artistically, all was not over yet. Indeed, there was a brief renaissance in film-making between 1930 and 1933, though it was restricted by tightened censorship. A victim was the American film, directed by Lewis Milestone, of Erich Maria Remarque's best-selling anti-war novel *All Quiet on the Western Front*. The novel itself had already annoyed the Right, and the film was picketed by the SA. Would-be patrons were intimidated, and inside the cinema stink-bombs were set off, even white mice released. One of the most enthusiastic picketers was the erstwhile Expressionist playwright, now a Nazi convert, Arnolt Bronnen. In the *Weltbühne*, Ossietzky raised his voice in protest, but his humane cry was lost in the roar of intemperate approval. Hindenburg was against the film, of course; the government bowed to right-wing pressure and banned it. But other films escaped the censor. G. W. Pabst's anti-war *Westfront 1918* appeared at the same time as *All Quiet*, and Hans Zöberlin's *Stosstrupp 1917* was produced immediately after Hitler came to power, though it is certainly neither less realistic than Pabst's film, nor especially chauvinistic. In the dying days of Weimar there were still films which questioned authority and presented a humanistic message, but more warily than those made six or seven years earlier. All the more remarkable is the achievement of Leontine Sagan's *Mädchen in Uniform* (Girls in Uniform), a study of authoritarianism in a school for officers' daughters, made in 1931 and based on a contemporary play. The girls' uniforms have the same striped pattern as those worn by inmates of the concentration camps.[21] Interestingly, *Mädchen* was universally acclaimed.

Other films of the early Thirties were less intense: Piel Jutzi's film of *Berlin Alexanderplatz* had little of the bite of the original novel, and Gerhard Lamprecht's *Emil and the Detectives*, while both anti-authoritarian and humanizing, had no political edge, nor did *The Captain of Köpenick*.[22] The advent of sound opened the way for filmed operetta; the most stylish were Erich Pommer's contemporary *The Three from the Petrol Station*, which broke new ground by using a modern everyday setting and ordinary people as heroes, and Eric Charell's *The Congress Dances*, a Viennese period piece set in 1814 (produced though not directed by Pommer). But of far higher quality was one of the last films Fritz Lang made in Germany, his first 'talkie', *M*, starring Peter Lorre and based on the career of a Düsseldorf child-murderer, Peter Kürten. The pre-production title was *Murderer Among Us*, and Lang was surprised by the reaction to its announcement:

> He received numerous threatening letters and, still worse, was bluntly refused permission to use the Staaken studio for his film. 'But why this incomprehensible conspiracy against a film about the Düsseldorf child-murderer Kürten?' he asked the studio manager in despair. '*Ach*, I see,' the manager said . . . and immediately surrendered the keys of Staaken. Lang, too, understood; while arguing with the man, he had seized his lapel and

caught a glimpse of the Nazi insignia on its reverse. 'Murderer among us':
the Party feared to be compromised. On that day, Lang added, he came of
age politically.[23]

Meanwhile, Arnold Fanck and Luis Trenker continued to make mountain films, and in 1932 Leni Riefenstahl took her first steps as a director
with the romantic tragedy *The Blue Light*, set in the Dolomites. The new
spirit of nationalism, which these films fed, had another opportunity to
express itself in the centenary year of Goethe's death, 1932. 'Official Germany celebrates Goethe,' wrote Carl von Ossietzky, 'not as a poet and
prophet, but as opium.'[24] Goethe's near-contemporary, Heinrich Heine,
a hero of the 1848 revolution, was a poet who stood on almost as high
a literary peak as Goethe. But he was also a Jew and, as Ludwig Marcuse
pointed out, had still to be given a monument of any sort, after 75 years
of proposal and protest.

The leading Nazis' own artistic taste was relatively straightforward,
and in their rivalry (Goebbels controlled film, Göring the State Theatre),
the two chief arbiters of 'German Art' allowed their minions a certain
degree of freedom. Eager to win the affection of working-class Berliners,
Goebbels was to be seen at Erich Carow's *Comedy Stage* in 1938, eschew-
ing the immaculate English suits he favoured by then for an old brown
jacket, in order to look the part. Both he and Hitler loved films. Goebbels
enjoyed *Die Nibelungen; Anna Karenina* and *Queen Christina* (both with
Garbo); and even *Battleship Potemkin*. He was not blind to real artistic
merit, and no doubt the anti-Semitic scenes in *Potemkin* made the
Bolshevik film easier to accept. His favourite was *The Blue Angel*, but as
it was officially considered degenerate and Marlene Dietrich was *persona
non grata*, this was kept a dark secret. Hitler also like the *Nibelungen*
and *Potemkin*, as well as Luis Trenker movies, and operettas. Of the
stage stars, his favourite was the deep-voiced Swedish *chanteuse* Zarah
Leander, who made her Berlin début in 1937.

Operetta and light comedy took over the thirty or so theatres that had
survived the slump of 1929–30, along with accepted classics and new
'nationalistic' plays by writers such as Hanns Johst and Arnolt Bronnen.
Two days before the book-burning of 10 May 1933, Goebbels said in the
course of a reception for leading theatre people that he had 'no intention
of restricting artistic endeavour', but any latitude was tolerated only for
the first few years of the Third Reich. The more confident the new
leaders became, the less was criticism permitted. In the classic language
of dictators, Hitler had stated in *Mein Kampf*: 'We demand legal prosecution of all tendencies in art and literature of a kind likely to disintegrate
our life as a nation, and the suppression of institutions which militate
against [these requirements].' By 1939, all criticism of the state was

muzzled; the concentration camps, the first of which was opened as early as March 1933, were soon overflowing with German dissidents.[25] The press was dominated by Nazi publications. Ironically, it was the house newspaper of the SS, *Das Schwarze Korps*, which very occasionally allowed itself to criticize the regime – but this was strategic criticism. Many thousands of Germans emerged on the morning of 31 January 1933 in brown uniforms they had not hitherto worn, and soon many more would join the Party – in *Das Schwarze Korps* these opportunists were referred to contemptuously by the 'old' Nazis as 'March Violets'.

As soon as he was in power, Hitler set about consolidating his position. The Communists still posed a serious political threat, and to counter it they had to be discredited. There is little doubt now that the Reichstag fire of 27 February 1933 was the work of Nazi agents, but the Communists were blamed, and it was soon used as an excuse to declare the party illegal and round up its leaders. The discovery of the apparently simple-minded Marinus van der Lubbe and his subsequent show-trial provided the NSDAP with a convenient scapegoat.[26] As yet, Hitler needed a gloss of respectability. Hindenburg was still alive, still (just) filling the role of father figure to the Germans; and for all his faults, Hindenburg was a man who at heart believed in correct procedure. New elections were therefore held on 5 March. They were a farce: opposition parties were terrorized and not allowed to campaign; all media were effectively taken over by the NSDAP in a propaganda drive masterminded by Goebbels, or else suppressed. Nevertheless, the NSDAP polled only 43.9 per cent of the vote nationally, and in Berlin only 34.6, whereas the Communists in Berlin polled 24.4 per cent (but only 12.3 per cent nationwide). To reinforce his position, at an NSDAP-dominated assembly at the Kroll Opera House (being used as a temporary Reichstag) Hitler had himself granted extraordinary and absolute executive powers in the interests of national security. A threatened Bolshevik coup was the trumped-up excuse. From now on Germany had a dictator.

But the Führer was still treading carefully. To ingratiate himself with Hindenburg and the army, he attended a service at a special Reichstag opening ceremony in the Garrison Church in Potsdam on 21 March: Potsdam was the spiritual cradle of Prussia and the home of the army. In the church Frederick the Great lay buried. 'I wasn't there myself,' remembers Ludwig von Hammerstein, 'but my father took my older brother Kunrat. All the conservative elements were there, so Hitler abandoned his quasi-military dress for a morning coat once again; but Prince Auwi (August-Wilhelm) wore the uniform of an SA *Obergruppenführer*. I remember how enthusiastic Fräulein von Oven, my father's secretary, was about the parades [she was later in the Resistance]. My father was less than enthusiastic, but it was a successful public relations exercise for Hitler.'[27]

Ten days later, on 1 April, a national Boycott Day was declared against all Jewish shops and enterprises. It only lasted the day: the Nazis could not yet afford to lose the Jewish contribution to the economy, and were still not absolutely secure in their position. This was just the first shot across the bows. Many Jewish concerns supplied uniforms and flags to the NSDAP. Julius Posener was appalled to find his uncle Paul happily renting a shop to the SA in the autumn of 1932.[28] But doctors, dentists and lawyers very quickly had their practices restricted. The Jewish professional classes were affected first, and many of them were among the first to emigrate. 'My family was composed of doctors and dentists,' says Wolfgang Nelki.

> We were all immediately affected, and that made for a big difference between us and Jews in other areas of work – labourers, for example, and technicians and petty officials continued to work for years under the Nazis; but as early as 31 March 1933 my father decided that we would all have to emigrate. He and my mother left that day. I remember that on Boycott Day two of my brothers opened the dental surgery. A policeman stood outside at the door and reminded patients that this was a Jewish practice, and they said, yes, they knew, and came in anyway. Those were unreal times. There was a Jewish shoemaker downstairs and the policeman warned his customers, too. I took a pair of shoes down to be soled and the policeman even warned me, but I went in, and as I did so, the Jewish shoemaker's Jewish wife came out of the back of the shop and called to the policeman, 'Your coffee's ready!'[29]

It has to be said that not all Jews had the foresight of Wolfgang Nelki's father; and not all Jews had his opportunity.

The exodus had begun even before Hitler's arrival in power. Tucholsky, Grosz, Erich Maria Remarque, the writer Fritz von Unruh, Erwin Piscator, Herwarth Walden, George Lukács, the philosopher Albert Ehrenstein, Rudolf Leonhard and Carl Sternheim had all left already; by no means all were Jews. In the face of a demonstration at the theatre where she was playing in a piece by the Jewish lawyer Max Alsberg, Tilla Durieux, by now married to the Jewish brewer Ludwig Katzenellenbogen, left on 1 April. Else Schiff-Bassermann, the Jewish wife of the actor Albert Bassermann, left at about the same time with her husband. On the train bound for Prague Durieux encountered the essayist Alfred Polgar, the newspaper editor Theodor Wolff, and many artists, actors and writers. Thomas Mann did not return from Switzerland; Lion Feuchtwanger (who had computed the plethora of syntactical errors in *Mein Kampf*) and Arnold Zweig left within the first two months of the Third Reich; Otto Klemperer and Bruno Walter left; others, like Ossietzky and Erich Mühsam, were arrested and sent to the camps, where many died. Many of those who went voluntarily into exile were subsequently stripped of their German citizenship by the Nazi administration. Georg Grosz was the first, on 8 March 1933. In August Feuchtwanger, Alfred Kerr, Heinrich Mann, Tucholsky, and Ernst Toller were stripped of theirs. In March 1934 Einstein – technically Swiss, but born in Ulm – lost his, and in November he was joined by Piscator and Wieland Herzfelde, who had taken his publishing concern to Prague. Brecht and Mehring lost theirs in 1935, and Thomas Mann and Arnold Zweig theirs in 1936. Fritz Kortner, who left in 1932 but returned as the Nazis' fortunes seemed to be on the wane, had just moved back into his flat when he heard the news on the radio that Hitler had been made Chancellor. 'Great,' he said ironically. 'Let's pack.' Steffie Spira narrowly escaped arrest and fled with her husband to Mexico, after internment and imprisonment in France. Like most Jewish businessmen, the Ullsteins were forced to sell up to Aryan buyers at 10 per cent of the value of their concern. Hermann Ullstein was relieved of his entire $25,000 of savings by the police as he left for England.[30] The Nazi 'cleansing' operation robbed Germany of its creative life-blood.

To make more room for his military processions, Hitler had the lime trees in Unter den Linden (the name of the street means 'Under the Limes') cut down, and the grass in Wilhelmplatz was covered with paving stones. New saplings were planted in 1934, but Berliners remembered an old march by Walter Kollo:

> *Solang' noch Untern Linden die alten Bäume blüh'n,*
> *kann nichts uns überwinden – Berlin bleibt doch Berlin!*
> (As long as the old trees bloom on Unter den Linden,
> Nothing can defeat us – Berlin will stay Berlin!)

Perhaps Fate knew the song.

13 Under the Third Reich

IN CONTRAST TO other major German cities, Berlin had not had a ghetto or seen a pogrom against Jews for 250 years.[1] Its reward had been a concentration of Jewish talent. Now, as the days darkened, Jews from the more oppressive provinces, especially to the east, started to migrate to the capital. In 1933 Greater Berlin had a population of 4,242,301, of whom 160,564 were Jews, and 700,000 supporters of Hitler. Oppression there was not yet quite complete; for example, Göring permitted a performance of Berg's opera *Lulu*, based on Wedekind's play, in 1934 – it was, to quote John Russell, 'in the nature of a last salute to the independent, free-tongued, inquisitive Berlin of the Twenties'. But in Berlin the Nazis had difficulty in drumming up sufficient numbers to mark the traditional Workers' Day, and in fact they found the capital an uncooperative city. Almost all the main administrative posts, both in government and in the Gestapo organization which took up residence in Prinz-Albrecht-Strasse, were taken by non-Berliners; the one prominent Berliner among them, Arthur Nebe, later joined the German resistance to Hitler.[2]

The Nazi byword was *Gleichschaltung* – which means 'bringing into line', or 'reduction to one level'. It was the first of many words to acquire a special Nazi meaning as the new power took grip. *Gleichschaltung* was a drastic move in a cosmopolitan city used to freedom, and the Nazis trod carefully at first. The country was still volatile, and civil war still a possibility. Nevertheless, we have seen how quickly the press was muzzled, and how fast prominent Jews in all areas of communication – which is as much as to say *most* prominent people in those areas – were deprived of their work. Those with exceptional foresight and somewhere to go left quickly. Others misjudged it, as was easily possible until the later Thirties. Still others would not, or could not, accept the situation. They did not see themselves as German Jews, but as Jewish Germans. A higher proportion of Jews than of non-Jews had been decorated in the First World War, and a higher proportion had died. Many still held honorary army rank. Many had been baptized. But Julius Streicher's slogan, 'The Jews are our Misfortune', caught on quickly, and spread. Mosse and Ullstein were *gleichgeschaltet*, and only Hugenberg's right-wing Scherl newspaper publishing house remained unscathed. Not only Jews were affected. Any members of the professions – Jewish or Gentile – holding contentious views were, in the course of the years leading up to 1939, gradually weeded out. Some slipped through the net, some left, some found menial jobs, some went to the camps. Many who depended on the language for their work, men like Alfred Kerr, Richard Tauber and Kurt Tucholsky, found their exile particularly grim. The ones to fare best were the scientists, and the musicians – whole bands, string quartets, popular entertainment groups like the Comedian Harmonists, were driven out.

Bloody and direct tactics were also used. In June 1933 twenty Communists and Social Democrats were rounded up by SA men who had taken unto themselves the role of 'ancillary police' in Köpenick, and tortured to death. Soon after, seventy more met the same fate: they were taken to SA bases and never seen again. Some corpses were sewn into weighted sacks and thrown into the Dahme River. Terror reigned on the streets and the police did nothing to counter it. Victims were afraid to *go* to the police for fear of further attack. Such violence continued until the 'ancillary police' role of the SA ceased in August 1933. Hitler, who detested Berlin, was showing the city who was boss.

Schools were also targeted. The Karl-Marx-Schule was closed and Fritz Karsen fled the country. The school was renamed after Kaiser Friedrich. Education for subnormal and handicapped children was reduced. The influence of the Hitler Youth and the League of German Girls was increased. From 1939, membership of the Hitler Youth became compulsory for children aged between 10 and 18. While offering all the attractions of the earlier youth movements, these Nazi organizations also indoctrinated children and turned them against rebellious or controversial parents. The two youth movements were sharply divided along sexist lines: boys were prepared for war, girls for motherhood and domesticity. The League of German Girls was called in German the *Bund deutscher Mädel*, or BdM. This led to a number of ribald jokes, as in German those initials could also stand for League of German Mattresses, or Useful Items for German Men. But under the Nazis, until the pressures of war forced them back to work, German women were condemned to subsidiary, passive and supportive roles. Fashions and hairdos for women were drab, based on folk-costume, and women were discouraged from wearing make-up or otherwise 'falsely' beautifying themselves.

The Church was also scheduled for Nazification – though this was more difficult. The Roman Catholic Church was a powerful, international organization with its headquarters outside Germany; the faith of its priests (as of those of the Evangelical sects) was unexpectedly strong, and it was impossible for the Nazis to suborn all the bishops. In Berlin, where more than three-quarters of the population were Protestant, a pro-Nazi Christian group sprang up in 1932 calling itself *Deutsche Christen*. It declared itself to be against liberalism, Judaism and Marxism, and targeted especially Pastor Martin Niemöller's community in Dahlem. The Dahlem group included the vicar of the Gedächtniskirche in the centre of town, Pastor Jacobi, and also Dietrich Bonhoeffer, then at the theological faculty of the university. Pastor Jacobi was a patient of the eminent Jewish ophthalmologist Oskar Fehr, and went to him one day for a new pair of spectacles: his had been broken in the course of a fist-fight with Pastor Hauk of the *Deutsche Christen*, who had wanted to put a photograph of Hitler on the high altar of the Gedächtniskirche.

On 11 November 1933, when he refused to answer a Nazi questionnaire about his racial ancestry, Niemöller was relieved of his post and suspended. Six hundred of his parishioners protested by telegraph to the authorities. Hitler invited Niemöller and the district bishops to a meeting on 25 January 1934, which ended in a sharp exchange of words between priest and dictator. Niemöller was branded a public enemy in the press. A bomb exploded in his house. But by early 1934 many of those opposed to the NSDAP were already in a concentration camp: one had been set up for Berlin (to relieve the so-called 'wild' camp at Columbiahaus) at Sachsenhausen-Oranienburg, just to the north of the city. This camp later gained notoriety as 'the homosexuals' Auschwitz', because of the number of male homosexuals who were cruelly worked to death there. Niemöller spent 1938 to 1941 there before being transferred to Dachau for the rest of the war. The Dahlem community, however, kept up its resistance after his arrest, sheltering Jewish victims of the regime, and 'U-boats', as Jews and political dissidents who went underground were known in the current slang.

The small and recently established Catholic community – 10 per cent of Berlin's population, with a bishopric only since 1929 – was also involved in resistance to the NSDAP. The Nazis conducted a smear campaign against them in the press between 1935 and 1937, culminating in an edict from Martin Bormann, on 12 April 1937, closing Catholic schools.

As under all dictators, individuals were terrorized; experienced men were chased from office because of their politics or race, beaten up by SA men in their homes, humiliated, or elbowed aside to make room for NSDAP appointees.

Hitler's character was not unique, or in many ways even remarkable. When he became Chancellor in 1933, he was nearing his 44th birthday. He was small and ugly, and the style of moustache he wore, fashionable at the time among the petty bourgeoisie, did little to improve his looks. He was ill-educated, not very bright, and personally rather boring, a failure in the professions of art and architecture he had hoped to pursue. It must also be said that he had great passion, manic self-belief, some humour, and artistic leanings which were not wholly discreditable. But it was the public image of Hitler that ruled Germany, not the man himself. The petty opportunist who got away with it, and possibly lost contact with his own sense of reality as he did so, was amplified into his charismatic personification of an embittered yet powerful group within the country. Just as the Second World War was an inevitable consequence of the First, so this anachronistic creature who thought that Europe was still the centre of world power was the result of the Weimar Republic's inability to extirpate the worst elements of militarism, nationalism and conservatism from its country's consciousness.

During Hitler's rise to power he inevitably had to mix with others more adept at the social arts and graces than he. To help him with this facet of his career, Frau Bechstein, wife of the piano manufacturer, took him under her wing, as Ludwig von Hammerstein remembers:

> We never met Hitler, but he came to visit my father at home early on – in 1928, I think, in Hardenbergstrasse. They sat on the balcony and talked. The connection with Hitler came through the Bechsteins because Frau Helene was a great admirer of his and taught him how and when to kiss a lady's hand, how to address people properly, the correct knives and forks to use – things like that; and she'd give dinner parties and invite him with conservative friends and contacts. My father had met Hitler at such a party and was not impressed, but the man was hungry for army contacts. After his visit he treated us to a free subscription to the *Völkische Beobachter*!

Heinrich Zille, the great Berlin caricaturist who was one of the darlings of the capital, with an annual ball at the Sportpalast named after him, died a year after his glittering 70th birthday gala in 1928. The last Zille Ball was in 1932. On 22 December that year, the last great reception by a Berlin theatre director was given at the Villa Kunz in Grunewald, following the First Night of Paul Abraham's operetta *Ball in Savoy* at the Grosses Schauspielhaus. The last guest to leave was Secretary of State Otto Meissner, who concluded his long career by serving Hitler. Others at the party were already in the course of selling up their houses and flats in Grunewald, Dahlem and Zehlendorf, in order to leave. The grand villas would soon have new owners. Carl Zuckmayer has this memory of the last great Press Ball, which took place on 29 January 1933.[3]

> In the Ullstein box . . . we met our friends the aviator Ernst Udet and the novelist Bruno Frank . . . None of the Ullstein brothers had appeared; Emil Herz, the firm's managing director, did the honours. He was forever refilling our glasses, saying each time, 'Drink up, go ahead – who knows when you'll be drinking champagne in an Ullstein box again.' At the bottom of our hearts all of us were feeling: Never again.
>
> Udet and I, who took brandy between the glasses of champagne, were soon in that condition in which one no longer guards one's tongue. 'Look at the tinware,' Udet said to me, pointing around the hall. 'They've all got their gew-gaws out of the mothballs. A year ago no one would have been caught dead with the stuff.'
>
> Sure enough, on many lapels and dinner jackets you saw the ribbons and crosses of war decorations, which in the past no one would have dreamed of wearing at the Berlin Press Ball. Udet took his *Pour le Mérite* from his neck – he always wore it under his white tie with evening dress – and put it into his pocket.
>
> 'You know what?' he proposed to me. 'Let's take our pants down and dangle our bare backsides over the railings of the box.' To worry my wife, who thought we were quite capable of carrying out such a stunt, we went so far as to loosen our braces. In reality, neither of us was feeling in a jocular mood.[4]

Soon after, Zuckmayer was forced to flee. Udet, the First World War fighter ace, stayed; but he committed suicide in 1942. Only a few people saw clearly what was coming. Before he left, George Grosz told Thomas Mann that in his opinion Hitler would last, not six months as some predicted, but six to ten years; that the Germans who had elected him deserved him; that Nazism was based on terror and slavery; and that within a few years there would be an alliance between Stalin and Hitler.[5] Such perception was given to few indeed.

Hedda Adlon remembered that on the night of Hitler's appointment to the Chancellery, the torchlit SA columns sang in triumph 'Soon we'll crush the French . . .' as they passed the French Embassy on Pariser Platz near the Brandenburg Gate. The blinds in the embassy remained drawn shut, as did Max Liebermann's. The Hotel Adlon continued to be a meeting place for the élite, though the élite was changing. On the night of the Reichstag fire, an I. G. Farben conference was taking place at the hotel, and the industrialist Carl Duisberg commented to the chemist Georg Kränzlein: 'This fire will be a beacon to lead all Germany into the arms of Communism in years to come.' It was only with the greatest difficulty that his cynical words were kept from the ears of the Security Service.[6]

The Adlons themselves lived with the Third Reich, but were not friends of it. Louis Adlon helped Dr Bernhard Weiss, the Jewish Deputy Chief of Police, to escape from Berlin when the time came. The Gestapo had the hotel bugged, but Louis and Hedda developed a code to warn 'honoured guests' of this. Louis himself survived the war, only to die at the hands of the Russians in the ruins of Berlin. His death was the result of an unfortunate misunderstanding: the Russians discovered and plundered the hotel's vast wine-cellar, where a fire broke out which gutted the building. The hotel had been turned into a German field-hospital, and the wounded inside couldn't escape the flames. The fire was filmed by the Russians; Adlon was, quite innocently, identified to them as the *Generaldirektor* of the hotel and they, understanding only the word *general*, arrested him. He died in captivity soon afterwards.[7]

Unity Mitford visited Berlin in 1936 and thereafter was a regular guest at the hotel. Hedda Adlon remembers that she 'shared the political ambition' of her sister Diana, who married her second husband, the British Fascist leader Sir Oswald Mosley, that year. Unity had visions of an alliance being reached between Germany and Britain if she were to marry Hitler, whom she admired, and with whom she fell in love.[8] 'She was delighted whenever she received an invitation from him, which occurred regularly. She always stayed at the Adlon . . . so we had a pretty fair idea to what extent the unsuspecting Unity was calculatedly enmeshed in the plans of the Reich Chancellery.' Hedda remembers her as looking very much the typical English upper-class girl, slim and sporty, with regular features, violet-blue eyes, and blonde hair that tumbled generously over her shoulders. 'She had brought her nippy little two-seater, an MG, over from England with her, and in it she made long tours throughout Germany.' When she was invited to the Chancellery, an orderly would arrive at the Adlon to escort her. Her friendship with Hitler became close enough for her to accompany him to Munich and Berchtesgaden. She even introduced her father and her brother to him when they were in Berlin. But it is unlikely that Hitler ever saw anything beyond political advantage in the prospect of a match with her, and in any case the outbreak of war shattered her ambitions in that direction. She was in Munich on the day war was declared, and attempted to shoot herself in the English Garden there. After a complicated brain operation and a long convalescence, delicate diplomatic manoeuvring enabled her to return to England via Switzerland.

Hitler's guests also stayed at the Adlon, like the delegation of French Air Force officers accompanying General Vuillemin, who were treated to a demonstration of the Luftwaffe's might. Another representative of a foreign power soon to feel the weight of the jackboot was President Hacha of Czechoslovakia, who was at the Adlon in March 1939: 'His manners had all the sweet courtesy of the old Austria, and I often asked myself why it had no effect on Hitler, who was Austrian himself."[9] In fact, Hitler kept the frail old man waiting until one in the morning to see him, and Hacha was then bidden to the Chancellery for a meeting which lasted until dawn. He returned to the Adlon broken and exhausted.

A trickle of artists adorned the dining-room and the bar, but the great days of the Adlon were gone, and those who had really illuminated the hotel had been driven out. Austerity and hypocrisy had set up home in Berlin, now. Among the last guests before the war, apart from the permanent gaggle of foreign journalists, were thirty-one members of the British Embassy waiting to go home after their embassy (across the Pariser Platz from the hotel) had been sealed in the presence of the Swiss Ambassador, who henceforward was to represent British interests in Germany.

Relations between the Nazi private armies and the Reichswehr continued to be difficult, and Hitler now needed the Reichswehr. He knew he had to curb the brown-uniformed hordes of the SA who had brought him to power and maintained him there so far, but who were now getting dangerously strong. Their leader, Ernst Röhm (who had started his career as a lift-boy at the Gourmenia Palace Hotel in Berlin), disagreed with Hitler over the role of the SA *vis-à-vis* the Wehrmacht, and represented a possible threat to the Führer's domination. By now, however, the black-uniformed SS had become an efficient and ruthless unit, one Hitler knew he could use with absolute confidence. While he hesitated over his course of action, Franz von Papen, now Vice-Chancellor but horrified by the turn events were taking, gave a speech at the University of Marburg, appealing against the excesses of the new regime. It was a brilliant piece of writing by his aide, Edgar Jung, and by engaging public opinion von Papen hoped to contain Hitler and bring him back into the fold of the conventional Right. Hindenburg could not live much longer, and once he was gone there would be no focus of control over the Nazis at all. The speech also contained attacks on Goebbels and his lies, and on the SA.[10]

Hitler, attending a conference of NSDAP leaders at the provincial town of Gera, hurried to Berlin to find that Röhm had already entrenched himself at Munich. Furious as he was with von Papen – Goebbels' press screamed invective against the Vice-Chancellor the following day – he would not accept his resignation, nor that of other 'moderate Right' members of his cabinet. Von Papen's speech had met with approval abroad – and among many thousands of Germans, with relief; Hitler could not afford to split his power base at this crucial stage. On the other hand, he needed the army as never before, and it was clear that matters were coming to a head with the SA. With the connivance of the army, a massacre was planned and carried out by SS units, principally in Munich, for 48 hours from dawn on June 30. This blood-letting, known as The Night of the Long Knives, permanently shattered the SA, which continued thereafter only as a small internal party-police organization. The homosexual Röhm was slain in his bed with his lover, and Hitler oozed moral indignation over his 'discovery' that this most trusted of his chiefs should have turned out to be a 'sexual pervert'. Thus ended a partnership that went back to the earliest days of the Nazi Party.

The Night of the Long Knives was used to rid the NSDAP of other thorns in its side. Gregor Strasser was murdered; Franz von Papen was arrested, and escaped only because the army took him under its direct protection. Most significant of all was the murder in their Neu-Babelsberg villa of General von Schleicher and his wife. One of Schleicher's closest aides, Kurt von Bredow, heard the news as he sat over tea at the Adlon Hotel the same afternoon. ' "I am going home," he said in a raised voice so that the waiters, well known as Gestapo agents, might hear. "They have killed my chief. What is there left for me?" '[11] That same evening he was shot when he responded to a ring at his front doorbell.

Hindenburg died on 2 August 1934, not before congratulating Hitler on having extirpated so many traitors from Germany's midst. On the same day the army was required to swear an oath of personal fealty to the Führer, who now merged the offices of Chancellor and President. Opponents of the regime were subjected to ever harsher treatment. Arnold Bauer was imprisoned twice by the Gestapo, once for six months, once for eighteen.

> Political detainees weren't tortured so much later, at least nowhere near as badly as in the early SA days in 1933 and 1934; but even so, when I was in prison in 1936 – I missed the Olympics, by the way – I was beaten black and blue, and bullwhipped, But I had been working for the underground press. There were simpler forms of protest. We all used to go to the annual performance of Beethoven's Ninth at the People's Theatre. That was one of the few traditions carried over from the Weimar days to the Third Reich. To attend and listen to the *Ode to Joy* was an inner way of saying No to the NSDAP. But Hitler had all the support of the Ruhr industrialists, and protest without backing goes nowhere.[12]

Bauer escaped relatively lightly because his lawyer told the authorities that he was *ein Beamtensohn* – 'the son of an official'; he was also a Gentile.

'One of my last assignments before leaving was to interview the actor Heinrich George for the Finnish magazine *Elokuva Aitta*,' remembers the journalist Alfred Fischer. 'In my opinion, he was the best actor of all. He gave the interview in his wine-cellar, stroking his pet Great Dane. He was very left-wing, but he could still afford to express such views, as this was only a couple of weeks into February 1933. I noticed that nevertheless he had pictures of Göring and Goebbels on his walls.' Later George, who stayed on under the Nazis, suffered the humiliation of being given one-line parts only in plays at the State Theatre, by then under the control of the lugubrious Franz Ulbrich from Weimar.[13] George was subsequently called up, and died a prisoner of the Russians. Among the 'overnight' Nazis who emerged after 30 January 1933, Fischer remembers especially the appalling Hans Belling. 'He ran a film magazine financed by his mother, never paid fees, and himself contributed to a book . . . called *Film-Jews Are Watching You*, in which many of his former associates were vilified. Work became harder and harder to find, especially for me, since I even look very Jewish, and Nazi laws affecting who was allowed to work in journalism began to be enforced from January 1934.'

'As a family, we were not victims of much direct SA terror,' remembers Henni Handler. 'But still we were forced to abandon our summer house to the east of the city in 1934 by the local Nazis, and, yes, we were beaten up a bit then.' A contemporary of hers adds: 'Being young – still children, really – sometimes it seemed like a bit of an adventure. We didn't take it that seriously at first. I even remember going for a walk in the Grunewald with a girl-friend and we were picked on by a Nazi – it was obvious that we were Jews – and he started to beat me up; but he didn't succeed. I beat him up in the end. But you had to know how to look after yourself.'

As the tension between the political parties became pronounced after 1929, the various party salutes had to be learned and recognized. The SPD salute was a clenched fist with the arm outstretched; the Communist salute was the same, but with the arm crooked. As for the Nazis:

> If people belong to the same social group, it is customary to raise the right arm at an angle so that the palm of the hand becomes visible. The appropriate phrase that goes with it is 'Heil Hitler' or at least 'Heil'. If one espies an acquaintance in the distance, it suffices merely to raise the right hand in the manner described. If one encounters a person socially – or through any other circumstances – inferior to oneself, then the right arm is to be fully stretched out, raised to eye-level; at the same time one is to say 'Heil Hitler'. The greeting should always be carried out with the left arm if one's right arm is engaged by a lady.[14]

The so-called *Hitlergruss* became compulsory, and though many chose to ignore it, it was risky to do so in the company of strangers, or when shopping, or in any public situation.

From 1933 on, measures restricting the Jews socially and professionally were set in motion and gradually increased. Laws enacted late in 1933 excluded Jews from involvement in the arts, literature, music and journalism at an editorial level; earlier their right to practise as lawyers, doctors, teachers, and so on had been curbed – Jewish doctors, for example, were downgraded to 'medical practitioners', and could only treat fellow-Jews. Jews had already been eliminated from the civil service. The most significant general step against the Jews was the enactment of the first Nuremberg Laws in the autumn of 1935: these isolated Jews socially, prohibited any form of sexual relationship between Jew and non-Jew (divorce was actively encouraged in the case of existing mixed marriages), and forbade Jews to work as domestics in non-Jewish households. Later, in the case of mixed-race Jews, the degree of an individual's Jewishness was defined by law. Schools and universities were progressively 'aryanized', and Jewish children were denied the right to public education. In the summer of 1935 certain park benches in the Tiergarten were painted yellow and allocated for Jewish use only. These benches were few in number and located in the least attractive parts of the park. Yellow in medieval times had signified sickness, and treacherous aggression. Yellow was also the colour associated with Judas, and in the Middle Ages Jews had often been obliged to wear yellow dress or yellow badges. It was in keeping with Nazi thinking to revive these primitive ideas.

The changes were introduced gradually, as the Nazis' original policy was to encourage Jews to leave. It was vain for any Jew to close his or her mind to what was coming, but it was also difficult for the average Jew to know where to turn. Foreign countries were not generous with visas, and often more money was needed to escape than was easily available. Alfred Fischer's colleague Gerd Neumann was able to emigrate to Palestine, for example; but only because he could afford to pay the £1,000 'capital certificate' demanded by the British Mandate Authorities. There would come a time when Jews would be permitted to take no more than 10 marks with them when they left; all property and valuables would be forfeit; holding a foreign bank account would become an offence punishable by death.

But in the beginning, few believed that Hitler would last long: it seemed impossible that such insane rule could. Nor were the Nazi organizations remarkable at first for their unity, or for their efficiency in enforcing regulations. 'Yellow stars and other markings, like armbands, didn't come in until much later – not until 1941,' remembers one Berlin Jewess.

I didn't leave until 1939, and almost right up until then restrictions were either not applied very strictly, or it was possible to circumvent them. I remember going to a ball, and at it an SA man in full uniform asked me to dance. What could I do? I danced with him. He was quite a young man. After we'd been dancing for a while I said to him: 'Isn't your racial instinct telling you anything about me?' And he blushed as red as a beetroot and said, 'You mustn't think we're all like that, Miss.' But that was in 1934. Later, I wouldn't have dared to take such liberties. Later, it could have meant the concentration camps. But this guy was just a nice, very young man.[15]

Stefan Zweig wrote the libretto for Richard Strauss's *The Silent Woman* in 1933. This was an embarrassment to the NSDAP, since a disgraced Jewish writer was now linked to the name of Germany's greatest living composer, who could not be touched. Strauss had accepted the post of President of the Nazi Chamber of Music, and his voluntary alignment with the Nazis was of great propaganda value to them in the face of their repudiation by most eminent artists. Strauss defended Zweig, but Zweig thought that his real motivation was the protection of his Jewish daughter-in-law and his half-Jewish grandchildren. From his exile in London Zweig refused to object to the performance of the opera, thereby robbing the Nazis of an excuse to stop its production, and Hitler was forced to allow it to go ahead in Dresden 'exceptionally'. However, it was immediately banned when the Security Service discovered that Strauss had been corresponding with Zweig about further collaboration, and Strauss was then obliged to resign his presidential post.

This was not the end of Zweig's persecution. In exile he heard the circumstances of his mother's death: her Aryan nurse could only stay by her bedside overnight if her Jewish cousin, a 60-year-old man, and the only relative able to be with her, left. The nurse was under 45, and was thus not allowed to be alone with a Jewish male, according to the latest Nazi legislation. Zweig's gloom in London was only alleviated by the arrival there in 1938 of his friend Sigmund Freud, driven out of the house he had occupied in Vienna since 1891. Freud had just published his *Moses and Monotheism*. Speaking of his fellow Jews, the psychoanalyst made an arid joke: 'Now that everything is being taken from them, I had to go and take their best man!' Freud died in London in 1939. Zweig killed himself in Brazil three years later.[16]

Hans Jackson remembers little anti-Semitism at school – he went to the Friedrichsrealgymnasium[17] in Kreuzberg, where most of his fellow-students were the sons of army officers; but he was forced to leave when he was fourteen. 'I remember too how they took over Jewish businesses. First, the assets and the bank accounts would be frozen so that the owner was immobilized, then the Nazis would arrive and make an offer to buy – which was an offer you couldn't refuse. It was that simple. It all started in Berlin around 1936 – a little later than elsewhere. Sometimes there was confusion: the SA smashed up Israel's department store one night, unaware that it had already been "aryanized"!'[18] 'I remember being terrified one day in the street,' says Ed Rosenstiel. 'I was collecting for the Jewish section of *Winterhilfe* (Winter Relief).[19] Suddenly I noticed a column of SA men and I ducked into a doorway to avoid having to salute the flag as they passed, but one of them had seen me, and he broke rank and ran across to me. I thought I was in for a beating, but he embraced me heartily. It was an old school chum, Wolf von Müller!'[20]

Inge Fehr, the daughter of the ophthalmologist Professor Oskar Fehr, was not even aware that she was half-Jewish until six months after the beginning of the Third Reich; the family had been baptized and brought up as Christians. Finding out – a BdM fellow-pupil at school informed her – came as an enormous shock. The wealthy bourgeois family lived in a 14-room flat and had five servants. The large Horch automobile was big enough to take all of them as well as the chauffeur and the nanny. Professor Fehr's clientele was international and included Luis Trenker, Max Schmeling, Hans Albers (who met his Jewish girl-friend secretly at the Fehrs'), and the family of Prince August-Wilhelm. Professor Fehr was deprived of his post as Director of Ophthalmology at Rudolf-Virchow-Hospital and downgraded, but was able to work privately in Berlin until 1938. Then, after enormous difficulties and tribulations, he fled with his family to Britain, where he was obliged to requalify. He did so in Edinburgh at the age of sixty, and ended with a Harley Street practice.

> On 15 September 1938 we heard that all cars belonging to Jews had to display a special 'Jewish' number. So we sold the car. The new numbers clearly identified any car that belonged to a Jew and most that did were smashed up or at least pelted with stones – but things were never quite so bad in Berlin as outside it, and we had a friend who lent us her 'Aryan' car. But there were other things we had to put up with. I remember taking our two pedigree dachshunds, Plisch and Plum, for their usual morning walk around the block when a female neighbour, exercising her dog, called it away from ours, saying: 'Don't play with those non-Aryan dogs.' I called Plisch and Plum away, and said loudly 'Don't play with that non-pedigree dog!'[21]

The Jewish population of Berlin did not decline between 1933 and 1938, partly because during the early years of the Third Reich the exodus was slow, and partly because those who left were replaced by refugees from provincial Germany. There were big Jewish organizations, such as the Central Society for German Citizens of the Jewish Faith, founded in 1893. Until 1937, its 'house magazine' continued to be published by Mosse and sold openly at kiosks throughout the city, and nationally. The Jews were not at first restricted in their activities within their own community. Indeed, they were allowed complete artistic freedom, beyond that allowed to Aryans, on the grounds that as they were already a degenerate race, degenerate art couldn't possibly pollute them! However, Gestapo officials attended all performances to note down the slightest speech or even inflection which could be regarded as seditious. Shakespeare was not above suspicion; Autolycus' 'I see this is the time that the unjust man doth thrive'[22] was warily applauded during a performance of *The Winter's Tale* in February 1939. Jewish cultural activity continued, albeit latterly in a restricted manner, until 1941. There were three theatre companies, an opera, two symphony orchestras, and several choirs, comprising nationally about 2,500 artists and an audience of 70,000. Tolerated by the Nazi regime as a means of containing the remains of the Jewish German population, the cultural movement became a symbol of hope and survival to a race determined not to be deprived of their identity or their heritage.[23] Their protector and persecutor was Hans Hinkel, their Nazi representative within the administration, whose love–hate relationship with Jewry led him to act as their advocate and defender to his peers, while also allowing them no leeway. Censorship was quite extraordinary. In a comedy by Ferenc Molnár, one of the characters had to address a line to his pale tan leather attaché case. It ran: 'Farewell, untrustworthy blond briefcase!' The Nazis had the word 'blond' replaced with 'beautiful'.

Berlin was still very much an international capital. Hitler wanted the approval of the rest of the world, and he wanted a major propaganda victory at the Olympic Games in 1936. At this stage the Nazis still gave active help to organizations encouraging Jews to emigrate. Jews were not subjected to extreme or consistent persecution until after the *Kristallnacht* outrage at the end of 1938, and the 'Final Solution' was not drawn up until the Wannsee Conference of January 1942. In the meantime, codes governing what Jews were or were not allowed to do in the field of culture reached dizzy heights of bureaucratic ridiculousness: the Jewish *Kulturbund* was allowed to perform Beethoven until 1937, but Schiller and the German Romantics had been 'withdrawn' from them in 1934. Goethe and the classical school, however, were permitted until 1936. Foreign writers who were permitted included J. B. Priestley and Ferenc Molnár – who waived their fees in the case of *Kulturbund* performances. Jewish orchestras were allowed to play Mozart's work until the annexation of Austria in 1938, and Handel was allowed until November 1938. He was not a Nazi favourite, because of his biblical themes and his desertion of Germany for England.

Meanwhile, in contemporary England, Neville Chamberlain enjoyed the triumph following his Munich meeting with Hitler, which was supposed to snatch peace from the jaws of war, but which in fact allowed the Führer to take over the strategically important Sudetenland.

14 A Cloud Across the Sun

■■■■■■ NAZI BERLIN WAS an austere place. Ersatz was a common term even before the war started, and although the new regime dealt dramatically with such problems as unemployment, by means of ambitious road-building programmes and by expanding the arms industry, these enterprises brought ordinary people little joy and little reward. The autobahns occupied between 5,000 and 10,000 hitherto unemployed men in Berlin during 1934, and the 226-kilometre-long Berliner Ring was constructed between 1935 and 1939. The road-building projects were part of Hitler's plan to transform Berlin into the capital of his new empire – when the city would be renamed Germania. To picture what Berlin might have become, one can still look at the Air Ministry building in Berlin built for Göring in 1935 by Emil Sagebiel, or the Nuremberg Stadium, or – if one seeks a smaller-scale parallel – central Bucharest today. Vast public building projects were envisaged for Berlin. Werner March designed the Olympic Stadium (which survived the war) for 1936; Albert Speer's plans for the new Chancellery were grandiose to a degree which reflected Hitler's megalomania: from the entrance, foreign diplomats would be obliged to walk 300 metres to the Reception Room, via a Hall of Honour, an Ante-Room, a Hall of Mosaics and a Marble Gallery – the aim was to humble them. The resurrection of improvements planned in the Twenties but shelved because of inflation also formed part of the Nazis' projects, but Hitler was interested in prestige projects above all. The building of cheap flats, for example, decreased sharply after he came to power.

Berlin itself was ruled by Stadtskommissar Julius Lippert, who had taken over from the last mayor, Gustav Böss's colourless successor Heinrich Sahm. For Berliners, life ran along strictly regulated tracks.

Life for the poor became harder as working women were obliged to leave their factory jobs in accordance with Nazi thinking about the role of women; they did not return until the authorities were obliged to recall them to replace men sent to fight.

Winterhilfe (Winter Relief) was another innovation of the NSDAP. So relentless did the process of collecting become – the collectors were usually SA but often Hitler Youth and BdM members as well – that between October and March householders and shops could purchase special plaques to put on their doors to fend off importunate box-rattlers. Where the money collected actually went is not recorded. Some may have gone to relieve the poor; some no doubt went to fund the National Effort. Richard Grunberger calls *Winterhilfe* 'the Third Reich's gratuitous ritual *par exellence*':

> From 1937 onwards, when Germany overcame the effects of the Depression and there were more vacancies than job-seekers, the Winter Relief campaign was a form of activity purely for its own sake, and as such exactly served the regime's aim of permanent emotional mobilization. Thus a vast collecting and publicity machine kept moving into top gear afresh each winter under manifestly false pretences; even wartime collections of comforts for the troops served less as antidotes than as levers for manipulating popular feeling and eliciting a self-sacrificing response.[1]

One aspect of *Winterhilfe* that became part and parcel of everyday life, and also neatly expressed the petty bourgeois mentality of the Nazis, was the *Eintopftag* (stew-day). On one day a month every German household ate one meal consisting of one course only – an all-in-one stew, or *Eintopf*. The money saved was sent to Winter Relief. Public figures would ostentatiously eat their *Eintöpfe* for the camera, and the army staple of pease pudding was a popular ingredient.

Reports in the international press about the way of life in National Socialist Berlin – the rigidly-enforced new laws, the measures taken against Jews, the joylessness of the city – were repudiated by the Nazi propaganda machine or dismissed as malicious misinterpretations. In 1936 the NSDAP enjoyed an ideal opportunity to invite the world to Berlin and demonstrate that a false impression had been given of the new regime. Hitler repudiated the Treaty of Versailles in 1935 and moved troops into the Rhineland in March 1936, but no one in the international community boycotted the Berlin Olympic Games, scheduled for August. The First World War was still fresh in politicians' memories, and peace at any price the desire uppermost in their minds. Even Winston Churchill, whose embarrassingly blunt line of 'Kill the Bolshie, kiss the Hun' indicated his support for German reconstruction after the First World War, did not raise his solitary warning voice until some time after

Hitler's accession to power; interestingly, however, his son Randolph, covering the German election campaign for *The Sunday Graphic* in July 1932, wrote: 'The success of the Nazi party sooner or later means war.'

The International Olympic Committee had chosen Berlin for the 1936 Olympics in 1930, and ratified their decision at an IOC plenary session in Barcelona a year later. As it became clear that the NSDAP would soon be in power in Germany, the President of the IOC asked the German delegate, Ritter von Halt, to confirm Hitler's ability to host the Games; Hitler expressed enthusiasm for the idea. Six days before he took power Theodor Lewald, an under-secretary in the Ministry of the Interior, convened the first meeting of the German Olympic Committee. But Lewald, awarded the *Adlerschild*, the highest accolade of the Weimar Republic, by Hindenburg for his services to sport, was half-Jewish, and Hitler now became convinced that after all the Olympic Movement was 'a piece of theatre inspired by Jews', unacceptable in the National Socialist State. It took all Goebbels' arts of persuasion, plus those of the *Reichssportführer*, Hans von Tschammer und Otten, and the *Reichsjugendführer*, Baldur von Schirach, to persuade him to change his mind. In fact, Nazi propaganda attempted to exploit Lewald's Jewishness to deny the regime's anti-Semitism, and no one in Berlin mentioned, for example, the 598 university professors and other teachers who had lost their jobs because of their race.[2] Even so, it was not without difficulty that Berlin kept the right to hold the games. Hitler's anti-Semitic policies were widely reported in the foreign press, his propaganda notwithstanding, and the chairman of the American Olympic Committee, Avery Brundage, proposed to let the games drop – as in 1916; or to transfer them to Tokyo or Rome; or to boycott them. His objections were overridden.

Hitler gave orders that all state, party and army facilities should be fully exploited to ensure that the Games would run smoothly, and be remembered as 'the greatest festival of all time'. The west side of the city was transformed by the major building works involved in preparing to host the Games. New underground lines were laid, and new *S-Bahn* tracks. No detail was left unchecked. Even the 7,000-odd prostitutes in the city who had been registered during the Weimar Republic but had had their official status removed by the NSDAP, now had it returned to them, and their numbers were reinforced by girls from the provinces. Women were allowed to wear their skirts 5 centimetres higher than the Party officially permitted – the hemline could now be 30 centimetres above the soles of the feet, instead of the usual 25.

The Party was eager to conceal its crimes in the most obvious, even ludicrous ways. Just as they later 'sanitized' and 'beautified' the model concentration camp at Theresienstadt for the benefit of Red Cross inspectors, so now in Berlin all traces of racism and oppression were removed or covered up. The yellow benches disappeared from the Tiergarten, the red display cabinets for *Der Stürmer*[3] magazine were removed, and in Berlin the magazine itself was withdrawn for the two weeks of the Games. All signs forbidding entry to Jews were taken down. Nevertheless, every effort was made to restrict contact between visiting foreigners and local Jews, and the official Games city-plan, although it showed the location of all churches and even a mosque, did not show where the synagogues were. Before the games started, an SS couplet went the rounds:

> *Wenn die Olympiade vorbei*
> *Schlagen wir die Juden zu Brei.*
> (When the Olympic Games are done
> We'll smash the Jews up bone by bone).[4]

And indeed, as soon as the last competitors had departed after the Games, Nazi rule returned to the city with a vengeance. Even during them, although Göring and Goebbels usually abandoned their uniforms for suits, the Führer stuck to his; and the story of his refusal to shake hands with the black American athlete Jesse Owens (who carried off four gold medals in six days, thereby spiking the Nazi *Untermensch* theory) is well known. The gold, silver and bronze medals for ladies' fencing were won by an Austrian, a Hungarian, and a German respectively – but, inconveniently, they were all Jewesses. In wrestling, the German champion was the Communist Werner Seelenbinder, who refused to give the Nazi salute when receiving his medal and did not flinch from telling athletes from abroad exactly what was happening in Germany. He was killed in a concentration camp in 1944. At the opening ceremony, the only nations whose teams did not give the Nazi salute were those of Great Britain and Japan.

Despite his initial reservations, Hitler followed the Games with enthusiasm and showed his every emotion openly – these were the days before the telephoto lens, and in any case Hitler was very unsophisticated. When Ilse Dörfield dropped the baton in the women's final of the 4 × 100 metres relay race on the last stretch, so that the Americans won, the Führer leapt to his feet, ripped his cap from his head, and crumpling it in his hands sank back into his seat, shaking his head.

During the games, the city was colourful. The latest women's fashion was two-tone jackets, and their brightness briefly outshone the brown and black uniforms and the dun-coloured civilian clothes of everyday life. Unter den Linden, the Lustgarten, and every other appropriate public place was decked with huge swastika banners. Largely thanks to the efforts of the German Olympic trainer Carl Diem of Berlin, a veteran of organized sport, Germany was victorious overall and carried off 42 gold medals; America, in second place, had to be content with 25. Berliners alone took 17 gold medals, plus 19 silver and 18 bronze.

'We went to the Games quite often,' remembers Helga Russow.[5] 'It was a great time for Berlin, and gave us a bit of a breather from the Nazis. Maybe we hoped it would never end. For a little while there was no *Hitlergruss*, no stupid songs, and we had a sense of belonging to the rest of the world again. But there was barely time to enjoy it before it was over.' 'I remember the stadium. It was as big as a city,' says Illa Walter.[6] 'The place was packed, and when Hitler entered and took his place all the Germans stood up. Fortunately there were plenty of foreigners there too and they didn't get up, and nor did I. I never used the *Hitlergruss* either. At least this time I didn't draw any attention to myself. The Games themselves were exciting; but I won't forget him making his entrance and the roar of the crowd as they stood up.'

The 1936 Olympic Games readily call to mind the work of the Nazi film maker Leni Riefenstahl, of whom mention has already been made. She was born in Berlin in 1902 and after studying Fine Art she briefly became a ballet dancer before embarking on a career as a film actress. She worked for Luis Trenker, who influenced her later work as a director, as did Fritz Lang, but her work for UFA was limited to parts in Wilhelm Prager's *Ways to Strength and Beauty* and two 'mountain' films by Arnold Fanck: *The Holy Mountain* and *The Great Step.* All these were made in the late Twenties.

Her first film as a director was *The Blue Light* in 1932, a romantic drama; but she did not come into her own until after the Nazis had seized power. Under Hitler's rule she made the so-called documentary films for which she is famous. They were actually pieces of arrant Nazi propaganda – though Riefenstahl disingenuously claimed to be apolitical, she was an enthusiastic banner-waver for the Führer – redeemed by brilliant and innovative cinematography.

The first was *Triumph of Faith* (1933), quickly followed by *Triumph of the Will* (1934–35), which documented the progress of the 1934 Nazi Rally at Nuremberg and sought to make heroes out of even the lowest of the Nazi thugs, such as Robert Ley, who are paraded before an idolatrous camera. Though a superb piece of film-making, it is perhaps not especially innovative – similar, and better, scenes can be recalled in any of Eisenstein's films, for example – and its endless march sequences accompanied by Nazi brass bands pall as the hours pass. In its day, however, it was responsible for major recruitment to the Party, and no doubt more than justified Hitler's commissioning of it.

As a producer and director, and Hitler's darling, Riefenstahl became one of UFA's major properties. All her films were distributed by the company and had their premières at the Ufa-Palast am Zoo cinema.

Triumph of the Will was followed by *Day of Freedom – Our Armed Forces* (1935), which Riefenstahl produced and directed.

The peak of her career was reached with the two Olympic films, *Festival of the People* and *Festival of Beauty* (1936–1938), again commissioned by Hitler, and given a gala première, as *Olympiade*, on Hitler's 49th birthday. In these films she developed the imaginative close-ups, unconventional camera angles and tracking shots she had shown herself so adept at in *Triumph of the Will*. Her achievement was to do for the Nazi cult of Strength-through-Joy what Thorak did in his idealized muscle-men statues, and what Veit Harlan did for the policy of anti-Semitism: she lent Nazism a counterfeit respectability by the application of an artistic imprimatur. As she was a more talented artist than either Thorak or Harlan, history has been more prone to forgive her.

She continued to thrive throughout the Third Reich, but after the war she was put under a ban by the Allies until 1952. Thereafter she continued her career, and in great age produced an acclaimed photo-essay on African tribesmen, but her career never again attained the heights it had achieved under the dictator whom she had done so much to glorify.

Germany's writers had already been 'cleansed'; now it was the turn of the artists. Nazi leaders had little real sense of what was valid in art, in so far as one can make an absolute judgement. In art, Nazi leaders 'knew what they liked'. This was either a flattering and sentimental depiction of German peasant life or (perhaps paradoxically) a version of the style that later became known in the Eastern Bloc as Socialist Realism: idealized people representing what might one day be, in idealized surroundings. The poor were picturesque and contented. Alternatively, strong-jawed, muscle-bound men and women in nude or semi-nude poses (never erotic, though sometimes pornographic) strove for the good of the New Germany. Leading exponents of the style were Arno Breker and Hitler's favourite sculptor Josef Thorak – nicknamed by the Germans 'Professor Thorax' on account of his predilection for massive, heaving musculature.

A committee of art arbiters was appointed to sort out what was seemly under the NSDAP from what was not. It comprised Count Baudassin, Wolf Willrich, the cartoonist Schweitzer, who drew under the name of Mjölnir (Thor's Hammer), and Adolf Ziegler. These men were responsible for the destruction of as many as 16,000 works of art, including a thousand by Nolde, 400 by Kokoschka, 200–300 each by Grosz and Dix, and many more by foreign painters including Cézanne, Picasso, Matisse, Dufy, de Chirico and Max Ernst. In 1939 alone, 4,000 paintings were burnt in the courtyard of the central Berlin fire brigade. There was an exhibition of 'degenerate' art at Karlsruhe as early as 1933, another at

Nuremberg two years later, and a huge one at Munich in 1937. No artistically viable criteria were applied. Broadly speaking, the artists involved stood accused of obsession with money and pornography.[7] Interestingly, the Munich exhibition attracted two million visitors, making it the most popular exhibition in the history of the Third Reich. The concurrent exhibition of New German Art attracted a fifth of that number, and the gallery built to house it was locally nicknamed 'The Munich Art Terminal', and 'Palazzo Kitschi'. Adolf Ziegler's 'painstakingly executed confections of lifeless nudity earned him the soubriquet "Reich Master of Pubic Hair".'[8] Numbed art critics managed to squeeze a little genuine criticism between the lines of their reviews. Paintings that escaped the torch were sold off in Lucerne in 1939, where those with the means could pick up a van Gogh self-portrait for $20,000, or a Gauguin for as little as $8,000. A picture by Picasso, *The Absinthe Drinker*, did not find a buyer.[9]

Music was similarly stigmatized; the Nazis' task was easy, as most prominent contemporary composers were either Jews or pupils of Jews. Berlin finally had to forego jazz, though later than in other parts of Germany; Jack Hilton was playing at the Scala as late as February, 1937.[10] Mozart's *Marriage of Figaro* and *Così fan tutte* were attacked because their librettist, Lorenzo da Ponte, was born a Jew. *The Magic Flute* was suspect because its theme was Freemasonry, but it found a surprising defender in the Führer himself, who declared at the 1938 Party Rally: 'Only a man lacking in national respect would condemn Mozart's *Magic Flute* because it may sometimes come into conflict with his own ideas.'[11] Classical plays also suffered. *The Merchant of Venice* was still permitted – superficially, at least, it showed the Jew as villain. But there were ideological problems to be overcome. For his production in Vienna in 1942, Lothar Müthel had the critic-turned-dramaturge Herbert Ihering adapt the play so that Jessica became the bastard child of Shylock's wife following an affair with a non-Jew – and so fit for marriage with the Aryan Lorenzo.

Arguments for and against the artists who stayed on in Germany are still vigorous today; in a biography of his father Max, Gottfried Reinhardt inveighs against them with cold dignity, on the grounds that they gave the Third Reich a veneer of respectability.[12] Of those who stayed, some were convinced Nazis while others were not at all politically engaged and merely did what was most expedient. Some became victims of their consciences. Take the film *Jew Süss* of 1940: its director was a former actor, Veit Harlan, and it starred Werner Krauss with, in the title role, Ferdinand Marian. As a punishment for their undoubted services to the Third Reich, Krauss and Harlan were both forbidden to practise their professions for a period after the war; thereafter, they resumed their lives and careers. But Marian (who had been forced by Goebbels to take on the role, under threat of having his licence to act revoked) was overcome by remorse, sought solace in alcohol, and died in a possibly suicidal car crash in 1945. The director of the State Theatre, Gustav Gründgens, having concurred with such actions as Goebbels' proscription in 1936 of *any* theatre criticism, left voluntarily for the Front in 1943, unable to carry on the balancing act of trying to serve both humanity and the Nazis.

'My reaction to the SA massacre in 1934 was "that is their business; I should leave those terrible people to do what they want to among themselves; basically it's nothing to do with me",' wrote the actor Bernhard Minetti in his autobiography.[13] It was four days after Minetti's 28th birthday that Hitler came to power; his account of life in the Third Reich is illuminating, and curiously indifferent. But perhaps in his indifference lies his honesty. At the time of writing he was still a working actor in Berlin, and much honoured there. Although his precise relationship with the NSDAP is the subject of some gossip, he maintains that he was never a member of the Party. His own account, under the heading 'A Question of Conscience', runs, in part:

> One developed a kind of self-protection by screening oneself off from events, and that was probably the beginning of that suppression of feelings which would absorb the entire nation later on. From early on I avoided expressing any political opinion. Soon one heard about concentration camps, but one did not conceive of them as Auschwitz or Maidaneck would be later. One regarded them as a kind of prison camp – from such a starting point the concept of a 'KZ'[14] remained more harmless than they in fact were after 1940 . . . Justice had resigned itself to [Hitler's] will. I don't say that to excuse artists, nor even myself. I can only refer to myself, to my nature, which combined with my intellect and my instincts to prescribe the way I should behave. I knew what it would mean to speak out against the regime. I wanted to act, and not sit in a 'KZ'. That was my reality, my nature . . . nobody forced me to it.[15]

It was hardly surprising that clairvoyants thrived in the late Twenties and early Thirties. People who felt themselves to be drowning clutched blindly at such straws. Among the many charlatans, one stands out: Erik Jan Hanussen.[16] Hanussen, who gave himself out to be a Danish aristocrat, was in fact a Bohemian from Prossnitz by the name of Hermann (or Herschel) Steinschneider. His background was not impeccable: a former journalist who had been involved in some petty blackmail, he had at one point written a series of pamphlets denouncing clairvoyancy. At the Apollo Theatre in Vienna he set up a strong-man act with a twist: the 'strong man' was a woman, Martha Farra, who appeared made up like Cleopatra, and performed her feats of strength while in a trance.

Hanussen insisted on his own technical crew, but when they went on strike for a larger cut, he and Martha told the Apollo management they couldn't perform because of a 'breakdown in the telepathic waves' – then fled Vienna. Investigation proved the act to have been a confidence trick. Hanussen had demanded, and got, 50 per cent of the box-office takings.

Hanussen then put his earlier research into the supernatural to use, and appeared in Berlin in 1929, giving displays of mind-reading and hypnosis in variety theatres. He developed a reputation and quickly became very rich. Styling himself 'the Magician of Berlin', he rented a large flat in Lietzenburger Strasse, one block south of Kurfürstendamm, which he called 'The House of the Occult'. It was furnished in a suitably Gothick style, and it was also bugged – a great novelty in those days: Hanussen eavesdropped as his assistants interviewed prospective clients, and was thus able to subsequently astonish those clients with his intimate knowledge. Among them was Wolf Heinrich, Graf von Helldorf, then head of the Berlin SA. Arthur Koestler met Hanussen in 1931 and describes him as a 'stocky, dark-haired man with quick movements, full of dynamic energy and not without charm'. He relates that Hanussen acted as Master of Ceremonies at drunken parties at Helldorf's Wannsee villa, in the course of which he would put pretty actresses into a trance and then induce them to 'react to the embraces of an imaginary lover'.

When Goebbels' magazine *Der Angriff* appeared, Hanussen developed the idea of publishing his own popular weekly, a *Guide to Your Stars*, for the masses who couldn't afford private interviews with him. As the fortunes of the NSDAP rose and his friendship with Helldorf grew, Hanussen turned his clairvoyance to political ends. In 1932 his magazine predicted absolute victory for Hitler. He also lent money to Helldorf, and let Helldorf have the use of his car, which sported the Nazi flag. But then Hanussen gave a party at his private flat in Kurfürstendamm during which his medium, Maria Paudler, went into a trance and predicted the Reichstag fire. In some way Hanussen was involved in the planning of this crime and, true to form, he was obliquely showing off about it.

This was too much. His brand new show at the Scala didn't do as well as expected – perhaps as a consequence. He next tried to gain control of no less a paper than the *Berliner Tageblatt*. His proposal was greeted with contemptuous disbelief by the managing director, Karl Vetter. Hanussen, furious, swore revenge and flung out of the *Tageblatt's* offices, giving Vetter three days to change his mind; but news of the interview reached the ears of the paper's SA commissioner, Ohst. 'Three days is all *he*'s got,' Ohst is reported to have said. Two days later, in fact, while Hanussen was having his usual pre-show coffee at the Grüner Zweig café next door to the Scala, the proprietress, Toni Ott, warned him that two plain-clothes policemen had been asking for him. He laughed off her

fears; but he did not reach the theatre that evening. He was driven off
in his own car and not seen alive again.

Those are the bones of Hanussen's story. It is not wholly verifiable.
Hanussen had kept Helldorf's IOUs with him in his wallet as a kind of
insurance. The Gestapo had discovered his real name, and that he was
Jewish. His body was found in a wood on the outskirts of the city, riddled
with bullets, and the IOUs were gone from his wallet. Ohst and Helldorf
were friends, but Hanussen's murder probably had more to do with his
implication in the Reichstag fire conspiracy than with the fact that
Helldorf owed him money, or that he had upset Ohst with his vainglorious attempt to take over the *Tageblatt* – though either would have
been more than enough to guarantee his death, as would his race.
Hanussen's story demonstrates how, in times like those, a fairground
mountebank could rise to become involved in political intrigue and
treachery at the highest level.[17]

Helldorf was made Chief of the Berlin Police; he subsequently joined
the Resistance to Hitler. Four years after the Hanussen affair, the *Daily
Express* carried a story[18] about an English showgirl called Grace
Cameron Dzino who had been shot dead with her four-year-old son by
her Turkish husband. Ismet Dzino had been Hanussen's secretary, and
Grace's marriage and her death had been predicted by the clairvoyant in
Berlin in 1931.

15 Towards War

▄▄▄▄▄ BERLIN HOSTED TWO major events in 1937 but they had little of the Olympic Games' international *élan*; nor was anything like the effort made for them in terms of publicity, budget, or regard for world opinion. The celebrations for the city's 700th birthday took place without the Führer, who was away in Bayreuth for the Wagner Festival. Even Göring, by now Premier of Prussia, took no part; his rival, Josef Goebbels, presided over the festivities. These were a sad portent of things to come: a massive procession followed by various concerts featuring military bands, and sports and athletics displays designed to show off German discipline and readiness for action. No attempt was made to conceal their inherent belligerence, and party-organized mass demonstrations worsened an already depressing picture. Some, however, found pleasure in them. Inge Fehr, who was fourteen at the time, enjoyed a spectacular show at the Olympic Stadium, with fireworks; her pleasure was innocent.

The times were certainly confusing: not a year earlier, she and a friend had been asked by a storm-troop cameraman to pose with a *Winterhilfe* collecting tin in the street and told that the picture would appear in the *Beobachter* with the caption, 'German Girls Give to the Winter Relief Fund'. Not much more than a year after the 700th birthday celebrations, she and her family were driven from their home, harassed by officials and forbidden to take anything of value with them. 'Once the packing was completed we were forbidden to buy any new goods. I became very defiant, and went out and bought myself a small leather case and a penknife.'[1] This story has a happy ending: the Fehrs managed to substitute for their own jewellery inferior items which deceived the SA; the real necklaces and rings were entrusted to Gentile Berlin friends, from whom almost every item was recovered after the war.

In September 1937, a year after declaring the Italian Empire, Mussolini paid a visit to his fellow dictator. Along with other pompous bunting, square white fluted columns were erected along Unter den Linden, topped with the new Nazi eagle clutching the swastika and dwarfing the poor little new lime trees. From the 27th to the 29th, Mussolini took part in army manoeuvres in Mecklenburg and gave a speech swearing eternal loyalty to the German Reich at the new Maifeld area immediately to the west of the Olympic Stadium. Hitler was anxious to impress Mussolini with German smartness and power. At least the uniforms of the Nazi organizations, now that they controlled the state income, had improved. Earlier they had been shabby and almost home-made, worn with lace-up motor-cycle boots instead of jackboots. By the end of the war, ordinary German soldiers' uniforms were made of ersatz cloth derived from wood fibre, but the SS still wore clothes tailored from wool.

Mussolini was accommodated at the old Palace of the State President, Hindenburg's residence when he led the country, a few steps from the Hotel Adlon in Pariser Platz. (Between them was the British Embassy.) Because of this proximity, the Hotel Adlon was charged with looking after Mussolini. To put him up in the Palace was a signal mark of honour, and Hitler wanted every detail of his stay perfect. However, something went wrong. The palace was old, and hot water had not been installed until Ebert became president. At the time, to save money, old pipes were reused, so when a tap was turned on, it took at least five minutes for hot water to flow. It happened that a thunderstorm broke during Mussolini's speech at the Maifeld, and by the end he was soaking wet. But the ceremonial drive back to the Palace had still to be made, in an open car as it had stopped raining by then, so that Mussolini might show himself to the people of Berlin. Hedda Adlon reports that the route teemed with sightseers,[2] and takes up the story:[3]

> Hitler hung his jacket around his guest's shoulders, and as they parted com-pany in the courtyard of the Presidential Palace he admonished [him] in a friendly way: 'Duce, take a hot bath immediately. Then drink a hot camomile tea. Then go straight to bed and have a good two hours' sweat!' This was in the afternoon. That evening there was to be a grand banquet in the Reich Chancellery in honour of Mussolini. Hitler asked, 'Duce, did you take my advice?' 'I wanted to,' replied the other, 'but there was no hot water.' Hitler's look turned stony. 'And what did you do?' he asked, tight-lipped. 'I went to the Hotel Adlon.' And that was the end of it; but not, alas, for Hitler. The man couldn't let anything go! Even before Mussolini had left, two Security Service officials came to the Adlon and arrested the director responsible for the management of the Presidential Palace. Their job was to investigate whether or not the lack of hot water had been a question of sabotage.

The matter was quickly cleared up and the unfortunate director exonerated, but Hitler still wouldn't let the matter drop. He went personally to the bathroom used by Mussolini and, watch in hand, checked for himself how long it took the hot water to flow.

That same year saw the première of Carl Orff's *Carmina Burana*; Gustav Gründgens was appointed General Director of the State Theatre; Albert Speer was appointed General Buildings Supervisor of Berlin; Pastor Martin Niemöller was sent to Sachsenhausen; the French liner *Normandie* won the Blue Riband previously held by the *Bremen*; and the old champion of right-wing militarism, Erich von Ludendorff, died.

In the course of 1938 and 1939 what came to be known as 'actions' against the Jews were stepped up. These included the wholesale arrest of Jews with criminal records – even if these were for traffic offences; the marking of passports with a 'J'; the termination of education for Jewish children and students; and the deprivation of various other rights – going to a public theatre, cinema, swimming pool, or park; using certain main streets; visiting a museum; owning a radio, or a pet . . .

Anti-Semitism was always worse outside Berlin – Illa Walter remembers the shock she felt when she drove from the city to the coast for a swim and encountered *Juden Unerwünscht* (Jews Unwelcome) signs for the first time at the limits of the seaside town. But matters reached their pre-war nadir with *Reichskristallnacht*: Crystal Night – the Night of the Broken Glass. Once again, a pathetic chain of events caused by frustration and misery was exploited by the NSDAP to its own ends. In March 1938 Poland, also anti-Semitic and afraid that Germany would repatriate Polish Jews, promulgated a law revoking the Polish citizenship of any nationals who had lived abroad for more than five years, unless they registered by 31 October 1938. Germany responded by rounding up Polish Jews within its territory to return them. As the Polish authorities refused to readmit them to Poland, several thousand people, officially stateless, were condemned to spend some weeks in wretched conditions in a no man's land at the frontier near Posen. Poland eventually relented, but not before the 17-year-old son of one couple condemned to this fate had registered his protest. Herschel Grynzspan (a student in Paris) shot and fatally wounded Ernst vom Rath, Third Secretary at the German Embassy in Paris. Two days later, on 9 November, Rath died, and by then Goebbels had used his shooting as an excuse to whip up the most appalling 'spontaneous' demonstration yet against the Jews. On the night of 9 November, Jewish property and synagogues were set on fire all over the country – though foreign Jews were not molested, and the head of the Security Service, Reinhard Heydrich, gave orders to his men that looters were to be dealt with ruthlessly. Care was also taken that fires should not be allowed to spread – hence, some synagogues in heavily built-up areas were spared, like the red-brick synagogue which still stands in a court-yard in Wörthstrasse, not far from Kollwitzplatz in the crumbling working class district of Prenzlauer Berg. The Mühlhausen synagogue was spared for the same reason. The SS took advantage of the chaos to arrest as many able-bodied (and preferably wealthy) male Jews as they could accommodate.

The smashed shop-window glass that gave the pogrom its name was later estimated to equal half the amount produced annually in Belgium, from where it had originally been imported. Seven thousand Jewish businesses were destroyed, 100 Jews killed, and many thousands beaten up, abused, arrested, or driven from their homes. The German Jewish community was fined 1 billion marks to pay for the damage done. After Kristallnacht, it was impossible for Jews who had remained to close their eyes to what would happen if they were to stay in Germany any longer. Even though they knew the importance of Jewish commerce to the economy, the NSDAP was moving in for the kill.

'My Jewish friends started to leave in a rush after Kristallnacht,' remembers Helga Russow.[4]

> I had to go to Paris after that, if I wanted to see them. Up until then it had all happened so slowly, so gradually. You could kid yourself that if you accepted this or that new measure, perhaps they wouldn't go any further, and you kept on hoping that somehow or other they wouldn't stay in power; but by the time 1939 came you found that you were trussed up like a turkey and it was too late to do anything about it. Their progress was such that you became acclimatized to the new way of thinking unless you were very careful. Now and then a new law would come in against the Jews which would give you a jolt, or a newspaper would be suppressed; but after Kristallnacht the beast was out of the cage.

'Kristallnacht brought a shocking realization of what was to come, and what we were capable of under National Socialism,' says Ludwig von Hammerstein.[5]

> It was followed by a tremendous sense of isolation – we only saw German newspapers, were only supposed to listen to German broadcasts. My father had given me a good radio and I could get stations like the BBC and Radio Moscow on it – anything that brought news from outside was a boon. It helped you believe that you still belonged to the community of nations, and it helped you to stay in touch with what was really happening, as opposed to what they told you was happening. I remember writing in my journal in September 1939: 'This war will simply be construed as a crime against the world and we will all be sucked under by it.' Mind you, I hid that book very carefully!

'Those of us [Jews] who were left were very worried after November

1938,' remembers Hans Jackson, who did not escape until the following year.[6] 'The later one left it, the harder it was to get out, until finally it was impossible. All the quotas filled up. People queued day in, day out, outside the embassies in Berlin, to go anywhere that would take them: Shanghai, Hong Kong, Brazil, Ecuador, Iran ... There was even a hotline that would tell you where visas were being released. But visas cost money. Within a week of Kristallnacht a Nazi representative turned up to enforce purchase of my father's shop.'

'I remember discussing the whole problem of leaving,' recalls a Jewish *Berlinerin*.

I was a trained dancer, and there was a chance to get out on a tour to South America, but my friend the comedian Max Ehrlich advised me against it. 'I don't think you'd make a very good whore,' he said, 'and that's what you'd be reduced to if you went on this trip.' But many women saved their lives by practising that profession ... A friend ... said we had better decide which of us lived in the higher block, and then we'd climb to the top of it, hold hands, and jump off. We were 19 and 22 years old, and that's how black we thought the future would be. The way Jews' rights were eroded, and the horrible things imputed to Jews in the National Socialist press conspired to make one terribly depressed ... But something else has worried me since: what kind of German would I have turned out to be if I hadn't also been Jewish, and therefore forced to leave?

This lady left finally when a rich, elderly patroness of her painter husband asked her to call.

My husband was considerably older than me, and reluctant to go. Frau Minden told me to go, with or without him. This was in December 1938. She gave me a deadline of two weeks, and that was the goad I needed. I arranged for a visa for domestic work with my sister, who was already in England. When I was ready to go, I saw Frau Minden again. She handed me a little box containing a brooch whose sale, she told me, would keep me for three years if I got into trouble. I still have the brooch – in a bank vault. I managed to smuggle it out, and took nothing else beyond the 10 marks I was allowed.

Two weeks later, Frau Minden committed suicide. She did it in an orderly way, with great dignity and no fuss, distributing her treasures to her friends beforehand, and disguising her death as heart failure. She was too old to start life afresh in a new country; she had no dependants, and she knew what was coming.

Early in the morning of 9 November 1938, the editors of the remaining dozen small Jewish newspapers in Berlin were bidden to the Police Praesidium in Alexanderplatz. There, having been kept waiting for the approved length of time, they were obliged to agree to the suspension of all their newspapers, magazines and periodicals. Their journey to

Alexanderplatz gave some of them their first view of the damage done on Kristallnacht. 'Don't forget that Berlin was a big city,' one remembers.

> On my way to my first meeting at the 'Alex' . . . I didn't see very much of the damage. It was intense, but localized. You shouldn't go away with the impression that the whole city was ablaze. Even the famous Oranien-burgerstrasse synagogue . . . wasn't as badly damaged as all that by the Kristallnacht fires. Like most of central Berlin, the real destruction occurred in the bombing of 1945. In November 1938 . . . the destruction wasn't spread evenly and consistently throughout the city.

The Oranienburgerstrasse synagogue, being in a built-up area, was pro-tected to some extent from the mob by a local police official.[7] 'Even the following day, there was barely anyone in Oranienburgerstrasse or Fasanenstrasse.[8] It was worse in the smaller towns around Germany, where the effect – and anti-Semitism itself – were both relatively greater.'

Kristallnacht was not quite the end. A very modest new Jewish paper was allowed in Berlin shortly afterwards, and this *Jüdische Nachricht-enblatt* appeared nationally twice a week until 1943.[9] Even the *Kultur-bund* and the State Organization for Jews in Germany were allowed to continue. The latter performed an indispensable role in the Jewish emigration process, which the Nazis were keen to maintain even though in the days following Kristallnacht they incarcerated 30,000 Jewish men in the concentration camps already established at Buchenwald near Weimar, Dachau near Munich, and Sachsenhausen near Berlin.

Nearly everyone who had briefly made Berlin seem the centre of the world was gone. The city felt empty, and was empty of the life it had known. But the spirit of the Berliner was not quite crushed. Ernst Lowenthal, who was still working for the Jewish community in Berlin after Kristallnacht, remembers:

> . . . a few days after Kristallnacht I had to take the underground to Kaiserhof station and go from there to collect some money from a bank in the imme-diate vicinity; but I knew that . . . I would have to cross a few streets that the Nazis had forbidden to Jews. I reached the bank without a problem, and even the journey back by taxi was fine, though we went, as my habit would have always been, by the quickest way – down Wilhelmstrasse and along Unter dèn Linden. I had to warn the driver that with me on board he would be better advised to take a different route – Jews weren't allowed on either of those streets, and he would have been in trouble too if any official had seen fit to stop us and check our papers. But all he said was, in the curt, tough-guy way Berliners like to speak: 'Look mate, *I* decide where I drive.'[10]

On 1 January 1939, male Jews were required to add 'Israel' to their name, and females, 'Sara'. On 15 March, Bohemia and Moravia were jointly declared a 'protectorate' of the Third Reich. On 1 September, on the strength of a trumped-up incident, Hitler invaded Poland.

Five and a half years and 363 bombing raids later, 20 square kilometres of central Berlin had been destroyed. One-third of the city's 1.5 million buildings were ruined, and 150,000 Berliners were dead. When the air-raids ended in April 1945, Russian artillery – 22,000 pieces of ordnance – fired shells into Berlin at the rate of one every five seconds. The Schloss was battered and burned. Later, the Communists dismantled what remained of it, except for Reinhold Begas' Neptune Fountain, which incongruously survives, and erected a modern People's Palace near its site. A concrete bunker built to house and protect classical paintings was hit and destroyed, though many other treasures, including the paintings from Wilhelm Bode's collection at the Kaiser-Friedrich-Museum, had been transported to a salt mine deep in the country for safe keeping, together with the country's gold reserves from the State Bank. On Göring's orders, art treasures had been sheltered, but many were destroyed, and many disappeared into Russia. For a time, even the Americans confiscated two hundred.

In the Tiergarten, a stables was hit and the horses that were not killed or maimed broke loose and galloped screaming down Kurfüstendamm, their manes and tails on fire.

When it was over, Berliners came out of the cellars and started to pick over the hills of debris for food, for fuel, for objects to barter. The people looked like scarecrows.

'I didn't want to come back to Germany,' says Steffie Spira.

> But my husband wanted to find out what had happened to his family, and we were actors. Gustav von Wangenheim had returned from Russia to take over the Deutsches Theater. He offered us automatic contracts.
>
> So we got back to Berlin. My abiding impression of the bombed city is that of the *Trümmerfrauen* – the women of the ruins – working their orderly German way through the piles of rubble, setting aside usable material in neat rows, ready to rebuild what had been lost.
>
> Which is all any of us can ever do, until the end.

Notes

References to chapters and notes given in brackets refer to this book.

TWILIGHT

Chapter 1: Götterdämmerung

1. See Alexander Reissner, *Berlin 1675–1945* (Oswald Wolff, 1984), pp. 115–16.
2. Conversation with the author.
3. Conversation with the author.
4. Conversation with the author, but see also Wolfgang Ribbe (ed.), *Geschichte Berlins, Band II: Von der Märzrevolution bis zur Gegenwart* (C. H. Beck, Munich, 1987), where a grim picture is painted, and where it is stated that theatres and museums had closed.
5. Otto Friedrich, *Before the Deluge* (Harper and Row, NY, 1972), pp. 70–1.
6. For more detail, see Bernt Engelmann, *Berlin, eine Stadt wie keine andere* (Bertelsmann, Munich, 1986), pp. 210 ff.
7. See Ribbe, op. cit., pp. 759 ff.
8. Translated by John Burgess, and quoted in Lisa Appignanesi, *The Cabaret* (Universe Books, NY, 1976).
9. Unlikely. Aurochs were extinct in northern Europe by the seventeenth century.
10. From the memoirs of Bernhard von Bülow, Chancellor, 1900–1909, quoted in Engelmann, op. cit., pp. 217–18.
11. I am indebted for this to Walther Kiaulehn, *Berlin, Schicksal eine Weltstadt* (Biederstein, Munich and Berlin, 1958).
12. Heinrich Himmler also aped the Teutonic Knights, some of whose attributes he sought to attach to his 'Order of the SS'.
13. Much of the material on the German military in this book is drawn from

The Nemesis of Power by John Wheeler-Bennett (Macmillan, 1954). The account here is taken from p. 15 of that work. See also Tirpitz, *My Memoirs* (London and New York, 1919).

14. Hindenburg (1847–1934) will play a major and increasingly inglorious role in this story. In an account which is rich in sonorous German names, his stands out, so I give it here in full: Paul Ludwig Hans Anton von Beneckendorff und von Hindenburg.

15. Tannenberg was a small town in central East Prussia. The battle against Samsonov's numerically superior army was fought 27–29 August 1914. The Battle of the Masurian Lakes was fought 5–15 September 1914. A pompous monument was erected at Tannenberg in 1927, but destroyed in 1945.

16. For a full discussion of this, see Wheeler-Bennett, op. cit., pp. 12 ff.

17. On all aspects of politics, see Erich Eyck's two-volume history of the Weimar Republic. Reference here is to Vol. 1, *From the Collapse of the Monarchy to Ebert's death and Hindenburg's Election*, translated by Harlan P. Hanson and Robert G. L. White (Harvard UP, 1962), pp. 5 ff.

18. Ibid., loc. cit.

19. *Untersuchungsausschuss über die Weltkriegsverantwortlichkeit, 4. Unterausschuss: Die Ursachen des deutschen Zusammenbruchs im Jahre 1918*, 12 volumes in 15 parts (Berlin, 1925–1929), Vol. II, p. 225.

20. Engelmann, op. cit., p. 220.

21. Max von Baden, *Erinnerungen* (Stuttgart, 1927), pp. 619–26, and quoted in Eyck, op. cit., p. 44.

22. Diary, 14 December 1893. Quoted and translated by Peter Gay in his *Weimar Culture, The Outsider as Insider* (Secker and Warburg, 1969), p. 3.

23. Gay, op. cit., p. 4.

24. See *Ausstellungsverzeichnis: neu Beginnen kannst du mit dem letzten Atemzug. 100 Jahre Freie Volksbühne* (Berlin Museum und Freie Volksbühne e. V., Berlin, 1990).

25. Ribbe, op. cit., quoting a letter cited in Michael S. Cullen, *Der Reichstag: Die Geschichte eines Monuments* (Berlin, 1983).

MORNING

Chapter 2: Death and Resurrection

1. There are several versions of this event. This one is taken from Engelmann, op. cit., p. 222.

2. *Berliner Tageblatt*, 10 November 1918. See also *Ursachen und Folgen*, Vol. III, p. 10.

3. This account is of necessity a summary. It is drawn from contemporary reports, but principal secondary sources which the reader in search of more detail might like to follow up are in: Engelmann, op. cit.; Eyck, op. cit., Vol. I; Friedrich, op. cit.; Ribbe, op. cit.; Wheeler-Bennett, op. cit. See also: Detlev J. K. Peukert, *Die Weimarer Republik* (Suhrkamp, Frankfurt/Main, 1987), which has been translated as *The Weimar Republic* by Richard Dawson (Allen Lane, The Penguin Press, 1991). It is much shorter and more broadly based than Eyck's work.

4. Adolf Hitler, *Mein Kampf* (My Struggle) (Paternoster Library, 1938 (10th Impression, Cheap Edition)), pp. 90–2. The translator's name is not given.
5. As with so much data relating to the period, conflicting dates and even places are given by various sources. The last diary entry is dated 30 September 1937 at Fournels. Kessler's diaries from 1918 to 1937 are entertaining and informative about Weimar Berlin. These are published as *Tagebücher*, ed. Wolfgang Pfeffer-Belli (Insel, Frankfurt/Main, 1961); paperback edition (which I refer to), 1982. An abridged version in English appeared in 1971 as *In the Twenties*, translated by Charles Kessler and published by Weidenfeld and Nicolson.
6. The large square in front of the Schloss. It is still there. The north side of it is still bounded by Schinkel's Altes Museum.
7. Big department stores.
8. George Grosz, *A Big Yes and a Small No*, translated by Arnold J. Pomerans (Allison and Busby, London and New York, 1982), p. 93.
9. Ibid., p. 94.
10. Kessler, op. cit., p. 126 (9 February 1919).
11. Kessler, op. cit., p. 91. There was strong Russian influence in Berlin at the time, and the German Communist Party was inaugurated on 1 January 1919 in the presence of a Russian delegation. It would have been immeasurably in the interests of Russia to see Germany become a Communist state.
12. Margaritte Ludendorff, *Als Ich Ludendorffs Frau war*, (Munich, 1929), quoted in Wheeler-Bennett, op. cit., p. 38.
13. Eyck, op. cit., Vol. I, p. 64.
14. Carl Severing, *Lebensweg*, Vol. II (Cologne, 1950), p. 374.
15. This and what follows is taken from Kessler, op. cit., pp. 143 ff (entries for March 1919). In the German, Kessler uses *Philisterium* (rather than *Philistertum*) for 'philistinism', to make a light pun on *Ministerium* (ministry).
16. The Kaiser's fourth son, and later a prominent member of the SA.
17. Greater Berlin was finally formed in April–October 1920. See Chapter 8: House of Bricks, House of Straw.
18. Conversation with the author.
19. Sources for this and what follows are in Ribbe, op. cit., and Hans J. Reichhardt, *Berliner Forum 7/79: Berlin in der Weimarer Republik – die Stadtverwaltung unter Oberbürgermeister Gustav Böss* (Presse und Informationsamt des Landes Berlin, 1979).
20. Quoted in Friedrich, op. cit., pp. 65–6. The original reporter of this incident was J. M. Keynes.
21. *The Diary and Letters of Käthe Kollwitz*, ed. Hans Kollwitz, translated by Richard and Clara Winston (Henry Regnery Co., Chicago, 1955), p. 43.
22. Diary entry for 8 December 1918, quoted in ibid., p. 89.
23. Quoted in Gay, op. cit., p. 9.
24. Kessler, op. cit., pp. 160–1.
25. For a full discussion of Weimar culture and thought, see Gay, op. cit., and Walter Laqueur, *Weimar: A Cultural History* (Weidenfeld and Nicolson, 1974).

Chapter 3: A Phoenix Arisen

1. For more detail on much of what follows, see especially Appignanesi, op. cit.
2. Ibid., p. 81.
3. Grosz, op. cit., pp. 98–101.
4. Ibid., p. 104.
5. Sources vary about whether it was in 1919 or 1920. As far as I have been able to ascertain, it was in 1919.
6. Grosz, op. cit., p. 106.
7. Stefan Zweig, *The World of Yesterday*, translated by Cedar and Eden Paul (Cassell Biographies, 1987), p. 61. Originally published in 1944 by Berman-Fischer Verlag zu Stockholm as *Die Welt von Gestern*.
8. Quoted in 'PEM' (Paul Erich Marcus), *Heimweh nach dem Kurfürstendamm* (Lothar Blanvalet Verlag, Berlin, 1952), p. 14.
9. The main shopping street of west Berlin, along with Tauentzienstrasse. In those days the Ku'damm (as Berliners call it) combined shops with cafés, hotels, and elegant apartment blocks. It was also the place for the evening promenade or *korso* in fine weather. One old Berliner remembered that the advent of neon street lighting destroyed its character. These days it is empty at night except for cinema-goers and gorgeous, hard-faced prostitutes dressed in tiny mini-skirts above Dietrich legs, and all carrying umbrellas: Berlin is a rainy city. This passage is from Zweig, op. cit., pp. 238–9.
10. I thought it worth trying for mood rather than literal accuracy here. The original is: *Die Liebe ist ein Zeitvertreib, Man nimmt dazu den Unterleib*, from Erich Kästner, *Fabian*, in *Gesammelte Schrifte für Erwachsene*, Band 2, Romane I (Droemer Knaur, Atrium Verlag, Zurich, 1969).
11. Ibid., p. 53.
12. 'PEM', op. cit., p. 42.
13. Kästner, op. cit., p. 83.
14. Edwin Rosenstiel, conversation with the author.
15. Zweig, op. cit., p. 198.
16. Quoted in Friedrich, op. cit., p. 34.
17. There would be much more to say about this film if space allowed. However, it is discussed in numerous film histories which provide several different interpretations. Although limited by its self-imposed interpretative theme, one of the best books on German film of the period is still Siegfried Kracauer, *From Caligari to Hitler: A Psychological History of the German Film* (Princeton UP, 1947). See also Lotte H. Eisner, *Die Dämonische Leinwand* (Fischer, 1987).
18. Kracauer, op. cit., p. 65.
19. Kessler, op. cit. What follows on the Treaty of Versailles is taken principally from Eyck and Wheeler-Bennett, who both carry very full accounts, but see also Peukert. The whole matter is far more complicated than the summary I have space for makes it appear.
20. Kessler, op. cit., pp. 82–3.
21. Eyck, op. cit., p. 92.

22. Ludwig, Freiherr von Hammerstein, in conversation with the author.
23. Carl Zuckmayer, *A Part of Myself*, transl. Richard and Clara Winston (Secker and Warburg, 1970), pp. 231–2.
24. Vladimir Nabokov moved to Berlin from Cambridge the next year. Under the pen name of 'Sirin' he embarked on his cycle of novels dealing with the Russian community in Berlin: *King, Queen, Knave*; *The Eye*; *The Defence*; *Laughter in the Dark*; *Despair*; and *The Gift*.

Chapter 4: Comedy, Tragedy, Politics and Money

1. Conversation with the author.
2. Principal secondary sources for what follows are Eyck and Wheeler-Bennett, from whom full accounts can be had. As so often, each version – and these are not the only two I have drawn on – differs slightly.
3. Kessler, op. cit., entry for 10 May 1920, pp. 227–8.
4. Ibid., 12 July 1920, p. 243.
5. The reduction in the offical armed forces was compensated for by an increase in secret armed forces and secret rearmament. See main text, below.
6. Eyck, op. cit., p. 186.
7. See Harry Kessler, *Walther Rathenau: sein Leben und sein Werk* (Hermann Klemm, Berlin, 1928), pp. 75 ff. Kessler's biography is sensitive, exhaustive and disinterested.
8. See Georges Kaeckenbeck, *The International Experiment of Upper Silesia, 1922–1937* (NY and London, 1942).
9. Kessler, *Rathenau*, p. 323. The circumstances surrounding Rathenau's appointment are complex.
10. Quoted in Kessler, ibid., pp. 356–7. A most beautiful short essay.
11. From General von Rabenau's biography of Seeckt, p. 316. Quoted in Eyck, op. cit., p. 203.
12. There are variations on this couplet. I have used the one quoted in Kessler's biography.
13. Kessler, *Rathenau*, p. 353.
14. Most of this account of the murder is taken from Kessler, ibid., pp. 357 ff.
15. The quotation (taken from Kessler) is in the *Vossische Zeitung* for 25 June 1922.
16. Kessler, *Rathenau*, p. 366.
17. Ibid., p. 370. See also Kessler's diary entries for 24–27 June 1922 inclusive.
18. Eyck, op. cit., p. 220.
19. Conversation with the author.
20. In Stefan Zweig, *Meisternovellen* (Fischer, Frankfurt/Main, 1970).
21. Tilla Durieux, *Meine erste 90 Jahren* (Rowohlt, Reinbek bei Hamburg, 1977), pp. 210–12.
22. Conversation with the author.
23. Conversation with the author.
24. Conversation with the author.

25. Conversation with the author.
26. Conversation with the author.
27. Eyck, op. cit., pp. 166–7.
28. Wheeler-Bennett, op. cit., p. 86. Pages 83–332 of his book give a full account of the intricacies of German military reconstruction, 1920–1934.

Chapter 5: Centre of the World

1. Zuckmayer, op. cit., pp. 274–5.
2. The speakers are Inge Samson, Erna Nelki, and Connie and Edwin Rosenstiel. All quotations are from various Berliners' conversations with the author.
3. Some sources say 1924.
4. Ossip K. Flechtheim, in conversation with the author.
5. Durieux, op. cit., pp. 216–17.
6. Kessler, *Tagebücher*, pp. 472–3.
7. Conversation with the author.
8. Quoted in Friedrich, op. cit., p. 144.
9. Many sources give 1922; 1921 is on the film's credits.
10. Kracauer, op. cit., develops a theme of the tyrant in his 'psychological history'. I recommend his book to those wishing to explore this possibility.
11. Kracauer, op. cit., p. 82.
12. This and several of the other films mentioned here are available on VHS video cassettes at the Goethe Institute Library, London.
13. See Laqueur, op. cit., pp. 230–49, for an interesting discussion about the German cinema at this time.
14. Conversation with the author.
15. For the song about Ebert, see Appignanesi, op. cit., pp. 132 f; for 'Petronella', p. 135 (my translation).
16. Very roughly, Master of Ceremonies during a cabaret show, who would have his own monologues and patter.
17. Appignanesi, op. cit., p. 141.
18. Translated by John Willett.
19. Kiaulehn, op. cit., p. 243.
20. Ibid., p. 250.
21. Reissner, op. cit., pp. 119–20.
22. Bernd Ruland, *Das was Berlin* (Hesta, Bayreuth, 1972), p. 110.
23. Lothar Fischer, *Tanz zwischen Rausch und Tod, Anita Berber 1918–1929 in Berlin* (Haude und Spener, Berlin, 1988).
24. 'PEM', op. cit., pp. 115–16.
25. The publisher, born in the little Slovakian town of Liptovsky-Mikulas. Fischer Verlag is still one of the largest publishing houses in Germany.
26. What follows on Weissenberg is largely based on Kiaulehn, op. cit., pp. 560–2 and 578–9.
27. Conversation with the author.

28. Walter Stoeckel, *Erinnerungen eines Frauenarztes*, ed. Hans Borgelt (Munich, 1966), pp. 412 f.
29. See Hedda Adlon, *Hotel Adlon, das Haus in dem die Welt zu Gast war* (Kindler, Munich, 1955).
30. I have been unable to verify this story but Hedda Adlon – probably not a 100 per cent reliable source – tells it like this.
31. There are several versions – variations on a theme – about how Dietrich was selected for the film. Dietrich's year of birth is now agreed to be 1901.

Chapter 6: Berlin Alexanderplatz

1. No one interested in the Berlin of the period should fail to read this great novel. The English translation (an excellent one by Eugene Jolas) was republished in London by Secker and Warburg in 1974.
2. This and succeeding Zuckmayer quotations are from Zuckmayer, op. cit.
3. In conversation with the author. See also Friedrich, op. cit., pp. 252–3, who draws a damning picture of Hirschfeld – the only voice I have come across raised against him.
4. Most of what follows is taken from 'Sling' (Paul Schlesinger), *Richter und Gerichtete* (Ullstein, Berlin, 1929), Part I – Grosse Prozesse, Chapter 1, Krantz. But see also Kiaulehn, op. cit., pp. 520–5, for a very full account.
5. Most of the information on murderers not drawn from contemporary reports is taken from Ruland, op. cit., Chapter XI.
6. Quoted in Friedrich, op. cit., pp. 353–4.
7. Arthur Koestler, *Pfeil ins Blaue* (Kurt Desch, Vienna, Munich and Basle, 1953), pp. 298–9. Originally published in English as *An Arrow in the Blue*.
8. See Erich Kästner's *Fabian* for a description of a very similar kind of place.
9. Alfred Joachim Fischer, *In der Nähe der Ereignisse* (Transit, Berlin, 1991), p. 37.
10. *Deutsche Allgemeine Zeitung*, 16 September 1923.
11. Ibid., 4 October 1923.
12. See Ruland, op. cit., pp. 235 ff.
13. See Anton Gill, *The Journey Back From Hell* (Grafton, 1988, and Morrow, NY, 1989).
14. Ruland, op. cit., p. 240.
15. One shouldn't make too much of this – *Heil* was a fairly common way of shouting approval of a leader.
16. The full story, and other criminal club stories, can be found in Ruland, op. cit., pp. 197 ff.
17. See Kiaulehn, op. cit., pp. 528–9.

NOON

Chapter 7: In the Jungle of the Cities

1. It is impossible to tackle fully the subject of the German theatre during the

Weimar Republic and after in one chapter. For more, see especially: Günther Rühle (ed.), *Theater für die Republik 1917–1933 im Spiegel der Kritik* (Fischer, Frankfurt/Main, 1967). This 1200-page work is comprehensive.

2. Zuckmayer, op. cit., p. 277.

3. Ibid., pp. 275–6.

4. Ihering: the alternative spelling, and the one used most often in contemporary documentation, is Jhering. Pre–1945, words which in their modern form begin with an I, frequently began with a J.

5. See Zuckmayer, op. cit., pp. 284 ff.

6. Even the fact that Chaplin's Tramp and Hitler both wore a toothbrush moustache may not be without significance – see Charles Chaplin, *My Autobiography* (Penguin, Harmondsworth, 1966), pp. 316 and 386.

7. Conversation with the author.

8. Converstion with the author.

9. See: Hermann Haarmann (ed.), *Alfred Kerr: Lesebuch zu Leben und Werk* (Klaus Siebenhaar, Thomas Wölk, Argon, Berlin, 1987); Akademie der Künste, ref: Sb 6302.

10. Conversation with the author.

11. See also Eberhard Spangenberg, *Karriere eines Romans: Mephisto, Klaus Mann und Gustaf* (sic) *Gründgens* (Ellermann, Munich, 1982).

12. Conversation with the author.

13. Kreuger was responsible for the acquisition of a Stradivarius by Marek Weber, band leader at the Adlon Hotel; the long and involved story is told in Adlon, op. cit., pp. 227–40.

Chapter 8: House of Bricks, House of Straw

1. For a detailed bureaucratic history of the city at this time, see Ribbe, op. cit., pp. 825–75.

2. *Gross-Berlin-Tagebuch*, pp. 102 ff.

3. See Reichhardt, op. cit. (Note 19, Chapter 2).

4. For the full story, see Christian Engeli, *Gustav Böss, Oberbürgermeister von Berlin, 1921–1930* (Stuttgart, 1971), pp. 226–47.

5. Conversation with the author.

6. Conversation with the author.

7. Conversation with the author.

8. Bendlerstrasse is now Stauffenbergstrasse. Tattersall's main branch was just to the south of Pariser Platz, on the edge of the Tiergarten, in Friedrich-Ebert-Strasse.

9. Conversation with the author.

10. Much of what follows is drawn from Eyck, op. cit., Volume II: *From the Locarno Conference to Hitler's Seizure of Power*, where the whole enormously complex story is lucidly expounded.

11. Friedrich von Rabenau (ed.), *Seeckt, aus seinem Leben 1918–1936* (Leipzig, 1940), p. 417 (26 June 1925).

12. Then Frau Golke.

13. Theodor Eschenburg, 'Die Rolle der Persönlichkeit in der Krise der Weimarer Republik', in Burghard Freudenfeld (ed.), *Stationen der Deutschen Geschichte 1919–1945* (Deutsche Verlags-Anstalt, Stuttgart, 1962).
14. Gustav Stresemann, *Vermächtnis*, Vol. II, p. 239 (and quoted in Eyck, op. cit., Vol. II, p. 32).
15. Georges Suarez, *Briand, L'Artisan de la Paix, 1923–1932* (Paris, 1952), Vol. VI, p. 129.
16. Stresemann Papers, 7334H and 7335H.
17. *Manchester Guardian*, 3 and 6 December 1926.
18. An area never satisfactorily cleared up was the judiciary. The statistician and *Weltbühne* contributor Emil J. Gumbel, in *Zwei Jahre Mord* (1920), pointed out that of 314 right-wing murderers tried, only one received a life sentence. The others were imprisoned for a group total of 31 years and 3 months – in some cases they were pardoned before the end of their term. Of the 13 Communists convicted of political murders, eight were executed, and the others were sentenced to a total of 176 years and 10 months. Also, of the 705 people charged with High Treason following the Kapp *putsch*, only one was sentenced, to 'five years of "honorary confinement".' See Grenville, *Tucholsky* p. 39 (Note 13, Chapter 10), and William Shirer, *The Rise and Fall of the Third Reich* (Simon & Schuster, New York, 1960), p. 85.
19. Inge Fehr Samson, in conversation with the author.
20. Eyck, op. cit., Vol. II, p. 178.
21. Ibid., p. 217.
22. For political parties' followers to wear uniforms was far more usual in those days, and not only in Germany. In Great Britain there were Sir Oswald Mosley's Blackshirts, and John Hargrave's Greenshirts. In 1937 the British government passed a Public Order Act banning political uniforms. The Greenshirts were far from being a Fascist organization. They were the champions of Social Credit, and endorsed by such men as Augustus John and Sir Compton Mackenzie.
23. Italics: in English in the original.
24. Entry for 3 October 1929.

Chapter 9: The Crystallizing Arts

1. See Gay, op. cit., pp. 121–2.
2. Ibid., p. 128, quoting Heinrich Mann to Felix Bertaux, 11 June 1923.
3. For an interesting discussion of *Neue Sachlichkeit*, see the catalogue *Neue Sachlichkeit and German Realism of the Twenties* (Arts Council of Great Britain, 1978).
4. Grosz, op. cit., p. 52.
5. Ibid., p. 52.
6. Nolde's work appeared in the 1937 Nazi Degenerate Art exhibition in Munich – see Chapter 14.
7. Lethal stuff!

8. This and what follows is taken from a conversation the author had with Professor Walter Huder.

9. See M. Kay Flavell, *George Grosz, A Biography* (Yale UP, 1988), p. 42. It seems incredible that all that happened on only sixty bottles of wine. They must have had reinforcements.

10. For a detailed analysis, see Julius Posener, *Fast so alt wie das Jahrhundert* (Siedler, Munich, 1990).

11. This and much of what follows is taken from a conversation the author had with Professor Julius Posener.

12. The Gestapo decree of 21 July 1933 indicated *inter alia* that Ludwig Hildesheimer and Vassily Kandinsky should be dismissed. The official Bauhaus notification of closure came on 10 August, giving 'financial difficulties' as the reason. Previously, Mies had even tried to engage Alfred Rosenberg, then Cultural Leader of the New Germany, as an ally.

13. See Friedrich, op. cit., p. 195 and the following pages in this excellent book for more on Schönberg, and a discussion of Thomas Mann's *Dr Faustus* in relation to him. I agree with Friedrich about the Lowe–Porter translation of Mann, while acknowledging the difficulty of the task – but we should have a new translation of his work by now.

14. Ibid., p. 201.

15. The comments which follow are from Boleslaw Barlog, *Theater Lebenslänglich* (Ullstein, Frankfurt/Main, 1990), pp. 194 ff, and from correspondence with Professor Barlog, who, it should be said, has a very generous nature. Barlog also remained in Germany during the Third Reich, but could not really have done otherwise.

16. Ibid., pp. 196 ff.

17. Ibid., p. 239.

18. A new biography of Karajan by Wolfgang Stresemann is in preparation.

19. Conversation with the author.

20. Conversation with the author.

21. And as such resented.

22. Kessler, op. cit., p. 362.

23. Gay, op. cit., p. 29.

24. For more, see ibid., pp. 34 ff.

25. Laqueur, op. cit., pp. 212 ff.

Chapter 10: Stopping a Catastrophe with a Typewriter

1. Ribbe, op. cit., pp. 894–5.

2. See 'PEM', op. cit., Chapter Five.

3. A history of the press in Weimar Germany has yet to be written. A biography by Klaus Täubert of Emil Faktor which encompasses a history of the *Börsen-Courier* is in preparation.

4. Quoted in Laqueur, op. cit., pp. 80–1.

5. See ibid., pp. 86 ff.

6. Quoted in Friedrich, op. cit., p. 371.

7. Zuckmayer, op. cit., p. 271.
8. Ibid., p. 230.
9. Ibid., p. 317.
10. Ibid., pp. 317–18.
11. Walter Huder, in conversation with the author. Tietz also owned KaDeWe, which still stands on the corner of Wittenbergplatz, and is still a famous department store, of the order of Selfridges or Bloomingdales.
12. For a Tucholsky anthology in English, see *The World is a Comedy – A Kurt Tucholsky Anthology*, translated and edited by Harry Zohn (Sci-Art Publishers, Cambridge, Massachusetts, 1957), from which I have quoted in this chapter.
13. Bryan P. Grenville, *Kurt Tucholsky – The Ironic Sentimentalist* (Oswald Wolff, London, 1981). See also the Tucholsky Archives in the Akademie der Künste, Berlin, and at Marbach; also Roland Links (ed.), *Kurt Tucholsky: Ausgewählte Briefe* (Volk und Welt, Berlin, 1983).
14. Walter Benjamin, *Melancholy of the Left* 1931.
15. Quoted in Appignanesi, op. cit., p. 105.
16. Klaus Täubert, in conversation with the author.
17. Erich Kästner in *Gesammelte Schriften* (Atrium Verlag, Zurich), Vol. V, p. 562. See also his praise of the Weimar days – *GS* Vol. V, p. 94: *Erste Hilfe gegen Kritiker*.
18. And see *GS* Vol. I, pp. 299 ff.
19. Zweig, op. cit., p. 277.
20. Conversation with the author.
21. Glaeser was a left-wing journalist and novelist who left in 1933, but returned in 1939 to edit the soldiers' paper, *Adler im Süden*. He remained under suspicion from the NSDAP, however. Goebbels, whose envious and embittered nature enjoyed its Walpurgisnacht on 10 May, sang out the names of writers as their books were thrown onto the fires.
22. Barlog, op. cit., p. 233.
23. She was Luiselotte Enderle.
24. Conversation with the author.
25. Sahl, op. cit., pp. 130 ff.
26. Conversation with the author.
27. See Koestler, op. cit., pp. 282 ff.
28. Ibid., p. 300.
29. Conversation with the author. See also Alfred Joachim Fischer, op. cit., pp. 25 f.
30. Conversation with the author.

Chapter 11: Sportpalast, Speedway and Ring

1. Conversation with the author.
2. Barlog, op. cit., p. 25.
3. See Curt Riess, *Das waren Zeiten* (Fritz Molden Verlag, Vienna, Munich, Zurich, Innsbruck, 1977), p. 110.

4. For much of what follows, see also 'PEM', op. cit., Chapter Eleven, and Ruland, op. cit., pp. 184 ff.
5. 'PEM', op. cit.
6. Alfred Fischer, in conversation with the author. Fischer's brother had lost his right hand in action during the First World War, and couldn't imagine that as a war veteran he'd be persecuted; but he was engaged politically, and when the Gestapo arrested him, they said: 'Watch your step or we'll cut your left hand off for you, you Jewish pig.' After his release, Herr Fischer made hasty arrangements to leave.
7. There is a museum dedicated to him in Indianapolis.
8. On ascent and descent. Once at cruising height, they could fly far above the little aeroplanes, and managed to inflict serious bomb damage on London.
9. Statistically: *LZ 127* was 235 metres long and contained 15 kilometres of struts.
10. Koestler, *Pfeil ins Blaue*.
11. Kessler, op. cit., entry for 4 June 1930.
12. See Gay, op. cit., pp. 77 ff, and p. 140.
13. Quoted in ibid., p. 87.

NIGHT

Chapter 12: House of Cards

1. Quoted in Friedrich, op. cit., p. 210.
2. For the effect of Nazi rule on education, see Gill, op. cit.; Elie Cohen, *Human Behaviour in the Concentration Camp*, translated M. H. Braaksma (Free Association Books, 1988); and Richard Grunberger, *A Social History of the Third Reich* (Weidenfeld and Nicolson, 1971; Penguin Books, 1974).
3. See Eyck, op. cit., Vol. II, Chapter IX.
4. See Geoffrey Dawson's editorial in *The Times*, 16 September 1930.
5. For more, see Eyck, op. cit., Vol. II, pp. 292 ff. See also Wheeler-Bennett, op. cit.
6. For more, see ibid., pp. 370 ff.
7. Ibid., pp. 388 ff.
8. Ibid., p. 394.
9. Ibid., p. 400 (quoting *Documents on British Foreign Policy*, Vol. III, p. 146).
10. Ibid., p. 404; and see Sir John Simon, *Retrospect* (Hamish Hamilton, 1952), p. 188.
11. *Vom Kaiserhof zur Reichskanzlei*, p. 101.
12. Speech, 3 March 1933.
13. Alfred Fischer, in conversation with the author.
14. Telegram from Isherwood to Auden. I am indebted to Jonathan Barker, former Arts Council Poetry Librarian, for this information.
15. Letter to Isherwood, written in German, 2 March 1946.
16. *Mr Norris Changes Trains* became available in the UK as a Methuen paperback in 1987.
17. Available in the UK in a Minerva paperback edition (reprinted 1990).

280 Notes

18. *Goodbye to Berlin.* See also especially the SA episode on pp. 247–8 of the Minerva edition, and the description of the Tiergarten on p. 231. While the film *Cabaret* scarcely does the book justice, the tawdry night-club is a perfect reconstruction.
19. Stephen Spender, *World Within World* (Hamish Hamilton, 1951), pp. 47 and 120–35, 142, 169, and pp. 174–5.
20. Akademie der Künste, Berlin, George Grosz Archive reference: Hbr 71/86/159–169.
21. See Kracauer, op. cit., pp. 226 ff.
22. *Kuhle Wampe, The Testament of Dr Mabuse,* and other films not mentioned here are referred to earlier in this book.
23. Kracauer, op. cit., p. 219.
24. *Die Weltbühne,* 236, quoted in Gay, op. cit., pp. 87–8.
25. See Gill, op. cit.
26. A very full account is given in Hans-Bernd Gisevius, *To the Bitter End* (Greenwood Press, 1975), pp. 62–81.
27. Conversation with the author.
28. Conversation with the author.
29. Conversation with the author.
30. Space does not permit a full discussion of the persecution of the Jews here. For more, see: Lucy S. Dawidowicz, *The War against the Jews* (Pelican, 1977), and Gill, op. cit. See also the fascinating book by Herbert Freeden, *Jüdisches Theater in Nazideutschland* (J. C. B. Mohr (Paul Siebel), Tübingen, 1964).

Chapter 13: Under the Third Reich

1. Engelmann, op. cit., p. 234.
2. A book on this subject by Anton Gill, entitled *An Honourable Defeat,* is in preparation for William Heinemann.
3. Some sources say it took place on 28 January. I have been unable to locate an original programme by which to verify the date.
4. Zuckmayer, op. cit., p. 322.
5. See Laqueur, op. cit., pp. 264–5.
6. At this stage, the Security Service (*Sicherheitsdienst*) was a branch of the Gestapo. To understand the bureaucracy of the Gestapo, with its 170-odd sub-departments, see Reinhard Rürup (ed.), *Topographie des Terrors,* (Arenhövel, Berlin, 1987). It is also available in an English translation, as *Topography of Terror.*
7. The Russians' misunderstanding of the prefix 'general' to a civilian title caused a nervous moment for Gustav Gründgens, too, who was *Generalintendant* of the State Theatre. He was saved by Ernst Busch. See Barlog, op. cit., p. 39.
8. See Adlon, op. cit., pp. 359–61.
9. Ibid., p. 374.

10. *Rede des Vizekanzlers von Papen vor dem Universitätsbund, Marburg, am 17 Juni 1934.*
11. Wheeler-Bennett, op. cit., p. 324.
12. Conversation with the author.
13. See Bernhard Minetti, *Erinnerungen eines Schauspielers* (Rowohlt, Reinbek bei Hamburg, 1988), p. 82. Minetti at first underwent similar humiliation.
14. E. Höflich, *Wie benehme ich mich* (Stollfuss, Bonn). Quoted in *Schwarzes Korps*, 5 September 1935, and in Richard Grunberger, *A Social History of the Third Reich* (Penguin Books edition, 1974), p. 114. A wonderful description of Nazi social awfulness is given in the same book, pp. 92–4.
15. Conversation with the author.
16. See Zweig, op. cit., pp. 277ff and pp. 318–19.
17. *Gymnasien* were academic grammar schools specializing in the humanities; *Realgymnasien* specialized in modern languages. The Nazis discontinued them, in line with their other changes to the education system, which included lowering the top leaving age by one year in order to free young men for the Front earlier.
18. Conversation with the author.
19. A form of charity collecting on behalf of the poor and, later, soldiers. The SA were the main collectors originally, and you refused to put money into their collecting tins at your peril.
20. Conversation with the author.
21. Conversation with the author.
22. *The Winter's Tale*, IV, iii, line 695.
23. The full story is told in Freeden, op. cit.

Chapter 14: A Cloud Across the Sun

1. Grunberger, op. cit., p. 109.
2. Ruland, op. cit. He gives a very full description of the Games, with statistics, pp. 39–65.
3. A rabid, quasi-pornographic anti-Semitic magazine produced by the *Gauleiter* of Franconia, Julius Streicher.
4. Ribbe, op. cit., p. 972.
5. Conversation with the author.
6. Conversation with the author.
7. See Grunberger, op. cit., Chapter 28.
8. Ibid., p. 538.
9. Laqueur, op. cit., pp. 266f.
10. I am indebted to the private theatre and concert programme collection of Professor E. G. Lowenthal.
11. *Fränkische Tagezeitung*, 20 August 1938; and see Grunberger, op. cit., p. 515.
12. Gottfried Reinhardt, *Der Liebhaber* (Knaur, Munich and Zurich, 1973), pp. 202–3.
13. Minetti, op. cit., pp. 139ff.

14. KZ = *Konzentrationslager* (concentration camp).
15. Minetti, op. cit., pp. 139–140.
16. I say 'charlatans'; but see Koestler, op. cit., pp. 354–7, for a story about Hanussen which demonstrates that the man may have had a genuine 'gift'. Sources differ about Hanussen's precise background. Compare Koestler's account with Kiaulehn's (op. cit., pp. 562–3). Much of my additional information about Hanussen is from 'PEM', op. cit., who gives full details – see especially pp. 68ff.
17. A feature film about Hanussen, who is something of a cult figure in Germany, appeared there recently (1991), starring Klaus Maria Brandauer.
18. 23 September 1937.

Chapter 15: Towards War

1. Inge Fehr Samson, in conversation with the author, and from her private memoir.
2. Adlon, op. cit., p. 362.
3. Ibid., pp. 363–4.
4. Conversation with the author.
5. Conversation with the author.
6. Conversation with the author.
7. See Heinz Knoblauch, *Der beherzte Revierversteher* (Morgenbuch, Berlin, 1990).
8. The other major Berlin synagogue was in Fasanenstrasse.
9. See 'Das war das Ende der jüdischen Presse in Deutschland', article by Ernst G. Lowenthal in *Allgemeine Jüdische Wochenzeitung*, Düsseldorf, 30 October 1953.
10. 'Es geschah vor 50 Jahren', article by Ernst G. Lowenthal in *Allgemeine Jüdische Wochenzeitung*, Bonn, 4 November 1988.

Bibliography

The corpus of work on the subject discussed in this book is truly vast, and the following selection of books is brief. I have added the word 'bibliography' in brackets to the entry for any volume which contains one which is particularly extensive or useful. The Wiener Library, London has an extension bibliography on the Weimar Republic, and there is a good selection of books on the period at the Goethe Institute Library, London. The majority of the individuals mentioned have either written autobiographies or had biographies written about them. I also have an extensive database, which may be accessed on application. Many more books not mentioned below will be found in the Notes to this volume.

AUTOBIOGRAPHY AND BIOGRAPHY

Jazz Cleopatra – Josephine Baker in her Time, Phyllis Rose (Vintage, 1991).
Theater Lebenslänglich, Boleslaw Barlog (Ullstein, Frankfurt/Main, 1990).
Tanz Zwischen Rausch und Tod: Anita Berber 1918–1929 in Berlin, Lothar Fischer (Haude and Spener, 1988).
Bertolt Brecht, Frederic Ewen (Calder and Boyars, 1970).
Winston Churchill: A Brief Life, Piers Brandon (Secker and Warburg, 1984).
The Amazing Blonde Woman: Dietrich's own Style, Patrick O'Connor (Bloomsbury, 1991).
Meine ersten 90 Jahren, Tilla Durieux (Rowohlt, Reinbek/Hamburg, 1977).
Die Tänzerin Valeska Gert, Fred Hildebrandt (Walter Hüdecke, Stuttgart, 1928).
In der Nähe der Ereignisse, Alfred Joachim Fischer (Transit, Berlin, 1991).
To the Bitter End, Bernd Gisevius (Greenwood Press, Boston, 1947).
A Small Yes and a Big No, George Grosz, trl. Arnold J. Pomerans (Allison and Busby, London and NYC, 1982).
Hitler, Joachim C. Fest, trl. Richard and Clara Winston (Penguin, 1983).

My Struggle, Adolf Hitler (Paternoster, 1938).
Erich Kästner, Helmut Kiesel (Beck, Munich, 1981).
Tagebücher, Harry, Graf Kessler, ed. Wolfgang Pfeiffer-Belli (Insel, Frankfurt/Main, 1982).
Pfeil ins Blaue, Arthur Koestler (Desch, Vienna-Munich-Basle, 1953).
Käthe Kollwitz, Arnold Bauer (Colloquium, Berlin, 1987).
The Diary and Letters of Käthe Kollwitz, ed. Hans Kollwitz, trl. Richard and Clara Winston (Henry Regnery, Chicago, 1955).
Aller Tage Abend, Fritz Kortner (Kindler, Munich, 1959).
Kortner Anekdotisch, ed. Claus Landsittel (Kindler, Munich, 1967).
Klaus Mann Zum 75. Geburtstag, ed. Klaus Täubert (Europäische Ideen, Berlin, 1981).
Erinnerungen eines Schauspielers, Bernhard Minetti (Rowohlt, Reinbek/Hamburg, 1988).
Fast so alt wie das Jahrhundert, Julius Posener (Siedler, Berlin, 1990).
Walther Rathenau, Harry, Graf Kessler (Klemm, Berlin, 1928).
Max Reinhardt: Ausgewählte Briefe, Reden, Schriften und Szenen aus Regie Büchern, ed. Franz Hadamowsky (Georg Prachner, Vienna, 1963).
Wie Max Reinhardt lebte, Helene Thimig-Reinhardt (Schulz, Starnberger See, 1973).
Der Liebhaber, Gottfried Reinhardt (Droemer Knaur, Munich, 1973).
Memoiren eines Moralisten, Hans Sahl (Luchterhand, Frankfurt/Main, 1990).
World within World, Stephen Spender (Hamish Hamilton, 1951).
Trab der Schaukelpferde, Steffie Spira (Kore, Freiburg, 1991).
Kurt Tucholsky - The Ironic Sentimentalist, Bryan P. Grenville (Oswald Wolff, 1983).
Kurt Tucholsky - Ausgewählter Briefe, ed. Roland Links (Volk und Welt, Berlin, 1983).
A Part of Myself, Carl Zyckmayer, trl. Richard and Clara Winston (Secker and Warburg, 1970).
The World of Yesterday, Stefan Zweig, trl. Cedar and Eden Paul (Cassell, 1987).

CULTURE

Barnouw, Dagmar, *Weimar Intellectuals and the Threat of Modernity* (Bloomington, Indiana UP, 1988).
Eisner, Lotte, *Die dämonische Leinwand* (Fischer, Frankfurt/Main, 1987).
Gay, Peter, *Weimar Culture: The Outsider as Insider* (Secker and Warburg, 1969 (bibliography)).
Grosz, George, *Ecce Homo* (Facsimile Edition, Grove Press, NYC, 1966).
Haarmann, Hermann (ed.) et al., *Alfred Kerr: Lesebuch zu Leben und Werk* (Argon, Berlin, 1987).
Hilbersheimer, Ludwig, *Berliner Architektur der 20er Jahre* (Florian, Kupferberg, 1967).
Kirsch, Karin, *Kleiner Führer durch die Weissenhofsiedlung* (DVA, Stuttgart, 1989).
Kracauer, Siegfried, *From Caligari to Hitler: A Phychological History of the German Film* (Princeton UP, 1947).

Kulas, Gertraude (ed.), *Neu Beginnen kannst du mit dem letzten Atemzug ... 100 Jahre freie Volksbühne* (Berlin Museum und Freie Volksbühne e.V., Berlin, 1990).
Laqueur, Walter, *Weimar, A Cultural History* (Weidenfeld and Nicolson, 1974 (bibliography)).
Rühle, Günther (ed.), *Theater für die Republik* (Fischer, Frankfurt/Main, 1967).
Wingler, Hans M., *Das Bauhaus*, (Rasch, Bramsche, 1962).

FICTION

This is a very broad area. Works which are important as a background to our period are the Berlin novels of Theodor Fontane and, in a different way, those of Vladimir Nabokov. See also works by Gottfried Benn and Stefan Zweig. The Weimar Republic is mirrored in Thomas Mann's *The Magic Mountain* and *Doctor Faustus*. The best novel of Weimar Berlin is Alfred Döblin's *Berlin Alexanderplatz* (see Note 1, Chapter 6). See also:

Boyd, William, *The New Confessions* (Hamish Hamilton, 1987).
Deighton, Len, *Winter* (Grafton, 1988).
Goll, Yvan, *Sodom Berlin* (Fischer, Frankfurt/Main, 1988).
Isherwood, Christopher, *Goodbye to Berlin* (Minerva-Mandarin, 1990).
— *Mr Norris Changes Trains* (Methuen, 1990).
Kästner, Erich, *Fabian* (Atrium, Zurich, 1969).
Kerr, Philip, *March Violets* (Penguin, 1990).
— *The Pale Criminal* (Penguin, 1991).
Zohn, Harry (ed./trl.), *The World is a Comedy – A Tucholsky Anthology* (Sci-Art, Cambridge, Mass., 1957).

GENERAL AND SOCIAL

Adlon, Hedda, *Hotel Adlon* (Kindler, Munich, 1955).
Appignanesi, Lisa, *The Cabaret* (Universe, NYC, 1976).
Baedekers Berlin 1927 (Leipzig).
Dawidowicz, Lucy, *The War Against the Jews 1933–1945* (Weidenfeld and Nicolson, 1975).
Engelmann, Bernt, *Berlin, eine Stadt wir keine andere* (Bertelsmann, Munich, 1986 (bibliography)).
Everett, Susanne, *Lost Berlin* (Contemporary Books, Chicago, 1979).
Freeden, Herbert, *Jüdisches Theater in Nazideutschland* (J. C. B. Mohr (Paul Siebeck), Tübingen, 1964).
Friedrich, Otto, *Before the Deluge* (Harper and Row, NYC, 1972 (bibliography)).
Gill, Anton, *The Journey back from Hell* (Grafton, 1988).
Grunberger, Richard, *A Social History of the Third Reich* (Penguin, 1979).
Grunfeld, Frederick von, *The Hitler File* (Weidenfeld and Nicolson, 1974).
Jansen, Wolfgang, *Glanzrevuen der zwanziger Jahre* (Hentrich, Berlin, 1987).
Kiaulehn, Walter, *Berlin, Schicksal einer Weltstadt* (Biederstein, Munich-Berlin, 1958 (bibliography)).

Kuhn, Volker, *Hoppla, wir beben* (Quadriga, Berlin, 1988).
Kunstamt Kreuzberg und Institut für Theaterwissenschaft der Universität Köln, *Weimarer Republik* (Elefanten Press, Berlin, 1977).
Mierau, Fritz (ed.), *Russen in Berlin* (Quadriga, Berlin, 1988).
'PEM', *Heimweh nach dem Kurfürstendamm* (Blanvalet, Berlin, 1952).
Reissner, Alexander, *Berlin 1675–1945* (Oswald Wolff, 1984).
Ribbe, Wolfgang (ed.), *Geschichte Berlins Band II: von der Märzrevolution bis zur Gegenwart* (Beck, Munich, 1987).
Riess, Curt, *Das waren Zeiten* (Molden, Vienna-Munich, 1977).
Ruland, Bernd, *Das war Berlin* (Hestia, Bayreuth, 1972).
Schebera, Jürgen (ed.), *Damals im Romanischen Cafe . . .* (Westermann, 1988).
Schebera, Jürgen, and Schrader, Bärbel (eds), *Kunstmetropole Berlin 1918–1933* (Aufbau, 1987).
Sich fügen – heisst lügen: 80 Jahre deutsches Kabarett (Schmidt und Bödige, Mainz, 1981).
Spiess, Volker (ed.), *Gauner, künstler, originale – die 20er Jahre in Berlin* (Haude und Spener, 1988).
Stein, Werner, *Kulturfahrplan* (F. A. Herbig, Munich, 1969).
Zeman, Z. A. B., *Nazi Propaganda* (OUP, 1964).

MILITARY

Cooper, Matthew, *The German Army 1933–1945* (Macdonald and Jane's, 1978).
Hart, Liddell, *The Other Side of the Hill* (Cassell, 1951).
Wheeler-Bennett, John W., *The Nemesis of Power* (Macmillan, 1954).

POLITICAL

Büsch, Otto, and Haus, Wolfgang, *Berlin als Hauptstadt der Weimarer Republik 1919–1933* (Dirk Nishen, 1988).
Eyck, Erich (trl. Harlan P. Hanson and Robert G. L. Waite), *A History of the Weimar Republic* (2 Volumes) (Harvard UP, 1967 (bibliography)).
Fest, Joachim C. (trl. Richard and Clara Winston), *The Face of the Third Reich* (Weidenfeld and Nicolson, 1970).
Freudenfeld, Burghard (ed.), *Stationen der deutschen Geschichte 1919–1945* (DVA, Stuttgart, 1962).
Hildebrandt, Horst (ed.), *Die deutschen Verfassungen des 19. und 20. Jahrhunderts* (Schöningh, Paderborn, 1975).
Peukert, Detrlev J. K. (trl. Richard Deveson), *The Weimar Republic* (Allen Lane, The Penguin Press, 1991).
Reichhardt, Hans J., *Die Stadtverwaltung unter Oberbürgermeister Gustav Böss* (Presse und Informationsamt des Landes Berlin, 1979).
Rürup, Reinhard (ed.), *Topographie des Terrors* (Arenhövel, Berlin, 1989).
Sapinsley, Barbara, *From Kaiser to Hitler* (Grosset and Dunlop, 1968 (bibliography)).
Wiskemann, Elizabeth, *Europe of the Dictators* (Fontana, 1966).

Index